TIME-SAVER DETAILS FOR EXTERIOR WALL DESIGN

Time-Saver Details for Exterior Wall Design

FRED NASHED, AIA

McGRAW-HILL

NEW YORK   SAN FRANCISCO   WASHINGTON, D.C.   AUCKLAND   BOGOTÁ
CARACAS   LISBON   LONDON   MADRID   MEXICO CITY   MILAN
MONTREAL   NEW DELHI   SAN JUAN   SINGAPORE
SYDNEY   TOKYO   TORONTO

Library of Congress Cataloging-in-Publication Data

Nashed, Fred.
    Time-saver details for exterior wall designs / Fred Nashed.
       p.   cm.
    Includes bibliographical references and index.
    ISBN 0-07-046082-5 (hardcover)
    1. Exterior walls—Design and constuction.   I. Title.
TH2235.N37   1995
721'.2—dc20   95-34805
                                               CIP

1 2 3 4 5 6 7 8 9 0   KGP/KGP   9 0 1 0 9 8 7 6

ISBN 0-07-046082-5

The sponsoring editor for this book was Joel Stein, the editing supervisor was Frank Kotowski, Jr. and the production supervisor was Suzanne W. B. Rapcavage.

It was set in Garamond by North Market Street Graphics.

Printed and bound by Quebecor/Kingsport.

McGraw-Hill books are available at special quantity discounts to use as premiums and sales promotions, or for use in corporate training programs. For more information, please write to the Director of Special Sales, McGraw-Hill, 11 West 19th Street, New York, NY 10011. Or contact your local bookstore.

This book is printed on acid-free paper.

To Gayle:
Wife, helper, counselor, and friend

Contents

ACKNOWLEDGMENTS   xi

DISCLAIMER   xiii

HOW THIS BOOK CAN HELP YOU   xv

PREFACE   xvii

PART 1   **FACTORS THAT INFLUENCE WALL DESIGN**   **1**

Chapter 1   **Forces of Nature**   **3**

1.1   **GENERAL**   3

1.2   **WIND**   3

   1.2.1   **Forces That Move Air**   3

   1.2.2   **Methods of Protection**   5

   1.2.3   **What Can Go Wrong**   6

1.3   **WATER**   6

   1.3.1   **Forces That Move Water**   6

   1.3.2   **Methods of Protection**   9

   1.3.3   **What Can Go Wrong**   19

1.4   **HEAT AND COLD**   20

   1.4.1   **Heat Transfer**   21

   1.4.2   **Methods of Protection**   23

   1.4.3   **What Can Go Wrong**   25

1.5   **EARTHQUAKES**   27

   1.5.1   **The Mechanics of Seismic Action**   27

   1.5.2   **Mitigation Measures**   30

   1.5.3   **What Can Go Wrong**   35

1.6   **MISCELLANEOUS FORCES**   36

   1.6.1   **Fire**   37

   1.6.2   **Electrolysis**   38

   1.6.3   **Sound**   39

   1.6.4   **Infestation**   41

   SUMMARY   42

Chapter 2   Structural and Other Design Considerations   45

2.1   GENERAL   45

2.2   STRUCTURAL CONSIDERATIONS   46

   2.2.1   Deflection   46

   2.2.2   Column Locations   50

   2.2.3   Cladding Support   54

   2.2.4   Loose Lintels   56

   2.2.5   Details   58

   2.2.6   Structure as an Element of Design   61

2.3   COST   62

   2.3.1   Controlling Costs   62

   2.3.2   Cost Evaluation Methods   64

   2.3.3   Design Decisions   68

   2.3.4   Strategies for Staying Within the Budget   69

   2.3.5   Other Issues Affecting Cost   70

2.4   OTHER DESIGN CONSIDERATIONS   71

   2.4.1   Durability   71

   2.4.2   Maintenance   71

   2.4.3   System Selection   73

   SUMMARY   74

PART II   EXTERIOR WALL DESIGN   77

Chapter 3   Wall Types and Fenestration   79

3.1   GENERAL   79

3.2   WALL TYPES   79

   3.2.1   Type Categorized by Function   79

   3.2.2   Design Philosophies   81

3.3   FENESTRATION   84

   3.3.1   Window Types   84

   3.3.2   Framing Systems   90

   3.3.3   Glazing   98

   3.3.4   Glass Treatments   103

   3.3.5   Window Treatments   106

   SUMMARY   107

Chapter 4   Wall Assemblies   109

4.1   GENERAL   109

4.2   UNIT MASONRY WALLS   109

   4.2.1   Historical Background   109

   4.2.2   Components   111

   4.2.3   Ornamentation   133

   4.2.4   Assemblies   136

   4.2.5   What Can Go Wrong   137

   SUMMARY   142

4.3   STONE WALLS   146

   4.3.1   Historical Background   146

4.3.2 **Components** 147

4.3.3 **Ornamentation** 151

4.3.4 **Assemblies and Details** 153

4.3.5 **What Can Go Wrong** 160

SUMMARY 162

4.4 **CEMENT-BASED SYSTEMS** 162

4.4.1 **Historical Background** 162

4.4.2 **Components** 164

4.4.3 **Ornamentation** 179

4.4.4 **Assemblies** 180

4.4.5 **What Can Go Wrong** 180

SUMMARY 185

4.5 **METAL CLADDING** 185

4.5.1 **Historical Background** 185

4.5.2 **Components** 186

4.5.3 **Ornamentation** 193

4.5.4 **Assemblies** 198

4.5.5 **What Can Go Wrong** 199

SUMMARY 203

4.6 **STUD-BACKED WALLS** 205

4.6.1 **Historical Background** 205

4.6.2 **Components** 206

4.6.3 **Ornamentation** 215

4.6.4 **Assemblies** 217

4.6.5 **What Can Go Wrong** 218

SUMMARY 219

Chapter 5 **Drawing the Wall Section** 221

5.1 **GENERAL** 221

5.2 **POINTS TO CONSIDER** 221

5.2.1 **Sources of Information** 222

5.2.2 **Wall Defenses** 222

5.3 **DRAFTING GUIDELINES** 223

5.3.1 **Drawing Hierarchies** 223

5.3.2 **Critical Dimensions** 229

5.3.3 **Step-By-Step Procedure** 230

SUMMARY 233

Conclusion 237

Glossary 239

Appendix A 247

Appendix B 253

Appendix C 257

References 263

Bibliography 265

INDEX 269

Acknowledgments

I wish to thank all those who helped to bring this effort to fruition. Special thanks are extended to Gayle Nashed for the countless hours she spent in wordprocessing, proofreading, and making helpful suggestions as well as for keeping our lives running smoothly during this long and arduous work.

Thanks are also due Wagdy Anis, senior associate at Shepley Bulfinch Richardson and Abbott, for including me in the deliberations of their production review committee where I participated in stimulating technical discussions that inspired some of the material in this book. Assistance from David Lund, Bruce Cole, and Katherine Meyer of SBRA is also appreciated as was the help from Julie Sullivan of Sullivan Design, who provided technical literature pertaining to the rain screen principle. I also wish to thank officials of the trade associations who granted me permission to include their material in this book, especially the BIA, PCI and AAMA.

Special thanks are due also to Joel Stein, senior editor at McGraw-Hill, for perceiving the merit of this subject and endorsing it for publication, and for his continuous support during the writing. Frank Kotowski's editing effort to smooth the text and Maggie Shapiro's work on the eye-catching cover design are also much appreciated.

Disclaimer

The information provided in this book is based on dependable sources including books, seminars, discussions with colleagues and industry representatives as well as the author's personal experience. While every effort has been made to present an error-free text, no warranties, express or implied, are given in connection herewith and no responsibility can be taken for any claims arising from its use. It is incumbent upon those entrusted with the production of construction drawings to refer to applicable codes, and use input from their consultants to base their contract documents upon.

How This Book Can Help You

This book is intended for use by project architects, job captains, technical advisers, interns, and students. The information included herein was gathered from many sources and presented in a concise, easy to comprehend manner to explain many of the systems most used in exterior wall construction. Understanding the principles behind wall design can help you avoid the pitfalls that are present in every aspect of wall detailing during schematic design, design development, construction drawings, shop drawing review, as well as give you the know-how to present your point of view in the field.

While some of you may not be currently involved in some of the wall types described in the text, inevitably you will during your career. This book will come in handy as a quick reference to bring you up to speed. The details, axonometrics, and perspectives give you an overview of each system and the text can be absorbed in a relatively short time. This is very important in today's fast-paced architectural practice.

For students, a summary is included at the end of each chapter to review the highlights of the topics contained in it. I have tried to avoid technical jargon and used easy-to-comprehend language throughout most of the book. My wife's questions about language she did not understand was invaluable in that regard since she is not an architect.

The bibliography at the end of the book is intended to direct you toward broadening your reading on the subject and providing more in depth information.

Preface

The building envelope, which comprises the exterior walls as well as the roof, represents one of the most challenging segments of architectural practice. The majority of professional liability litigation, cost overruns, and client discontent is concentrated in this area. While there are many excellent books dealing with the general topics of building construction, drafting, construction drawings, masonry, precast concrete, structures, cost estimating, energy conservation, etc., I could not find any that dealt specifically and in depth with the subject of exterior walls. After finishing this book, I now have a deeper understanding of the saying, "Only fools dare where angels fear to tread." This subject requires the author to be an expert on the subjects of science, structural engineering, mechanical engineering, building materials, fenestration, chemical engineering (sealants, sealers), and the list goes on. In an ideal world, the book should have been written by a panel of world famous experts on each of these subjects. This approach would, however, have one drawback. These experts would use technical language understandable only to other experts in each of the topics. They would load it with equations, and use hard-to-understand technical terms and jargon used in their individual disciplines. This would deter all but the hardiest of souls from proceeding to the bitter end.

Approaching this subject in this manner would be akin to the way technology is taught in most architectural schools. We have all had to endure the trauma of plodding through structural and mechanical calculations only to discover that the majority of us have no use for it and that all we needed to know was a general comprehension of these systems in a way that would let us communicate effectively with our consultants. That is the approach I took when I wrote and illustrated Chaps. 1 and 2 after I noticed how woefully unprepared many graduates are. They dread encounters with the consultants or take on a cocky attitude to hide their lack of understanding of these issues.

In another book of mine, *Time-Saving Techniques for Architectural Construction Drawings,* I divided the tasks assigned to the project team into four main categories starting with the least challenging and progressing to the most difficult. This book addresses the most challenging of these categories, namely, the task of developing trouble-free wall sections based on sound design principles. I remember the first time I was entrusted with the task of drawing wall sections for a project. I muddled along as best I could and produced a set of drawings which I thought at the time was pretty good. They were not, and the project architect went into a frenzy of redlining to correct them. Forty years later, after being in charge of many major projects, I am still refining the methodology of doing this assignment properly.

Metric equivalents are included in the text as well as in App. A. These equivalents are rounded off. For example, an inch is represented as 25 mm rather than 25.4 mm. Superscripted numbers are listed in the References after the appendices. They point the reader to the source upon which the text was based.

I have tried to cover as much territory as possible but, because this subject is so vast and because new materials and technical innovations are being introduced constantly, no book can be considered the final word. My goal is to provide a good start for the person entrusted with developing detailing and drawing wall sections so that he or she will continue to keep abreast of the latest developments and seek more in-depth information from other sources.

It is my hope that this book will shed some light on a subject that is often assigned to junior staff who are constantly being challenged to produce a flawless set of construction drawings with so little preparation.

Fred Nashed

TIME-SAVER DETAILS FOR EXTERIOR WALL DESIGN

PART I

Factors That Influence Wall Design

This book is divided into two parts. Part I addresses the issues that affect wall design. The chapters included in this part explain the function of the defenses built into any kind of exterior wall: defenses such as the vapor retarder, the air barrier, sealers, sealants, dampproofing, and waterproofing. Having a clearer understanding of these crucial elements of the wall is the best insurance against inadequate detailing and faulty execution, two of the problems that result in leakage, litigation, and client dissatisfaction.

While understanding the forces of nature is the most important background information needed to detail the wall properly, other elements of the design are also important. Structural issues such as the effect of deflection on wall panels, the relationship of the cladding to the supporting structure, and the distribution of forces around openings are examples of structural considerations that need to be addressed early on in the design process.

Other considerations such as the factors that cause cost overruns and the measures to take to reduce them are often overlooked by the designer. Not only does this cause consternation for the client and possibly require awkward explanations, but it also can require the designer to spend time and effort to modify the contract documents and resubmit them for rebidding, an activity that can result in making the project unprofitable for the architect. Chapter 2 also addresses the issues of cost, maintainability, and the methodology of evaluating products to choose the most appropriate ones to specify.

While Part I may sound like "all work and no play," I have tried to make it as easy to comprehend and as informative as possible. It is not loaded with equations or formulas, and the use of difficult jargon has been avoided. It is essential that the reader assimilate the information included in this first part before proceeding to Part II which deals with the "fun" part—wall and window types and assemblies and the proper way to draw and dimension them. In other words, the nuts and bolts of exterior walls.

CHAPTER 1

Forces of Nature

1.1 GENERAL

Wind, rain, temperature changes, earthquakes, and other forces of nature have a profound effect on exterior cladding. Each section of this chapter is organized into two parts. The first describes the effect of the natural force on the exterior cladding, and the second addresses the methods used to protect against it. A description of what can go wrong is also included where needed.

Understanding the rationale behind the arrangement of components that comprise a wall assembly helps the designer to detail the means of protection properly. Items such as air barriers, vapor retarders, dampproofing, waterproofing, sealants, and sealers are representatives of these components. The quality of light is also an important element of design. Chapter 4 touches lightly upon that subject by describing glass treatments. While this does not do justice to this vast subject which includes building orientation and the various shading elements, this subject falls more in the realm of design than in that of this book.

The last part of this chapter deals with influences that are not, strictly speaking, forces of nature but are, nevertheless, important items to take into consideration during detailing. Fire can have a catastrophic effect on buildings and their occupants. Electrolysis can cause severe corrosion in metals, noise pollution can make interior space uncomfortable and in certain cases even unusable for the purpose for which it was constructed, and protection against insect and bird infestation must be implemented.

Detailing a wall without being thoroughly familiar with the rationale behind its construction elements is an invitation to failure. Understanding these issues can help avert problems and result in sound, long-lasting construction. It also helps the architect to make the right decisions during shop drawing review and in the field.

1.2 WIND

Air currents can infiltrate through joints around doors and windows and through minor shrinkage cracks, imperfect joint sealants, or other paths created by thermal or structural movement. Unless these air currents are stopped by a carefully constructed air barrier, building occupants will be subjected to uncomfortable air drafts in winter; mechanically conditioned (heated or cooled) interior air will exfiltrate and be replaced by exterior, unmodified air, wasting energy; and water vapor will condense inside the wall assembly causing corrosion and damage to its concealed components. Air currents can also drive rain through these imperfections causing water leaks.

Air pressure against the building envelope can be caused by

- Wind pressure
- The stack effect
- Mechanical pressurization

This section explains the mechanics of air currents and describes the methods used to resist them.

1.2.1 Forces That Move Air
WIND PRESSURE

Wind is one of the most potent forces of nature. Hurricanes and tornadoes can demolish buildings and cause death and destruction in their wake. Their velocities can reach an awesome 200 mph (322 km/h). Wind speed is affected by terrain and altitude. High winds occur in flat, open country and coastal zones. Rough terrain, forests, and urban areas slow it down. Hilltops and the upper floors in high-rise buildings experience accelerated wind speeds. Building codes usually define zones for different wind pressures to be used in design calculations. These are used by the structural engineer as the basis for the design of shear walls, moment connections (see Chap. 2), and exterior cladding support calculations. The architect uses them as the basis for determining glass thickness and window mullion depth during discussions with manufacturers' representatives. Most building codes list the intensity of these pressures up to 60 ft (18 m). For greater heights, the structural engineer should be able to provide the architect with that information (see also App. C). For high-rise buildings, design wind pressure is usually arrived at by placing a model of the building and its surroundings in a wind tunnel and attaching pressure sensors to the facade to determine the expected design pressures. While this adds to the design cost, it has been proven to be cost effective in most cases. It provides a solid basis for the design that may effect savings over empirical or theory-based calculations. Wind exerts positive pressure on one side of the building and negative pressure (suction) on the opposite side [Fig. 1.1(a)]. Wind also creates turbulence and negative pressures at the zones adjacent to corners and over the top of angular buildings [Fig. 1.1(b)].

Architectural features such as projecting columns can channel air flow downwards and create high-pressure air currents at street level that can become hazardous to pedestrians [Fig. 1.2(a)]. An arcade or projecting canopies can provide protection in this situation. Horizontal projections such as balconies or sunscreens channel wind horizontally toward the corners [Fig. 1.2(b)]. Architects must be aware of these issues during schematic design. Creating a breezeway in the middle of a building [Fig. 1.2(c)] can attract strong positive and negative air currents that can interfere with entrance door operation, increasing the wind chill factor near them, and creating stresses on the cladding and windows that may exceed the limits mandated by the building code. Air flow tends to remain attached to rounded or curved surfaces [Fig. 1.2(d)].

Exterior soffits must also be designed to resist wind forces. They should not be constructed like interior ceilings but rather be attached to braced structural members. A performance specification stipulating that soffits be supported by light gauge framing and that the shop drawings be stamped by a structural engineer is one of the ways to ensure proper design.

THE STACK EFFECT

This is a phenomenon that occurs in high-rise buildings. In winter, heated air rises to the top floors through elevator and duct shafts, stairs, and other penetrations between floors. This warm air is replaced at lower floors by cold air entering the building through main entrances and other access points. This air movement creates interior pressure against the walls in upper floors and exterior pressure against the bottom half of the building [Fig. 1.3(a)]. Main lobby doors opening to the exterior in high-rise buildings are sometimes hard to push outward

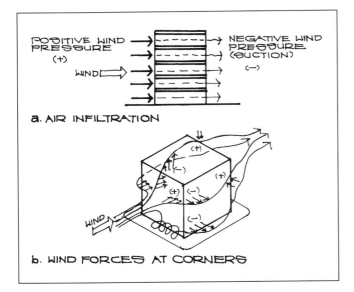

Figure 1.1   The effect of wind pressure on buildings.

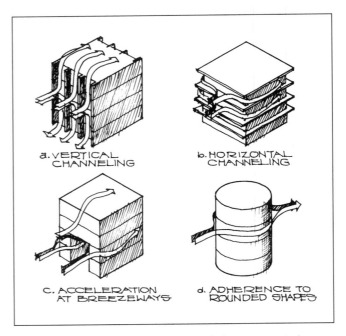

Figure 1.2   The effect of architectural design on wind behavior.

in winter because of the cold air pressing against them at that level. Revolving doors and vestibules with double sets of doors usually solve this problem. To a much lesser degree, the process is reversed in summer because the interior cooled air gravitates toward the bottom half of the building.

This upward movement of air is referred to as the *stack effect* because it resembles the movement of air in a smoke stack where the air is drawn through the hearth, is heated, and rises to the top creating a draft.

MECHANICAL PRESSURIZATION

In an effort to reduce cold air infiltration at lower floors, mechanical engineers may opt to increase the pressure inside the building [Fig. 1.3(*b*)]. While this measure will counter the pressure on lower floors, it will increase the interior pressure against the walls in upper floors. The net result is dubious. While a reduction of infiltrating cold air at lower floors will reduce the energy needed to heat that air, an increase in exfiltration in upper floors caused by the combined forces of the stack effect and mechanical pressurization will cause more energy loss at this zone [Fig. 1.3(*c*)].

Since upward migration of air is inevitable in winter and the connection between floors through shafts and stairwells is rather hard to seal, the most practical solution to lessen this migration would be to pressurize these air conduits. Whenever a door is opened in a stair or elevator shaft, air will exit instead of entering and moving to other floors. Incidentally, this is the measure used when a fire alarm activates the stair pressurization system to prevent smoke from entering a fire exit in a high-rise building.

Wind pressure from the exterior is the determining design factor for exterior wall cladding. The stack effect is only a contributing element that must be considered especially in tall buildings.

1.2.2 Methods of Protection
AIR BARRIERS

An impervious air barrier included in the wall assembly and sealed around the perimeters will minimize the volume of air passing through the wall. It will reduce the potential for discomfort caused by air drafts or damage to the wall assembly caused by wind-driven water or condensing vapor. It can be placed in any part of the wall assembly. Gypsum wallboard used as an interior wall finish can qualify as an air barrier provided it is extended all the way to the structure and sealed around the perimeter. A polyethylene vapor retarder can qualify if supported on both sides to resist both positive and negative wind pressure, which can be quite substantial. Sheathing covered with an air barrier such as Tyvek can also function in that capacity. Placing the air barrier on the side of the wall facing the interior is preferred because, at that location, it is protected from thermal fluctuations. These fluctuations can subject it to harmful stresses resulting in the eventual failure of seams.

Air barriers must be sealed around all interruptions. Gaps at a barrier's interface with floor slabs, spandrel beams, or columns will prevent the barrier from performing its intended function properly.

Durability is another prerequisite for the material chosen to function as an air barrier. This is especially important if it is located in an inaccessible part of the wall assembly. The material must be unaffected by ultravio-

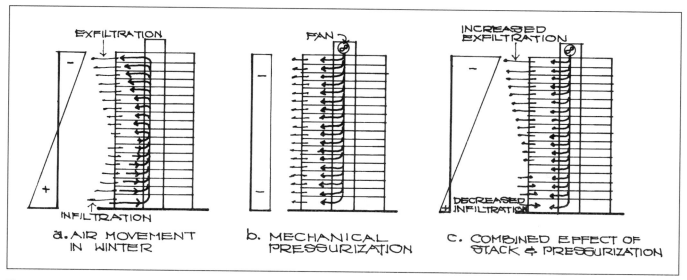

Figure 1.3 The stack effect.

let rays if, during the course of construction, it is exposed to the sun for any length of time. It must also be compatible with the tapes and sealants it comes in contact with. Special care must be given to building corners where movement from two directions occurs and around doors and windows.

1.2.3   What Can Go Wrong

Wall appearance may be deceptive. Walls that may appear to be air-impermeable will let in enough air pressure to dislodge items attached to them in the absence of a well detailed and properly installed air barrier. Figure 1.4(*a*) shows an example of adhered rigid insulation panels that became detached as a result of negative air pressure in the absence of an air barrier.

In a similar manner, an unsupported polyethylene vapor retarder can be forced by air pressure to detach from the wall and become ineffectual [Fig. 1.4(*b*)]. Extending the wallboard all the way to the deck to provide the needed structural support prevents this from happening.

Another example of a detail commonly used in commercial and industrial construction is shown in Fig. 1.5(*a*). Note the absence of linkage between the air barrier and roof membrane. Figure 1.5(*b*) shows the proper way to detail this junction.

1.3   WATER

Water, like wind, is one of the major forces of nature. Flooding rivers and seismic-impelled ocean tsunami (strong ocean currents created by the vibrations from an earthquake) can devastate entire regions. There is no known defense against the awesome force of a tsunami other than to construct the building in a manner similar to wartime bunkers, anchor it with deep foundations, leave the premises well ahead of time (if the time can be predicted with any accuracy), and hope for the best. The best defense against river flooding is to avoid construction on low-lying flood-prone areas.

The behavior of water in the form of rain or groundwater is more manageable and is much easier to anticipate and defend against. Wind-driven rain seeks entry through entry points in the cladding such as cracks and joint sealant imperfections causing water leaks. If the temperature drops below the freezing point, water lodged in these cracks will freeze, expand, and cause damage to the wall. Understanding the forces that move water and the methods of protection against them is required before one can develop trouble-free details.

1.3.1   Forces That Move Water

In addition to wind force, it is important to have an understanding of how water seeks entry into the cladding. Water is moved by the following forces:

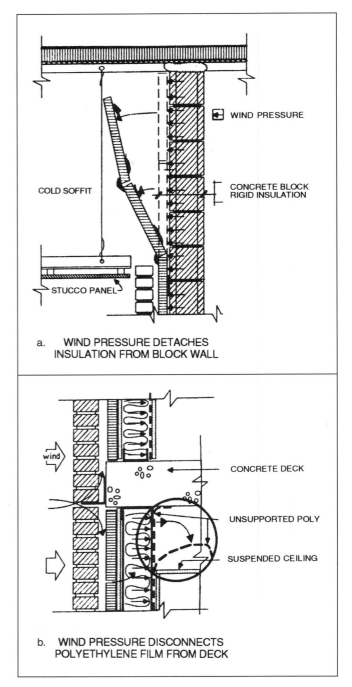

a.   WIND PRESSURE DETACHES
      INSULATION FROM BLOCK WALL

b.   WIND PRESSURE DISCONNECTS
      POLYETHYLENE FILM FROM DECK

Figure 1.4   The effects of wind pressure in the absence of an adequate air barrier. (Reproduced by permission; R. L. Quirouette, *The Difference Between a Vapour Barrier and an Air Barrier,* Building Practice Note #54, National Research Council Canada, Ottawa, 1985)

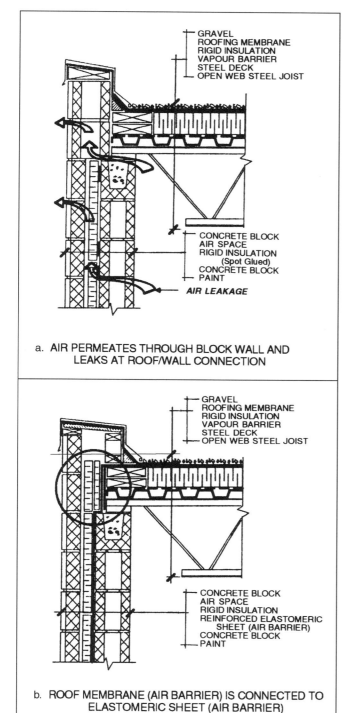

a. AIR PERMEATES THROUGH BLOCK WALL AND
   LEAKS AT ROOF/WALL CONNECTION

b. ROOF MEMBRANE (AIR BARRIER) IS CONNECTED TO
   ELASTOMERIC SHEET (AIR BARRIER)

Figure 1.5 The importance of providing a linkage between an air barrier and the roofing membrane. (Reproduced by permission; R. L. Quirouette, *The Difference Between a Vapour Barrier and an Air Barrier,* Building Practice Note #54, National Research Council Canada, Ottawa, 1985)

- Gravity
- Kinetic energy
- Surface tension
- Capillary action
- Hydrostatic pressure
- Vapor migration

A description of each follows.

GRAVITY

If horizontal joints are sloped in the wrong direction, water, pulled by gravity, will be directed toward the interior rather than the exterior of the building [Fig. 1.6(*a*)]. Whenever possible, flashing should also be sloped to prevent long-term standing water from occurring. Providing a positive slope in horizontal surfaces is a standard design practice. It applies to joints between wall panels, window sills, and copings. The latter should be sloped toward the roof to prevent dirt from streaking the facade.

KINETIC ENERGY

This is the tendency of raindrops to continue to travel carried by their own momentum even after the impelling force (wind) ceases. Placing a dam, baffle, or labyrinth in the path of the water prevents it from entering the cavity [Fig. 1.6(*b*)]. This measure is also effective against rainwater impelled by air currents.

SURFACE TENSION

Water tends to cling to the surface even in defiance of gravitational pull. Water traveling across soffits and window heads are examples of this phenomenon. Providing a gap or drip in its path interrupts the flow [Fig. 1.6(*c*)].

CAPILLARY ACTION

Porous materials absorb water through their pores and conduct it toward the dry side of the wall. The rate and speed of water flow depends on the thickness of the wall and the porosity of the material. This rarely poses a problem if the walls are thick because, by the time water travels part way through the material, the rain would have already stopped and the drying process begins.

This mechanism allows hairline cracks and narrow joints or fissures to convey water much more rapidly causing leaks. In cavity walls, water conveyed in this fashion trickles on the back of the front wythe and is directed by the flashing to exit through weepholes. Narrow joints should either be widened or provided with wider gaps to act as breaks to the flow of water [Fig. 1.6(*d*)].

To avoid cracking in brittle materials, control joints are provided at intervals to accommodate thermal

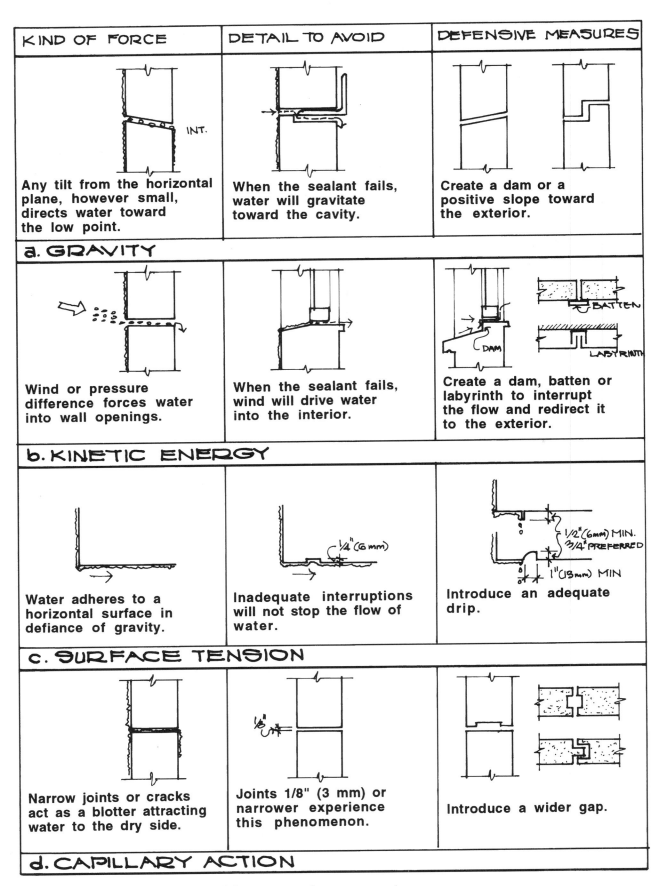

KIND OF FORCE	DETAIL TO AVOID	DEFENSIVE MEASURES
Any tilt from the horizontal plane, however small, directs water toward the low point.	When the sealant fails, water will gravitate toward the cavity.	Create a dam or a positive slope toward the exterior.
a. GRAVITY		
Wind or pressure difference forces water into wall openings.	When the sealant fails, wind will drive water into the interior.	Create a dam, batten or labyrinth to interrupt the flow and redirect it to the exterior.
b. KINETIC ENERGY		
Water adheres to a horizontal surface in defiance of gravity.	Inadequate interruptions will not stop the flow of water.	Introduce an adequate drip.
c. SURFACE TENSION		
Narrow joints or cracks act as a blotter attracting water to the dry side.	Joints 1/8" (3 mm) or narrower experience this phenomenon.	Introduce a wider gap.
d. CAPILLARY ACTION		

Figure 1.6 Forces that move water and the measures taken to counter them.

8

movement as well as any differential movement between the cladding and support structure. Reinforcement is also provided in masonry walls to control cracking. Figure 1.7 shows a joint designed with all the defense mechanisms mentioned above.

HYDROSTATIC PRESSURE

Water from rivers, lakes, reservoirs, and rain seeps through porous ground strata to accumulate as groundwater. The top surface of this water is referred to as the *water table*. Hydrostatic pressure is the force that this water exerts against underground structures. The deeper the structure (basement), the higher the pressure and the higher the possibility that water will force its way through any imperfection in the waterproofing membrane.

Groundwater level rises and falls depending on the amount of rainfall or melting snow as well as site contours. It is closer to the surface in low-lying sites and farther from the surface at higher elevations. It flows slowly toward lower ground.

MOISTURE MIGRATION

Humidity is water vapor suspended in the air we breathe. It is caused by water evaporation from falling rain and bodies of water such as rivers, lakes, and oceans. Inside buildings, vapor is augmented by human activities and bodily metabolism. Cooking, bathing, coffee-making, and sweating raise indoor humidity levels.

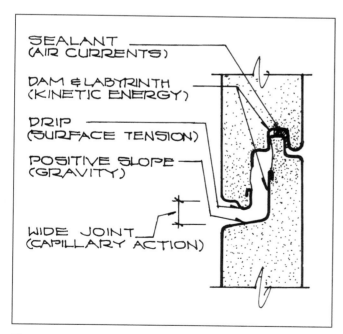

Figure 1.7 A joint designed to resist forces that move water. (Metal sandwich panel by Robertson.)

Water vapor acts like a gas. It can travel through seemingly impenetrable materials such as polyethylene vapor retarders, gypsum board, and concrete walls. This movement occurs at different rates. Its travel through polyethylene is so slow that it can be disregarded. It also travels through still air from areas of high vapor pressure (warm areas) to areas with lower vapor pressure (cold areas). Air currents move vapor at a much faster rate and increase the potential for damage by condensation inside a wall. The percentage of humidity in the air is also regulated by the mechanical system to maintain a comfortable and healthy atmosphere. If humidity is too high, we feel hot and sweaty. If it is too low, skin loses its moisture and nasal passages become too dry. Water vapor, if allowed to travel unhindered through a wall assembly, will condense when it reaches a temperature where the air becomes saturated and unable to carry the water droplets. This temperature is referred to as the *dew point*. These water droplets have the potential of freezing within the wall assembly and causing damage to its components.

1.3.2 Methods of Protection

Protecting exterior cladding against leakage and water vapor damage is of prime importance to the long-term endurance of the walls and comfort of the occupants. In addition to the measures already described to resist water migration caused by gravity, kinetic energy, surface tension, and capillary action, the following measures of protection are used:

- Sealants
- Sealers
- Dampproofing
- Waterproofing
- Vapor retarder

The following is a description of each of these measures.

SEALANTS

Joints between wall panels and around window and door frames must be sealed to prevent water from entering the wall assembly. Sealants used to close the gaps between these components are elastomeric materials with high cohesion and adhesion properties. Cohesiveness allows the sealant to stretch and contract without cracking, and high adhesion allows it to maintain its attachment to the sides of the joint without separating when stretched. They are exposed to ultraviolet (UV) rays, acid rain, freeze-thaw cycles, and other factors that eventually cause them to fail and necessitate periodic reapplication. The longevity of the sealant is dependent on its quality, the skill of the applicator, and the condition of the surfaces to which the sealant is to adhere. As a general rule, exterior sealants last between 10 and 15 years if applied properly.

Sealants are identified by their modulus of elongation which describes the ratio between the force required to elongate the sealant a certain amount and the resulting elongation. Moderate to high-modulus sealants represent the bulk of sealants used in exterior applications. Most good sealants are capable of an elongation range between 200% and 600%, allowing the joint to move ±25%. Wider joints require a stiffer sealant to prevent sagging. Consult with the sealant manufacturer for specific recommendations before making the final selection. Architects may choose from three joint designs: single-stage, two-stage, and rain screen joints.

1. Single-stage joints [Fig. 1.8(a)] offer a single line of defense. They require perfectly prepared substrates, accurate width-to-depth ratio and perfect tooling of the sealant as well as proper mixing of the ingredients if the sealant is prepared by mixing two components.

2. Two-stage joints [Fig. 1.8(b)] provide a backup seal to act as insurance against the failure of the exterior seal. The inner seal is protected from UV rays and other sealant degrading elements and can last a long time. This type of joint costs more initially but is more dependable than single-stage joints and is designed according to the same principles as a cavity wall with weepholes to drain the cavity between the sealants.

3. Carrying the two-stage design a step further, joints can be designed according to the rain screen principle (see Sec. 3.2.2). These joints [Fig. 1.8(c)] are similar to the two-stage design, but the cavity is weeped at each level and is widened in the middle to reduce air velocity. A perforated gasket may be substituted for the exterior sealant. The more frequent weeps, vents, or perforations (gasket) help equalize the pressure within the cavity with the exterior air pressure to stop air currents from forcing rain into it.

The back seal in both the two-stage and the rain screen designs may be applied from the front or the back. Front application requires a wider joint, approximately ¾ in (20 mm) wide, to allow enough space for the insertion of a special extension nozzle attached to the caulking gun. It also requires accurate placement of the backer rod. Applying the sealant may also be done from inside the building. This requires accessibility for initial application as well as for subsequent maintenance. This can be extremely difficult if not impossible in most cases because spandrel beams, slab edges, or columns are usually in the way. However, if the perimeter beams

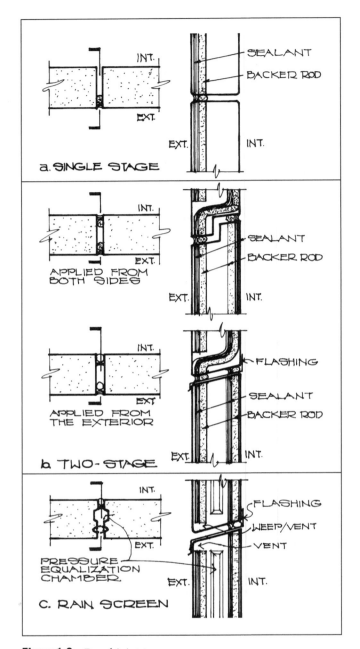

Figure 1.8 Panel joint types.

and columns are placed at some distance from the slab edge, applying the sealant from the interior becomes feasible.

Joint width is determined by panel material, size, and color. These are all strong factors affecting the rate of thermal movement. Other determinants include structural deflection due to live load. Dead load is not considered a factor since deflection caused by the weight of the structure would have already occurred before the cladding is attached. The dead weight of the wall panel itself, however, must be taken into account. Concrete column shrinkage in multistory structures and construction tolerances are also factors in determining joint width. Under any circumstances, exterior control joints must not be less than ½ in (13 mm), and ¾ in (20 mm) is preferred.

Metal panels become substantially hotter than the adjacent air temperature. They expand more than other materials especially if the panel is aluminum. Large panels experience more movement than small ones and require wider joints. For example, if the rate of expansion is 1%, a 10-ft (3 m) panel would expand 0.1 ft (30 mm) while a 2-ft (0.6 m) panel would elongate 0.02 ft (6 mm). Characteristics of other materials such as concrete shrinkage and brick elongation must also be considered.

The designer must choose a sealant capable of handling the calculated movement. For example, if during the final construction document checking, the architect notices that the specifications call for a sealant capable of a 25% movement while the calculated movement based on the final selection of panel size, material, color, and thermal range is 50%, a sealant substitution is made or an intermediate joint is added at the center of the panel.

The Precast/Prestressed Concrete Institute (PCI)[1] recommends the following equation to calculate the width of a joint. It is applicable to any cladding material.

$$J = \frac{(100A)}{X} + B + C$$

where:
J = Minimum joint width, in.
X = stated movement capability of the sealant in percent.
A = calculated movement of panel from thermal changes = (coefficient of thermal expansion) (change in temperature) (panel length)
B = material construction tolerances
C = seismic or other considerations as appropriate.

The following example illustrates the use of this equation. (Note: Items shown in [ ] for this example are the metric equivalents.) Concrete panels of 15 feet [4.57 m] length, expecting a temperature change in the concrete of 120°F [48.89°C], with a material or construction tolerance of 0.25 inches [6 mm], are to be sealed with a sealant having ±25 percent movement capability (as determined by ASTM C719). The coefficient of thermal expansion of the concrete is 6×10^{-6} in./in./deg. F [0.0000169 mm/mm/deg. C]. The calculated movement of the panel from thermal change is as follows:

$$A = (6 \times 10^{-6} \text{ in./in./deg. F}) (120 \text{ deg. F}) (180 \text{ in.})$$
$$= 0.130 \text{ in.}$$
$$[0.0000169 \times 48.89 \text{ deg. C} \times 4572 = 3.77 \text{ mm}]$$
$$X = 25\%$$

Construction tolerance = 0.25 in. [6 mm]
No seismic considerations

The calculated minimum joint width is as follows:

$$J = \frac{(100 \times 0.130 \text{ in.})}{25} + 0.25 \text{ in.} = 0.77 \text{ in.}$$

$$[J = \frac{100 \times 3.77}{25} + 6 \text{ mm} = 21 \text{ mm}]$$

If joint width determined is perceived by the designer to be too wide, another sealant having a greater movement capability should be selected. For example, if movement capability is ±50 percent, the joint width in the example becomes 0.51 in. [13 mm].

Refer to Table 1.1 for coefficients of expansion for common building materials to use in the equation above. In the absence of information about change in temperature, use a temperature difference of 130°F (54°C). Table 1.2 shows the properties of field-molded sealants. It is included in this subsection to assist the reader in the selection of an appropriate sealant based on joint characteristics.

Sealant manufacturers usually indicate the relationship between joint width and sealant depth. As a general rule, the depth is half the width but not less than ¼ in (6 mm) or more than ⅝ in (16 mm). The sealant must adhere to two sides only to avoid being overstressed. Tooling the joint forces the sealant against the sides and back to ensure that this adhesion occurs and that the sealant is shaped into an hourglass profile. Backer rods are usually manufactured from polyurethane or polyethylene and sized 30 to 50% larger than the maximum joint width [the joint width in winter plus a construction tolerance of ±⅛ in (3 mm)]. Polyethylene includes a gas in its formulation and must not be punctured during placement to prevent the gas from escaping and forming a bubble in the sealant causing it to fail. There are two kinds of backer rods—open- and closed-cell. The first kind may allow vapor escaping from the interior to pass right through and exert pressure behind the sealant causing it to eventually fail. This can happen if no other means of venting the vapor is provided. Closed-cell rods do not pose this problem.

Determining the right joint width, selecting the right type of sealant, and having the sealant applied by a skilled applicator can result in a sealed joint capable of accommodating temperature extremes and resisting continuous movement for a relatively long time.

SEALERS

Sealers or water repellents are chemical formulations designed to reduce or eliminate the water permeability

Material		Density		Coefficient of Thermal Expansion	
		lb/ft³	kg/m³	in/in/°F	mm/mm/°C
Wood (seasoned)					
Douglas fir	parallel to grain	32	510	0.0000021	0.0000038
	perpendicular to grain			0.000032	0.000058
Pine	parallel to grain	26	415	0.0000030	0.0000054
	perpendicular to grain			0.000019	0.000034
Oak, red or white	parallel to grain	41–46	655–735	0.0000027	0.0000049
	perpendicular to grain			0.000030	0.000054
Masonry					
Limestone		160	2560	0.0000044	0.0000079
Granite		165	2640	0.0000047	0.0000085
Marble		165	2640	0.0000073	0.0000131
Brick (average)		100–140	1600–2240	0.0000036	0.0000065
Concrete masonry units		100–140	1600–2240	0.0000052	0.0000094
Concrete					
Normal weight concrete		145	2320	0.0000055	0.0000099
Metals					
Steel		490	7850	0.0000065	0.0000117
Stainless steel, 18–8		490	7850	0.0000099	0.0000178
Aluminum		165	2640	0.0000128	0.0000231
Copper		556	8900	0.0000093	0.0000168
Finish Materials					
Gypsum board		43–50	690–800	0.000009	0.0000162
Gypsum plaster, sand		105	1680	0.000007	0.0000126
Glass		156	2500	0.0000050	0.0000090
Acrylic glazing sheet		72	1150	0.0000410	0.0000742
Polycarbonate glazing sheet		75	1200	0.0000440	0.0000796
Polyethylene		57–61	910–970	0.000085	0.000153
Polyvinyl chloride		75–106	1200–1700	0.000040	0.000072

Table 1.1 Coefficients of thermal expansion for common building materials. (Reproduced by permission; Edward Allen, *Fundamentals of Building Construction Materials and Methods,* John Wiley & Sons, Inc., 1990)

of exterior wall surfaces. Sealers are of limited duration and must be reapplied periodically as part of a maintenance program. If properly constructed, most wall assemblies usually do not require the application of a sealer to the exposed surface. However, if the wet appearance of the wall after a rain shower is objectionable, the architect may elect to apply a sealer to the surface. Single-wythe concrete masonry unit (CMU) walls require a sealer to prevent water seepage into the interior. Sealers should have a perm rating approximately five times the rating for the vapor retarder to allow water vapor escaping through imperfections in the retarder to vent to the exterior without hindrance.

DAMPPROOFING

Unlike waterproofing, dampproofing is not intended to resist hydrostatic pressure. It is usually used above ground except for residential construction where builders sometimes use dampproofing below grade when the site is known to have a low water table.

Dampproofing materials come in many forms. Below grade, bituminous emulsions may be sprayed, brushed, or troweled on foundation walls (residential construction). Fibrated emulsions may be used on masonry backup walls above grade if their perm rating is much higher than the vapor retarder's rating. Mortar parging (mortar troweled onto the surface of the walls) is also used in this application. Over sheathing, 15-lb felt is used. Membranes, known as *house wrap* are also used as a combination air barrier–dampproofing.

WATERPROOFING

This type of protection is used to defend underground structures against leakage and/or hydrostatic pressure. Retaining walls located below grade are usually constructed of cast-in-place reinforced concrete for nonresidential buildings. While thick, high quality concrete is dense enough to prevent water from seeping from one side of the wall to the other, it usually develops hairline cracks between pours and in other locations

	Polysulfides		Polyurethanes		Silicones		
	One-Component	Two-Component	One-Component	Two-Component	One-Component	One-Component	Two-Component
Chief Ingredients	Polysulfide polymers, activators, pigments, inert fillers, curing agents, and nonvolatilizing plasticizers	Base: polysulfide polymers, activators, pigments, plasticizers, fillers, Activator: accelerators, extenders, activators	Polyurethane prepolymer, filler pigments & plasticizers	Base: polyurethane prepolymer, filler, pigments, plasticizers, Activator: accelerators, extenders, activators	Siloxane polymer pigments & fillers acetoxy system	Siloxane polymer pigments: alcohol or other non-acid cure	Siloxane polymer pigments: alcohol or other non-acid cure
Primer Required	usually	usually	usually	usually	usually	occassionally	occassionally
Curing Process	chemical reaction with moisture in air & oxidation	chemical reaction with curing agent	chemical reaction with moisture in air	chemical reaction with curing agent	chemical reaction with moisture in air	chemical reaction with moisture in air	chemical reaction with curing agent
Tack-Free Time (hrs.) (ASTM C679)	24	36-48	24-36	24-72	1	1-2	½-5
[1]Cure Time (days)	7-14	7	7-14	3-5	7-14	7-14	4-7
Max. Cured Elongation	300%	600%	300%	500%	300%	400-1600%	400-2000%
Recommended Max. Joint Movement	± 25%	± 25%	± 15%	± 25%	± 25%	± 25% to + 100, − 50%	± 12½% to ± 50%
Max. Joint Width	¾"	1"	1¼"	2"	¾"	1"	1"
Resiliency	high	high	high	high	high	moderate	high
Resistance to Compression	moderate	moderate	high	high	high	low	low
[2]Resistance to Extension	moderate	moderate	medium	medium	high	low	low
Service Temp. Range °F	− 40 to − 200°	− 60 to + 200°	− 40 to + 180°	− 40 to + 180°	− 60 to + 350°	− 60 to + 300°	− 60 to + 300°
Normal Application Temp. Range	+ 40 to + 120°	+ 40 to + 120°	+ 40 to + 120°	+ 40 to + 120°	+ 20 to + 160°	+ 20 to + 160°	+ 20 to + 160°
Weather Resistance	good	good	very good	very good	excellent	excellent	excellent
Ultra-Violet Resistance, Direct	good	good	poor to good	poor to good	excellent	excellent	excellent
Cut, Tear, Abrasion Resistance	good	good	excellent	excellent	poor	poor-excellent	excellent knotty tear
[3]Life Expectancy	20 years +	20 years +	20 years +	20 years +	20 years +	20 years +	20 years +
Hardness Shore A (ASTM C661)	25 - 35	25 - 45	25 - 45	25 - 45	30 - 45	15 - 35	15 - 40
Applicable Specifications	FS:TT-S-00230C ASTM C920 19-GP-13A (Canadian)	FS:TT-S-00227E ASTM C920 19-GP-24 19-GP-3B (Canadian)	FS:TT-S-00230C ASTM C920 19-GP-13 (Canadian)	FS:TT-S-00227E ASTM C920 19-GP-24 (Canadian)	FS:TT-S-00230C FS-TT-S-001543A ASTM C920 19-GP-9B (Canadian)	FS:TT-S-00230C FS-TT-S-001543A ASTM C920 19-GP-18 (Canadian)	FS:TT-S-00227E USASI A-116.1 ASTM C920 19-GP-19 (Canadian)

[1]Cure time as well as pot life are greatly affected by temperature and humidity. Low temperatures and low humidity create longer pot life and longer cure time; conversely, high temperatures and high humidity create shorter pot life and shorter cure time. Typical examples of variations are:

Two-Part Polysulfide

Air Temp.,	Pot Life	Initial Cure	Final Cure
50°	7-14 hrs.	72 hrs.	14 days
77°	3-6 hrs.	36 hrs.	7 days
100°	1-3 hrs.	24 hrs.	5 days

[2]Resistance to extension is better known in technical terms as modulus. Modulus is defined as the unit stress required to produce a given strain. It is not constant but, rather, changes in values as the amount of elongation changes.

[3]Life expectancy is directly related to joint design, workmanship and conditions imposed on any sealant. The length of time illustrated is based on joint design within the limitations outlined by the manufacturer, and good workmanship based on accepted field practices and average job conditions. A violation of any one of the above would shorten the life expectancy to a degree. A total disregard for all would render any sealant useless within a very short period of time.

Table 1.2 Comparative characteristics and properties of field molded sealants. (Reproduced by permission; Precast/Prestressed Concrete Institute, *Architectural Precast Concrete,* 1989)

due to shrinkage or "creep." In the absence of waterproofing, wall imperfections will result in damp or flooded basements especially in the presence of hydrostatic pressure. To prevent this seepage, a waterproofing membrane is applied to the wall surface. This membrane must be protected from backfill with a protection board or rigid insulation. To relieve the hydrostatic pressure on the wall, a drainage medium [composed of a 12-in (300 mm) layer of gravel or prefabricated composite drainage panels] is placed against the waterproofing or rigid insulation and wrapped around a perforated drainage pipe. This pipe must be located at least 6 in (150 mm) below floor level but not less than 4 in (100 mm) above the bottom of the footings to avoid undermining the foundation. A strip of

neoprene or synthetic rubber, referred to as a *waterstop,* is also placed at junctions between pours (cold joints) to impede the seepage of water (Fig. 1.9).

Composite drainage panels incorporate a high-strength woven textile filter fabric bonded to a three-dimensional, impact-resistant polymeric core (Fig. 1.10). The fabric prevents water from conveying fine silt into the drainage pipes causing them to eventually clog. A protection board is required to protect the drainage panel from tree roots and frost heave. Rigid insulation can also perform that function. Gravel drainage necessitates the placement of a protection board to protect the waterproofing from the impact of gravel during the backfilling operation. Other drainage panels incorporating insulation are also available.

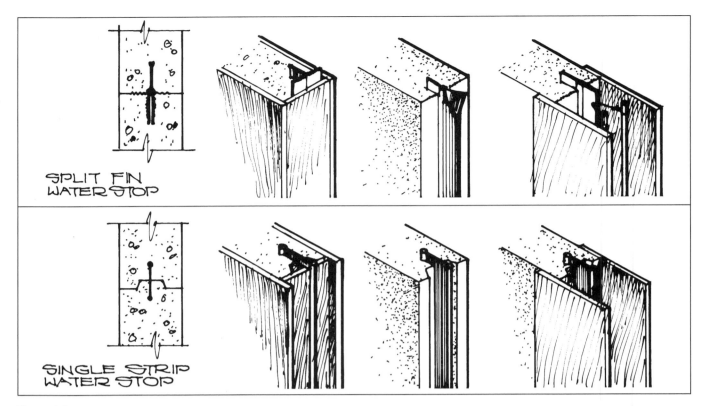

Figure 1.9 Water stops.

Before waterproofing is applied, the wall surface must be inspected and approved by the waterproofing subcontractor. Any voids must be filled, protrusions must be removed, and the wall must be dry before work begins.

Waterproofing membranes are divided into three main types—fluid-applied, adhered or mechanically-fastened sheets, and clay or cement formulations. Fluid-applied membranes have the advantage of being without seams. Some products are applied cold, while others require heating before application. They may be mopped, sprayed, brushed, or rolled onto the surface.

Sheet membranes are manufactured under strict quality control measures with uniform thickness. They may be field-adhered, self-adhering, or mechanically fastened. This latter type is attached either with stainless-steel bars fastened to the wall through the membrane

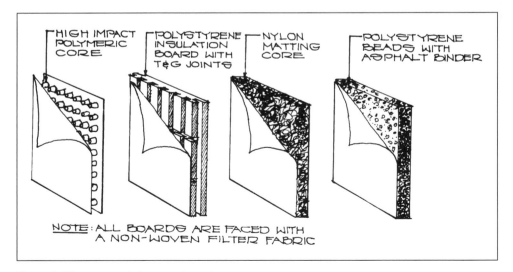

Figure 1.10 Types of drainage boards.

and covered with a flashing strip of the same material as the membrane or by discs that are attached directly to the wall and to which the membrane is heat-welded without a through-membrane penetration.

Sheet waterproofing seams must be inspected carefully before backfilling is allowed to start. Some experts believe that heat-welded seams are more dependable and durable than glued seams. Sheet waterproofing is easier to flash around pipe penetrations than field-applied elastomeric membranes. Figure 1.11 shows a typical sheet membrane application.

Bentonite is a special clay that expands 10 to 15 times its original volume when saturated with water forming a waterproof gel. It is self-healing if damaged and is produced in sheets composed of a layer of sodium bentonite adhered to a woven polypropylene mat or encased within corrugated biodegradable Kraft paper panels. It is applied by mechanically fastening the sheets or panels to the wall while overlapping the edges.

Cement formulations are composed either of Portland cement and iron oxide or cement combined with proprietary chemicals. The first mixture is usually referred to as *ironite*. Iron oxide expands in the presence of water to fill the voids preventing water from passing through. The second mixture forms crystals in the concrete to make it waterproof. These products are useful in applications where it is difficult to apply waterproofing from the exterior. Elevator pits are an example. They are easy to inspect and repair if leakage should occur. Both types are approximately 1 in (25 mm) thick.

VAPOR RETARDERS

Water vapor can condense within a wall assembly causing rot or corrosion to its components. It can saturate the insulation causing loss of thermal resistance (R-value) and, if allowed to pass to the exterior, can cause damage to exterior finishes by rupturing paint films or freezing and expanding within small cracks enlarging them and eventually spalling the material.

To prevent these problems from occurring, a vapor barrier is required in most locations to stop the vapor before it enters into the wall (Fig. 1.12). Because these "barriers" have perforations caused by fastener penetrations, imperfect seals around perimeters, and the barrier itself may allow minute amounts of vapor to pass through the material, vapor barriers are referred to in technical literature as *vapor retarders*. To qualify as a retarder, the material must have a permeance (perm) rating of 1.0 or less. One perm is equal to 1 grain (gr) of water transmitted through 1 ft²/h per inch of mercury vapor pressure difference. [Expressed in metric form as 15 ng transmitted through 1 m²/s when the difference in water pressure is 1 Pa.) Table 1.3 lists perm ratings for

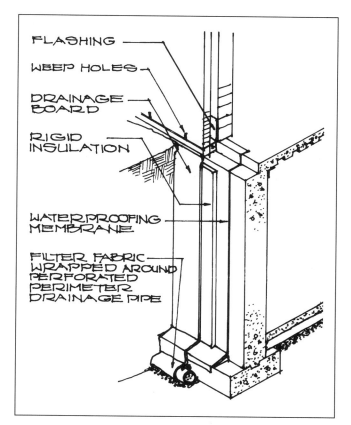

Figure 1.11 Example of a sheet membrane application.

some common building materials. The last segment lists materials suitable for use as vapor retarders. Materials located downstream from the vapor retarder must have a perm rating at least five times the value of the rating for the retarder to allow any escaping vapor to vent to the exterior. To check a wall section, the architect must make a list of all the materials included in the assembly starting from one side and proceeding to the other. The perm rating is then written opposite each material (Fig. 1.13). If a material located downstream from the retarder has a lower rating than it should, a material with a higher rating is substituted or a way for venting the vapor is introduced into the assembly. Building exteriors faced with metal panels or other impervious materials must either have an impervious vapor barrier (metal) on the warm side of the insulation to prevent any vapor from entering the wall assembly or be installed in such a way that a vented cavity between the metal panels and an insulated backup wall is introduced in the design.

Condensation occurs when water vapor reaches its *dew point,* the point at which air becomes saturated and unable to carry water. In a wall assembly, condensation usually occurs at a surface rather than in the middle of insulation. Roos[2] stated that,

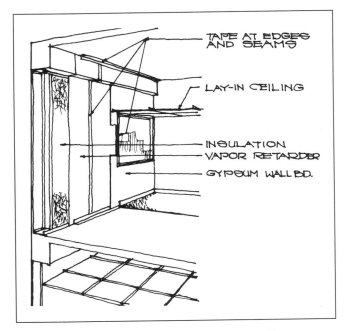

Figure 1.12 Vapor retarder in a stud wall assembly.

The heat resistance of the insulation is such that during winter the location of the dew point falls within the insulation. Theoretically, the resulting condensation should occur within the insulation. This, however, does not occur. Condensation, when it does happen, does not form at the location of the dew point within the insulation, but on the inside surface of the sheathing.

The principle involved is this: Whenever the dew point occurs within a material, condensation will not occur until the flow of water vapor encounters the surface of another material of greater resistance to the flow of water vapor. That is, as long as the air can keep on moving, it will carry the moisture along with it and will not deposit the moisture until it reaches a surface that resists its flow and is colder than the dew point.

The most widely used vapor retarder is a 4-mil sheet of polyethylene placed directly on the studs or furring channels and covered by the wallboard which acts as an air barrier. The ideal membrane should have good tear and puncture resistance in addition to low permeability.

Foil-faced wallboard, if used as a vapor retarder, must be supported by a structural member at both horizontal and vertical edges to prevent the taped joints from separating and allowing vapor to migrate through the joints. This means adding horizontal stud tracks at these locations. Sheet material such as polyethylene provides the least number of seams which are potential vapor migration points.

Vapor retarders must be placed at the warm side of the wall. In colder regions, the warm side is adjacent to the building interior. In hot, humid climates, its position is reversed especially if the building is mechanically cooled. In dry, temperate zones, a retarder may not be necessary.

A vapor retarder must be combined with an air barrier to provide an adequate defense against both vapor migration and uncomfortable air currents. In the absence of an air barrier extending the full height of each floor and sealed against the structure, wind pressure will accelerate vapor migration through imperfections in the retarder and may even rupture it causing major problems. The importance of including a continuous uninterrupted air barrier in conjunction with a vapor retarder in wall sections is sometimes ignored. A common practice by some architects is to end the wallboard a short distance above the hung ceiling to save money, not realizing that the wallboard also functions as the air barrier. This becomes critical when the space between the ceiling and the floor slab is used as a return-air plenum creating suction on the interior face of the vapor retarder and increasing the possibility of its failure. Of course, this does not apply in all instances.

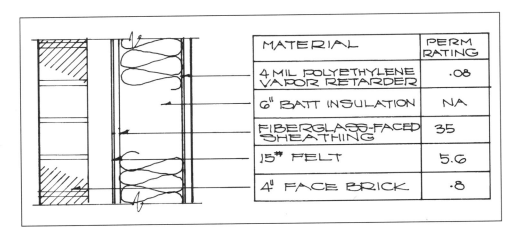

MATERIAL	PERM RATING
4 MIL POLYETHYLENE VAPOR RETARDER	.08
6" BATT INSULATION	NA
FIBERGLASS-FACED SHEATHING	35
15# FELT	5.6
4" FACE BRICK	.8

Figure 1.13 Perm rating analysis of a wall assembly.

Material	Thickness, in.	Permeance, Perm	Resistance[h], Rep	Permeability, Perm-in.	Resistance/in.[h], Rep/in.
Construction Materials					
Concrete (1:2:4 mix)				3.2	0.31
Brick masonry	4	0.8[f]	1.3		
Concrete block (cored, limestone aggregate)	8	2.4[f]	0.4		
Tile masonry, glazed	4	0.12[f]	8.3		
Asbestos cement board	0.12	4–8[d]	0.1–0.2		
With oil-base finishes		0.3–0.5[d]	2–3		
Plaster on metal lath	0.75	15[f]	0.067		
Plaster on wood lath		11[e]	0.091		
Plaster on plain gypsum lath (with studs)		20[f]	0.050		
Gypsum wall board (plain)	0.375	50[f]	0.020		
Gypsum sheathing (asphalt impregnated)	0.5			20[d]	0.050
Structural insulating board (sheathing quality)				20–50[f]	0.050–0.020
Structural insulating board (interior, uncoated)	0.5	50–90[f]	0.020–0.011		
Hardboard (standard)	0.125	11[f]	0.091		
Hardboard (tempered)	0.125	5[f]	0.2		
Built-up roofing (hot mopped)		0.0			
Wood, sugar pine				0.4–5.4[b]	2.5–0.19
Plywood (douglas fir, exterior glue)	0.25	0.7[f]	1.4		
Plywood (douglas fir, interior glue)	0.25	1.9[f]	0.53		
Acrylic, glass fiber reinforced sheet	0.056	0.12[d]	8.3		
Polyester, glass fiber reinforced sheet	0.048	0.05[d]	20		
Thermal Insulations					
Air (still)				120[f]	0.0083
Cellular glass				0.0[d]	∞
Corkboard				2.1–2.6[d]	0.48–0.38
				9.5[e]	0.11
Mineral wool (unprotected)				116[e]	0.0086
Expanded polyurethane (R-11 blown) board stock				0.4–1.6[d]	2.5–0.62
Expanded polystyrene—extruded				1.2[d]	0.83
Expanded polystyrene—bead				2.0–5.8[d]	0.50–0.17
Phenolic foam (covering removed)				26	0.038
Unicellular synthetic flexible rubber foam				0.02–0.15[d]	50–6.7
Plastic and Metal Foils and Films[c]					
Aluminum foil	0.001	0.0[d]	∞		
Aluminum foil	0.00035	0.05[d]	20		
Polyethylene	0.002	0.16[d]	6.3		3100
Polyethylene	0.004	0.08[d]	12.5		3100
Polyethylene	0.006	0.06[d]	17		3100
Polyethylene	0.008	0.04[d]	25		3100
Polyethylene	0.010	0.03[d]	33		3100
Polyvinylchloride, unplasticized	0.002	0.68[d]	1.5		
Polyvinylchloride, plasticized	0.004	0.8–1.4[d]	1.3–0.72		
Polyester	0.001	0.73[d]	1.4		
Polyester	0.0032	0.23[d]	4.3		
Polyester	0.0076	0.08[d]	12.5		
Cellulose acetate	0.01	4.6[d]	0.2		
Cellulose acetate	0.125	0.32[d]	3.1		

Table 1.3 Typical water vapor permeance and permeability values for common building materials. See App. A for metric equivalents. (Reproduced by permission; American Society of Heating, Refrigeration and Air Conditioning Engineers, *Handbook of Fundamentals*, 1989)

Other wall components such as metal cladding or precast concrete if sealed properly, function as air barriers.

Air barriers and vapor retarders must interface with window and door perimeters without any gaps. Gasket seals must also seal the gap between exterior doors and their frames.

Soffit areas pose a special problem for locating the vapor retarder. Because of the many hangers or structural supports and bracings for the soffit, it is usually impractical to install a continuous retarder. In addition, this area is usually not designed to support a worker to tape the joints, and the clearances between the soffit and the supporting floor are usually inadequate to work in. There are two common locations for the insulation. The first is to attach it hard against the underside of the floor, and the second is to lay it directly on the soffit as

Material	Weight, lb/100 ft²	Permeance, Perms Dry-Cup	Wet-Cup	Other	Resistance[h] Rep Dry-Cup	Wet-Cup	Other
Building Paper, Felts, Roofing Papers[g]							
Duplex sheet, asphalt laminated, aluminum foil one side	8.6	0.002	0.176		500	5.8	
Saturated and coated roll roofing	65	0.05	0.24		20	4.2	
Kraft paper and asphalt laminated, reinforced 30-120-30	6.8	0.3	1.8		3.3	0.55	
Blanket thermal insulation backup paper, asphalt coated	6.2	0.4	0.6–4.2		2.5	1.7–0.24	
Asphalt-saturated and coated vapor retarder paper	8.6	0.2–0.3	0.6		5.0–3.3	1.7	
Asphalt-saturated, but not coated, sheathing paper	4.4	3.3	20.2		0.3	0.05	
15-lb asphalt felt	14	1.0	5.6		1.0	0.18	
15-lb tar felt	14	4.0	18.2		0.25	0.055	
Single-kraft, double	3.2	31	42		0.032	0.024	
Liquid-Applied Coating Materials	**Thickness, in.**						
Commercial latex paints (dry film thickness)[i]							
Vapor retarder paint	0.0031			0.45			2.22
Primer-sealer	0.0012			6.28			0.16
Vinyl acetate/acrylic primer	0.002			7.42			0.13
Vinyl-acrylic primer	0.0016			8.62			0.12
Semi-gloss vinyl-acrylic enamel	0.0024			6.61			0.15
Exterior acrylic house and trim	0.0017			5.47			0.18
Paint–2 coats							
Asphalt paint on plywood			0.4			2.5	
Aluminum varnish on wood		0.3–0.5			3.3–2.0		
Enamels on smooth plaster				0.5–1.5			2.0–0.66
Primers and sealers on interior insulation board				0.9–2.1			1.1–0.48
Various primers plus 1 coat flat oil paint on plaster				1.6–3.0			0.63–0.33
Flat paint on interior insulation board				4			0.25
Water emulsion on interior insulation board				30–85			0.03–0.012
	Weight, oz/ft²						
Paint–3 coats							
Exterior paint, white lead and oil on wood siding		0.3–1.0			3.3–1.0		
Exterior paint, white lead-zinc oxide and oil on wood		0.9			1.1		
Styrene-butadiene latex coating	2	11			0.09		
Polyvinyl acetate latex coating	4	5.5			0.18		
Chlorosulfonated polyethylene mastic	3.5	1.7			0.59		
	7.0	0.06			16		
Asphalt cutback mastic, 1/16 in., dry		0.14			7.2		
3/16 in., dry		0.0			—		
Hot melt asphalt	2	0.5			2		
	3.5	0.1			10		

[a]This table permits comparisons of materials; but in the selection of vapor retarder materials, exact values for permeance or permeability should be obtained from the manufacturer or from laboratory tests. The values shown indicate variations among mean values for materials that are similar but of different density, orientation, lot, or source. The values should not be used as design or specification data. Values from dry-cup and wet-cup methods were usually obtained from investigations using ASTM E96 and C355; values shown under others were obtained by two-temperature, special cell, and air velocity methods. Permeance, resistance, permeability, and resistance per unit thickness values are given in the following units:

Permeance	Perm	= gr/h · ft² · in. Hg
Resistance	Rep	= in. Hg · ft² · h/gr
Permeability	Perm-in.	= gr/h · ft² · (in. Hg/in.)
Resistance/unit thickness	Rep/in.	= (in. Hg · ft² · h/gr)/in.

[b]Depending on construction and direction of vapor flow.

[c]Usually installed as vapor retarders, although sometimes used as exterior finish and elsewhere near cold side, where special considerations are then required for warm side barrier effectiveness.

[d]Dry-cup method.

[e]Wet-cup method.

[f]Other than dry- or wet-cup method.

[g]Low permeance sheets used as vapor retarders. High permeance used elsewhere in construction.

[h]Resistance and resistance/in. values have been calculated as the reciprocal of the permeance and permeability values.

[i]Cast at 10 mils wet film thickness.

Table 1.3 (cont.) Typical water vapor permeance and permeability values for common building materials. See App. A for metric equivalents. (Reproduced by permission; American Society of Heating, Refrigeration and Air Conditioning Engineers, *Handbook of Fundamentals*, 1989)

the work progresses. The only possible way to create a retarder is to seal the floor slab. This can be achieved either by applying a low-perm paint or sealant to the top of the slab or to spray a low-perm sealant on the underside of the slab or metal deck. The insulation is then attached to the underside, and the space between the soffit and the slab is vented to the exterior. This allows any vapor escaping from the floor above to migrate to the exterior rather than condense and damage the soffit. The first method should be exercised with caution to ensure that other materials such as carpet or tile adhesives are compatible with the sealer.

Placing the insulation directly on the hung soffit creates a relatively cold volume between the insulation and the slab causing cold floors and possible condensation problems. Mechanical engineers sometimes remedy this problem by heating the soffit plenum area. This author believes that the solution described above is a better approach to soffit design.

1.3.3 What Can Go Wrong

When dealing with defense mechanisms against water leakage, architects must pay heed to Murphy's law which states, "If anything can go wrong, it will." Nothing is more aggravating to a client, short of total collapse or the burning of the structure, than the occurrence of a leak. The following is a review of what can go wrong with each of the defenses described in the preceding subsection.

SEALANTS

While today's sealants are dependable and durable, several things can prevent them from performing properly. For instance, if the backer rod is not placed at the proper depth, the sealant can fail [Fig. 1.14(*a*)]. Another cause for failure is if the sealant is applied to an improperly prepared substrate. The surfaces intended to receive the sealant must be dry and free from release agents, sealers, or incompatible primers, and the sealant must be applied at an appropriate temperature, usually not less than 40°F (4.4°C). Hot temperatures are also unsuitable for sealant application. In addition, the time of construction can have a bearing on the performance of the sealant. Joint widths become narrower during the summer months and widen during winter. This is due to the fact that adjacent panels experience thermal expansion and contraction depending on the temperature. In most cases, the design calls for a certain joint width regardless of the time during which the building is constructed. If the panels are erected during the cold season, they will expand during the hot season resulting in a joint that may be too narrow to function properly [Fig. 1.14(*b*)].

Sealant effectiveness is dependent, to a certain extent, on the skill of the applicator. Mixing two-part sealants such as polysulfides or polyurethanes may be done improperly resulting in a sealant that does not have the cohesiveness required to handle the joint movement. The applicator may also omit tooling the sealant to give it the proper profile and force it against the sides for proper adhesion. The applicator may also apply the sealant while the surfaces are still covered with dew or are still wet after a recent rain resulting in poor adhesion. Primers required by certain manufacturers may also be omitted by a careless applicator resulting in sealant failure.

These are a few of the things that can go wrong with a sealant. Diligent field inspection and the performance

of random water pressure tests can lessen the probability of sealant failure. Designing the joints without sealants according to the rain screen principle (see Sec. 3.2.2) is another way to avoid sealant problems and the costly periodic maintenance associated with them. This approach, however, is very hard to explain to clients and requires the services of a consultant who is very knowledgeable in this application.

SEALERS

As mentioned before, sealers are not necessary except in a few cases where the cladding is a porous single wythe material such as CMU. If a sealer is used, the architect must avoid formulations that have a tendency to yellow or change color over time. Some sealants may give the wall a permanent wet look that may be objectionable to the designer. To avoid this possibility, the architect should ask the manufacturer's representative to arrange for a site visit to an actual project where the product was used. A sealer can contaminate joints intended to receive a sealant which is incompatible with it. Care must be exercised to either mask the joint or clean it prior to the application of the sealant. Some sealers can also have a low-perm rating that results in trapped vapor and the problems associated with it.

DAMPPROOFING

Most problems associated with dampproofing concern the liquid-applied kind. Its perm rating may be too low

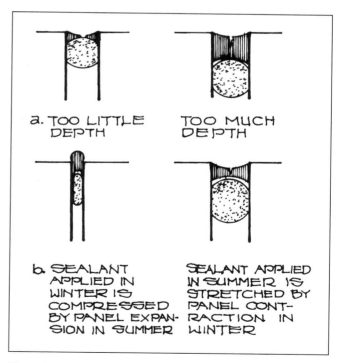

Figure 1.14 Examples of improper sealant application.

resulting in trapped moisture between it and the vapor retarder. Applying these products below grade is a tenuous proposition. The substrate may crack causing leaks and, since dampproofing membranes are not intended for application below grade, they should not be specified in that location. Careful detailing is required to ensure that the membrane interfaces properly with control and expansion joints as well as with different materials and junctions with shelf angles and window frames.

WATERPROOFING

The success or failure of a waterproofing membrane is not only dependent on the quality of the product used but also on the skill and experience of the subcontractor entrusted with the job. This is especially true when a liquid-applied membrane is specified. Maintaining the minimum thickness specified is not a task for the novice. Here again, diligent field supervision, random testing, and a good warranty issued by a reputable manufacturer requiring that the applicator have a minimum number of years of experience go a long way toward ensuring a long-lasting membrane.

Prefabricated sheet membranes are as good as their seams. Clay sheets enclosed in corrugated Kraft paper are vulnerable to damage. Parts of sheets may break and fall off the wall causing parts to be left unprotected. Field supervision can ensure a proper application. Once waterproofing is buried, it is very hard to pinpoint the source of a leak or to take corrective action.

Applying the cavity wall design approach to retaining walls, where the budget permits, is a good design policy especially where access to the exterior during construction is impractical. This is the case when foundation walls are constructed according to the slurry wall method or where the concrete is poured against sheet piles or wood lagging. This design requires a masonry wall to be constructed as a screen to mask any seepage that may occur (Fig. 1.15). The cavity is drained by a sloped gutter ending in a sump with a float-activated ejection pump. An access panel is required to service the pump.

VAPOR RETARDERS

As stated in Sec. 1.3.1 under Moisture Migration, water vapor can damage a wall if it is allowed to condense inside the assembly. To demonstrate how serious this problem can get, Quirouette,[3] an acknowledged Canadian authority on the subject of exterior cladding, states that a narrow, unsealed gap around an electric outlet (Fig. 1.16) with a total area of 1 in² (645 mm²) would let 30.9 lb (14 kg) of water into the wall under 9.3 mph (15 km/h) wind pressure in a month. This demonstrates the importance of proper detailing and field inspection to

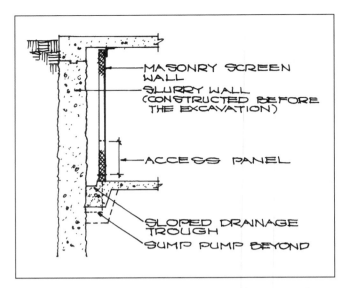

Figure 1.15 A drained cavity used in lieu of waterproofing.

ensure that both the air barrier and the vapor retarder are continuous and properly executed.

Finally, using a membrane to waterproof a backup wall can trap moisture between the vapor barrier and that membrane. Self-adhering membranes such as bituthene or adhered EPDM are examples of that application. If used, a waterproof membrane should function also as the vapor retarder. Rigid insulation, in that case, would be placed over the waterproofed sheathing in cold regions, and insulation would be placed in the interior only in hot, humid regions where air conditioning is used.

While it is important that every effort should be made to ensure that the vapor retarder provides a continuous membrane sealed around its perimeter, it does not have to be absolutely perfect. Minor imperfections like pinholes or unsealed laps placed over studs [and covered by the gypsum wallboard (GWB)] do not seem to cause any appreciable added infusion of vapor.

1.4   HEAT AND COLD

This section provides information pertinent to the subject of wall insulation. It explains the methods by which heat travels and the types of insulation used to shield the atmosphere within the building.

Unless a project is very small, architects depend on the mechanical engineering consultant to design the heating, ventilation, and air conditioning (HVAC) system. This encompasses design of the equipment: air-handling units, boilers, heating coils, chillers, heat pumps, etc., as well as the duct network.

One of the first steps undertaken by the engineer is to calculate the heat loss through the building envelope:

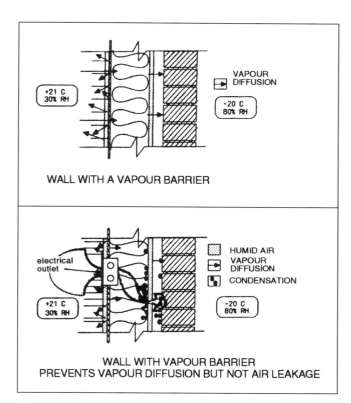

WALL WITH A VAPOUR BARRIER

WALL WITH VAPOUR BARRIER
PREVENTS VAPOUR DIFFUSION BUT NOT AIR LEAKAGE

Figure 1.16 Water diffusion through an electric outlet. (Reproduced by permission; R. L. Quirouette, *The Difference Between a Vapour Barrier and an Air Barrier,* Building Practice Note #54, National Research Council Canada, Ottawa, 1985)

exterior walls (including windows), roof, and ground floor slab. This information is the basis used for sizing the equipment to compensate for the required thermal modifications.

To enable the engineer to perform this task, the architect provides a set of preliminary drawings which include floor plans showing the shape and orientation of the building, building elevations showing window and door areas, and typical wall sections containing as much information about exterior wall construction as possible. This information must include a description of all materials used in the assembly indicating thickness, width of air cavities, information about window glass and frames, as well as any reflective films to be used in the walls and windows.

Based on this information the engineer determines the coefficient of heat transmission, or U-value, for the building envelope. This is the overall heat transfer from the interior to the exterior in winter and vice versa in summer. Each component (walls, roof, and slab-on-grade) is calculated in this manner. The engineer also determines the optimum shading coefficient for the windows. This is the ratio of solar heat gain through the chosen glass (tinted, reflective, etc.) to the gain through

a single thickness of clear glass ⅛ in (3 mm) thick. The lower the shading coefficient, the lower the solar heat gain. This information is given to the architect who checks the final design to make sure that the building envelope conforms to the U-value (R = 1/U) upon which the mechanical engineer sized the equipment.

1.4.1 Heat Transfer

The building envelope, if left without protection from temperature fluctuations could render the interior unbearably hot in summer and freezingly cold in winter. These extremes are most clearly felt in hot, humid areas in the summer and cold regions in the winter. Weather is not the only factor affecting the temperature inside a building. Other factors include the area of windows and doors; the number of occupants, their ages, and what activities they perform; heat generated by the occupants, lighting, and electrical or electronic equipment; as well as the effect of building orientation. One of the important factors affecting energy consumption, however, is heat flow through walls and roofs. Heat travels from warm to cold areas by

- Convection
- Conduction
- Radiation

The following is a brief description of each.

CONVECTION

Convection is heat transferred by air currents. As air is heated, it expands, becomes lighter, and moves upward in the wall cavity and is supplanted by cooler air moving in the opposite direction adjacent to the cold side of the wall [Fig. 1.17(a)]. This continuous movement transfers heat from the warm side to the cold.

CONDUCTION

Conduction is heat transfer in a solid body or liquid. When you touch a hot pot, the heat you feel is the result of heat traveling by conduction from the heating element to the side of the pot. Metals are good conductors while wood, plastics, and similar materials are considered as insulators. In wall assemblies, heat travels through studs and slab edges. This is referred to as *thermal bridging*. Window frames, if not thermally broken by a plastic insulator, will conduct heat at an accelerated rate. Figure 1.17(b) shows an example of a thermally broken window.

RADIATION

Radiation is the transfer of heat by light waves. The sun's rays traveling through the vacuum of space is a

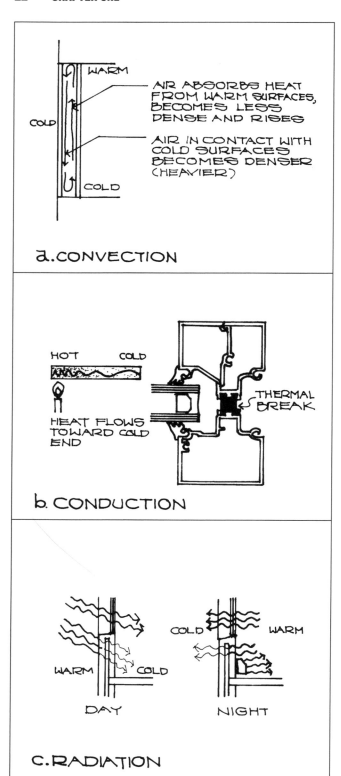

a. CONVECTION

b. CONDUCTION

c. RADIATION

Figure 1.17 How heat is transferred from hot to cold areas.

prime example. Heat travels by radiation until it is interrupted by an opaque object which absorbs the heat and transfers it by conduction to the rest of the material [Fig. 1.17(*c*)]. If the material is reflective, such as aluminum foil, it will reflect most of the heat and absorb the remaining fraction.

In wall assemblies, radiation transfers solar heat through air spaces. It also transfers internal heat toward the exterior. The largest portion of radiant heat travels through windows.

1.4.2 Methods of Protection

Insulative materials are usually included in the wall assembly in nontemperate regions. The thickness of insulation is determined by the available space within the wall thickness and by the cost of insulation. This thickness must be balanced against the cost of the heating and cooling system and fuel costs. There is a point of diminishing returns beyond which added insulation is not cost effective. In a similar process, evaluating the acoustical performance of insulation is required in noisy environments. Resilient, high-density materials insulate against vibration while materials with open, porous surfaces absorb sound. Designers must examine the characteristic of the insulative materials before making final decisions. They must review whether the material is flammable requiring protection with a fire-resistive material like wallboard. They must also find out the perm rating to determine whether it will impede water vapor migration and cause condensation in the assembly.

To slow heat transmission to and from the exterior, three defense mechanisms may be used:

- Resistive insulation
- Reflective insulation
- Capacity insulation (also known as thermal mass)

The following is a review of the three insulation types mentioned above.

RESISTIVE INSULATION

Materials used in construction resist the passage of heat at different rates depending on their physical characteristics and thickness. This resistance is referred to as the *R-value*. Some materials provide a far greater insulative resistance than ordinary construction materials. In most cases, they are used exclusively for that purpose and referred to as *insulation*.

R-values are listed in most technical literature on the subject of heating and cooling. For architects, *Architectural Graphic Standards*[4] contains a table listing the R-value for most building materials used in wall construction. Insulation must always be indicated on the drawings by its R-value rather than by its thickness, because thermal resistance is rarely the same for the same thickness produced by different manufacturers.

R-values are additive. This means that, after determining the R-value for each component of the wall assembly, these values can be added to arrive at the total resistance R_T for the assembly. There are, however, a few factors to be taken into consideration. These factors are

1. Air films adjacent to the interior and exterior surfaces of the wall and air in cavities offer resistance to heat transfer. Table 1.4 gives information regarding R-values for air in these locations. Calculating the R-value for the wall assembly is the responsibility of the mechanical engineer. On rare occasions, the project architect may have to make a rough calculation to check whether a change in the detailing will impact the R-value of the wall in a substantial way. Figure 1.18 shows a sample calculation. Of course, the easiest way is to pick up the phone, call the engineer, and ask.

2. Framing members, such as studs, reduce the overall R-value of the assembly because they offer less resistance to heat flow than the adjacent insulation. Likewise, other elements, such as slab edges, can interrupt perimeter insulation and reduce its effec-

tiveness. These elements are referred to as thermal bridges because they act as a bridge over the insulative heat barrier providing easy access to heat flow. They are allowed for in the calculation done by the mechanical engineer.

The following is a description of the most commonly used types of insulation for walls:

Batt Insulation. This type is commonly used to fill the wall cavity between studs. Batts are manufactured from fiberglass and are produced in standard widths to fit snugly between studs spaced 16 and 24 in (400 and 600 mm) on center. There is a slight width difference between batts intended to fit between wood studs and those produced to fit between metal studs. Batts should not be compressed to fit in a narrower space because they lose some of their R-value with compression. This type of insulation ranges in thickness from 3½ in (90 mm), for an R-value of 11, to 8 in (200 mm) for an R-value of 25. This product is manufactured in regular and high-density batts. Some sizes are produced in three densities, each with a different R-value. Batt insulation may be unfaced or have Kraft paper or foil facers.

Semirigid Insulation. This type is manufactured from fiberglass or mineral wool fiber with a thermosetting binder in 24 × 48 in (600 × 1200 mm) panels as well as custom sizes. Thicknesses range from 1 to 4 in (25 to 100 mm) with an R-value of approximately 3.25 per inch. Semirigid insulation may be unfaced or foil-faced and is also produced in several densities. It is used in curtain walls or attached to masonry. A denser type of mineral wool is used to prevent fire from migrating between floors. It is referred to as fire-safing insulation.

Rigid Insulation. Rigid insulation is manufactured from polystyrene, polyisocyanurate, phenolic foam, and high-density fiberglass. Thicknesses vary from ½ to 4 in (13 to 100 mm). Panel sizes vary according to the application. Plastic-based insulation such as polystyrene and polyisocyanurate is flammable and must be protected by gypsum board or other flame-resistant materials if placed facing the interior. There are two kinds of polystyrene, expanded polystyrene and extruded polystyrene. Expanded polystyrene (EPS) or beadboard, as it is called in the field, is of a lesser density and R-value (approximately 3.5 per inch) than extruded polystyrene which is more impact resistant. Both kinds are used to insulate masonry or concrete walls and exterior insulation and finish systems (EIFS).

Expanded polystyrene is also used as inserts in CMU cells. The extruded kind is used as insulation around foundations, as sheathing, and in precast panels. It has an average R-value of approximately 5.4 per inch. Polyisocyanurate panels have a higher R-value of approxi-

Position of Surface	Direction of Heat Flow	Surface Emittance, ϵ					
		Non-reflective $\epsilon = 0.90$		Reflective $\epsilon = 0.20$		$\epsilon = 0.05$	
		h_i	R	h_i	R	h_i	R
STILL AIR							
Horizontal	Upward	1.63	0.61	0.91	1.10	0.76	1.32
Sloping—45°	Upward	1.60	0.62	0.88	1.14	0.73	1.37
Vertical	Horizontal	1.46	0.68	0.74	1.35	0.59	1.70
Sloping—45°	Downward	1.32	0.76	0.60	1.67	0.45	2.22
Horizontal	Downward	1.08	0.92	0.37	2.70	0.22	4.55
MOVING AIR (Any position)		h_o	R	h_o	R	h_o	R
15-mph Wind (for winter)	Any	6.00	0.17	—	—	—	—
7.5-mph Wind (for summer)	Any	4.00	0.25	—	—	—	—

Notes:
1. Surface conductance h_i and h_o measured in Btu/h·ft²·°F; resistance R in °F·ft²·h/Btu.
2. No surface has both an air space resistance value and a surface resistance value.
3. For ventilated attics or spaces above ceilings under summer conditions (heat flow down), see Table 5.
4. Conductances are for surfaces of the stated emittance facing virtual blackbody surroundings at the same temperature as the ambient air. Values are based on a surface-air temperature difference of 10°F and for surface temperatures of 70°F.
5. See Chapter 3 for more detailed information, especially Tables 5 and 6, and see Figure 1 for additional data.
6. Condensate can have a significant impact on surface emittance (see Table 3).

Table 1.4 Surface conductances and resistances for air. See Appendix A for metric equivalents. (Reproduced by permission; American Society of Heating, Refrigeration and Air Conditioning Engineers, *Handbook of Fundamentals,* 1989)

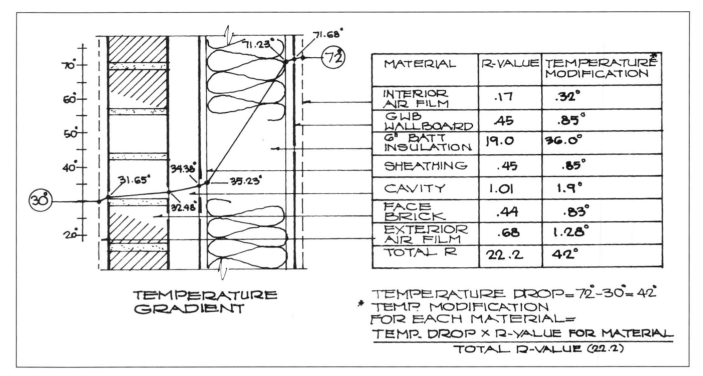

MATERIAL	R-VALUE	TEMPERATURE MODIFICATION*
INTERIOR AIR FILM	.17	.32°
GWB WALLBOARD	.45	.85°
6" BATT INSULATION	19.0	36.0°
SHEATHING	.45	.85°
CAVITY	1.01	1.9°
FACE BRICK	.44	.83°
EXTERIOR AIR FILM	.68	1.28°
TOTAL R	22.2	42°

TEMPERATURE DROP = 72°–30° = 42°
* TEMP. MODIFICATION
FOR EACH MATERIAL =
TEMP. DROP × R-VALUE FOR MATERIAL
TOTAL R-VALUE (22.2)

Figure 1.18   The R-value of a wall assembly.

mately 7.5 per inch. They are used in metal sandwich panels and prefabricated waferboard-faced panels for residential and light commercial construction. Both extruded polystyrene and polyisocyanurate panels are also used to insulate roofs.

Loose Fill. Perlite and vermiculite are lightweight granular materials used to fill the cells of CMU walls to increase their R-value. This form of insulation is not as effective as rigid or semirigid insulation used to cover the entire wall surface because the CMU cell walls act as thermal bridges interrupting the insulation and transferring heat from one side to the other. They are also used to fill the cavity in cavity walls.

REFLECTIVE INSULATION

To resist radiant heat traveling through a wall cavity, reflective films such as aluminum foil are sometimes used to face one side of the cavity. Foil is usually used as a facer for a more rigid material such as Kraft paper or gypsum board. It must face a cavity to be effective in reflecting radiative heat.

CAPACITY INSULATION

Some materials such as masonry and concrete acquire heat at a slow rate during the day and release it at a similar rate during the night. This has a dampening effect on heat fluctuations resulting in energy savings. Adobe buildings in New Mexico are an example that comes to

mind. The thick walls of these dwellings are built of mud bricks that keep the interior cool during the heat of the day. By sunset, the heat would have traveled through the thickness of the wall and reached the opposite side heating the interior. Szokolay,[5] an Australian authority on the subject, developed diagrams comparing the behavior of a ⅜-in (10 mm) polystyrene sheet, defined as a zero-mass element, to a 9-in (230 mm) solid brick wall during a 24-h period. Both materials have the same R-value, but their response to heat is different. Figure 1.19(a) shows the difference in heat gain rates during a 24-h period and Fig. 1.19(b) shows that the peak of heat flow through the brick wall is delayed by some 7 h behind that of the insulating material. The difference in the amplitude of heat flow is represented by the equation: $f = sQ/sQ_0$ where f = the decrement factor (Table 1.5), sQ = daily mean heat flow, and sQ_0 = zero-mass element (polystyrene). Mr. Szokolay developed Table 1.5 indicating U-values, time lag, and decrement factor values for numerous multilayer constructions. Some building materials shown in the table have different dimensions from what we are accustomed to in the United States. These drawings and tables are presented here to illustrate a point. Architects usually do not get involved in these calculations.

Capacity insulation is very effective in dry hot climates with hot days and cold nights. Hot, humid climates with hot nights as well as cold climates with little difference in

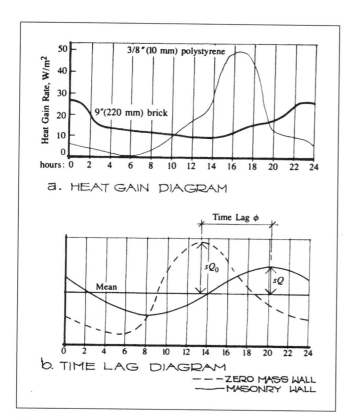

Figure 1.19 Comparison between the periodic heat flow of a brick wall and a zero mass element. (Reproduced by permission; H. J. Cowan, ed., *Handbook of Architectural Technology,* Van Nostrand Reinhold, 1991)

temperature between night and day usually require the placement of insulation at the exterior of the wall. The reason is that the sun's rays entering through windows warm the interior. Masonry walls absorb that heat and release it slowly during the night. If the insulation is installed on the interior face of the wall, it would interfere with this process and reduce the ability of the wall to transmit the heat absorbed from the sun to the interior. It also prevents the wall from absorbing heat from the interior.

Shading entire walls with overhangs, balconies, or trees and using double roofs and light colors are all ways to reduce interior temperature in such climates.

1.4.3 What Can Go Wrong

Unlike air barriers, defenses against water leakage, and vapor migration, very little can go wrong with a thermal barrier (insulation). The following are a few issues to guard against.

CONDENSATION

If condensation occurs within the insulation, it will lose much of its R-value. Leakage from the exterior or vapor exfiltration must not be allowed within the wall assembly.

FOIL-FACED MATERIALS

Architects entrusted with detailing projects located in states other than where they normally practice must check with a local architect or engage the services of a local mechanical engineer before they include a foil-faced material or another vapor retarder in the wall assembly. As mentioned before, the location of the vapor retarder varies depending on the temperature and relative humidity of the zone. This means facing the interior in cold climates, the exterior in hot or humid climates, and the use of nonfaced insulation in temperate, dry climates.

THERMAL BRIDGING

Any interruption in the insulation results in thermal bridging. The interrupting material, in most cases, contributes little resistance to heat transfer. Apart from EIFS and some sandwich panel systems, wall sections will include thermal bridging in the form of metal studs, masonry ties, slab edges, metal lintels, shelf angles, and other components of the wall assembly. While most of these items are taken into consideration by the mechanical engineer, the architect should make every effort to minimize their area or provide insulation to reduce heat transfer through them. In doing so, he or she would be saving energy and reducing the potential for the accumulation of condensation on these cold surfaces. Placing rigid insulation over the sheathing or poured insulation in the cavity are two of the most commonly used methods to reduce the effect of thermal bridging.

OVERDESIGN

Most architects are so busy detailing the project, solving problems, preparing specifications, managing the team, attending meetings, etc., that they take a shortcut to determine the R-value of the wall assembly. They ask the mechanical engineer about the R-value and choose an insulating material having the same value instead of adding the R-value of the other components of the wall assembly including cavities. While this is erring on the safe side by providing more insulation than is necessary, it results in unnecessary expense to the owner. The extra cost results from the added cost of unnecessary insulation and the oversizing of mechanical equipment.

The proper procedure is to request a printout of the data used as a basis for calculating the U-values from the engineer. Double check the wall and window areas against those shown on the final drawings to ascertain

	U-value, Btu/ft² h °F	Admittance, Btu/ft² h °F	U-value W/m² K	Admittance, W/m² K	Time Lag, hours	Decrement Factor
Walls						
brick, single skin, 4.5 in. (110 mm)	0.58	0.74	3.28	4.2	2.6	0.87
9 in. (230 mm)	0.40	0.83	2.26	4.7	6.1	0.54
13 in. (335 mm)	0.30	0.83	1.73	4.7	9.4	0.29
brick, single skin, 4.5 in. (110 mm) plastered	0.53	0.72	3.02	4.1	3.0	0.83
9 in. (230 mm) plastered	0.38	0.79	2.14	4.5	6.5	0.49
13 in. (335 mm) plastered	0.32	0.79	1.79	4.5	9.9	0.26
brick, cavity, 11 in. (270 mm) plastered	0.26	0.77	1.47	4.4	7.7	0.44
same with 1 in. (25 mm) EPS in cavity	0.13	0.81	0.72	4.6	8.9	0.34
same with 1.5 in. (40 mm) EPS in cavity	0.10	0.83	0.55	4.7	9.1	0.32
same with 2 in. (50 mm) EPS in cavity	0.08	0.83	0.47	4.7	9.2	0.31
concrete block, solid, 8 in. (200 mm) + plasterboard	0.32	0.44	1.83	2.5	6.8	0.35
same but foil-backed plasterboard	0.25	0.32	1.40	1.82	7.0	0.32
same + 1 in. (25 mm) EPS (no cavity)	0.16	0.21	0.93	1.2	7.2	0.30
same but 1 in. (25 mm) cavity + 1 in. (25 mm) EPS + plasterboard	0.12	0.18	0.70	1.0	7.3	0.29
same but lightweight concrete	0.12	0.32	0.68	1.8	7.4	0.46
same but foil-backed plasterboard	0.11	0.26	0.61	1.5	7.7	0.42
same + 1 in. (25 mm) EPS (no cavity)	0.09	0.19	0.50	1.1	8.2	0.36
same but 1 in. (25 mm) cavity + 1 in. (25 mm) EPS + plasterboard	0.08	0.18	0.46	1.0	8.3	0.34
concrete block, hollow, 4 in. (100 mm) inside plastered	0.44	0.67	2.50	3.8	2.4	0.89
same, 8 in. (200 mm) inside plastered	0.43	0.72	2.42	4.1	3.0	0.83
concrete, dense, cast, 6 in. (150 mm)	0.61	0.93	3.48	5.3	4.0	0.70
same + 2 in. (50 mm) woodwool slab plastered	0.22	0.30	1.23	1.7	6.0	0.50
same but lightweight plaster	0.20	0.30	1.15	1.7	6.3	0.49
concrete, dense, cast, 8 in. (200 mm)	0.54	0.97	3.10	5.5	5.4	0.56
same + 2 in. (50 mm) woodwool slab plastered	0.21	0.39	1.18	2.2	7.7	0.36
same but lightweight plaster	0.19	0.30	1.11	1.7	7.6	0.35
concrete precast panel, 3 in. (75 mm)	0.75	0.86	4.28	4.9	1.9	0.91
same + 1 in. (25) cavity + 1 in. (25) EPS + plasterboard	0.15	0.18	0.84	1.0	3.0	0.82
concrete precast, 3 in. (75) + 1 in. (25) EPS + 6 in. (150 mm) lightweight concrete	0.10	0.40	0.58	2.3	8.7	0.41
same but 2 in. (50 mm) EPS	0.07	0.42	0.41	2.4	9.2	0.35
brick veneer, 4.5 in. (110 mm) + cavity + plasterboard	0.31	0.39	1.77	2.2	3.5	0.77
same but foil-backed plasterboard	0.24	0.30	1.36	1.7	3.7	0.75
same with 1 in. (25 mm) EPS or glass fiber	0.14	0.19	0.78	1.1	4.1	0.71
same with 2 in. (50 mm) EPS or glass fiber	0.09	0.16	0.50	0.9	4.3	0.69
same, 1 in. (25 mm) EPS + foil-backed plasterboard	0.12	0.18	0.69	1.0	4.1	0.71
block veneer, 4 in. (100 mm) + cavity + plasterboard	0.28	0.37	1.57	2.1	4.1	0.72
same but foil-backed plasterboard	0.22	0.30	1.24	1.7	4.3	0.69
same with 1 in. (25 mm) EPS or glass fiber	0.13	0.19	0.74	1.1	4.7	0.65
same with 2 in. (50 mm) EPS or glass fiber	0.08	0.16	0.48	0.9	4.9	0.62
same, 1 in. (25 mm) EPS + foil-backed plasterboard	0.12	0.18	0.66	1.0	4.7	0.64
framed, single fibrous cement or galvanized steel sheeting	0.91	0.92	5.16	5.2	0	1
same + cavity + plasterboard	0.39	0.39	2.20	2.2	0.3	1
same + 1 in. (25 mm) EPS or glass fiber	0.15	0.19	0.86	1.1	0.5	0.99
same + 2 in. (50 mm) EPS or glass fiber	0.09	0.16	0.53	0.9	0.7	0.99

Table 1.5 Thermal properties of some building elements. (Reproduced by permission; H. J. Cowan, ed., *Handbook of Architectural Technology,* Van Nostrand Reinhold, 1991)

	U-value, $Btu/ft^2 h °F$	Admittance, $Btu/ft^2 h °F$	U-value $W/m^2 K$	Admittance, $W/m^2 K$	Time Lag, hours	Decrement Factor
Walls						
framed, 0.75 in. (20 mm) timber boarding	0.53	0.53	3.00	3.0	0.4	1
same + cavity + plasterboard	0.29	0.32	1.68	1.8	0.8	0.99
same + 1 in. (25 mm) EPS or glass fiber	0.13	0.18	0.76	1.0	1.0	0.99
same + 2 in. (50 mm) EPS or glass fiber	0.09	0.16	0.49	0.9	1.2	0.98
framed, tile-hanging + paper + cavity + 2 in. (50 mm) EPS + plasterboard	0.10	0.14	0.54	0.78	1.0	0.99
same but 4 in. (100 mm) EPS or glass fiber	0.06	0.12	0.32	0.71	1.0	0.99
wood frame, single 0.25 in. (6 mm) glass	0.88	0.88	5.0	5.0	0	1
double glazing	0.51	0.51	2.9	2.9	0	1
metal frame, single 0.25 in. (6 mm) glass	1.06	1.06	6.0	6.0	0	1
same but discontinuous frame	1.00	1.00	5.7	5.7	0	1
metal frame, double glazing	0.63	0.63	3.6	3.6	0	1
same but discontinuous frame	0.58	0.58	3.3	3.3	0	0
roof glazing, single 0.25 in. (6 mm) glass	1.16	1.16	6.6	6.6	0	1
double glazing	0.81	0.81	4.6	4.6	0	1
horizontal laylight + skylight,						
ventilated	0.67	0.67	3.8	3.8	0	1
unventilated	0.53	0.53	3.0	3.0	0	1

Table 1.5 (*cont.*) Thermal properties of some building elements. (Reproduced by permission; H. J. Cowan, ed., *Handbook of Architectural Technology,* Van Nostrand Reinhold, 1991)

that no changes have occurred in the elevation since the information was transmitted and specify the appropriate insulation. If a change in the design has occurred since the architect furnished the drawings to the engineer, that change must be communicated to him or her and the appropriate design change made accordingly.

1.5 EARTHQUAKES

The state of California comes to mind at the mention of earthquakes, but one look at a map of the United States showing earthquake epicenters (Fig. 1.20) indicates that while the western part of the United States experiences the bulk of seismic activity, the rest of the country is not unaffected. Most architects consider the aspects of the design related to withstanding earthquake forces to be the sole responsibility of the structural engineer. While this assumption may be tolerated in zones 1 and 2 (Fig. 1.21), it is rather risky when applied to zones 3 or 4. The architect who, in most building projects, makes design decisions must become thoroughly familiar with this subject. Building form, the location of supports and openings, and other decisions determined during the schematic phase can have a profound effect on how the building behaves during an earthquake. With time, this familiarity may even produce innovative solutions that can become a new standard applied to future buildings.

This section touches briefly on the mechanics of seismic action, describes the do's and don'ts of building form as well as the measures employed to add to their safety.

1.5.1 The Mechanics of Seismic Action
SEISMIC MOVEMENT

The earth's crust is divided into several large segments or plates floating on molten rock (Fig. 1.22). Convective currents in this liquefied material cause the plates to move at an almost imperceptible pace. When two abutting plates move against each other (Fig. 1.23), stresses build up at any obstruction impeding their movement. When these stresses exceed the resistance of the obstruction, a sudden slippage occurs along the length of the juncture between the plates creating vibrations radiating in all directions from the obstruction. The plates are referred to as *tectonic plates,* the juncture is known as a *fault,* and the obstruction is the *epicenter* of the vibration or earthquake. Earthquake vibrations are complex. Paul Weidlinger of Weidlinger Associates, consulting engineers describes the movements as follows:

> What we perceive as the shaking of the ground is a wave motion propagating outward from the location where the energy was released.
>
> The first wave known as the P-wave travels at about 14,000 mph, and it alternatively pushes and pulls on the foundations of buildings in the direction of its travel. Another wave, the S-wave, comes later, since it has only half the speed, but it tends to displace the foundations at right angles to the P-wave motion. Not only does it shake side to side, but also up and down at one half the frequency.[6]

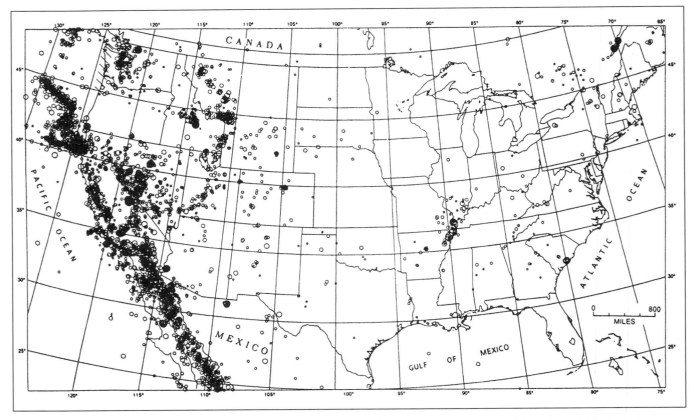

Figure 1.20   Earthquake epicenters and magnitudes in the Continental United States and parts of Canada and Mexico. (Reproduced by permission; Construction Specialties, Inc.)

The Uniform Building Code lists the following factors as the basis for seismic design:

1. Seismic hazard zone

2. Dynamic characteristic of the building

3. Type of structural system

4. Subsoil conditions

5. Importance of the building

6. Weight of the building

Unsuitable building designs in earthquake-prone regions can be catastrophic and very costly in economical terms. The 1985 Mexico City earthquake which measured 8.1 on the Richter scale killed more than 20,000 people and caused damage in excess of $4 billion. The 1994 earthquake in Los Angeles which measured 6.7 on the Richter scale caused damage in excess of $30 billion and left more than 25,000 people homeless.

Even single-story structures are not immune from the intense earthquake motion. For instance, the 1976 Tangshan earthquake in the People's Republic of China measuring 7.8 on the Richter scale killed more than 250,000

people and demolished the city which was 80% single-story nonreinforced masonry construction.[7] This demonstrates the pressing need for collaboration between all design professionals to continue monitoring the measures taken to produce earthquake-resistant designs and devise new mitigation measures to reduce the damage and loss of life.

IRREGULAR STRUCTURES

Symmetrical buildings located on level ground having uniform soil characteristics have a better chance of withstanding an earthquake than irregularly shaped buildings constructed on a site with varied soil conditions. Unfortunately, not all buildings located in seismically active zones can be designed under these conditions. The site may have a pronounced slope with several soil strata having different bearing capacities and movement reactions. The street pattern may create triangular sites that result in asymmetrical buildings.

While it is true that seismic forces may attack building foundations from any angle, it is assumed that they act perpendicular to the facades (Fig. 1.24). The reason being that if the shock wave hits the building at an

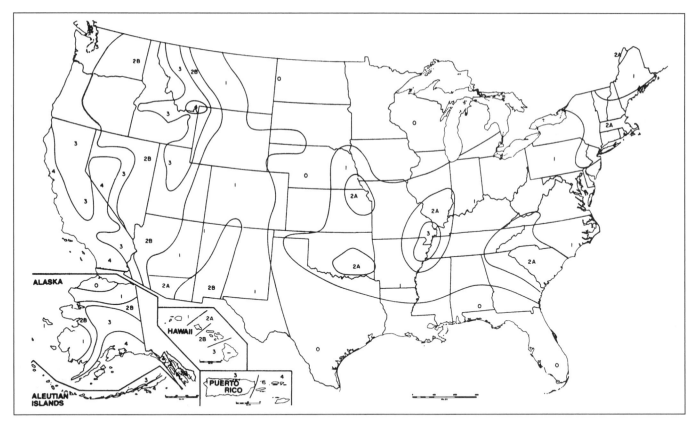

Figure 1.21 Seismic risk map of the United States. (Reproduced by permission; International Conference of Building Officials, *Uniform Building Code,* 1994 ed.)

angle, each side of the building will share in resisting the force. Designing each side to bear the full force of the earthquake is a more conservative approach.

The Structural Engineers Association of California (SEAOC), in its commentary portion on *Recommended Lateral Force Requirements and Commentary* (1975), listed more than 20 types of irregular structures or framing systems that have a higher potential for sustaining damage in an earthquake.[8] These designs present real challenges for the structural engineer resulting in much higher costs. Where possible, architects should avoid them in zones 3 and 4. Figure 1.25 illustrates a few of those types.

Earthquake movement can play havoc with *soft stories*. These are stories where the structure is less stiff than the rest of the building due to added height, discontinuities in columns, and omission of bracing elements such as spandrels or shear walls. Designers should also avoid these conditions if at all possible.

An earthquake will seek any weakness in the structure and concentrate on it. This includes, in addition to the conditions mentioned above, discontinuities in the floor diaphragm such as stairs or shafts. These elements create a weakness in the diaphragm that can prevent it

from transmitting lateral movement to stiffening vertical structural elements. Locating these openings at the intersection between wings, which is the usual choice, aggravates this weakness.

Asymmetrical or irregular plans produce different volumes that offer different resistances to movement. For instance, one wing of an L- or T-shaped building resists movement better than the other [Fig. 1.26(*a*)]. The same is especially true if the building is triangular in plan. This condition is further aggravated by the fact that the core, with its stiffening element, is usually located near one of the sides of the triangle [Fig. 1.26(*b*)].

POUNDING

One problem that caused much of the damage in the earthquake in Mexico City mentioned above is that adjacent buildings pounded against each other during the temblor (Fig. 1.27). One measure to take in this situation is to try to match the height of the existing neighboring building and leave a wide gap between the two buildings. A similar situation can occur if the building is bisected by an expansion joint. In this case, the structural engineer can design a wide expansion joint based on calculations that define the expected movement of the

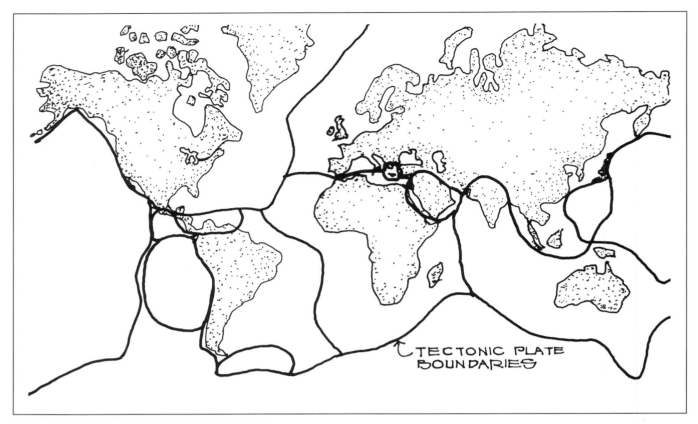

Figure 1.22 Continental tectonic plates.

two sides to prevent them from pounding against each other. Seismic joints can reach a width of 24 in (600 mm) and require special seals at exterior walls (Fig. 1.28). This can pose a challenge to the designer trying to minimize the impact of the joint on the esthetics of the elevation.

1.5.2 Mitigation Measures

To provide some protection from the impact of earthquake shock waves, several mitigation measures are employed. These include

- Stiff structures
- Base isolation
- Tuned mass damper

The following is a brief description of these design strategies.

STIFF STRUCTURES

Stiffening the structure to resist lateral forces can take several forms. It can be accomplished by introducing what is commonly referred to as *shear walls* constructed of either solid walls or trussed frames extending from the foundation to the top of the building in both orthogonal orientations. Because this solution is also used to resist wind pressure, it is used to stiffen most structural frames regardless of the seismic zone they are located in. For that reason, it is addressed in Chap. 2 (see Sec. 2.2.1) which deals with structural issues.

Elements such as heavy equipment must be located in a manner that does not conflict with this concept, add eccentricity to the loading, or act in a manner similar to an upside down pendulum.

Brittle veneers such as tiles should be avoided as a finish on walls subject to shear deformation. Window frame isolation in these walls is also essential to minimize glass breakage. Exit door frames should be designed with shock-absorbing perimeters to prevent them from getting stuck and preventing the occupants from evacuating the building during the emergency (Fig. 1.29).

Stiff or heavy buildings tend to attract more seismic force than light or flexible buildings. The heavier the building, the greater is the horizontal load assumed to be acting on each floor. While the stiff structure approach provides relative safety to the occupants, considerable damage to the structural frame may still occur. This approach to seismic design can be likened to a car traveling along a bumpy road without shock absorbers. On the other hand, a more flexible frame will accom-

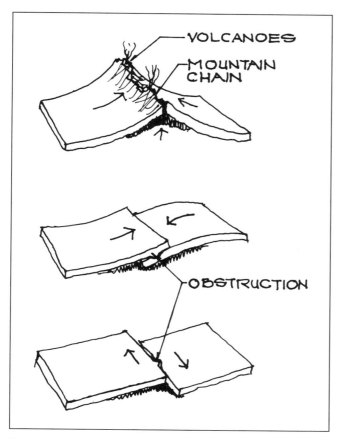

Figure 1.23 Types of tectonic plate movements.

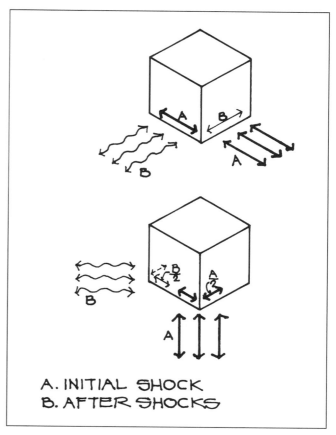

A. INITIAL SHOCK
B. AFTER SHOCKS

Figure 1.24 Design based on the premise that seismic forces are acting perpendicular to the facade assumes the severest case of loading.

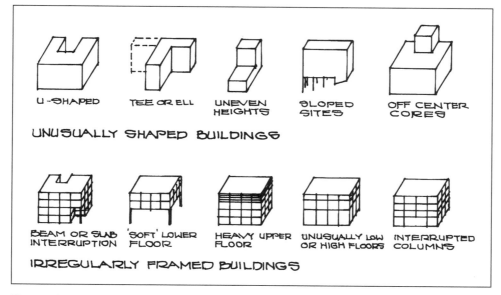

Figure 1.25 Buildings that are most susceptible to earthquake damage.

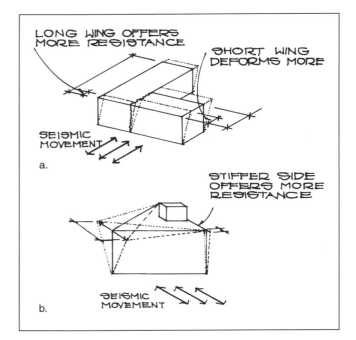

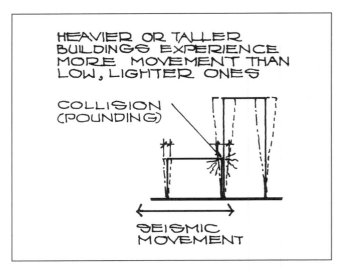

Figure 1.27 Damage caused by pounding.

Figure 1.26 The effect of seismic movements on irregularly shaped buildings.

modate more movement but may result in heavy damage to the interiors.

BASE ISOLATION

A more sophisticated approach to mitigation of seismic movements is to design the foundation in such a way that it would absorb the bulk of ground movement without transmitting that movement to the superstructure. This is referred to as *base isolation*. This approach is recognized by the 1991 Uniform Building Code and is considered by many to be a safer and more economical design strategy applicable to both new construction and restoration projects. It is currently applied to medium- and low-rise buildings.

Frank Lloyd Wright was the first to use this approach in his design for the Imperial Hotel in Tokyo in 1922. His base isolation design consisted of driving 8-ft (2.4 m) tapered wooden piles into the ground, retracting them, and immediately filling the holes with concrete. These concrete pins, spaced 2 ft (600 mm) apart supported jointed footing courses and rested on very weak soil conditions. The system functioned well to absorb shock waves in a subsequent severe earthquake with relatively little damage to the superstructure compared to other buildings in the area.

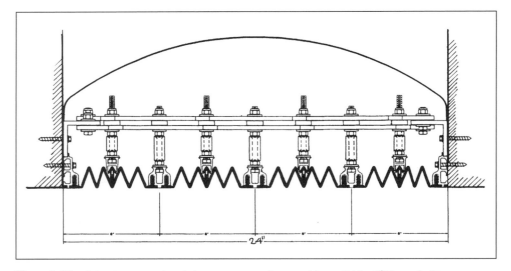

Figure 1.28 Seismic expansion joint covers can be as wide as 24 in (600 mm). (Reproduced by permission; Construction Specialties, Inc.)

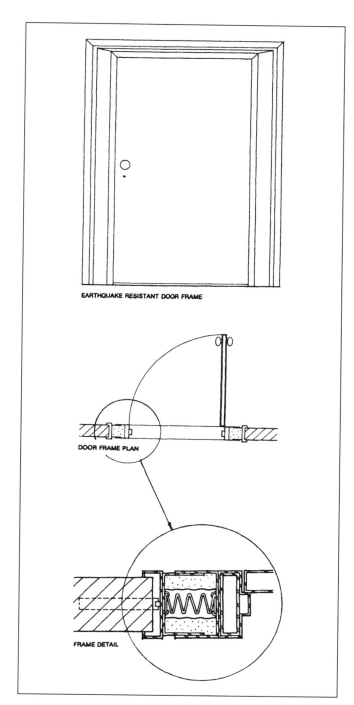

EARTHQUAKE RESISTANT DOOR FRAME

DOOR FRAME PLAN

FRAME DETAIL

Figure 1.29 An exit door designed for safe operation during an earthquake. (Reproduced by permission; Richard Rush, "Building in the Path of Nature's Wrath," *Progressive Architecture,* Penton Publishing, February 1980)

Engineers in New Zealand, a nation located in a seismically active zone, introduced two systems using base isolation in the early eighties. The first was used on a relatively large four-story government building and employed laminated steel and rubber pads with a cylin-

drical lead core [Fig. 1.30(*a*)] to support the building. These supports are capable of allowing the building to move up to 8 in (200 mm) without rupture. They have a dampening effect similar to a car's shock absorber. Similar designs have been successfully used on other projects in the United States. Another design for base isolation utilizes a concave steel plate supported on a sliding hemisphere [Fig. 1.30(*b*)]. This support system was invented by Victor Zayas, president of Earthquake Protection Systems. To allow the building to move, a gap, sometimes referred to as a *moat,* is usually left around the perimeter of the building to allow it to move. It is bridged over by a sliding plate.[9]

Buildings using base isolation technology must provide flexible connections for all utilities. Items that normally rest on the ground such as storefronts and first-floor elevator shafts and pits must be hung from the floor above and isolated from ground movement (Fig. 1.31).

Base isolation allows the structure to move as a unit with minimum distortion and damage. The bulk of the movement is absorbed by the foundation. Theoretically, both the interior finishes and exterior cladding should survive an earthquake without sustaining any significant damage. However, base isolation does have limitations. The superstructure has to be made stiff to prevent racking as it moves which adds 3 to 4% to the initial construction cost. This is a good investment in seismically active zones but is not suitable for high-rise buildings.

TUNED MASS DAMPERS

A measure used in high-rise buildings to resist both wind pressure and seismic movement is a system referred to as a *tuned mass damper.* The damper is a heavy element located at or near the top of the building and activated by a mechanism to provide an equal and opposite reaction to lateral movement. This results in canceling or minimizing the kinetic effect on the building.

One of the first applications of this design was introduced in the Centerpoint Tower in Sydney, Australia by incorporating the water tank in the design of the damper. A more recent installation created by the engineering firm of LeMessurier and Associates is a 400-ton block of concrete constructed as part of a motion dampening system at the top of Citicorp Bank Tower in New York City (Fig. 1.32).

PROTECTING THE CLADDING

During an earthquake, a differential movement, referred to as *structural frame drift,* occurs between floors (see Fig. 2.7). The extent of this movement depends upon the stiffness of the structure and the intensity of the earthquake. For infill panels such as stud-backed plaster, tile, or similar cladding the designer must take frame drift

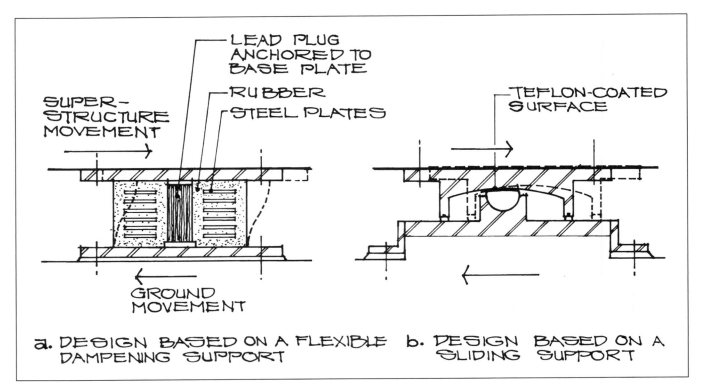

Figure 1.30 Base isolation systems.

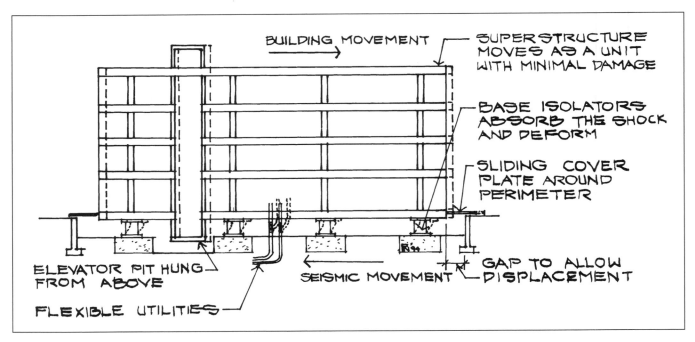

Figure 1.31 Base isolation measures to minimize damage.

into consideration. This can be achieved by designing the structure for minimum drift and providing a wider joint between the wall panel and the structural frame (see Fig. 2.9). Designing the joint to protect the interior against noise, weather, and fire is of the utmost importance. Foamed polyurethane backed by an intumescent fire-resistant sealant can provide the required protection.

Wall panel supports must be designed to allow movement between wall panels and the structural frame. This can be achieved by either allowing the connections to deform or by allowing the fasteners to slide through slots (a slotted connection) or oversize holes (see Fig. 2.8).

In seismic zones, lightweight cladding, such as metal or glass fiber–reinforced concrete (GFRC), systems are advantageous because their low mass does not give as much momentum to seismic movement as heavier systems. As a result the stress on the structure as well as on the connectors is reduced.

Precast or stone panels placed at building corners should be designed with the joint placed at the corner in the form of a quirk with a wide joint rather than using a single-piece corner panel. The first arrangement avoids stresses that can cause cracking.

FUTURE POSSIBILITIES

It is conceivable that a hovercraft-like system using an air or water cushion can be devised to provide the ulti-

mate base isolation solution by lifting the building from its foundation. Although this may sound too far-fetched, there are actual structures that utilize these systems. One example is the Aloha Stadium in Hawaii (Fig. 1.33) designed with four movable grandstands resting on air bearings designed according to the same principle used in hovercraft to reconfigure the seating as shown. Another mobile structure is the Mile High Stadium in Denver which uses bearings to achieve a similar function (Fig. 1.34). Using a similar system triggered by a motion detector calibrated to respond to seismic movement could provide safety to buildings in severe seismic zones. The triggering mechanism should differentiate between normal everyday vibrations and the distinctive earthquake movements.

An example of such a triggering mechanism was created by a company in New Zealand which introduced an earthquake sensor to trigger emergency equipment and shut down dangerous machinery during an earthquake.[10] Other measures used in base isolation designs to isolate utilities, elevators, and cladding can be utilized in this design also. To my knowledge, no building using the air or water cushioning approach is planned at this writing.

1.5.3   What Can Go Wrong

Earthquakes are unpredictable. Anything can and usually does happen during a severe earthquake. The amount of

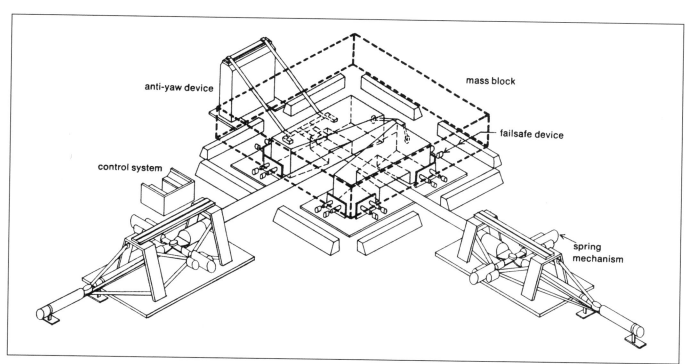

Figure 1.32   Tuned Mass Damper at the top of Citicorp Bank Tower in New York City. (Reproduced by permission; *Architectural Record,* "Engineering for Architecture," mid-August 1976)

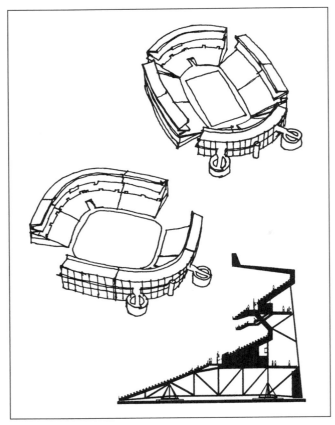

Figure 1.33 The Aloha Stadium in Hawaii. Charles Luckman Associates, Architect. Air film system by Rolair Systems. (Reproduced by permission; *Architectural Record,* "Innovation," mid-August 1976)

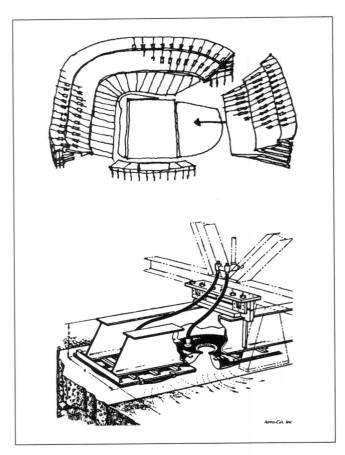

Figure 1.34 Mile High Stadium in Denver, Colorado. DMJM, Inc., Architect. Lifting system by Aero-Go, Inc. (Reproduced by permission; *Architectural Record,* "Innovation," mid-August 1976)

damage and the extent of destruction depends on the mitigating measures used and the severity of the earthquake.

1.6 MISCELLANEOUS FORCES

Section 1.5 addressed one of the most potent forces of nature that come to bear on exterior walls. This part of the text deals with a few natural phenomena that affect construction to a lesser degree but are, nevertheless, quite important. Whereas leakage, deterioration, drafts, and temperature fluctuations are very important, their effect takes a relatively long time to be considered hazardous to the occupants. Fire, on the other hand, can devastate a building and cause loss of life in a matter of hours. Fortunately, there are measures to prevent that from happening. Electrolysis has the potential for eating through a metal resulting in the eventual failure of a connection. Acoustics play an important role in the quality of life within an enclosed space. Insect and bird infestation also have an effect on buildings.

These are by no means all the natural forces and phenomena that buildings are subjected to. Lightning is another awesome force of nature. A lightning bolt seeks the highest element to use as a conduit from the clouds to earth. Codes define the necessary measures required to provide a safe passage for this tremendous energy. These measures usually include a metal network around the highest points of the roof connected to heavy copper rods leading to a grounding network. In steel-frame buildings, the frame itself is usually used in lieu of the rods. Rods are placed within a polyvinyl chloride (PVC) pipe encased in the columns in concrete-frame structures. When a building is surrounded by or is situated in close proximity to taller buildings, it is usually not required to have lightning protection. Because the task of designing the grounding system is handled by the electrical engineer, lightning is not addressed in this section. The architect must, however, review the electrical drawings to make sure that nothing shown therein impacts the architectural details.

Light is another phenomenon that has an effect on sizing fenestration and the introduction of shading devices. This is a rather broad subject that affects the designer more than the detailer. An element of it is dealt with briefly in Chap. 3 where glass treatments such as tinting or reflective coatings are addressed.

The following selection of miscellaneous forces is discussed:

- Fire
- Electrolysis
- Sound
- Infestation

1.6.1 Fire

The effect of fire on buildings can be devastating. The codes define the fire-rating requirements for exterior walls. This is based on their proximity to walls of adjacent buildings. The closer the buildings, the higher the rating. Windows in these walls are also required to be rated or protected by fire sprinkler heads.

Once a fire starts in a multistory structure, it can travel from floor to floor if certain measures to stop it are ignored. Here again codes are specific about describing these measures. Fire-safing insulation is usually introduced between the edge of floor slabs and the exterior wall and sealed to prevent smoke from migrating between floors (Fig. 1.35). Some codes also stipulate that part of the exterior cladding be rated to prevent flames from traveling from floor to floor. All-glass curtain walls are especially vulnerable if this is not observed because the heat of the flames shatters the glass. In the absence of that barrier, there is a definite danger of fire migration between floors. United States Gypsum Company (USG) has tested a system that protects the spandrel glass and the vertical mullions (Fig. 1.36). The company states that the test was monitored by representatives from Underwriters Laboratories (UL), but as of this writing, the design has not been included in the UL Directory.

Confining a fire within a limited space and preventing it from migrating from floor to floor or from building to building is of prime concern to all architects. Defensive measures must be designed in conformance to the building code and executed properly to prevent unnecessary loss of life and damage to property. Designers must investigate and document the combustion toxicity of every material they specify to reduce the danger to building occupants.

Codes specify flame spread and smoke generation limits for interior wall finishes and, as stated earlier, fire-rated GWB is required to separate flammable rigid insulation such as polystyrene from the interior. This applies to all materials in the building especially carpeting, furnishings, and wall covering.

The best defense against the spread of a fire is a sprinkler system in conjunction with fire protection for the structural frame. The UL Fire-Resistance Directory lists several fire-rated wall assemblies. For exterior walls, masonry and precast construction with 1-, 2-, 3-, or 4-h ratings are available. Floor assemblies framing into the wall must also be protected. Cementitious or fiber spray is normally used on steel spandrel beams and columns. To determine the fire rating, an actual part of the assembly is subjected to fire under controlled conditions to determine the length of time it can last without failure. This means that any change from the components described in the approved design may result in noncompliance. Of course, a change to a heavier structural member is acceptable.

Table 1.6 gives information about the thickness of fireproofing relative to the fire rating on columns. It is useful in developing wall section details (see also Chap. 5). Be sure to allow an adequate clearance between the sprayed spandrel beam and the exterior wall to provide space for screw-attaching the wallboard to resist wind pressure. Allow a minimum ½ in (13 mm) between column fireproofing and the furring studs enclosing it. Thin-film intumescent fireproofing is applied like paint with a brush or roller or by spraying it onto exposed steel. If exposed to fire, the film softens and expands to form a layer up to ⅜ in (100 mm) thick providing protection up to 1½ h. Intumescent protection ranging in thickness from ¼ to ¾ in (6 to 20 mm) in thickness can also be applied as a thicker sprayed mastic coating which presents a rougher pebbled finish or troweled smooth surface suitable for exposed exterior use. It provides up to 3 h of fire protection. This method of fireproofing costs more than other fire-resistive treatments and is usually specified where the structure is designed to be exposed to view.

Cementitious fireproofing is a Portland cement–based, sprayed-on fireproofing applied to unprimed steel columns, beams, and, in some cases, the metal deck to provide up to 4 h of fire protection. Most cementitious fireproofing is not suitable for exposure to weather. Certain types are formulated for interior applications in unenclosed buildings like parking garages and mechanical rooms. Check with the product representative before making the final selection.

Sprayed-on fiber fireproofing applications are dry mixes containing mineral fibers. They are dry pumped and wetted at the spray nozzle. This method provides the same protection as cementitious fireproofing but usually is applied at a greater thickness. It has a lesser density and cohesion than the cementitious type and is easier to damage especially during construction prior to enclosure within the furring. It is, however, less costly

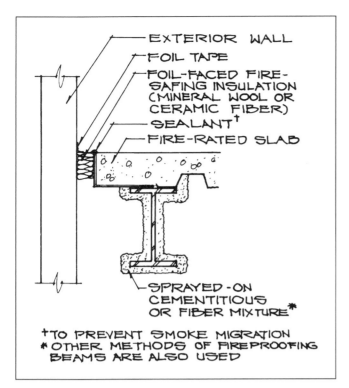

Figure 1.35 Placing a fire stop to fill the gap between the slab edge and wall panel prevents fire and smoke from traveling from floor to floor.

which makes it the preferred method for commercial construction. Some articles that appeared in technical literature have questioned the effect of the fibers on the health of building occupants especially when the area between the ceiling and the floor slab is used as a return-air plenum. To this author's knowledge, as of this writing no proof has been established that this is the case.

1.6.2 Electrolysis

Electrolysis, otherwise referred to as galvanic action or galvanic corrosion, is the tendency of one kind of metal to corrode when placed in contact with another metal in the presence of a solution (usually impure water). This solution acts in a similar fashion to an electrolyte in a battery. Figure 1.37 lists some of the metals commonly used in construction. The farther apart the metals in the list, the more corrosion will occur in the "less noble" metal. For instance, if magnesium is in contact with gold in the presence of an electrolyte, magnesium will suffer extensive corrosion in a relatively short period of time. The Specialty Steel Industry of the United States[11] points out that galvanic action also depends on the relative surface area of each material. If stainless-steel fasteners are used to join carbon-steel plates in the presence of water, very little corrosion will occur. If, on the other hand, carbon-steel rivets are used to fasten stainless-steel plates in a wet environment, the rivets will corrode quickly. As is

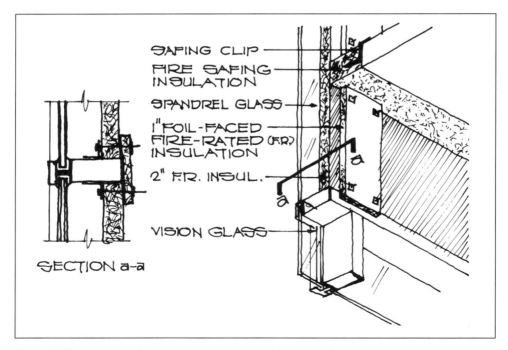

Figure 1.36 Spandrel glass protection as proposed by United States Gypsum Company.

TYPE	HOUR RATING	SPRAY THICKNESS RANGE IN INCHES (mm)	
		FOR W10 X 49 COLUMNS	FOR W14 X 228 COLUMNS
CEMENTITIOUS SPRAY	3/4	3/8 to 11/16 (10 to 17)	1/4 (6)
	1	7/16 to 7/8 (11 to 22)	5/16 to 3/4 (8 to 19)
	1 1/2	3/8 to 1 3/8 (10 to 35)	1/2 to 1 1/8 (13 to 29)
	2	3/4 to 1 1/16 (19 to 43)	3/8 to 15/16 (10 to 24)
	3	1 to 2 3/16 (25 to 56)	11/16 to 1 5/16 (17 to 28)
	4	1 3/16 to 2 7/8 (30 to 73)	1 1/16 to 2 1/8 (27 to 54)
FIBER SPRAY	1	5/8 to 1 3/16 (16 to 30)	3/8 (10)
	1 1/2	1 1/8 to 1 3/16 (29 to 30)	7/16 to 9/16 (11 to 14)
	2	1 1/4 to 2 1/2 (32 to 64)	1/2 to 13/16 (13 to 20)
	3	1 5/8 to 2 3/8 (41 to 60)	13/16 to 1 1/4 (20 to 32)
	4	2 1/8 to 3 3/16 (54 to 81)	1 1/16 to 1 7/8 (43 to 48)

NOTES:
1. Two sizes of columns form the basis of the x-series of column fireproofing designs in the UL Directory. These thicknesses are applicable to columns with an equal or greater than the $\frac{\text{Weight}}{\text{Perimeter}}$ $(\frac{W}{D})$ ratio shown. Designs covering tube and pipe columns as well as smaller and larger columns are also included in the directory.

2. This table is based on information derived from the 1992 directory. It is applicable to designs where the spray follows the contour of the column. Spray with a radiused thickness at flange corners requires a thicker application.

3. Spray thickness is affected by column size, type of mixture (cementitious or fiber) and the formulations produced by different manufacturers. The rating is based on actual fire tests.

Table 1.6 Thickness of fireproofing sprayed on columns. (Based on the Underwriters Laboratories, Inc., *Fire-Resistance Directory,* Vol. 1, 1992)

widely known, corrosion is more severe in areas subject to industrial pollution or salt air. Zinc used in galvanizing steel is considered a sacrificial coating. It corrodes if a more nobel metal is placed against the steel and in so doing, protects the steel for a prolonged period. The amount that is corroded is deposited on the other metal and continues to isolate the two metals. Eventually, the zinc layer will migrate and expose the steel causing it to rust.

To prevent electrolysis from causing problems, specifications usually call for isolating dissimilar metals by painting the contact surface with zinc chromate fol-

lowed by another coat of bituminous paint or a similar measure such as tape or plastic shims (Fig. 1.38).

1.6.3 Sound

In most cases, outside noise does not pose a problem because a sealed exterior wall usually provides adequate protection against sound transmission into the building. Certain types of buildings such as hospitals, schools, libraries, and recording studios may require special detailing to provide acceptable interior sound levels in noisy locations. An unusual site condition such as close proximity to an airport or a noisy freeway also requires special mitigation measures. This subsection provides some background information.

Sound is transmitted either through the air or by setting parts of the structure to vibrating. The first kind is referred to as *airborne sound* and the second as *structure-borne sound*. Exterior air-borne sound, in most cases, does not pose a problem except in buildings with operable windows. Structure-borne sound is usually caused by a high-decibel sound source such as a jackhammer or a diesel or jet engine that sets the wall to vibrating and is reradiated into the interior to become audible as air-borne sound.

If the building is designed with operable windows, residents usually close them when the noise becomes annoying. Specifying a high quality tight-fitting window is usually sufficient to reduce exterior noise to acceptable levels for the majority of cases.

To lessen the effect of structure-borne sound, the most effective measure is to provide a barrier at the source. You may have noticed walls erected on the sides of freeways for that purpose. This, however, cannot be achieved in projects such as an airport hotel or sensitive occupancy buildings abutting a noisy environment. Under these circumstances, the acoustical engineer conducts a preliminary survey to determine the intensity of noise at the site. If the occupancy calls for a noise level inside the building not to exceed 20 decibels (dB) while the exterior noise level, based on the survey, is 65 dB, the exterior wall sound transmission class (STC) rating should be 65 − 20 = 45 dB.

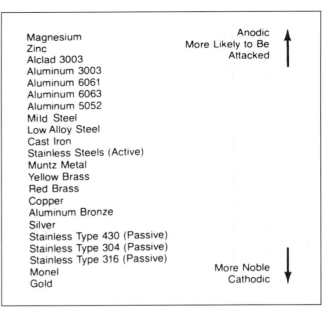

Magnesium
Zinc
Alclad 3003
Aluminum 3003
Aluminum 6061
Aluminum 6063
Aluminum 5052
Mild Steel
Low Alloy Steel
Cast Iron
Stainless Steels (Active)
Muntz Metal
Yellow Brass
Red Brass
Copper
Aluminum Bronze
Silver
Stainless Type 430 (Passive)
Stainless Type 304 (Passive)
Stainless Type 316 (Passive)
Monel
Gold

Anodic
More Likely to Be
Attacked ↑

More Noble
Cathodic ↓

Figure 1.37 Galvanic series of metals and alloys in seawater. (Reproduced by permission from the International Nickel Company, Inc., NY, NY)

Measures to raise the STC rating of the building envelope include

■ Improving window performance by using multiple glazing or laminated glass or specifying the use of special acoustic windows. The emphasis is on win-

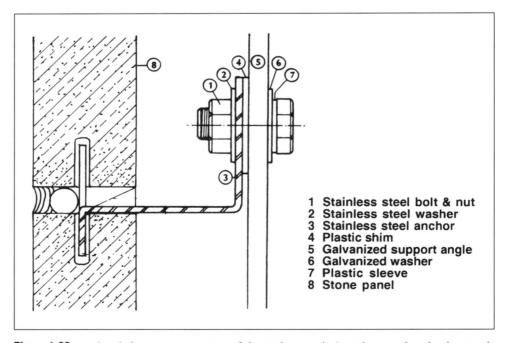

1 Stainless steel bolt & nut
2 Stainless steel washer
3 Stainless steel anchor
4 Plastic shim
5 Galvanized support angle
6 Galvanized washer
7 Plastic sleeve
8 Stone panel

Figure 1.38 A detail showing separation of dissimilar metals (stainless steel and galvanized steel) to prevent electrolysis. (Reproduced by permission; Wiss Janney Elstner, Associates)

dows because they are the weakest link in the exterior defense system.

- Increasing the wall mass without increasing its stiffness. Sheet lead is an example of a material that adds substantially to wall mass without adding perceptibly to its stiffness. It is usually used to provide sound isolation in interior partitions but under certain circumstances can be used in exterior walls and roof assemblies.

- Acoustical nonsetting, nonskinning, and nonhardening sealants can be used as an air barrier in panel joints to seal flanking sound transmission paths.

- Panel support hardware can also be buffered with rubber or neoprene pads to prevent structure-borne vibration from being transmitted to floor slabs.

- Interior wallboard may be supported by resilient channels instead of being fastened directly to the studs.

- In extremely sensitive areas such as recording studios, the usual approach is to create a "room within a room" (Fig. 1.39). When executed properly, this measure isolates the space from any structure-borne sound transmission.

All these measures incur added costs. The room within a room approach also adds more thickness and weight to the walls which must be taken into account in space planning and structural calculations.

1.6.4 Infestation

Exterior wall assemblies are subject to damage or dirt caused by insects, birds, and, in some areas, rodents. Wood is the most vulnerable type of construction because it is organic in nature and can be consumed by insects such as termites and carpenter ants as well as wood-consuming fungus that causes rot in the presence of water.

Birds can build their nests in the most unlikely places. They perch on ledges, sills, copings, and beam tops. Their droppings can mar and stain facades as well as fall on pedestrians below. Rodents can infest basements

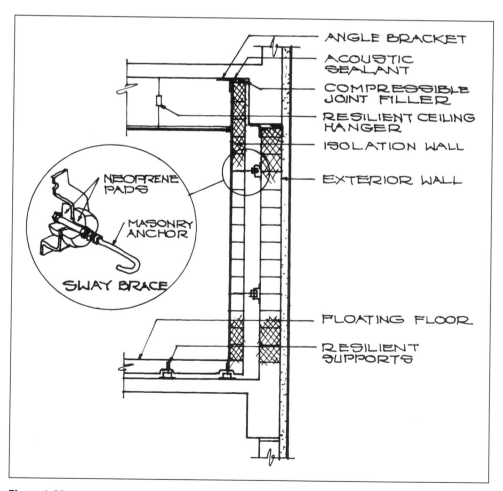

Figure 1.39 The room within a room design concept.

and spread disease. They can gnaw their way through wood and cause damage to walls.

Certain measures can be taken to protect against the potential damage caused by these creatures. Where wood is used, the most effective treatment against termites is to poison the soil. This approach is constantly being challenged due to its impact on the environment. Specifiers must check with the Environmental Protection Agency (EPA) to find out what is currently allowable before specifying chemicals to be used in that regard. Pressure-treated wood must be used if it comes in contact with or is close to the soil, and periodic inspection must be conducted by a well-trained inspector to detect infestation in its early stages. Because the most prevalent type of termite depends on moisture for its survival, a well-drained site conducting water away from walls is important so that during dry spells all moisture can evaporate leaving the termites to perish or migrate to another location.

Bees and wasps can build their hives within cavity walls if they gain access to the cavity. This can prevent water from draining properly through weepholes. To prevent this from happening, weepholes must be stuffed with a material such as fiberglass. Pea gravel placed in the cavity to aid in drainage is also a good deterrent. Intake louvers must be protected by bird screens for the same reason. Insects are usually caught in the intake filters placed inboard of the louvers. If insect screens are placed directly behind the intake louvers, insects caught in the screens may eventually reduce the flow of air.

To protect walls against birds, all horizontal planes should either have a steep slope (approximately 35 degrees) or a wire bird deterrent may be installed (Fig. 1.40). Another approach, and a more humane one, is to consider birds as a delightful part of the environment, install awnings at street level to protect pedestrians and clean the facades periodically.

SUMMARY

Forces of nature can have a profound effect on today's thin wall construction unless defense mechanisms are included in the details. Wind forces can drive rain into the wall assembly causing leaks. Air currents can accelerate the diffusion of vapor from the interior into the wall corroding studs and causing damage to other components including insulation. They can also cause rain to be sucked into the assembly causing leaks and uncomfortable drafts. These drafts also require the HVAC system to work harder to compensate for heat loss in winter and heat gain in summer. To prevent this from happening, an air barrier structurally capable of resisting these air currents and properly sealed around its perimeter must be included in the wall assembly.

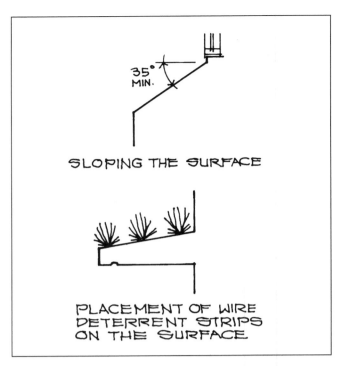

Figure 1.40 Measures used to deter birds from perching on horizontal surfaces.

This barrier must be combined with a vapor retarder placed at the warm side of the wall to stop vapor migration before it has a chance to infiltrate into the wall. The location of the retarder varies depending upon the climate. Cold climates require that the retarder be located on the side of the wall facing the interior, while hot humid climates require it to be located near the exterior face of the wall. Temperate zones may not require any retarder. Other elements in the wall assembly must have a perm rating at least five times the perm rating of the retarder.

In addition to vapor migration, forces that move water include gravity, kinetic energy, surface tension, and hydrostatic pressure. To protect against these forces, joints and soffits must include certain configurations designed to prevent water from proceeding into the wall. Sealants, sealers, and dampproofing above grade and waterproofing coupled with perimeter drainage below grade provide the needed defenses. Each of these protective measures requires careful detailing and field supervision to perform properly.

Building interiors must also be protected from heat and cold. Heat is transmitted by convection, conduction, and radiation. Convective air currents transfer heat from one side of a cavity to the other. Conduction conveys heat by acceleration of the molecules of certain materials such as metals. Studs in wall assemblies act as thermal bridges to convey heat from the warm side to the cold. Radiation accelerates heat through space by means of electromagnetic waves and affects the interior mainly through the windows.

Resistive, reflective, and capacity insulation are three types of insulation used to resist heat transfer through walls. Materials used as resistive insulation are bad conductors of heat. They are rated according to their effectiveness in resisting heat transfer by their R-rating. These materials include batt insulation, semirigid or rigid insulation, loose fill, and foams. Each type is appropriate for specific wall assemblies.

Reflective insulation is used to resist radiant heat traveling through wall cavities. Materials faced with aluminum foil are used in this capacity to reflect radiant heat across cavities. Reflective and low-e glass (see Chap. 3) perform the same function for windows.

Capacity insulation, also known as thermal mass, utilizes heavy masonry or concrete walls to dampen the thermal highs and lows by slowing heat transmission through the wall. It is most effective in hot, dry climates with a high thermal difference between night and day. In climates with small diurnal temperature differences, insulation placed on the exterior of the wall enhances its performance by letting the wall absorb the heat gain through the windows and releasing it gradually after sunset to provide warmth during cold nights. In hot regions, placing the insulation on the exterior reduces the demand for constant air conditioning during the night.

Seismic activity is another force of nature that can have a catastrophic impact on buildings located in severe seismic zones. Earthquakes are more prevalent than most people realize. Fortunately, design can play a role to mitigate their impact. Structures can be stiffened by including shear walls, braced frames, or moment connections in the structural frame. These measures, however, attract seismic forces giving the occupants a rough ride similar to a car traveling on a rough road without shock absorbers. A more intelligent approach referred to as base isolation introduces elements in the foundation that act as shock absorbers to prevent the bulk of the shocks from being transmitted to the superstructure. A third defense mechanism is used to counter high-rise sway caused by wind and seismic movements and is referred

to as a tuned mass damper. It is composed of a heavy weight manipulated by computer-activated mechanisms and placed near the top of the building to provide a counter action to lateral forces, dampening their effect.

Other natural phenomena affecting buildings include fire, electrolysis, noise, and infestation.

Measures to prevent the spread of fire include

1. Spraying cementitious or fiber formulations on the structural frame
2. Specifying fire-rated wall assemblies and windows
3. Placing sprinkler heads at windows
4. Sealing gaps between slab edges and the wall with a fire-safing material (dense mineral fiber) and a sealant to prevent smoke migration between floors

Electrolysis is the tendency of a metal to erode when in contact with another metal in the presence of moisture. Providing an isolation medium between the two metals prevents this from occurring.

Noise-sensitive buildings such as hospitals and libraries may require extra measures to protect against noise from specific noise sources such as freeways and airports. This can be achieved by specially designed windows and acoustical sealants. Some buildings such as recording studios may require total isolation of critical interior spaces from the vibration transmitted through the building envelope or frame. This is achieved by implementing the room within a room design approach. An acoustical engineer is usually involved in this type of design.

Finally, certain measures can be used to protect against insect and bird infestation. Using ecologically acceptable methods approved by the EPA is the safest approach to eradicating harmful insects such as termites. Sloping horizontal surfaces that are potential perches for birds or attaching wire spike deterrents to those surfaces are methods usually used to bar birds from buildings. A passive method is to let the birds add to the liveliness of the environment, clean up after them, and protect pedestrians by installing canopies above the sidewalk.

CHAPTER 2

Structural and Other Design Considerations

2.1 GENERAL

Before the advent of specialization in the building professions, master builders wore many hats. They designed the building, developed its details, sized its structural members, and supervised its construction. Those early architects developed their skills over a long period of apprenticeship to older, more experienced master builders. They all gained some of their know-how from buildings that collapsed when they reached beyond the bearing capacity of the building material that was used or when lateral forces caused the walls or roof to collapse. An example that comes to mind is the introduction of the flying buttress in Gothic architecture. These half arches (Fig. 2.1) were introduced to resist the thrust of the vaulted roofs supported by high walls no doubt after a major cathedral showed instability or collapsed during construction.

Today, while project architects are still responsible for the overall design, they depend on their consultants to produce construction drawings for the structural, mechanical, cost estimating, and other specialized aspects of the project. While specialization makes it possible for architects to concentrate on architectural design, the project manager, as head of the design team, must have enough background information to suggest alternatives to resolve conflicts between the architectural drawings and the drawings generated by other disciplines. This information also comes in handy during the coordination process at the end of the project.

Technically speaking, the structural frame of a building is designed to resist gravity and lateral forces caused by wind pressure and earthquake movement. These forces determine the size of structural frame members and the detailing of its connections or the design of its reinforcement. The structural engineer sizes columns and beams to resist gravity loads, designs shear walls or rigid frames to resist lateral loads caused by wind and seismic forces, and determines the locations of cladding supports. These supports must be designed to isolate the cladding from the movements of the supporting structure to avoid damage. While these movements are relatively small, they have the potential for causing cracks in the cladding.

The intent of the section addressing structural issues is to focus on exterior walls, explaining in simple terms the reasoning behind some of the structural concepts from an architect's point of view rather than engage in calculations and formulas. Architectural designers almost never do their own structural calculations when they prepare drawings for public buildings. They need, however, to develop a constant awareness while exploring architectural concepts. This awareness will enable them to propose solutions that are more economical, easier to build, and more in harmony with their architecture. It will also enable them to interface better with the structural engineer and give them the confidence to propose bold concepts for an imaginative and honest architecture.

Architects must also be aware of the cost implication of every decision they make especially during the

Figure 2.1 Notre Dame De Chalons Cathedral from Viollet-Le-Duc's book, *Dictionnaire Raisonné de L'architecture Française du XIè siècle.* (Reproduced by permission; Barry Bergdoll, "The Legacy of Viollet-le-Duc's Drawings," *Architectural Record,* mid-August 1981)

design development phase. Seemingly minor decisions such as adding a few inches to the floor-to-floor height in a multistory building can add up and result in a substantial increase in the area of an expensive cladding system as well as the overall length of the columns supporting the building. This can spell the difference between staying within the budget or having to make changes in the quality or scope of the project to bring the costs back in line.

The issue of durability must always be in the back of the architect's mind to ensure that the building will not deteriorate until well beyond its projected useful life.

Ease of maintenance coupled with a periodic inspection plan recommended to the owner can prolong the life of the building and prevent potential problems from reaching a dangerous level. It is a good policy to present the owner with a maintenance package similar to the owner's manual for a car at the conclusion of the job. This would give a good impression and go a long way toward ensuring that the building would give long-lasting and trouble-free service. Wall designs should incorporate redundant defenses and be designed with the assumption that if anything can go wrong, it will. The selection process for these systems or materials should be approached in a methodical fashion by developing a selection matrix evaluating each product against evaluation criteria before final selections are specified.

This chapter addresses structural, cost, and other design considerations.

2.2   STRUCTURAL CONSIDERATIONS

The topics discussed here include:

- Deflection
- Column locations
- Cladding support
- Details

2.2.1   Deflection

Deflection is the sagging that occurs in a structural member as a result of its own weight (dead load) and the application of other loads such as furniture and people (live load) as well as the weight of the cladding. The most familiar example is the slight sagging that occurs in the middle of a beam or the free end of a cantilever. This is referred to as a vertical deflection [Fig. 2.2(a)]. Another example is the horizontal displacement that occurs in structural studs as a result of the forces imposed on them by wind. On a larger scale, high-rise buildings, acting as vertical cantilevers fixed to the ground, experience horizontal deflection and act in a similar fashion to horizontal cantilevers [Fig. 2.2(b)].

VERTICAL DEFLECTION

Spandrel beams supporting wall panels should be designed for minimum deflection by increasing their depth (stiffness). This reduces the tendency of joints to narrow at the top and widen at the bottom. It also prevents damage to the window frame and glazing. An even better solution is to support wall panels directly on the columns to avoid the effect of beam deflection altogether [Fig. 2.3(a)]. Should the design call for frequent vertical panel joints, fake joints referred to as *rustications* can be introduced to give the desired appearance. In addition to

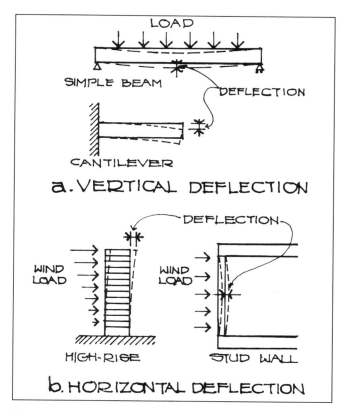

Figure 2.2 Deflection.

avoiding deflection problems, this solution also reduces the total length of costly joint sealants and their potential maintenance and leakage problems. Mounting the cladding panels on a truss spanning between columns is an approach often used in stone cladding.

Deflection also occurs in cantilevers. A perfectly safe cantilever will sag at its free end. This sagging can give the building occupants a feeling of insecurity because it impels them toward the edge. It also gives the structure a bouncy feeling that is unsettling to most people. I can recall while I was working in Fort Worth that a group from the office would meet for lunch in a nice cafeteria located on a circular cantilevered mezzanine in a new high-rise downtown. We would sit at a table at the perimeter of a rather long cantilever. Every time a person passed, we could feel the area bounce with each step. We used to wonder if the resonance would eventually cause it to collapse. Since I have not heard of such a catastrophe in Fort Worth in the past 15 years, I assume the balcony was safe. This anecdote illustrates the psychological effect of deflection and should make architects hesitate before insisting on limiting the depth of excessively long cantilevers. Long cantilevers can also cause elements of the facade to rotate [Fig. 2.3(b)] resulting in a potential leakage problem at the joints between window frames and other elements of the facade.

To minimize this type of sagging, deeper (stiffer) cantilevers than those dictated by the most economical design can be proposed in certain cases. A strut or brace can support the free end or shorten the cantilever to achieve the same result. The designer should ask the structural engineer about the amount of deflection to be expected and evaluate its impact.

Another area of concern associated with vertical deflection is the effect of spandrel beam deflection on studs. Metal studs used as backup for masonry, stucco, or other finish systems must be designed to accommodate horizontal deflection. If no gap is left between the bottom of the beam and the top stud track, the floor load will be transmitted from the beam to the studs causing them to buckle. Figure 2.3(c) illustrates what can happen and the usual method of mitigating this problem. Note that all items attached to the studs and the structure above must be detailed to accommodate this movement. Avoid fastening the sheathing or wallboard to the top 2 in (50 mm) of the studs, and allow dampproofing a generous overlap at this location.

The bulk of vertical deflection in concrete- or steel-framed structures occurs shortly after the concrete slab is poured (dead load). This initial deflection is of little concern vis-a-vis wall panel design because, by the time the contractor starts to attach the panels, the frame dead load deflection would have already occurred and panel supports can be adjusted or shimmed to accommodate it. Heavy panels like precast or limestone cause further deflection in the structure. Live load adds to it especially if heavy equipment or a crowded occupancy is located in the space adjacent to the panels. The sum of these last two deflections as well as thermal movement must be considered by the designer to determine joint widths between panels. The architect should ask the structural engineer about the maximum deflection that is expected to occur after the floor slab is poured as a result of the superimposed loads described above and detail the exterior walls accordingly.

HORIZONTAL DEFLECTION

To resist lateral forces, stiff elements are incorporated in the structural frame to strengthen it. These elements can be either sheer walls, rigid frames, or framed tubes.

Shear walls may be located in the building core(s) or the exterior perimeter of the building. These walls are located in both orthogonal orientations to function as stiffening elements to prevent the structure from racking (Fig. 2.4). Trussed frames can take the form of a horizontal letter K or an X and are commonly referred to as K- or X-bracing. Diagonal bracing is also used (Fig. 2.5).

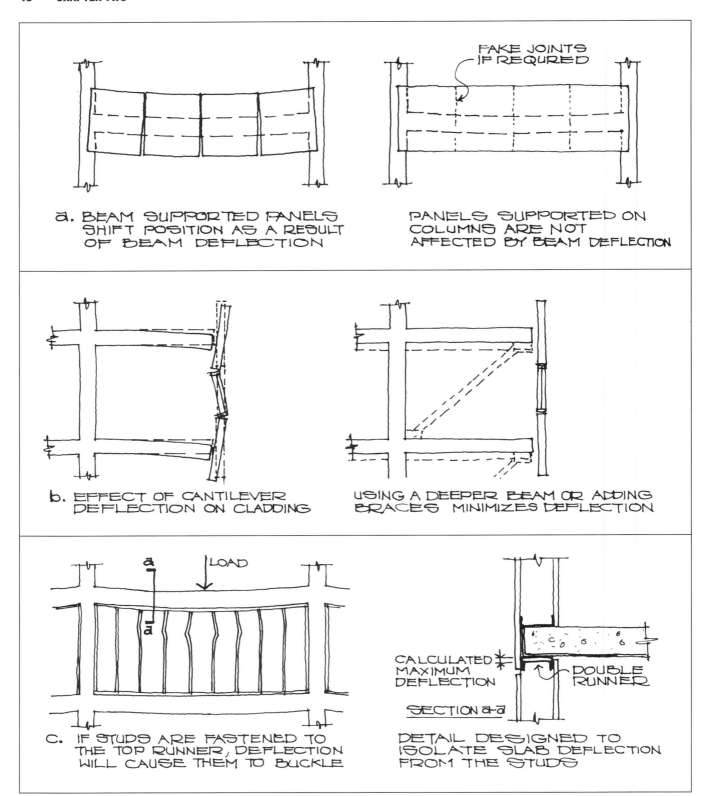

a. BEAM SUPPORTED PANELS SHIFT POSITION AS A RESULT OF BEAM DEFLECTION

FAKE JOINTS IF REQUIRED

PANELS SUPPORTED ON COLUMNS ARE NOT AFFECTED BY BEAM DEFLECTION

b. EFFECT OF CANTILEVER DEFLECTION ON CLADDING

USING A DEEPER BEAM OR ADDING BRACES MINIMIZES DEFLECTION

LOAD

c. IF STUDS ARE FASTENED TO THE TOP RUNNER, DEFLECTION WILL CAUSE THEM TO BUCKLE

CALCULATED MAXIMUM DEFLECTION   DOUBLE RUNNER

SECTION a-a

DETAIL DESIGNED TO ISOLATE SLAB DEFLECTION FROM THE STUDS

Figure 2.3 The effects of deflection on cladding.

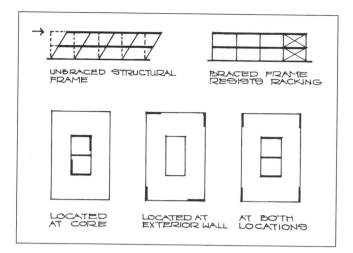

Figure 2.4 Shear wall locations.

During the schematic phase, the architect must discuss the location of these walls if they occur at the core with the structural engineer to avoid having to make substantial changes to the plans later. Shear walls located at the perimeter obviously impact the design of the building exterior and must be developed in close collaboration between the two disciplines.

Rigid frames aim to stiffen the connections between beams and columns to reduce the racking movement (Fig. 2.6). Rigid frames with moment-resisting connections (connections resisting rotation), contrary to their name, tend to give the structure a certain suppleness that dissipates the energy transmitted by lateral forces. This suppleness allows the structure to deform ever so slightly causing the columns to deform temporarily. This deformation is referred to as a *structural frame drift* (Fig. 2.7). Cladding supports attached to frames must be designed to accommodate their movement (deformation) without causing excessive damage to the cladding or letting it detach from the structure (Fig. 2.8). If exterior wall panels are fitted within the frame, they will sustain damage as a result of that displacement. To prevent that from happening, wall panels must be provided with a soft joint wide enough to accommodate the frame deformation (Fig. 2.9). This solution requires a rather stiff structure to minimize the effect of deformation on the panel. It also requires that all sealed joints be readily accessible for eventual reapplication (see also Sec. 1.5).

Another method of stiffening the structure is to design the exterior envelope as a tube with closely spaced columns at the perimeter (Fig. 2.10). The most famous example of this approach is the Sears Tower in Chicago. It was formed by multiple tubes constructed according to that principle (Fig. 2.11). Diagonal bracing may be introduced to transform the exterior framing into a giant truss acting as a tube cantilevering from the foundation

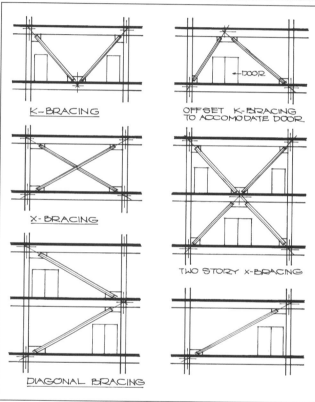

Figure 2.5 Forms of bracing. (Photograph by Tom Beddall)

(Fig. 2.12). Obviously, framed tube design involving high-rise buildings of that magnitude is addressed by an extremely limited segment of the profession. It is mentioned here for general information since the subject of deflection and deformation is being addressed.

Horizontal deflection also affects exterior wall studs whether the finish is applied directly to the sheathing or the studs are used as backup for masonry. Stud gauge, width, and spacing must be determined by a structural engineer. This would normally be done by the structural consultant if it is defined within the scope of services described in the architect-engineer agreement. If that is

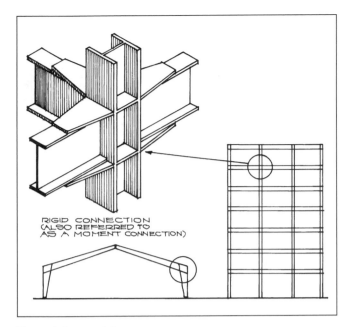

Figure 2.6 Rigid frames.

not the case, a performance specification stating the allowable deflection and the design wind pressure as defined by the code (or wind tunnel testing) may be used. This specification should require the shop drawings to be stamped by a structural engineer registered in the state. The architect must check these drawings for conformance with dimensions and detailing, and the structural engineer must check the calculations used to determine the size, spacing, and gauge of the studs.

The head, jambs, and sill of rough openings for large windows must be designed to resist the loads transferred to them from the area occupied by the window. Multiple studs at the jambs and light-gauge box beams at the head and sill will perform this task for large openings (Fig. 2.13).

2.2.2 Column Locations

The location of exterior columns relative to the exterior wall requires careful consideration. Columns can be either attached to or detached from the wall and located in one of five positions (Fig. 2.14). Each of the positions shown has its advantages and disadvantages. Designers

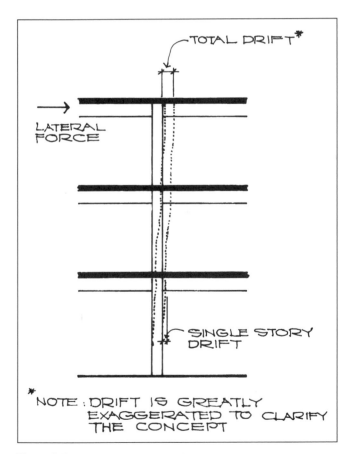

Figure 2.7 Structural frame drift.

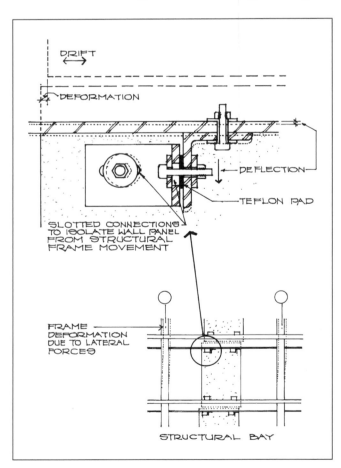

Figure 2.8 Panel supports designed to prevent frame drift and beam deflection from being transmitted to the panel.

---

must weigh this decision carefully before arriving at a final decision. The following is an evaluation of each position.

FREE-STANDING, EXTERIOR (FIG. 2.15)

Advantages:

1. The column does not encroach on the occupied space. This allows the designer to plan the interior space without worrying about conflicts between furniture or partition layouts and column location.

2. Column and beam grid give an interesting three-dimensional look to the facade.

3. Shading and/or window-washing platforms can be integrated in the design.

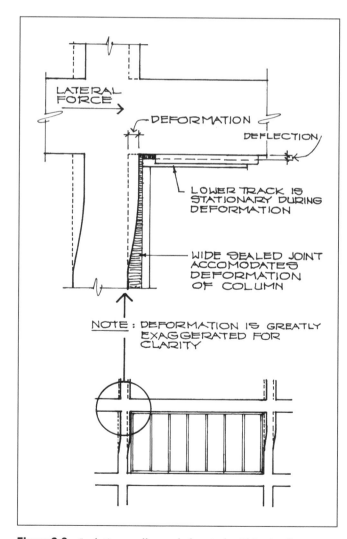

Figure 2.9 Isolating wall panels located within the frame from the structural frame deformation.

Figure 2.10 The structural tube concept. An office tower in Boston. (Skidmore, Owings and Merrill, Architects)

Disadvantages:

1. Beams connected to the core are required to span over a longer distance.

2. In steel-framed buildings, the part of the structural frame placed outside the insulated envelope is exposed to temperature extremes causing them to expand and contract while the interior columns are exposed to very little temperature fluctuation. This differential movement can cause stresses in the connections especially in multistory buildings. Wrapping the exposed part of the frame in thermal insulation can reduce this problem at added cost. Check with the structural engineer to determine whether the thermal movement poses a problem when using this design.

ATTACHED, EXTERIOR (FIG. 2.16)

Advantages:

1. Similar to the advantages listed above.

2. The design shown is suitable for elevations with a dominant vertical organization. It does not incorporate shading or a window-washing platform.

Disadvantages: Similar to those listed above.

Figure 2.11 The Sears Tower, Chicago. (Skidmore, Owings and Merrill, Architects)

Figure 2.12 The John Hancock Tower, Chicago. (Skidmore, Owings and Merrill, Architects)

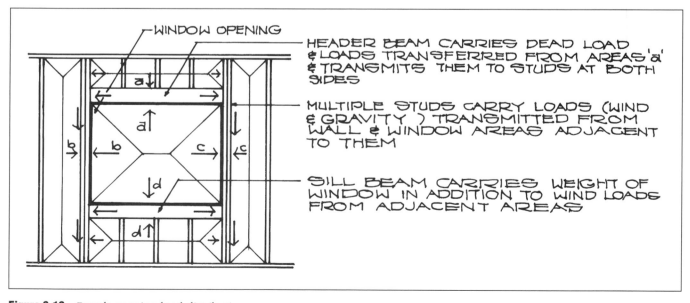

HEADER BEAM CARRIES DEAD LOAD & LOADS TRANSFERRED FROM AREAS 'a' & TRANSMITS THEM TO STUDS AT BOTH SIDES

MULTIPLE STUDS CARRY LOADS (WIND & GRAVITY) TRANSMITTED FROM WALL & WINDOW AREAS ADJACENT TO THEM

SILL BEAM CARRIES WEIGHT OF WINDOW IN ADDITION TO WIND LOADS FROM ADJACENT AREAS

WINDOW OPENING

Figure 2.13 Rough opening load distribution.

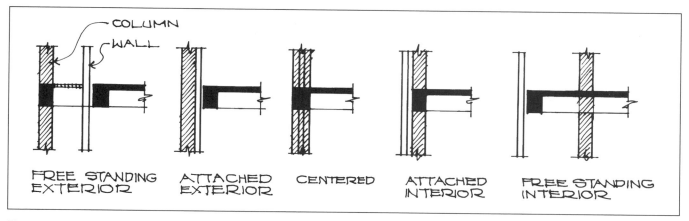

Figure 2.14 Options for exterior column position in relationship to cladding.

CENTERED (FIG. 2.17)

Advantage: Reduced column encroachment on interiors.

Disadvantages:

1. Column and beam are exposed to weather and must be insulated to avoid thermal bridging (see Sec. 1.4.3).

2. The junction between wall, column, and beam requires careful detailing to prevent structural frame deformation from transferring stresses to the cladding causing damage.

3. It is difficult, if not impossible, to seal the vapor retarder at its junction with the beams and columns if they are covered with sprayed-on fireproofing. Welding a continuous zee strip to the beam flange as shown is one way to solve this problem.

ATTACHED, INTERIOR (FIG. 2.18)

Advantage: This is one of the most often used column locations in steel construction. It encloses the frame, allows tolerable column interference with interior planning, and provides continuity for the cladding.

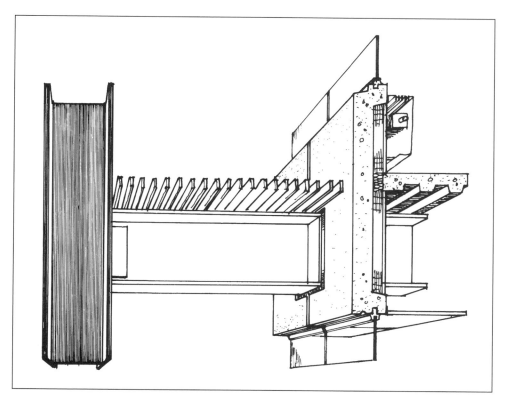

Figure 2.15 Freestanding column, exterior.

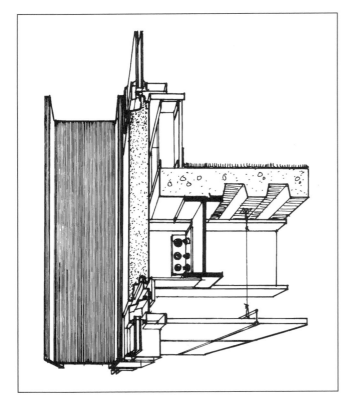

Figure 2.16 Attached column, exterior.

Disadvantage: The narrow clearance between the beam and cladding may interfere with screwing the gypsum board to the studs. A minimum clearance of approximately 12 in (300 mm) is required to apply the screws.

FREESTANDING, INTERIOR (FIG. 2.19)

Advantages:

1. Structurally advantageous for concrete frames.
2. No column interference with the cladding.

Disadvantages:

1. Column location interferes with interior planning. This solution is, however, suitable for buildings that require perimeter aisles or corridors or where column spacing coincides with the location of permanent partitions. It is also suitable for open office planning.
2. Deflection requires careful study if the cantilever is long.

The relative locations of the columns, spandrel beam, and wall cladding must be considered to minimize the disadvantages listed above.

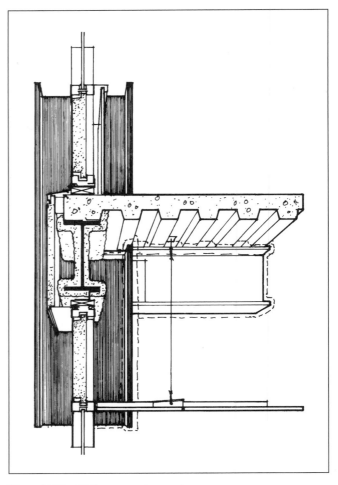

Figure 2.17 Wall centered on column.

2.2.3 Cladding Support

Different kinds of cladding require different kinds of support. Solid walls and stud walls clad in thin veneer systems such as stucco or tile are supported directly on the floor slab. Masonry veneers are usually supported on continuous shelf angles attached to the structure. Panelized systems such as precast, stone, truss-backed stone, GFRC, or metal curtain walls are supported on clip angles or specialized hardware (Fig. 2.20). Supports must allow the cladding to expand and contract. They must also be designed in such a manner that they can be adjusted to allow for clearances and construction tolerances (see Sec. 2.2.5).

MASONRY VENEER SUPPORT

A shelf angle, also known as a relieving angle, fastened to the structural frame is the usual method used to support masonry veneer walls. The architect must stipulate that the shelf angles be interrupted at control joints to allow both the brick wall panel and the angle to accommodate thermal movement. This movement

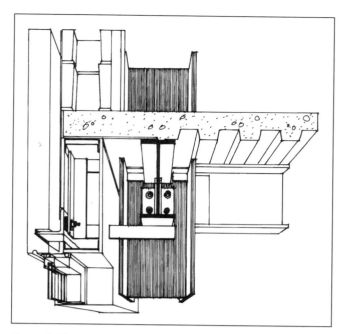

Figure 2.18 Attached column, interior.

should not be hampered by the metal ties which must be a product designed to accommodate it. Veneers also expand vertically and must be allowed to do so without restriction. This is usually accomplished by providing a sealed soft joint between the top of the veneer and the bottom of the shelf angle. This joint must

also be sized to accommodate structural deflection (see Fig. 4.30).

Shelf angles may be attached directly to the edge of the slab or the spandrel beam or hung from the structure at window heads (Fig. 2.21). Bracing attached to the shelf angle prevents the wall from rotating. Unless the cladding is lightweight, shelf angles should not be supported on metal studs designed to resist lateral forces only. The location of the horizontal leg must be coordinated between the architect and the engineer. The engineer is concerned about the location of the support both in relationship to the top of the slab and the size of the angle, its hangers, and bracing. The architect is concerned about the location of the horizontal leg in relationship to brick coursing or stone joints as well as the overall width of the horizontal joint which includes the angle leg thickness and the soft joint below it.

In masonry construction, shelf angles are usually furnished by the miscellaneous-iron subcontractor and, in many cases, attached by the mason after the steel installer has finished and left the job. This can cause problems since relieving angles are structural members that require a specific torque for the bolts that the mason may not be aware of or trained to perform. The specifications should spell out that the final torquing is the responsibility of the steel subcontractor if a slotted connection is used. A better solution is to attach the shelf

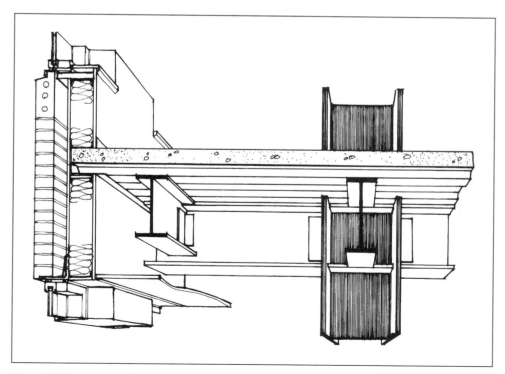

Figure 2.19 Freestanding column, interior.

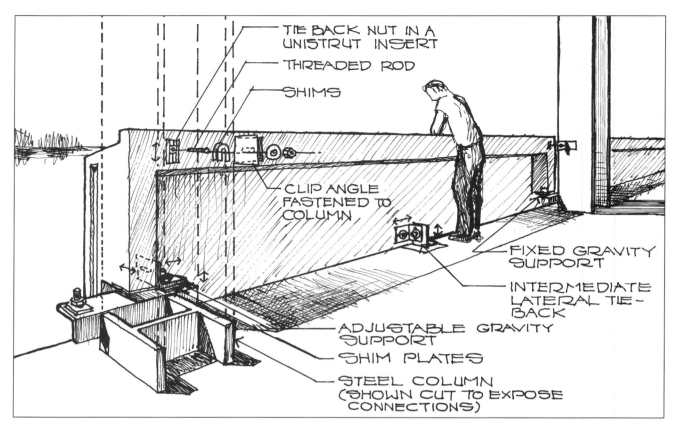

Figure 2.20   An example of panel support hardware and its adjustments.

angle to clip angles that can be adjusted vertically with shims. This approach prevents any chance of slippage.

PANEL SUPPORT

Large exterior wall panels are usually supported at four or more points. The number of support points depends on the size of the panel. There are usually two groups of supports: load-bearing and lateral restraint supports. This group of supports must be designed with only one fixed load-bearing support, while all the others are allowed to move slightly (Fig. 2.22). This design accommodates thermal expansion and contraction as well as provides the basis for statically determinate calculations. The PCI illustrates 10 principles for panel connections (Fig. 2.23). These connections must be accessible for initial installation. They must be designed with enough clearance to allow the installer to make adjustments to both the panel and supporting structure tolerances. Slotted connections accommodate the slight movements expected in nonfixed supports, and adjustment bolts accomplish the alignment procedure. The structural engineer determines the location of panel supports, and the architect makes sure that they do not conflict with architectural detailing. These details may not show the supports entirely and depend on a performance specifi-

cation indicating the lateral loads to be resisted and the required tolerances, or the architect may include suggested connections based on a dialogue with a panel manufacturer. If the second method is used, a general note must be added to show that these connections indicate intent only and that the actual connections shall be designed by the fabricator and approved by the architect, or wording to that effect. Personally, I prefer the second method because it helps anticipate potential problems that the connections may pose vis-a-vis adjacent elements of the wall. Shop drawings must be checked by the architect to make sure that the panel dimensions are correct and that the connections do not conflict with interior space. Copies are sent to the structural engineer who checks the locations and size of supports for adequacy and ascertains whether the panel weight is within design limits.

2.2.4   Loose Lintels

Lintels are horizontal structural members that span over wall openings to carry the wall above. The weight of that wall is transferred to the opening jambs. Loose lintels are handled by the mason. They are not mechanically attached to any part of the structure but rather rest on the two sides of the opening. The lintel bearing—the

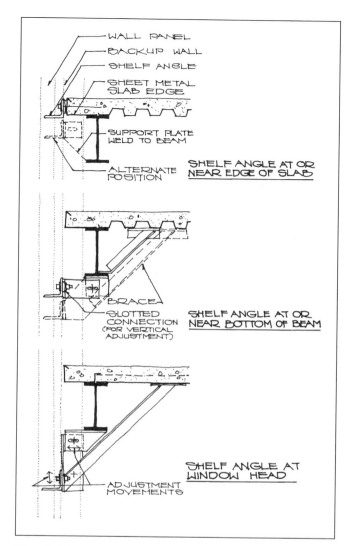

Figure 2.21 Shelf angle support positions in a steel-frame building.

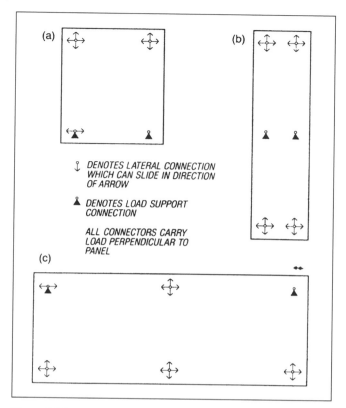

Figure 2.22 Connections for cladding panels in areas of low seismic activity. (Reproduced by permission; Precast/ Prestressed Concrete Institute, *Architectural Precast Concrete,* 2d ed., 1989)

distance between the side of the opening and the end of the lintel—is usually 4 in (100 mm) for small openings and 8 in (200 mm) for larger openings in masonry construction. One rule of thumb used by many designers is to allow 1 in (25 mm) for every foot (300 mm) of opening width.

LINTEL SIZES

The most common angle size used for lintels is $3\frac{1}{2} \times 3$ in (89×75 mm) placed with the $3\frac{1}{2}$-in leg horizontal. At least two-thirds of the brick width must bear on that leg. Another rule of thumb is to size the vertical leg by allowing $\frac{1}{2}$ in (13 mm) for every foot (300 mm) of clear opening. Architectural Graphic Standards[4] also contains tables for sizing most types of lintels.

Loose lintels may be constructed of precast (also called cast stone), reinforced concrete block, stone, or steel. Steel angles are the most commonly used type of lintel because they are usually less costly, are lightweight, and are easy to install. In most locations subject to rain, they must be galvanized. They may be combined with other angles or structural shapes to carry thick masonry walls.

In concrete masonry walls, as an alternative to steel angles, lintel block is used as a form and reinforcement is placed inside the U-shaped units and grouted to support the wall above. The structural engineer usually includes a lintel schedule indicating the size of the lintel, bearing width, and reinforcement (if cast stone, CMU, or site-cast concrete) for each opening width. The architect must make sure that all opening widths are covered because, in many cases, these schedules cover openings up to a width of 8 ft (244 m) only. Figure 2.24 shows some commonly used lintels.

ALTERNATE SPANNING METHODS

Wall openings may also be spanned by arches. Strip window heads are either extended to the bottom of the spandrel beam, or a steel shelf angle is hung from the beam and braced back to the structure (Fig. 2.21).

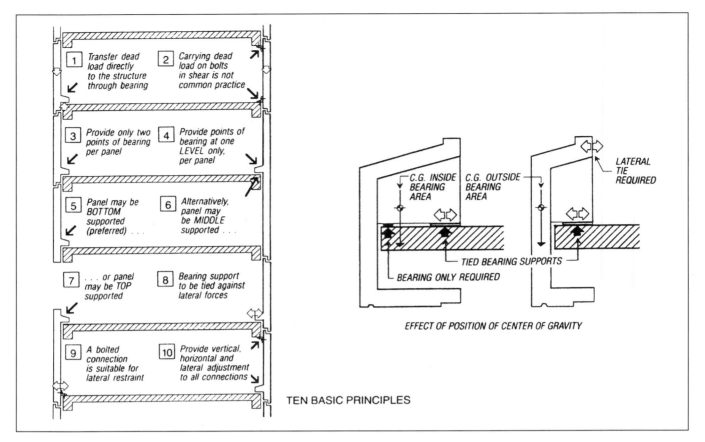

Figure 2.23 Design principles for cladding panel connections. (Reproduced by permission; Precast/Prestressed Concrete Institute, *Architectural Precast Concrete,* 2d ed., 1989)

In some cases, it is cheaper to choose a spandrel beam that is deeper than the size dictated strictly by structural loading to avoid the costly material and labor involved in erecting the miscellaneous steel hangers and braces required for supporting the window head and wall cladding at a point lower than the beam. In any case, the window head must be detailed to allow for deflection either by a slotted connection between the frame and the clip angles holding it or by installing a receptor (Fig. 2.25).

Wood lintels are referred to as headers. In light framing construction, they are cut from 2-in (50 mm) nominal thickness stock in pairs or threes shimmed to fit flush between the stud faces. Wide openings may be spanned by an engineered member such as glued laminated timber (glulam), laminated veneer, parallel strand, or laminated composite lumber as an alternative to multiple 2-in (50 mm) stock headers. Studs placed at the jambs are usually doubled or tripled to carry the added load that would have normally been carried by the studs that were omitted to create the opening. One stud on each side extends all the way to the floor beams and is nailed to the side of the header. The rest of the studs

provide support under it. Headers may be omitted if the window extends all the way to the underside of the floor beams.

2.2.5 Details

CLEARANCES

In wall construction, clearance is the space provided between the wall cladding and the structural frame to accommodate the construction tolerances allowed for both the frame and the cladding. Construction tolerances are the acceptable deviations from perfect execution.

In most instances, the nature and complexity of the construction process precludes perfect execution of the construction drawings. In spite of the fact that most buildings may look perfect, there is no such thing as 100% accuracy in the assembly of the myriad parts that form a structure. Columns will be slightly out of plumb, slab edges will not be perfectly straight or even parallel to each other throughout the height of the building, wall panel dimensions will deviate from the design dimensions, their corners may not be a true 90°, and they may have a slight warp. To prevent these devia-

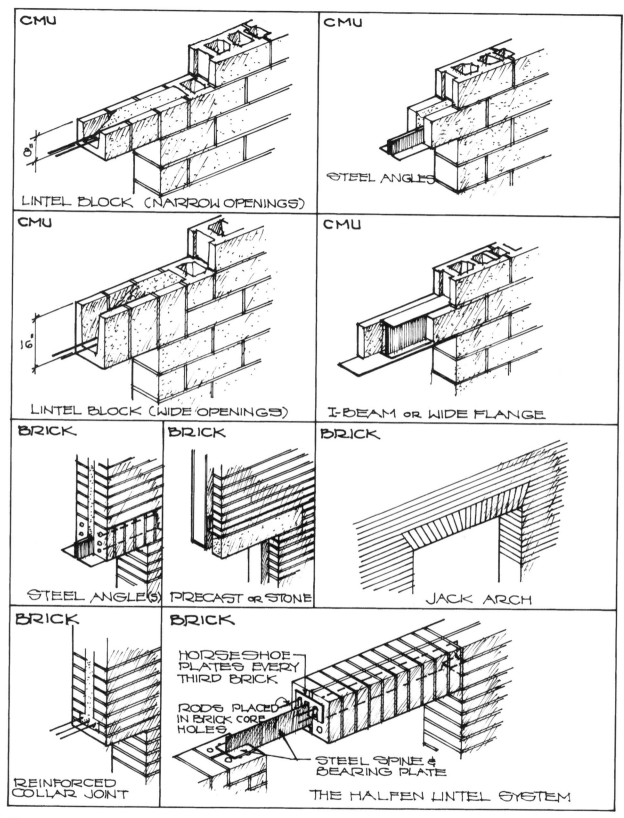

Figure 2.24 Some commonly used lintels.

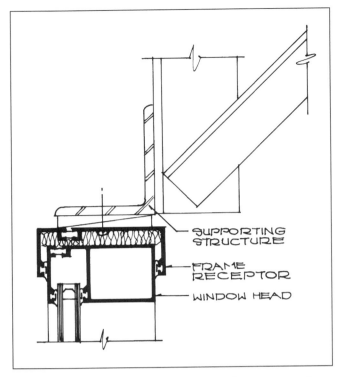

SUPPORTING STRUCTURE

FRAME RECEPTOR

WINDOW HEAD

Figure 2.25 Window head detail designed to accommodate deflection.

tions from getting out of hand, the specifications set limits within which inaccuracies will be tolerated. These limits are called *tolerances*. Architects should refer to these tolerances before deciding upon the width of the clearance. This width should include the tolerance for the structure throughout the length and height of the building plus the tolerance for wall panels plus a gap to allow the panels to move without friction against the frame. Table 2.1 shows acceptable tolerances for concrete and steel structural frames. Refer to industry standards for each cladding system to determine the acceptable tolerance for wall panels produced by each manufacturer.

Clearances should also be wide enough to allow the curtain wall installer to work comfortably. This means accommodating both the worker and whatever tool is being used to complete the installation.

In theory, tolerances allow the architect to refuse shoddy work if it exceeds the specified acceptable tolerances. In practice, outright refusal is almost never invoked because of the delays, added costs, and legal ramifications that such action would entail. Allowing enough tolerances, making frequent site visits, and limiting rejections to totally unacceptable work can go a long way toward achieving good results.

VERTICAL JOINTS

There are no hard and fast rules to determine the location of building expansion joints. The structural engineer usually determines their location based on several factors including intersections of building wings, building wings with substantial height difference, buildings supported on soils with different bearing capacities, and long buildings (Fig. 2.26).

The coefficients of thermal expansion for the structural frame and the cladding as well as other factors are calculated to determine the extent of the expected movement (see Chap. 4 for more information). To determine the width of an expansion joint, the movement for each side of the building is divided by two and an allowance is made for the compression of the joint filler [Fig. 2.27(a)]. This aspect of joint width determination depends on the type of joint filler used [Fig. 2.27(b)].

The structural engineer calculates the expected joint movement for the structural frame, and the architect calculates the cladding movement taking into consideration the input from the engineer. Based on this information and the desired look of the joint, a joint cover is selected to accommodate the movement. A dialogue with the joint cover manufacturer is important before the final selection.

Ideally, expansion joints should provide total separation between the two sides. This usually requires a double column at the joint [Fig. 2.28(a)]. In some cases, however, the architectural design requires the impact of the joint on the facade to be minimized. A slip joint as shown in Fig. 2.28(b) accommodates thermal movement by allowing one side to slide on a haunch or cantilever attached to the column supporting the other side.

Seismic movement can cause building wings to collide and act as battering rams. This fact must be taken into consideration in determining the number of joints and their location and width for buildings located in seismic zones 3 and 4. Section 1.5 provides more information about seismic movements.

Control joints occur at more frequent intervals than expansion joints. These intervals are determined by the coefficient of thermal expansion of the material used. In many cases, they are located at column centerlines.

HORIZONTAL JOINTS

Some materials such as brick and certain kinds of marble expand over time in addition to their thermal expansion and contraction. If that dimensional increase is not accommodated, brick will push against the underside of shelf angles and spall. Marble is a denser material and, if restrained against movement, will distort and bow

VARIATION OR TOLERANCE	CAST-IN-PLACE CONCRETE	STEEL
Variations from the plumb, or column tolerances	¼ inch per 10 feet but not more than 1 inch Valid to 100 feet height. No tolerances suggested above 100 feet	1 to 1000, no more than 1″ towards building nor 2″ away from building line in the first 20 stories; plus 1/16″ for each additional story up to a maximum of 2″ towards building or 3″ away from building line
Tolerances in levels	In 10 feet . . . . ± ¼″ Up to 20 ft bay . . . . ± ⅜″ In 40 ft or more . . . . ± ¾″	Erection tolerances for levels normally not stated, as levels should be governed by close manufacturing tolerances
Variations from the linear building lines in relation to columns and walls	In any bay . . . . ± ½″ In bay 20 ft max. . . . . ± ½″ In bay 40 ft max. . . . . ± 1″	As set by column alignments Closer for elevator columns
Tolerances in beams and columns	Cross section dimensions ⎤ ———— − ¼″ + ½″	1 to 1000 in alignment Section tolerances are close
Tolerances for placing or fastening of other materials such as connection hardware in relation to building lines	From specified location . . . . ± ¼″	Not established

Table 2.1 Relevant erection tolerances for cast-in-place concrete structures and structural steel. (Reproduced by permission; Precast/Prestressed Concrete Institute, *Architectural Precast Concrete,* 2d ed., 1989)

into disk shapes in a phenomenon called *hysteresis* (see Sec. 4.3.5).

Both vertical and horizontal joints should be analyzed to allow for these movements in relationship to the movement of the supporting structural frame. Concrete frames shrink over time (see Sec. 4.4.5), while steel frames expand and contract depending on temperature. Most architects follow the recommendations of the cladding manufacturer's representatives or choose a width from another project that did not develop problems. It is helpful, however, to be aware of all the forces affecting the cladding. Checking the recommended width by a simple calculation based on the thermal coefficients of the materials and building frame and choosing a good sealant helps to ensure that problems do not occur at a later date.

SLAB EDGE

Supporting the slab edge in steel construction may be accomplished by one of the methods shown in Fig. 2.29. While the structural engineer controls the method, size, and detailing of slab edges, the architect must evaluate the impact of that detailing on the defenses outlined in Chap. 1. Frequent angles supporting the slab edge and penetrating the vapor retarder are potential leakage points for vapor and are very hard to check in the field for proper taping. The same difficulty is encountered with air barriers. In addition, one must realize that slab edge supports

can add measurably to the cost in multistory construction. A sheet-metal closure costs less than a bent plate. A bent plate costs less than sheet metal supported by steel angles and so on. The following is a list of questions to be asked before deciding on a final solution:

1. Is the backup wall easy to seal against the slab?
2. Is this the most lightweight solution?
3. Does it entail an excessive amount of welding?
4. Is the cladding supported by the slab edge heavy?

2.2.6 Structure as an Element of Design

Exterior architecture is influenced by many factors such as the architecture of surrounding buildings, historical antecedents, solar exposure, proportions, and the type of occupancy. The type of structure should also be an important shaper of the design. The structural frame can have an organizing influence on the design, providing a repetitive rhythm not unlike the drumbeat in a musical piece. There are several ways in which the structure can be honestly expressed. It can combine the function of both supporting structure and cladding (see Fig. 4.83). A bold structural concept can shape the building and draw attention to it (Fig. 2.30). Supports can be consolidated and combined with other functions to make a bold statement (Fig. 2.31). The structure can be expressed albeit clad in a protective skin (Fig. 2.12).

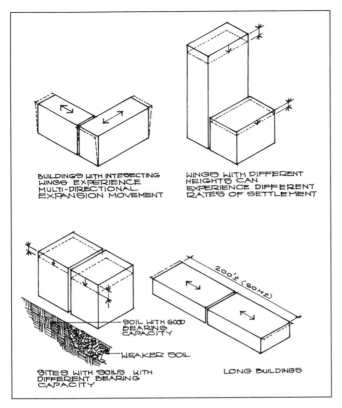

Figure 2.26 Locations requiring expansion joints.

2.3 COST

2.3.1 Controlling Costs

The total cost of the project includes several items besides the cost of construction. One must be aware of the total picture to appreciate the importance of life-cycle costs. Most architects, however, have their hands full trying to keep the costs within the budget allocated for architectural construction alone. One look at Fig. 2.32 shows that architectural construction drawings represent less than 35% of the total project cost for most public buildings. In fact, it may even be less than that in certain types of projects such as laboratories (Table 2.2). Before the initial meeting with the consultants, the project architect should determine whether the project budget is tight, average, or generous and, based on this evaluation, impress upon them to conduct their designs accordingly. After all, it does not make sense to allow two-thirds of the work to proceed with complete disregard for the budget while the architect tries to cut costs for the most visual 35% of the project. Should the bids come in over the budget, these individuals must devise ways to reduce the costs of their designs. It is always a good policy, when the architect perceives that a project has a tight budget, to design the project as frugally as possible for the base bid documents and include upgrades of materials or systems referred to as *add*

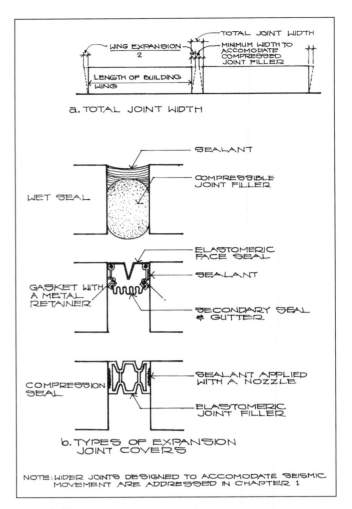

Figure 2.27 Expansion joint details.

alternates to be priced separately by the bidders. This stratagem can achieve two goals. The first is to ensure that the project stays within the budget, avoiding the mad scramble after the bids have been submitted to devise ways to cut costs and explain to the client why this occurred. The second is that the low bidder usually retains the part of the submitted cost that is allocated to overhead, taxes, contingency, etc., after cutting the cost of the items that were deleted. This means that if an item that normally costs $100,000 is deleted from the contract, the overall costs would be reduced by approximately $85,000. The added effort for defining add alternates can be minimal. For example, if the cladding is designed to be precast panels, the alternate can be to specify a stone veneer for these panels. This type of alternate requires an added section in the specifications and minimal, if any, extra drawings. In a similar manner, if the other disciplines include one or two alternates that do not entail a substantial extra drawing effort, the cost of the project can be controlled.

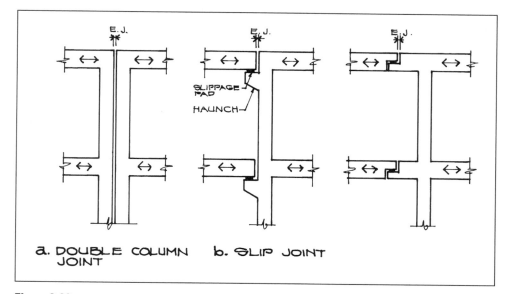

Figure 2.28 Expansion joints at columns.

Another factor that has a bearing on overall cost is the economy of size. Large projects generate large volumes of materials. As a result, contractors can negotiate lower unit prices from manufacturers. Large projects also generate intense competition between contracting firms. These factors usually result in lower bids.

MARKET CONDITIONS

Architects have a hard time predicting market conditions especially during the early stages of schematic design (SD). At the end of each phase, SD, design development (DD), and construction drawings (CD), the architect presents the owner with a cost estimate. These estimates are either prepared by the architect (SD phase) or by a professional cost estimator. Because construction drawings are usually prepared well in advance of actual construction, estimators must make certain assumptions about the value of money and market conditions at the time of bidding. These two issues are hard to predict with any amount of accuracy. Other issues, such as the possibility of labor shortages due to a strike or a surge in construction activity or material shortages, can also affect their estimate.

Allowance must also be made for market conditions. During a booming economy, contractors are much in demand and shortages in materials and labor sometimes occur. As a result, prices are raised and contractors have to allocate higher contingency amounts for unforeseen condition in their bids. The opposite is true during a stagnant economy when contractors are hurting and are willing to reduce their profit margins to stay in business.

Knowledgeable owners usually allow an adequate contingency in their budget to cover many possibilities including the difference between initial and final estimates, omissions and mistakes in contract documents requiring change orders, market conditions and changes requested by the client after the bids are received, as well as other unforeseen factors.

LABOR AND MATERIALS

Shortages of materials such as steel for the structural frame can occur during the booming economy referred to above. This can result in a longer lead time for the delivery of steel components to the site. This, in turn, can cause delays in other trades resulting in a delay in project delivery. If this happens, a penalty referred to as *liquidated damages* is usually imposed on the contractor. This penalty is commensurate with the length of the delay. This is one of the reasons why contractors submit inflated bids under these circumstances.

Another cost issue is the location of the project. Sites located at or close to crime-ridden areas of the city can result in higher costs because the contractor will add a contingency to cover the expected vandalism and pilferage of construction materials. Materials and Labor will cost more at remote sites.

Projects for government entities usually require the use of union labor. This type of labor usually produces high-quality execution but may cost more than non-union work. To guard against excessive labor costs especially on tight-budget projects, architects should consider using shop-fabricated, panelized wall systems as a base bid and detail the labor-intensive system as an

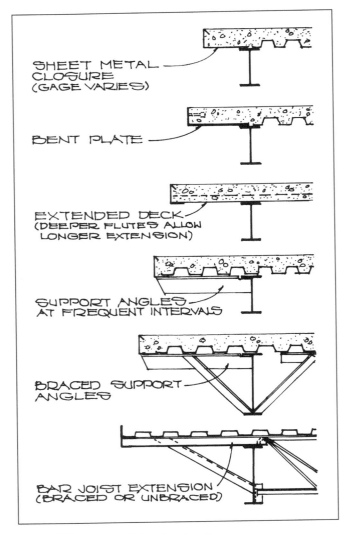

SHEET METAL CLOSURE (GAGE VARIES)

BENT PLATE

EXTENDED DECK (DEEPER FLUTES ALLOW LONGER EXTENSION)

SUPPORT ANGLES AT FREQUENT INTERVALS

BRACED SUPPORT ANGLES

BAR JOIST EXTENSION (BRACED OR UNBRACED)

Figure 2.29 Typical slab edge details.

add alternate to give the unions a competitive system to bid against. In addition, government controlled projects can be delayed by red tape and a disproportionate amount of paperwork.

2.3.2 Cost Evaluation Methods

The effect of choosing the wrong systems or materials for large, multimillion dollar projects can add substantial amounts to the cost or result in a shortening of the life of the building. Evaluation methods such as life-cycle cost comparison and value engineering were introduced to prevent that from happening.

LIFE-CYCLE COSTS

This evaluation method is used during the latter part of the schematic design phase or at the beginning of design development to compare initial costs to the costs incurred over the life of the building. A less durable

item chosen for its visual appeal and low initial cost may prove to be more expensive in the long run than an alternative that will last longer and require less maintenance. Life-cycle costs include initial, operating, maintenance, and replacement costs. All these costs must be adjusted to equivalent values at the time of construction to provide an even basis for comparison.

Initial costs of materials and labor are readily available from cost estimating publications such as the *Means Cost Guide*.[12] They can also be taken from recent projects undertaken by the architect. One word of caution—the cost quoted by the representatives, in most cases, does not include the general contractor's overhead and profit. Allow 15% to cover these expenses.

Initial costs obtained at the start of the project must be projected to equivalent costs at the estimated time of construction. For example, if the cost of an item is $1000 at the start of the SD phase, it may escalate to $1080 or more after the construction drawings are completed. This is caused by inflation and the length of time between initial and final estimates.

Operating costs apply to systems with moving parts such as elevators, escalators, dock levelers, and other equipment. It also applies to items under the control of the mechanical, electrical, and plumbing (MEP) consultant who, in certain cases, controls a greater percentage of the project than the architect (Table 2.2).

Since the architect, in most instances, heads the design team, he or she must become familiar with the different HVAC systems to be able to discuss alternatives with the consultant if cost issues arise.

Maintenance costs for the exterior may include window washing, periodic wall cleaning or painting, as well as items that are performed at longer intervals such as reapplication of sealant or tuck-pointing of brick. Some materials such as polished granite are durable and require very little maintenance, while others, such as painted stucco, may require more frequent repairs and repainting.

When a material or system reaches the end of its projected useful life, it may have to be replaced due to obsolescence, corrosion, or deterioration. Replacing it usually requires major expenditures to cover the cost of removing the old system and installing its replacement. This item does not usually apply to exterior walls which are expected to last as long as the structure. Unless, of course, a cheap, untested, or poorly detailed system is used.

THE VALUE OF MONEY

All the costs described above must be projected to reflect the value of the dollar at the time of construction to provide a sound basis for comparing life-cycle costs

Figure 2.30   Dulles International Airport, Chantilly, Virginia. (Eero Saarinen, Architect)

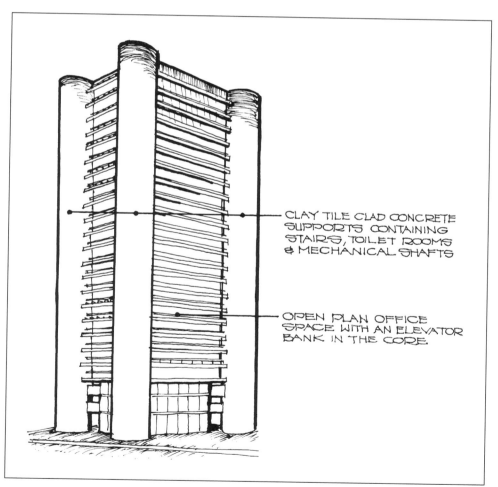

CLAY TILE CLAD CONCRETE
SUPPORTS CONTAINING
STAIRS, TOILET ROOMS
& MECHANICAL SHAFTS

OPEN PLAN OFFICE
SPACE WITH AN ELEVATOR
BANK IN THE CORE

Figure 2.31   Knights of Columbus Office Tower, New Haven, Connecticut. (Roche, Dinkeloo & Associates, Architects)

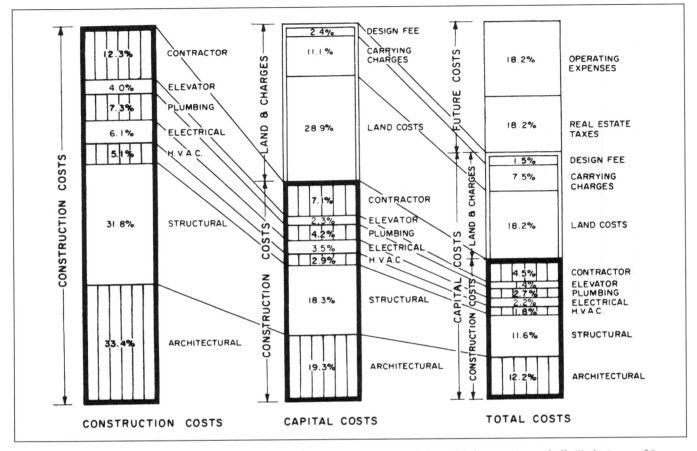

Figure 2.32 Construction costs in perspective. (Reproduced by permission of the publisher; W. B. Foxhall, *Techniques of Successful Practice for Architects and Engineers,* McGraw-Hill, Inc., 1975.)

of the different alternatives. An item that may cost $1700 ten years from now, can cost only $1000 in today's economy. The value of money is hard to predict in spite of the fact that there are computer programs designed to facilitate this process. To compute these values, the estimator must first make assumptions about the rate of inflation which may not be accurate. The assumed rate of inflation will, however, apply to all the choices being compared and usually results in the right selection.

VALUE ENGINEERING

This activity is sometimes used in conjunction with life-cycle cost estimates for large projects. The value engineering process brings together experienced representatives from each discipline to explore less costly alternatives than the ones chosen by the design team entrusted with the project. This group of individuals, who had no involvement in the project, are instructed to make any suggestion, however far-fetched it may be, to trigger constructive new concepts from other members of the group during several brainstorming sessions. It is an intense, exciting, and fruitful process. It is also

exhausting and may be inadvertently steered toward cheapening the project.

The value engineering approach usually proceeds in six phases:

1. Information
2. Function
3. Idea generation
4. Judicial analysis

Building Type	Architectural	Structural	M E P
Office Building	40%	25%	35%
Educational	40%	20%	40%
Hospital or Lab	35%	15%	50%
Retail	35%	30%	35%

Table 2.2 Rough percentages indicating the relative costs of architectural and engineering services.

5. Recommendation

6. Presentation

The information phase explores all the facts, determines the costs, identifies the functions, sets the worth of each function, and evaluates the value of these functions. The second phase classifies the functions into basic, secondary, supporting, or unnecessary. It analyzes them, eliminates unnecessary ones, and selects those that need value improvement. The third is the most interesting one. It utilizes the creativity of the participants, who are, in some cases, more experienced than members of the design team and bring a fresh, unbiased eye to the proceedings, to create, brainstorm, and introduce new thoughts to the process. It seeks to eliminate or reduce unnecessary items or frills from the project, challenge concepts, and explore maintenance and cost issues.

After the idea generation phase, a set of design criteria are developed and all the ideas introduced are evaluated against them. Those that do not measure up are dropped. Authorities in the field may be consulted during this analysis. Similar ideas may be grouped and a weighted evaluation process using a matrix is employed to develop recommendations. Life-cycle costs are also considered.

At the close of the value engineering encounter, the team manager gathers the material and makes a presentation to the project designer(s) supported by a written report.

To illustrate the way value engineering works, I will cite an example from my own experience. During the value engineering effort for the multibillion-dollar Deer Island sewage treatment plant project to reduce pollution in Boston harbor, one of the objectives stated by the designer was to design all the new buildings to harmonize with the style of a very old steam pumping station. This deteriorated brick building was to be restored at great expense and converted into an administration and information center displaying the existing historical steam pumping equipment. This design decision meant that all the new buildings had to be constructed of brick featuring fake arches, crenellations, corbels, and other costly embellishments imitating the existing building.

I suggested changing the objective so that the new buildings would be designed as a simple backdrop contrasting in material and color with the old building to let it stand out as a unique focal point instead of trying to compete with it. This change would have saved a substantial amount of money. Unfortunately, the majority would not be swayed by such a "revolutionary" approach and decided to stay with the original objective contributing to substantial cost overruns.

This example shows that value engineering does not necessarily follow pure logic or cost considerations only but is often swayed by other factors such as the prevailing tastes and philosophy of the participants as well.

THE INTUITIVE APPROACH

Intuition is the method used on all smaller projects. It depends on the experience and gut feel of the project architect. As one gains experience, one can usually tell which materials cost less or last longer and which assemblies and details inspire contractors to hike their prices and other factors that affect the overall costs of the project.

The following is a partial listing of cost control strategies:

- One of the most important and unrecognized tools to combat the added costs caused by change orders is to produce near-perfect contract documents that gain the respect and trust of the general contractor. A well-coordinated set of construction documents with details covering all conditions and keyed back to their source and supported by a tight specification for all disciplines can thwart the efforts of the experienced specialist employed by the contractor to find inconsistencies that can be used to request lucrative change orders. These individuals recognize the difference between a good set of drawings and a shoddy one. The good set usually inspires confidence that no major problems will occur during construction, and contractors will be less likely to inflate their bids to cover the unforeseen circumstances resulting from gaps in the information included in the contract documents.

- Shop-fabricated assemblies allow for more efficient use of labor and are not subject to adverse weather conditions during fabrication. In many cases these assemblies cost less especially if they don't have to be brought in from long distances and the hoisting equipment is already on the job.

- Code interpretation can have a significant effect on cost. Misinterpretation of the occupancy or selecting a more restrictive type of construction than the one allowed by the code are examples. For instance, selecting a type of construction that requires the steel frame to be sprayed instead of dividing the building into smaller segments to allow the use of an unprotected frame needs to be evaluated carefully before a decision is made.

- Using the least number, size, grade, or thickness of a component to achieve the desired result is a good policy to prevent unnecessary expense. This, of course, must be based on industry standards and sound calculations.

Making a presentation to the owner about the probable cost of an item, whether a finishing material or an assembly, must be prefaced with a statement that many factors can affect the cost and that it cannot be predicted accurately. As pointed out in the preceding text, many factors can raise or lower the price, and the architect has no control over most of them.

2.3.3 Design Decisions

THE OVERALL CONCEPT

The outline of the building plan can have a profound effect on the overall cost. Exterior walls that have many ins and outs increase the length of the wall [Fig. 2.33(a)]. These walls with their expensive finish and fenestration usually represent one of the most expensive components of the project. The same applies to wall sections. Bay windows, balconies, and, to a lesser degree, deep-set windows add to the cost [Fig. 2.33(b)].

Decisions that affect the floor-to-floor height in multi-story buildings must be evaluated carefully. A few extra unnecessary inches added at each level can add several extra feet to the overall height resulting in a substantial increase in the cost of the cladding. That is why developers demand a concerted effort between the architect and the mechanical and structural engineers to pare down the clearances between the ducts, beams, main fire sprinkler pipes, light fixtures, and ceilings to minimize these dimensions. This can mean running the ducts through holes or cutouts in the beams at noncritical locations, positioning them in shorter bays where the beams are shallower, or devising other solutions to achieve the same goal (see Fig. 5.9).

DETAILING

The following simple precautions can be taken to avoid cost overruns in the area of detailing:

- Designs that mandate exotic materials and a high degree of skill and precision in the construction of cladding components obviously cost more than those that use standard materials, detailing, and methods of construction. Concentrating on a few focal points such as entrances on which to use choice materials while using less costly construction on the rest of the building is used in many cases to reduce construction costs while maintaining aesthetic appeal.

- Using a unique material produced by a single manufacturer (single sourcing) is usually an invita-

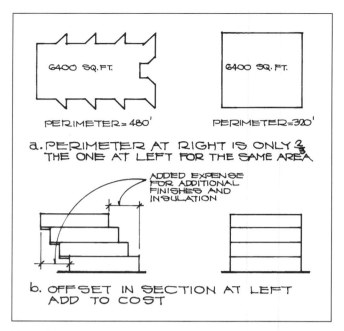

Figure 2.33 Increased perimeter cladding adds to the cost of the projects.

tion to inflated costs due to lack of competition. Government work usually requires a detailed memorandum justifying this decision and, unless truly necessary, may disallow it. Also on-site assembly, rather than shop-assembled and panelized panels, needs to be evaluated before a final decision is made.

- Designs that subdivide the wall into little areas or require the use of many different materials and finishes will inflate the overall cost of the assembly. Each different material may require installation by a different trade causing a scheduling nightmare and possible delays. Little panels require an excessive amount of sealed joints adding to the cost of material and labor to say nothing of the increased likelihood of leakage and increased maintenance costs.

To digress from the subject of cost for a moment, using a disproportionate number of different materials requires the architect to produce more details and more sections in the specifications to cover each material and more shop drawing checking and site visits to make sure that each one is constructed properly. All these reasons would seem to point toward the wisdom of using as few materials as possible on the exterior. Unfortunately, some designers tend to believe that the more complicated the design, the better the aesthetics. This is contrary to the approach used by the majority of world-famous architects to produce buildings of enduring beauty.

THE WEIGHT FACTOR

The overall weight of the cladding can also affect cost. Heavy cladding requires a stronger supporting structure and more elaborate foundations as well as the added expense of leasing heavier cranes to carry it. Opting to use GFRC over precast panels may not represent a savings in panel costs, but, because the panels weigh a fraction of the weight of precast panels, savings in the cost of the structural frame and foundations can be important enough to sway the decision in favor of GFRC, especially if the bearing capacity of the soil is poor or the building is located in a seismically active zone. Exterior walls that can be erected without the need for leasing hoisting equipment or erecting scaffolding can save money. Metal stud systems assembled on each floor and raised manually into position are an example.

CUSTOM DESIGN

Custom-designed components usually cost more than off-the-shelf products. The urge to design from scratch should be used judiciously especially on projects with limited budgets. Creating new designs and products is a time-honored tradition. One can still find fine examples of well-crafted items created by Frank Lloyd Wright and Paolo Soleri and other notable designers.

Today, one can usually find a product that would achieve a similar aesthetic result at a lower cost compared to the custom design that the architect sketched. The designer should search through Sweet's catalog[13] and individual product literature before creating a unique design. In addition to saving money, this approach will avoid any liability for problems that may develop later. This is especially true for complicated products such as custom lighting fixtures or windows. All new products of that type require the expertise of a person specializing in that area. One must consider that every new product usually requires modifications to iron out any flaws before being mass-produced. An architectural project unlike a car does not offer a second chance for taking corrective action and refinement.

IMPORTED MATERIALS

While imported products and building materials can give a project a unique appearance or enhance its aesthetics, delay in delivery due to dock worker strikes, shipping mishaps, or other circumstances unique to overseas operations may hold up construction or prevent the contractor from meeting the deadlines. This usually triggers penalties commensurate with the length of the delay. Contractors may increase their bid amount to cover this contingency. An example is cited in Sec. 4.3.4.

2.3.4 Strategies for Staying Within the Budget
DEFINING ADD ALTERNATES

Because of the uncertainties of market conditions (Sec. 2.3.1), architects have a hard time predicting whether the bids will be within the budget. I worked once in an office where we used to play a game of "guess what range the bids will come in at." The one who came closest received a prize.

When a project attracts bids that are substantially over the budget, the office must identify means of reducing the amount. This can mean spending many hours poring over the drawings to come up with a list of suggestions that have the least impact on the design. Items such as finishes, fenestration, and landscaping are the most likely to suffer in the process to say nothing of the reduced profitability for the office caused by the added hours spent on this activity.

As was mentioned previously, deleting items that were included in the bid is not as cost effective as adding items to a bid that came in below the budget. A better approach is to prepare the construction drawings according to minimum acceptable design standards. Identify areas that the architect would like to upgrade and have the bidders price them separately. If the bids come in lower than the budget, the owner selects some or all of the add alternates to be included in the contract. Add alternates are listed in the specifications, and each is provided with a blank space for the bidder to fill in the total or unit price.

This approach provides the architect with some control over the budget and avoids the mad scramble and expense required to bring the cost down if the bids are too high. It is no guarantee that this will not happen, but it is a step in the right direction.

CONTINGENCIES

Impressing upon the client to set aside a higher contingency amount to cover the difference between the bid and the cost estimate during a booming economy is a good policy. This is especially relevant for projects that are to be executed according to an accelerated schedule or fast-track. A *fast-track* project requires the preparation of construction drawings in several packages before the design development phase is completed (Fig. 2.34). Construction also begins before the construction drawings are finished. The potential for oversights and conflicts resulting from shortcomings in coordination between the disciplines is usually higher than a conventionally built project.

Raising the budget contingency amount can help cover the costs associated with these inevitable inconsistencies. While the fast-track method of construction is rather stressful on all the professionals involved in the project, it shortens the construction period and allows the owner to draw rent revenue from the property to start repaying the loan earlier than conventionally built projects. This results in a reduction in financing charges which can be quite substantial on large projects such as high-rise buildings.

COORDINATION

Uncoordinated drawings generate claims from the contractor that can add appreciably to the total cost of the project. To improve coordination between the disciplines, the architect must set a schedule at the start of the project in collaboration with the consultants. The schedule must require that the consultants deliver their completed drawings to the architect at least 4 or 5 weeks prior to the final deadlines. This period allows the architect to check the full construction set, write comments about discrepancies and inconsistencies, convene a meeting to resolve these issues, return their drawings for corrections, and have the architectural team make the necessary corrections and additions to the architectural set. As a consultant performing that task for major architectural firms, I have seen examples where the ceiling height stated on the reflected ceiling plans differed by as much as 2 ft (600 mm) from the actual ceiling height arrived at after adding the depth of

the beam, the intersecting ducts, the lights, and sprinkler system. This condition may require a costly remedial action requiring added costs to reconfigure the ducts and possibly to modify the structure as well as reduce the ceiling height. Issuing the drawings without going through this process can result in added costs both to the client and the architect who must spend time and money to issue change orders and face the unpleasant task of explaining to the client the reason why the drawings were not done right the first time around.

2.3.5 Other Issues Affecting Cost

DISCONTINUED PRODUCTS

Specifying a material manufactured by a company that has gone out of business, omitting a material from the specifications, or specifying a performance that cannot be met by the named acceptable products may result in costly substitutions. To produce a tight specification, the architect must check the required performance against the list of acceptable products and contact each manufacturer to make sure that the company is still in operation and that the product has not been modified or discontinued.

Using the Con-Doc system (see Chap. 5) for keying materials used in wall sections directly to the numbers used in the specifications ensures that all materials are covered.

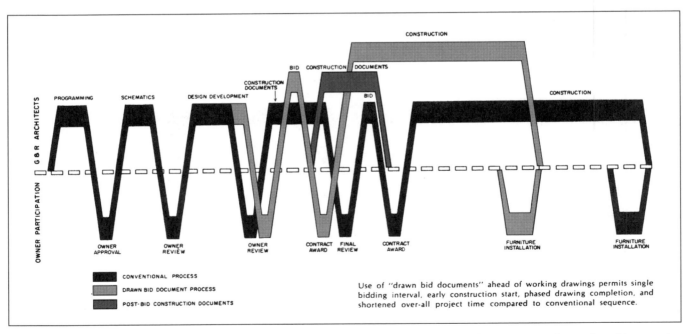

Figure 2.34 Comparison between the fast track (drawn bid) and conventional methods of construction. (Reproduced by permission of the publisher; W. B. Foxhall, *Techniques of Successful Practice for Architects and Engineers,* McGraw-Hill, Inc., 1975. All rights reserved.)

CHECKING SHOP DRAWINGS

Shop drawings are the detailed drawings submitted by the general contractor to the architect to be reviewed for conformance to the design intent. They must be reviewed in a methodical way against the details they are based on. One must be aware of the interrelationships between different assemblies to make certain that conflicts will not occur. For example, an omission in the listing of door hardware in a project containing a thousand doors can add up to a tidy sum. The same principle applies to door sizes. Mistakes or omissions can also be generated by consultants. Approval of shop drawings based on wrong information in the original construction drawings can be very costly.

While the contractor is responsible for checking the drawings and is required to bring any inconsistencies in the drawings to the attention of the architect prior to placing the bid, in many cases, the issue of a major and costly mistake will be brought to the attention of the owner coupled with a plea for payment to cover the added cost. This puts the architect in a weak position that is very hard to defend. If this occurs several times during the course of the job, the owner may sue to recover the added costs from the architect and the architect may lose credibility on the job.

2.4 OTHER DESIGN CONSIDERATIONS

2.4.1 Durability

Architects must strike a delicate balance between durability and cost. Choosing materials that will endure for a very long time without deteriorating, detailing them thoughtfully, testing them to make sure that the methodology used by the erector conforms to the design intent, and making frequent site visits to avoid costly mistakes is the ideal sought by most designers. Unfortunately, not all projects are funded to achieve this ideal. Compromises have to be made to stay within the budget.

LIFE EXPECTANCY

Most projects are required to have a theoretical life expectancy of 50 years. Anything beyond that period is considered a bonus. Of course, public buildings such as museums and courthouses are expected to last much longer. Assigning a limited number of years for the expected life of a building is not necessarily a bad thing. Technology is evolving at a fast pace and most structures become obsolete even before their projected useful life expectancy is over. Developer economics can also play a part in determining the useful life of a building. This author has witnessed the demolition of a relatively new, fully leased high-rise building in Houston to make way for an 80-story tower. A short while

after the demolition, during the design development phase of the new building, the bottom fell out of the Texas economy and the new project was canceled. This resulted in the addition of a fine new parking lot to downtown Houston.

Today, change is the only constant. Buildings that are designed to accommodate that change—if one can foresee what that change is going to be—are the ones that will last longest. Although this fact applies more fully to building interiors, exterior wall systems are not immune from obsolescence. Aesthetic trends change requiring buildings to have extensive face lifts or recladding, and window technology and energy savings may require building refenestration. For these reasons, designing an expensive wall system to last a long time beyond the foreseeable future is not necessarily the goal to aim for in every case. An ideal to strive for is to design the cladding for easy disassembly and replacement if at all possible.

REDUNDANCY

Exterior cladding constructed as a barrier wall (see Sec. 3.2.2) must be designed properly and executed perfectly to provide the protection expected to prevent leakage. Unfortunately, such perfection is very hard, if not impossible, to expect from a system composed of many parts, constructed by many trades, and supervised by very few. Things can and do go wrong requiring costly remedial action and continuous monitoring as well as very thoughtful detailing to minimize the inevitable problems.

A better approach is to assume that the primary system will fail sooner or later and provide a redundant backup system. Masonry cavity and veneer walls (see Sec. 4.2) as well as curtain walls designed according to the rain screen principle (see Sec. 3.2.2) are examples of that approach.

2.4.2 Maintenance

Building maintenance is the activity that prevents buildings from deteriorating rapidly, falling into disrepair, and losing their value. It is not unlike car maintenance. It falls into two categories: measures inherent in the initial design to prevent deterioration referred to as *preventive maintenance* and, the more widely known, *periodic maintenance*.

PREVENTIVE MAINTENANCE

The goal of preventive maintenance is to minimize the need for periodic maintenance or to reduce the items that need to be attended to. The following recommendations help illustrate this approach:

■ In stone-clad buildings choose a dark, polished stone surface for exterior walls to minimize the need for periodic cleaning. This is especially important at the bottom of the wall to a minimum height of 7 ft (2.1 m) in areas subject to graffiti or vandalism.

■ Use recessed windows instead of flush-mounted windows to eliminate the need for more frequent cleaning to remove dirt streaking. Constant glass exposure to polluted water washing over other materials can cause permanent etching of the glass surface.

■ Minimize areas where birds can lodge and soil the facade and passersby with their droppings. One effective method is to slant the surface 45°. If this is not possible, a wire bird repellent product can be used (see Fig. 1.40).

■ Designate the heaviest gauge recommended by the Sheet Metal and Air Conditioning Contractors National Association's (SMACNA) handbook[14] or even heavier metal for gutters and downspouts where they form part of the design to avoid gutter damage. If downspouts are exposed to damage by cars, place bumpers or bollards in front of them.

■ Horizontal rustication or horizontal board imprints in forms for exposed concrete tend to collect dirt which soils the facade when washed down by rain. If the design calls for these features, bevel the lower side at 45°.

■ Avoid a surface that requires periodic painting especially on durable materials such as brick or concrete. Materials that require protection such as wood should be protected with a more durable penetrating stain to extend the periods between applications.

These measures do not represent additional costs in many cases but effect substantial savings during the life of the building and help keep the exterior attractive for longer periods of time.

PERIODIC MAINTENANCE

Polishing metal parts at building entrances, cleaning sidewalks, and window washing are examples of periodic maintenance.

Window washing can be staged from the ground level using ropes and pulleys attached to the top. One individual hanging precariously on a platform does the work. This primitive method is usually used on low-rise and, in some cases, medium-rise buildings. Another more sophisticated and safer approach is to use a mechanized stage hanging from retractable or removable

davits located on the roof (Fig. 2.35). This is the most prevalent method used to clean high-rise windows. A third, more advanced, method is to use a fully automated washing rig operated by a person on the roof. While this latter type is used in Japan, it is not commonly used in the United States.

The designer should consult with the owner and regulatory authority to ascertain which system is contemplated for the building and is allowed within the jurisdiction. Anchor pins may be required at certain heights. These may be fastened either to the window frame or to the wall.

Rigs are hung from davits mounted on pedestals anchored to the structure, some davits are mounted on the back surface of parapets or on wheels attached to rails looping around the roof, and yet others are custom-designed for the project to solve challenging conditions. The designer should discuss with product representatives the requirements for the project, the cost, code requirements, roof protective measures, and anchoring devices. Some consultants specialize in designing these systems.

PERIODIC INSPECTION

Establishing a program of periodic inspection and maintenance can help prevent small problems from becoming big ones and ensure that the building maintains its appearance.

Conducting a yearly inspection in the spring is a wise investment that can help the owner avoid costly repairs later on. An experienced inspector can detect leakage points such as areas where the sealant has failed. Efflo-

Figure 2.35 Window washing rig.

rescence can indicate that weepholes in a cavity wall are plugged or that the vapor retarder is flawed. Rust stains can indicate that steel lintels or concrete reinforcement is being corroded by moisture. These illustrate a few obvious symptoms that indicate the need for inspection. If left uncorrected, these symptoms can become severe problems requiring major repairs or even replacement at a cost that can reach double or more the initial cost spent to construct the wall. While the architect has no control over the owner's decision to initiate these inspections, he or she can explain their importance using the analogy of car inspections.

2.4.3 System Selection

The wall system selection process is affected by many factors including

- Urban context
- Project budget
- Building type
- Weather and soil conditions

It is also affected by the architect's method of gathering information and how this information is evaluated. The following subsections address these factors and the process used by many architects to choose between different systems.

THE URBAN CONTEXT

There are two schools of thought affecting the choice of wall cladding materials in an urban setting. The first is to let the building blend with its surroundings by using materials similar to those used in the majority of buildings in the neighborhood. This is the prevalent trend. Examples of this approach are all around us.

The second approach is to choose materials and construction systems that contrast with the building's surroundings. The goal here is to draw attention to the building and create excitement. People either love it or hate it. Examples of this approach are more prevalent in Europe. They include the Pompidou Cultural Center and the Louvre plaza pyramid. Both are located in Paris and both created a furor of protest similar to that which occurred when the Eiffel tower was built. Now, they are showcases embraced by almost everybody.

PROJECT BUDGET

This is an obvious determinant or criterion that has a profound effect on the choice of the wall system to be used on the project. A precast system costs almost twice as much as a brick cavity wall system. It is usually not considered for tight-budget projects. Generously budgeted projects, on the other hand, allow for a wide vari-

ety of choices and require careful evaluation of each system before a final choice is made.

BUILDING TYPE

Courthouses, museums, headquarters for large corporations, and some government buildings require the use of more durable materials and rich detailing. Other types, such as commercial and multifamily residential construction, can do with a less durable type of construction. This is partly because the first type of building, in addition to having to present a prestigious image, is required to last for a very long period of time, while the second type becomes obsolete more quickly. Of course, there is the difference in budgets between the two types to act as a determinant in the choices made.

WEATHER AND SOIL CONDITIONS

A wall system appropriate for Alaska is usually not suitable for Arizona and vise versa. Local weather conditions and architectural styles and available materials differ from one region to another. A heavy system such as precast may not be appropriate for locations where soil bearing capacity is low or in seismically active locations.

THE SELECTION PROCESS

One of the main sources of information is the product representative. Some of these individuals are well informed about their product and are a rich source of information about what it can or cannot do. However, others are less so. These individuals should not be confused with impartial sources of information such as university seminars and consultant input. Representatives are in the business of selling their product. Many will be less than complimentary when comparing their product to competitive products that may be superior to theirs. They may also suppress shortcomings of their product for obvious reasons, or they may just honestly not know the facts.

It is incumbent upon architects to educate themselves continuously by attending seminars and symposia and reading technical literature to be prepared to ask meaningful questions and review product literature properly. They must seek the name of the technical person in the manufacturer's home office to get more accurate answers before specifying the material.

The questions to ask should include:

- How many years has the product been on the market?
- What is the cost of the product installed? This includes materials, labor, and, an additional amount to cover overhead and profit for the general contractor (12 to 15%).

- What standard details are available?

- What is the type and duration of the warranty?

- Does the representative have addresses of buildings where the product was used?

- Can he or she provide names and phone numbers of architects that used the product?

- What are the availability and delivery times?

- What comparable products are listed as equal in quality?

The architect, of course, should not depend solely on the information provided for the last item on this list. This question is usually asked when the product has very limited competition. This information is transmitted to the specification writer to research whether these products are truly equal.

Based on the interviews with product representatives, the architect can then develop a weighted product comparison matrix to evaluate the performance of the different products. Weighted means that each desired feature is assigned a value. This is usually from 1 to 5. One being least and 5 being the most desirable (Fig. 2.36). The product with the highest total and most favorable comments is the one selected.

The following is a list of criteria that may be considered during the evaluation process:

1. Weatherability, maintainability, and durability

2. Physical attributes such as dimensions, weight, color, R-value

3. Cost

4. Ease of erection and in some cases disassembly (space frames, for example)

5. Is it recyclable? Does it incorporate recycled materials?

6. Is it produced by an established and reputable manufacturer represented by a knowledgeable local representative?

SUMMARY

Structural members are designed to resist gravity and the lateral forces of wind and seismic action. Exterior wall panels must be mounted in a way that will minimize the effect of structural frame movements on them. Deflection in response to gravity, frame deformation in response to wind, seismic forces, and thermal expansion and contraction are examples of these movements. Deflection can be vertical such as the sagging that occurs at midspan or at the tip of cantilevers, or it can be horizontal affecting vertical studs and high-rise buildings. Supporting wall panels directly on the columns avoids vertical joint problems associated with beam

deformation. Using deeper or braced cantilevers minimizes problems associated with their sagging.

Several design strategies are used to resist the effect of lateral forces on the structural frame. Solid shear walls or cross-bracing can be introduced at exterior walls or building cores in both orthogonal directions. Rigid frames composed of moment connections or deeper spandrels can be constructed to stiffen the connections between beams and columns, the exterior framing can be designed as a truss or a tube formed by closely spaced columns, or the cladding itself can be integrated into the structure to provide the needed stiffness.

Columns may be placed at different locations in relation to the cladding. Each position has its advantages and disadvantages. The relationship between the column and the wall can affect the detailing of the vapor retarder and the air barrier in addition to the interior organization of the building. The designer must consider this decision very carefully.

Shelf angles are structural members designed to carry masonry veneer. They may be attached directly to the structure or hung from it. They should be adjusted by the mason to fit properly in the wall and torqued by the miscellaneous-iron worker.

Panelized systems are usually supported by clip angles or similar hardware designed to accommodate thermal and structural frame movements. Because supports are designed by the fabricator in most cases, architects should investigate their impact on the interior furring and allow space for their installation but not necessarily draw them.

Vertical and horizontal expansion joints are designed to accommodate thermal, lateral, and seismic movements. Vertical joints also allow buildings to adjust to different soil bearing capacities and different rates of settlement caused by different building heights. Subdividing the cladding areas prevents the buildup of stresses that can cause cracking. Special wide joints are introduced in buildings located in seismic zones 3 and 4 to prevent the destructive pounding that can occur between adjacent wings.

Designers must allow adequate clearances to accommodate the specified tolerances allowed for imperfect execution of the building frame as well as the cladding components. An additional gap should also be left to allow for slight deviations from the tolerances and to prevent friction between them. Having too much clearance is preferable to too little.

Lintels are beams designed to resist gravity and lateral forces imposed on them by the weight of the wall (in load-bearing walls, a portion of the floor load is also borne by lintels). Lintels transfer these loads to the jambs of the opening. Wind forces imposed on the win-

Evaluation Criteria

Manufacturer	Product Description	Core Material	Max. Panel Size	Thickness	Joint Description	Type of Finish	Fastener	Warranty	Cost	Weight	Comments
A	2" Metal Sandwich Panel with Pressure-equalized Joints	Polyiso. (5)	36" x 30' (3)	2 inches (2)	Rain Screen (5)	Kynar 500 (5)	Concealed (5)	20 Yr. (5)	$21 (4)	34 ÷ 8 = 4.25	Low R-value / Size is inappropriate
B											
C											
D											
E											

Annotations:
- *Average Weight*
- *Number of Weights*
- *Total of Weights*
- *Weight (from 1 to 5)*

Figure 2.36 Example of a product evaluation matrix.

dow glass area are transferred to the lintel, jambs, and sill. These members must be designed to resist these forces. That is why multiple studs are placed at the jambs and light-gauge box beams are sometimes placed at the top and bottom of wide openings in stud walls. Loose lintels are structural beams transferring their load to both sides of a masonry opening. They can be constructed from steel angles, CMU, stone, precast or site-cast concrete, and wood or its derivatives.

Expressing the structure as an element of design can add to the overall aesthetics. This approach can take several forms. Integrating the load support function in the cladding is one approach; expressing the structure to make a bold statement is another. These approaches provide an honest expression of the structure instead of hiding it. It is analogous to the introduction of alloy wheels in car design instead of hub caps. Other issues include cost, durability, redundancy, and maintenance.

Managing the costs of a project is a task that starts at the conceptual phase and continues throughout the project. If it is done right, it results in maintaining good relations with the client and may generate repeat work. If the project exceeds the budget, the architect must justify the reasons to the client and take remedial action that can cut into the fee.

Estimating costs is a complicated and time-consuming task. For any sizable project, it is entrusted to a professional cost estimator. The cost of money at the time of construction (inflation) must be factored in, market conditions must be assessed, the effect of the design on labor and material costs must be allowed for, and the impact of the systems chosen on life-cycle costs must be evaluated. Sole practitioners usually use the intuitive approach because the project budget does not allow them to use any other method. This contrasts with the practice of employing value engineering on very large projects to brainstorm ways to reduce costs and/or improve performance.

Several design strategies can be employed to avoid cost overruns. Designs employing many ins and outs which increase the area of an expensive cladding system must be avoided in low-budget projects. Floor-to-floor heights must be optimized for the same reason, and expensive detailing and materials should be concentrated at focal points. Using off-the-shelf products instead of one-of-a-kind, custom designs is advisable if the standard product has a comparable aesthetic impact. These hand-crafted, imaginative designs should be reserved for projects with large budgets that can absorb the extra cost. Finally, projects that emulate the "many-colored coat of Joseph" by incorporating as many build-ing materials and pieces as possible in the facade in the erroneous belief that this approach adds to the aesthetics should be avoided. They add to the cost of the building, increase the possibility of leakage, and add to the time and cost of producing the drawings. In most cases, the architect ends up losing money on the project.

The architect should advise the owner to allocate an adequate contingency to cover unforeseen circumstances. This is especially important if the project is to be constructed according to the fast-track or design-build methods. Architects should also include add alternates to the drawings and specifications to control costs. Some alternates can even be defined in the specifications without the need for additional drawings. This approach represents a minimal effort on the part of the architect.

Architects must also plan the project to allow time at the end for a thorough final check to coordinate the information within the architectural set as well as between the drawings of the different disciplines.

The life expectancy of the materials and systems should match the planned durability of the building. One of the most durable elements in a building is the exterior cladding. It should be designed and detailed with care to avoid premature deterioration. Its components should be tested to prove that they will perform as intended and modifications instituted if problems are detected during the test. Redundancy should be included in the design to ensure that if one line of defense against the elements is breached, another will take over its function.

Maintenance can be made part of the design by choosing easy to maintain materials featuring colors and textures that do not accent dirt. This approach is referred to as preventive maintenance. Periodic maintenance is in the purview of the owner. Examples include window washing, reapplying failed sealants, and re-pointing masonry. Architects should impress upon owners the importance of instituting a program of periodic inspection and maintenance.

A process of data gathering and evaluation of a cladding system and fenestration is required before making the final selection of these products. Sources of information include the product representatives, the technical advisor at the fabricator's headquarters, seminars, and technical literature. An evaluation matrix listing the desirable criteria should be constructed to evaluate the information gathered from product representatives, and the products that achieve the highest scores selected.

Exterior Wall Design

This part, unlike Part I which deals with concepts and issues that influence wall design, deals with the physical makeup of exterior walls. It identifies walls and the fenestration installed in them by type. It explains the rain screen pressure-equalized principle in a relatively understandable way, and it addresses the rather complicated components of fenestration with special emphasis on how to detail the frames in a manner that would minimize leaks.

Because of time constraints, I narrowed the scope of Chap. 4 to focus on five of the wall assemblies most used to enclose public buildings. The reader will notice that reference to wood construction is almost totally absent from this chapter. The reason is that while wood-framed walls represent a sizable percentage of total construction, the majority of that type of construction is used in housing. While some public buildings are constructed of wood, it is rarely, if ever, used for these purposes in the parts of the country where this author worked.

The final chapter deals with the proper way to draw, dimension, notate, and reference building sections, wall sections, and section details.

CHAPTER 3

Wall Types and Fenestration

3.1 GENERAL

Exterior walls provide a protective enclosure that performs several functions which include protecting the occupants from inclement weather, providing security, preventing dust and pollutants from accessing the enclosed space, and reducing external noise levels.

Categorizing walls by type is rather difficult. Walls have different functions; some are load-bearing and others act as cladding attached to a supporting structure. They have different physical compositions; some are single-thickness walls, while others are constructed as double-thickness cavity walls. Finally, they can be designed according to different design philosophies that require them to act as an impervious barrier wall or as a pressure-equalized rain screen using the force of the wind to deny wind-driven rain access into cavities. A wall may combine more than one of the descriptions listed above. For example, a wall may be described as a load-bearing cavity wall designed according to the rain screen principle.

Walls are also constructed from different materials, including masonry, concrete, metal, and glass to form different assemblies conforming to construction principles set by tradition and experience. Wall assemblies are treated as an independent topic covered in Chap. 4.

This chapter surveys the different aspects of wall design and attempts to provide some information about the different design philosophies currently being used. Fenestration is also addressed in this chapter since it forms an integral part of the wall. Individual window panes are usually called *lites,* a derivative of the word *lights*. The design and detailing of window systems requires architects to possess a certain familiarity with window types, framing systems, and the glazing incor-

porated in them. In addition, the architect must determine the design wind pressure mandated by the code based on calculations, on a discussion with the structural engineer, or, in the case of high-rise buildings, on wind tunnel tests. Based on this information, the depth of the mullions and the glass thickness can be determined from graphs issued by the manufacturer.

Leakage through exterior walls is almost as frequent as roof leakage. In many cases, it is caused by poor detailing around window frames. Window details must ensure that the joints around the window are detailed and sealed properly to avoid this problem. Because of the importance of this subject, architects must continue to educate themselves by attending seminars and reading the numerous books dealing with it. This chapter gives an overview of window design. It is by no means comprehensive in its coverage of this complicated and ever-evolving subject.

3.2 WALL TYPES

A wall may be constructed to carry the loads superimposed on it by the roof or floor(s) above it and to transfer these loads to the foundation. These walls are referred to as *load-bearing walls*. Alternatively, the load may be carried by a structural frame, in which case the exterior wall acts only as an infill or cladding attached to the frame carrying its own weight and resisting wind or seismic loads only. These walls are referred to as *curtain walls*.

3.2.1 Type Categorized by Function
LOAD-BEARING WALLS

Solid load-bearing masonry walls dominated construction throughout history until the advent of the Industrial

Age introduced more advanced methods of construction. These massive walls functioned reasonably well as barriers by providing security and barring noise, wind, and rain. Their thermal mass evened out temperature fluctuations. When it rained, moisture infiltrated part way into the wall and was released to the exterior in the form of vapor when the sun warmed the building. This usually happened before water had traveled all the way through the wall thickness.

While this conventional method of construction was suitable in the past, it is rarely used today because of cost, time, and space constraints. Present-day construction methods and economics almost mandate that walls be much thinner and lighter. Currently, solid load-bearing walls are used mostly in some residential and low-rise industrial buildings such as manufacturing plants and warehousing. They are also used in some high- and medium-rise hospitality buildings (hotels and motels) because the repetitious short spans between partitions make this type of wall economically attractive in this application. Further discussion of these load-bearing partitions is, however, outside the scope of this book because the partitions are not exterior walls.

One of the disadvantages of thin load-bearing walls is that they offer only one line of defense against air and water penetration into the building and, unlike cavity walls, they have no way to redirect water that may leak through this line of defense to the exterior unless the joints are constructed as a two-stage design (see Sec. 1.3.2).

Load-bearing walls may be constructed of reinforced masonry, poured-in-place (site cast) or precast concrete, steel, or wood studs. Bearing walls may also be constructed as a cavity wall composed of two wall thicknesses separated by an air space (cavity). This design provides a second line of defense. Should the outer wall thickness develop leaks, the water will trickle down the back of this outer barrier and be directed to exterior weepholes by a metal or flexible barrier referred to as *flashing* (see Fig. 4.32).

Cavity walls are usually constructed of masonry units, but the design can be applied to other materials. In masonry cavity wall construction, the inner and outer wall thicknesses (wythes) are tied together with masonry ties or joint reinforcement to allow the assembly to act in a manner similar to solid walls. The inner wythe may be of the same material as the outer wythe, or the outer wythe may be considered as a veneer with a different backup such as CMU or steel studs (wood studs are used in residential construction).

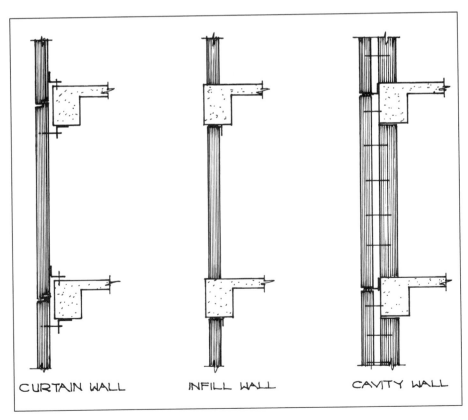

Figure 3.1 Curtain wall types.

Because wind gusts may blow water through openings in the outer wythe across the air cavity, and mortar droppings may get wet and convey moisture to the inner wythe, dampproofing that inner surface and the placement of flashing at weepholes is advisable.

Cavity walls are a refinement over single-thickness walls. They provide an added line of defense against leakage and should be used whenever budget constraints permit.

CURTAIN WALLS

Non-load-bearing walls support only their own weight in addition to lateral loads (wind and/or earthquake movements). They may be constructed as a single-thickness curtain wall attached to the slab edge, supported directly on the structure as an infill between spandrel beams, or they may be constructed as a cavity wall (Fig. 3.1). Curtain wall weight varies from the relatively heavy precast and masonry veneer to lightweight assemblies such as GFRC; stud assemblies faced with tile, EIFS, and stucco; all-glass cladding; and metal walls. Lightweight systems result in a lighter support structure and foundation. They also effect savings in material, transportation, and hoisting costs. Stud systems must be designed to deflect as little as possible especially if they provide support for a stiff veneer such as brick or a brittle facing such as stucco or tile.

3.2.2 Design Philosophies

Walls may be designed according to one of two design philosophies. They may be detailed and constructed to present an impervious skin sealed against water and air penetration (referred to as the *barrier wall* approach), or they may be designed in a way that provides an opposing force to resist the wind pressure that drives rain into the inevitable wall imperfections. This is referred to as the *pressure-equalized* approach, also known as the rain screen principle.

Before reading the descriptions of these philosophies, the reader is advised to review Secs. 1.2 and 1.3 that describe the forces of wind and water. Understanding how air currents behave and the mechanics of water movement will make it easy to understand the rationale behind the defensive measures integrated into wall design and the zones of maximum vulnerability. One must also understand the conditions under which water will leak.

WIND EFFECT ON CAVITIES

Wind travels at much higher speeds at building corners. That difference in speed causes air entering the cavity through any flaws in the wall to accelerate parallel to the facade to join the faster moving air at the corners.

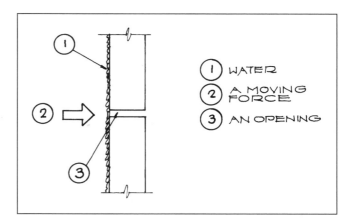

Figure 3.2 Conditions required before a leak can occur.

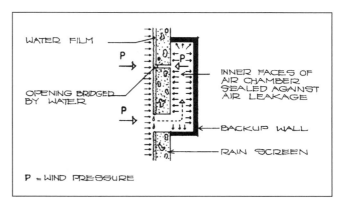

Figure 3.3 The pressure-equalization concept. (Reproduced by permission; J. K. Latta, *Walls, Windows and Roofs for the Canadian Climate,* The National Research Council Canada, Ottawa, 1979)

The same movement occurs near the top of the building. Rain carried by these air currents can drench the surface of the backup wall at these locations increasing the chance of leakage. As will be described later, creating air barriers within the cavity prevents this from happening.

CAUSES OF WATER LEAKAGE

Three conditions are required before a leak occurs: an opening, water, and an air current to push the water through the opening (Fig. 3.2). If one of these conditions is eliminated, no leakage can occur. Barrier walls try to eliminate the first condition by sealing all openings. Eliminating the second condition, namely water, is currently considered to be impractical, although some researchers believe that it may be conceivable to take advantage of the fact that building facades get wet unevenly during a rainstorm. Most of the water is deposited at the perimeter while the central part remains relatively dry.

Pressure-equalized wall design aims to eliminate the third condition, namely, the air currents that push water into wall openings. It achieves this by integrating three components into the wall design: an exterior facing, or rain screen; a drained cavity divided into relatively airtight compartments; and air vents protected from water infiltration. The following subsections describe both design philosophies in detail.

BARRIER WALLS

This design philosophy requires all joints and potential leakage points to be sealed to provide an impermeable skin around the building. While excellent sealants are available for this purpose, their performance depends, to a large extent, on several factors. These factors include the skill of the applicator, field conditions, proper surface preparation, proper mixing of the sealant (if it is a two-part mix), as well as the control of joint width and depth (see Sec. 1.3.2). Even under ideal conditions, sealants will eventually deteriorate as a result of continuous exposure to ultraviolet rays, ozone degradation, pollutants, the freeze-thaw cycle, and the continuous movement caused by thermal fluctuations. In spite of all these factors, most barrier walls are used extensively and perform satisfactorily for relatively long periods of time.

The most successful designs used in barrier walls employ a backup system. This may take the form of a two-stage sealed joint in single-thickness panelized systems such as precast assemblies, or it may take the form of a cavity wall design which provides for drainage.

RAIN SCREEN WALLS

As mentioned earlier, the rain screen design philosophy aims to eliminate the force that pushes water into the wall. The design is, in essence, a cavity wall subdivided into compartments made as airtight as possible. Each compartment is drained with weeps which are usually placed in a location sheltered from water infiltration. These weeps have a dual function. In addition to the drainage function, they act as air vents allowing air to enter into the cavity to increase its pressure and equalize it with the wind pressure. Once this occurs, air movement into the cavity is stopped and the goal of eliminating the force that pushes water is achieved. This process takes only an instant, a span of time that is usually not long enough for water to enter the cavity. Vents may also be placed in locations other than weepholes.

J. K. Latta of the National Research Council (NRC)[15] uses a pertinent analogy to illustrate the pressure-equalization idea. He theorizes that if air can be mechanically pumped into the cavity so that the pressure inside is raised to equal or exceed the exterior wind pressure, rain would not move toward the interior. Since this is impractical, using the power of the wind itself to pressurize the compartment (Fig. 3.3) is an even better proposition since this does not require the use of energy in the pressurization process and the resulting opposing pressure will be modulated by the intensity of the wind. A strong or gusting wind creates a strong counter pressure in the cavity, and a mild breeze creates a mild opposing pressure. In other words, the design creates pressure equalization on both sides of the rain screen.

Compared to other cladding systems, modern rain screen design is still in its formative stages. It is conducted according to rules of thumb. Research is continuing to try to determine the ratio of the lateral load carried by the rain screen to the load carried by the backup wall, the ratio between the cavity volume and the area of the vents [currently recommended to be less than 300 ft (100 m)], and the effect of air leakage within the cavity on the size of the air vents. This last issue is determined by lab tests and is very difficult if not impossible to determine in an actual wall assembly. The reason is that leakage can be caused by imperfections in the backup wall, the partitions between compartments, or in the wind screen itself. All these parameters are variable and hard to predict. Dalgliesh and Garden of Canada's NRC have this advice:[16]

> By compartmentation of the cavity, the range of pressure differences acting on any cavity compartment may be greatly reduced. It is proposed that until further pertinent information becomes available vertical closures should be provided at each outside corner of a building and at 4-foot intervals for about 20 feet from the corners. Horizontal closures should be used near the top of the wall. It is also considered advisable that both vertical and horizontal closures be positioned up to 30 feet on centers over the total wall area. It should be noted that these cavity closures (or partitions) need not provide a complete air seal but must be sufficient to allow the appropriate pressure difference between cavity compartments to develop. It is possible to follow a similar approach to deal with the problem of achieving pressure equalization in spaces or cavities where abrupt variations occur at projections and recesses.

Window jambs and heads can be considered as part of this partitioning of the cavity.

All-glass and all-metal curtain walls are currently the best applications of this system because their materials are impermeable to air infiltration. In all-glass curtain walls, the rain screen principle is applied to the mullions and spandrel panels only (Fig. 3.4). These are designed with vent or weepholes in the soffits of the horizontal mullions to pressurize the cavities. The wall is naturally subdivided into small compartments, and the backup of each cavity is all metal with gaskets acting as an air barrier. All-metal curtain walls may be designed as a barrier wall with all joints sealed or gasketed, or they may be designed as a rain screen. This latter design is carried out within the joint (see Fig. 1.7), with baffled open joints and a partitioned cavity (see Fig. 4.117), or it may be designed without partitions

(Fig. 3.5). While this last mentioned system is a well-designed rain screen, it is not pressure-equalized.

The rain screen principle can be applied to other curtain wall designs especially panelized systems such as precast, GFRC, and preassembled stone or brick panel systems (Chap. 4). Masonry cavity walls have all the prerequisite of a pressure-equalized system except for vertical compartmentalization of the cavity. The brick veneer acts as the rain screen, the full head joint weeps act as the pressurization vents, the gypsum wallboard

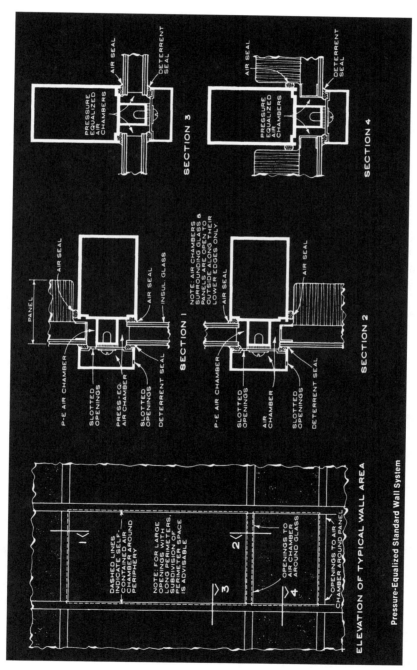

Figure 3.4 Pressure-equalized mullions in a glass curtain wall.

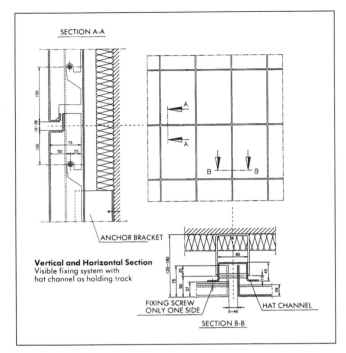

SECTION A-A

ANCHOR BRACKET

Vertical and Horizontal Section
Visible fixing system with
hat channel as holding track

FIXING SCREW
ONLY ONE SIDE

HAT CHANNEL

SECTION B-B

Figure 3.5 An example of a metal rain screen, non-pressure-equalized system. (Pohl Europanel, Pohl, Inc.)

interior finish acts as the air barrier, and the shelf angles placed at every story (or every other story) subdivide the facade into horizontal compartments. To qualify as a true pressure-equalized design, vertical compartmentalization must be created to prevent horizontal air currents inside the cavity from drawing outside air and water into it (Fig. 3.6). Augmenting the vertical barriers

created by window jambs and creating more barriers near the building edges (Fig. 3.7) would complete the rain screen requirements. The partitions do not have to be perfectly airtight but should be constructed as tight as possible to drastically reduce air velocity and prevent rainwater borne by it from infiltrating into the cavity. Research and testing are required to determine the most effective type of partitioning medium and vertical joint design. Alan Dalgliesh states,[17]

All rain screen cladding systems are designed to resist rain penetration but only the Pressure-Equalized Rain screen (PER wall) makes use of the air barrier to minimize the main force that pushes water into the wall. An air barrier is already needed to control air leakage, so the only additional cost involved is the provision of lateral stops to break the cavity up into compartments.

Although an unpressurized cavity wall may also prevent rain from getting into rooms, the PER wall is better because in addition, it keeps the cavity itself freer from moisture. The drier environment within the wall reduces the rate of deterioration of structural connections as well as the veneer itself. Water within the wall cavity is a major factor in deterioration. A properly designed and installed air barrier is a key component in defending against moisture accumulation within the wall, both from rain penetration and from water vapour exfiltrating from humid rooms.

3.3 FENESTRATION

3.3.1 Window Types

Exterior windows may be classified as

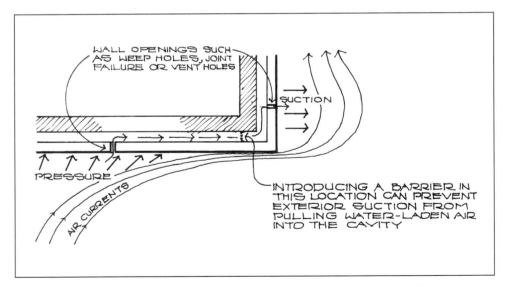

WALL OPENINGS SUCH AS WEEP HOLES, JOINT FAILURE OR VENT HOLES

SUCTION

PRESSURE

AIR CURRENTS

INTRODUCING A BARRIER IN THIS LOCATION CAN PREVENT EXTERIOR SUCTION FROM PULLING WATER-LADEN AIR INTO THE CAVITY

Figure 3.6 Air acceleration within the cavity is caused by exterior pressure differences at the corners and top of buildings.

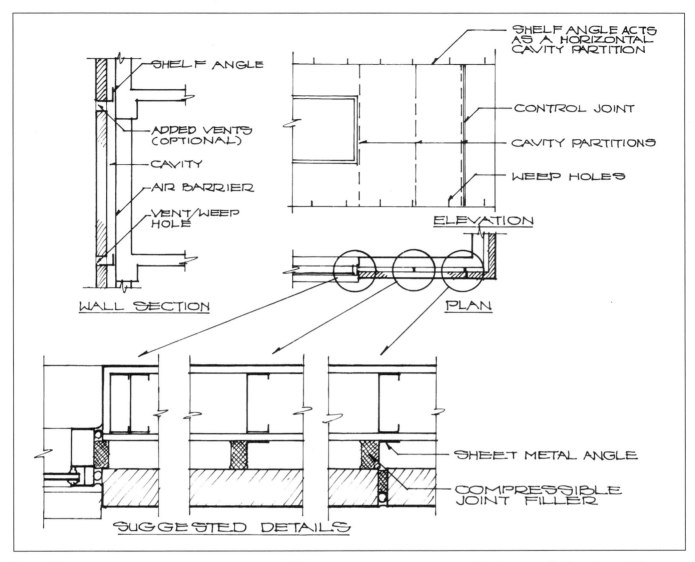

Figure 3.7 Creating partitions in a masonry cavity wall to convert it into a pressure-equalized system. Shelf angles, window jambs, and control joints can be integrated in the partition network.

- Punched windows
- Strip windows
- Storefronts
- Curtain walls

The first two are distinguished by their shape. Most storefront mullions are designed to span over a single story. Curtain walls are engineered to form the closure for multistory buildings. The following is a brief description of each type.

PUNCHED WINDOWS

This type of window is surrounded by an opaque wall. Figure 3.8 shows the different types of windows used in this design. Operable windows are used on a limited basis in public buildings but are very common in residential construction including multistory condominiums and apartment buildings. These types are also used in restoration projects in conjunction with an exterior trim referred to as *panning* (Fig. 3.9) simulating the profiles of existing, deteriorating wood trim. Panning may be produced from custom extrusions copying the existing wood window trim, or it may be fabricated from standard panning extrusions that may or may not imitate the original.

The architect must define the rough window opening (the width and height of the wall opening set to receive the window) allowing ½ in (13 mm) for the joint between the frame and the opening. This width makes provision for construction tolerances of ± ⅛ in (3 mm)

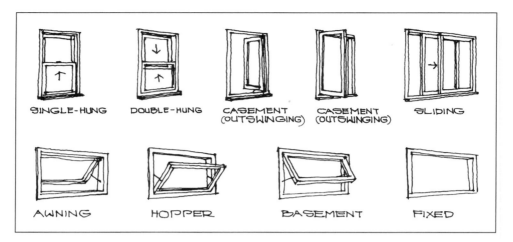

Figure 3.8 Types of punched windows.

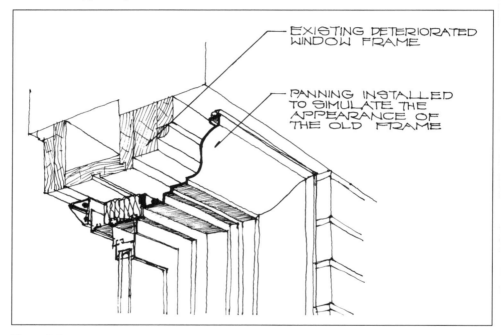

Figure 3.9 An example of a panning extrusion.

added to ⅜ in (10 mm) for the sealant. A ⅜-in (10 mm) gap is also acceptable for small windows.

STRIP WINDOWS

Strip or ribbon windows are common in office buildings and clerestories. The window mullions may occur at the head and sill only with the glass spanning between them. In this case, the glass is referred to as having a two-side support (the head and sill mullions). Its thickness is determined by graphs that are different from those used for a four-side support window. This latter designation applies to windows that have vertical mullions spanning between the head and sill.

The first design is suitable for open office plans without partitions or for exterior walls abutting continuous corridors. Vertical mullions should be spaced in multiples appropriate to the spacing of partitions located behind them. In many cases, a 5-ft (1.5 m) module is chosen because it allows for a minimum room dimension of 10 ft (3 m) as well as larger offices and conference rooms.

Strip windows transfer half the wind load pushing against the window to the wall above and the other half to the wall under the sill. The architect, in collaboration with the structural consultant, must design the walls to provide adequate support below the window and bracing at the window head.

STOREFRONTS

Most mullioned storefront systems are designed to span between the finished floor and the structure above. They are usually designed to span approximately 10 ft (3 m), and the mullions are, in most cases, 4 × 2 or 4½ × 2 in (110 × 50 mm) (Fig. 3.10). Storefronts are usually located at ground level, although, in residential multistory construction and multistory shopping malls, they may be located at all levels. Most of these systems are drained through the vertical mullions rather than through weepholes in the horizontal mullions as is the case with curtain walls. All-glass assemblies (Fig. 3.11) may also be used as storefronts.

Doors are an element of this system. To detail doors properly the architect must determine the type and location of the door closer. If it is floor-mounted, the required depression may be required to be shown on the structural drawings. This type of closer gives a neat, uncluttered appearance to the door but is harder to service than closers placed at door heads. The threshold detail must include a bead of sealant placed under the sill to prevent air infiltration and water leakage. Should a card-access security system or a physically handicapped access button be included in the design, the location of the card reader or button must be shown on the elevation and be connected to a power source shown on the electrical drawings.

Aluminum storefronts are usually less sophisticated and costly than curtain wall systems. Using a curtain wall system in applications where a storefront is adequate without a strong justification is a waste of money.

CURTAIN WALLS

Curtain wall systems are designed for applications where the mullions must extend in front of two or more floors. They are engineered specifically to withstand high winds and to span more than 10 ft (3 m). Most curtain walls are designed according to the rain screen principle with weep/vent holes located in the horizontal mullions. They may be either off-the-shelf, pre-engineered systems stocked and marketed by one of the major manufacturers or custom-designed in collaboration with a consultant specializing in curtain walls. A consultant advises the architect on the way certain details should be developed including the design of mullions if custom extrusions are used. Contrary to popular belief, a customized die fabricated to produce a custom extrusion profile does not represent a sizable investment especially on fair-sized projects. In most cases, the consultant does not produce a set of construction drawings. He or she develops a performance specification and leaves the actual design of the curtain

wall to the curtain wall subcontractor. That consultant checks the shop drawings for conformity to the specifications and must be actively involved in field testing. For major projects, testing may include the construction of a full-scale mock-up combining typical as well as special conditions. In most cases, the architect requests static wind testing, dynamic water testing, testing for the structural integrity of the system, and a thermal cycling test to measure condensation and the overall U-value of the wall. The consultant should also be entrusted with field testing at random locations on the building during the construction phase and with proposing corrective action if required. Because the test panel is assembled by the same personnel that will do the actual erection, these tests serve as a training venue, a dry run if you will, for the system.

A wind tunnel test is usually required for high-rise buildings to determine the wind pressures on which to

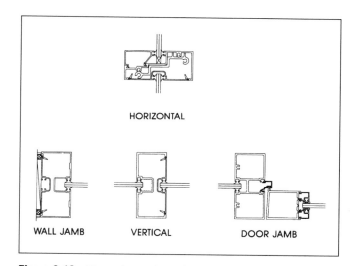

Figure 3.10 Typical storefront framing.

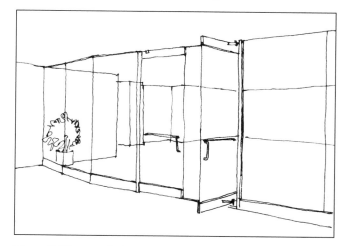

Figure 3.11 An all-glass assembly used as a storefront.

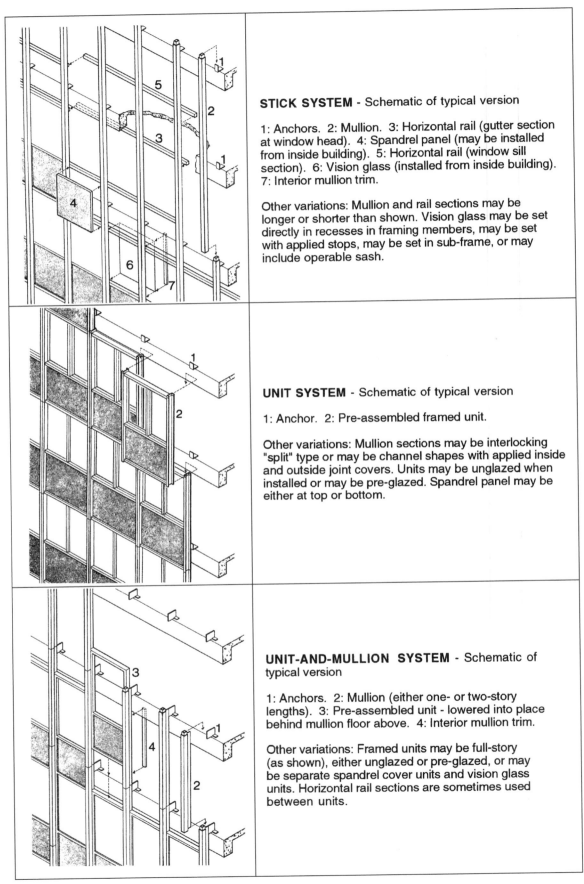

STICK SYSTEM - Schematic of typical version

1: Anchors. 2: Mullion. 3: Horizontal rail (gutter section at window head). 4: Spandrel panel (may be installed from inside building). 5: Horizontal rail (window sill section). 6: Vision glass (installed from inside building). 7: Interior mullion trim.

Other variations: Mullion and rail sections may be longer or shorter than shown. Vision glass may be set directly in recesses in framing members, may be set with applied stops, may be set in sub-frame, or may include operable sash.

UNIT SYSTEM - Schematic of typical version

1: Anchor. 2: Pre-assembled framed unit.

Other variations: Mullion sections may be interlocking "split" type or may be channel shapes with applied inside and outside joint covers. Units may be unglazed when installed or may be pre-glazed. Spandrel panel may be either at top or bottom.

UNIT-AND-MULLION SYSTEM - Schematic of typical version

1: Anchors. 2: Mullion (either one- or two-story lengths). 3: Pre-assembled unit - lowered into place behind mullion floor above. 4: Interior mullion trim.

Other variations: Framed units may be full-story (as shown), either unglazed or pre-glazed, or may be separate spandrel cover units and vision glass units. Horizontal rail sections are sometimes used between units.

Figure 3.12 Types of curtain wall assemblies. (Reproduced by permission; American Architectural Manufacturers Association, *Aluminum Curtain Wall Design Guide Manual,* 1979)

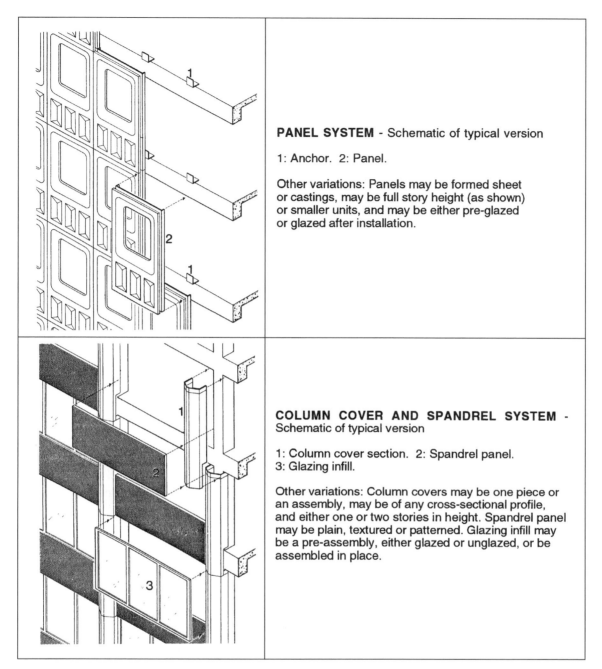

PANEL SYSTEM - Schematic of typical version

1: Anchor. 2: Panel.

Other variations: Panels may be formed sheet or castings, may be full story height (as shown) or smaller units, and may be either pre-glazed or glazed after installation.

COLUMN COVER AND SPANDREL SYSTEM - Schematic of typical version

1: Column cover section. 2: Spandrel panel. 3: Glazing infill.

Other variations: Column covers may be one piece or an assembly, may be of any cross-sectional profile, and either one or two stories in height. Spandrel panel may be plain, textured or patterned. Glazing infill may be a pre-assembly, either glazed or unglazed, or be assembled in place.

Figure 3.12 (*Continued*) Types of curtain wall assemblies. (Reproduced by permission; American Architectural Manufacturers Association, *Aluminum Curtain Wall Design Guide Manual,* 1979)

base the design. It requires the placement of a model of the building and its immediate surroundings in a wind tunnel. Sensors are attached to the facades to determine pressure (both positive and negative) intensities. These intensities are used in the design of the structure. The cost of conducting such a test may range between $20,000 and $30,000 and requires 6 to 8 weeks. It may result in savings of double or triple that amount in construction costs.

Off-the-shelf systems are pretested which means that water and air infiltration tests are not required to prove that the system will perform as designed. They are the norm for low-, medium-, and some high-rise buildings. This, however, is no substitute for field testing the system during installation to ensure that it is being installed and detailed properly.

Curtain wall systems may be assembled according to one of the methods shown in Fig. 3.12. Unit and mullion systems, also referred to as stick systems, are the most prevalent kind because they are economical and go up fast. There is a growing trend, however, toward factory-built preglazed, preinsulated full bay panels to minimize field work. The designer must allow an adequate clearance between the curtain wall and the supporting structure. The American Architectural Manufacturers Association (AAMA) states that, as a general rule, a minimum 2-in (50 mm) clearance must be allowed. The higher the structure, the wider the gap. The American Institute of Steel Construction's (AISC) Code of Standard Practice states that the allowable tolerance for columns is 1 in (25 mm) toward or 2 in (50 mm) away from the building line in the first 20 stories plus 1/16 in (1.5 mm) for each additional story.

Mullion size is determined by the intensity of wind pressure dictated by the building code or wind tunnel testing. Building codes usually contain a map defining wind velocities. These velocities are further defined by what is termed *exposure* which is determined by the surrounding terrain and height above grade. This information is then transformed through the use of equations into the design pressure used as a basis to determine mullion depth and glass thickness. The AAMA in collaboration with the American National Standards Institute publishes load tables based on exposure C providing precomputed wind velocity pressures (VP) at different elevations from grade. Design structural test and water test pressures corresponding to these wind velocities are also listed. *Exposure C* is defined as open terrain with scattered obstructions having heights less than 30 ft (9 m). Refer to App. C for more information on the subject of computing wind pressure. Manufacturers of standard, preengineered systems, also provide easy-to-use graphs for that purpose (Fig. 3.13). Different methods are used to support the mullion (Fig. 3.14). The method chosen for the project is determined through consultation with the window manufacturer and the structural engineer. It is recommended that fasteners used in contact with aluminum be manufactured from stainless steel having a minimum chromium content of 16% when used in locations subject to moisture to avoid galvanic action.

The AAMA recommends that detailed anchorage methods should be shown on the architectural drawings rather than on the wall contractor's shop drawings. This clarifies the scope of the work for all subcontractors involved in metal decking, rebar, concrete, steel framing, fire-proofing, and other work and invalidates any justification for later back charges on the grounds that extra work, not shown on the drawings, was required.

As of this writing, there is no rated fire assembly included in the UL *Fire-Resistance Directory* for an all-glass curtain wall. The directory does include a 3-h rated assembly for a mullion assembly with aluminum spandrel panels. USG has conducted a full-scale fire test on a glass curtain wall with observers from UL for an all-glass curtain wall assembly. USG seems to indicate in its literature that a UL design may result in the future (Fig. 1.36). In the meantime, constructing a fire-rated GWB partition behind the spandrel or using a fire-rated metal spandrel will provide that protection.

All-glass curtain walls are not as popular as they used to be in the seventies and early eighties because of changing design philosophies and economics. They are not as energy efficient as curtain walls incorporating opaque spandrel panels. However, they are still incorporated in some projects as a design feature or to act as an envelope for the whole building especially in temperate zones. They may make a comeback if glass insulation technology improves their R-rating to the point where they can compete with the overall rating and cost of opaque walls.

3.3.2   Framing Systems

The choice of a window framing system depends upon several factors which include

- *Window type.*   Punched, strip, storefront, curtain wall.
- *Building type.*   Residential, commercial, institutional, etc.
- *Design details.*   Width and depth of mullion, fixed window, or operable sash.
- *Budget.*   The choice is more limited for low-budget projects.
- *Geographical location.*   Weather extremes require thermal breaks and insulated glazing, features which may not be required in temperate zones.

Window frames may be constructed of wood, vinyl, metal, or rubber gaskets (Fig. 3.15). Structural glazing is also used. The following is a description of each.

WOOD AND VINYL FRAMES

Almost half of all window frames are assembled from wood. They provide a warm, homey look and better insulation than their metal counterparts. This is why they are preferred in residential construction. They can be painted, given a natural finish, or be clad with PVC or aluminum on the exterior to protect them from the weather.

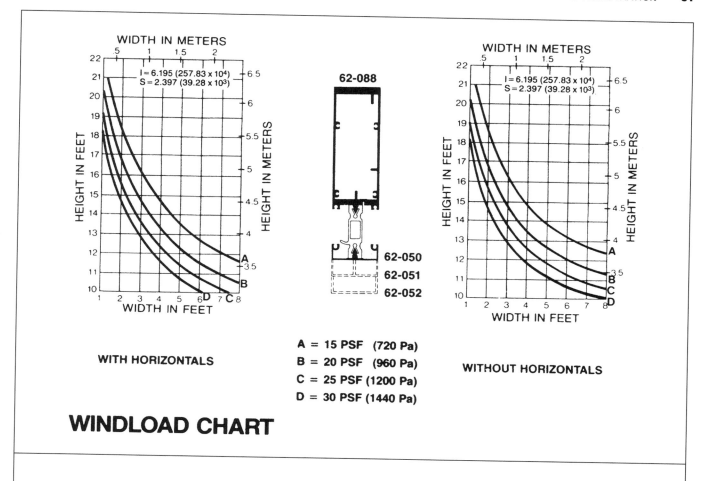

WIDTH IN METERS

I = 6.195 (257.83 x 10⁴)
S = 2.397 (39.28 x 10³)

HEIGHT IN FEET

HEIGHT IN METERS

WIDTH IN FEET

WITH HORIZONTALS

62-088

62-050
62-051
62-052

A = 15 PSF   (720 Pa)
B = 20 PSF   (960 Pa)
C = 25 PSF (1200 Pa)
D = 30 PSF (1440 Pa)

WITHOUT HORIZONTALS

WINDLOAD CHART

KEY

A – ¼″ GLASS W/¼ POINT LOADING

B – ¼″ GLASS W/⅛ POINT LOADING

C – 1″ GLASS W/¼ POINT LOADING

D – 1″ GLASS W/⅛ POINT LOADING

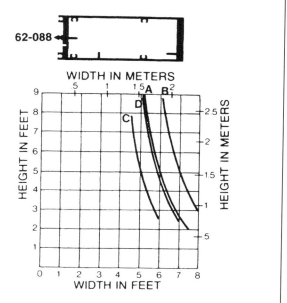

62-088

WIDTH IN METERS

HEIGHT IN FEET

HEIGHT IN METERS

WIDTH IN FEET

DEADLOAD CHART

Figure 3.13 Examples of charts used to size mullions. (Arcadia, Inc.)

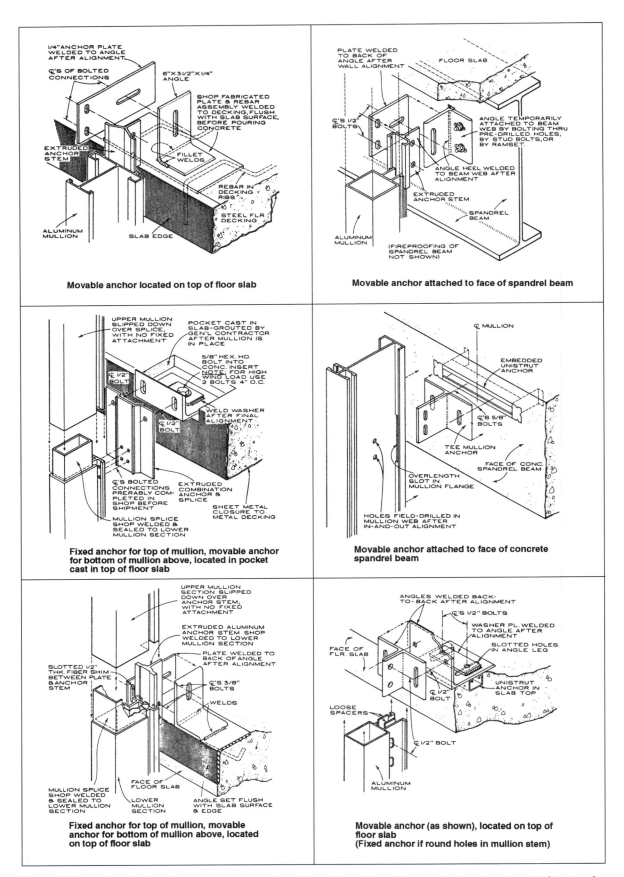

Figure 3.14 Methods of anchoring a curtain wall mullion. (Reproduced by permission; American Architectural Manufacturers Association, *Aluminum Curtain Wall Design Guide Manual,* 1979)

Wood and PVC windows are available in the same types used in aluminum punched windows (Fig. 3.8). They are stocked in standard sizes but can be ordered in custom, design-specific sizes at extra cost.

METAL FRAMES

Aluminum is the metal most widely used for window frames. Other metals include steel, stainless steel, and bronze. Aluminum is durable, will not rust, and can be anodized or painted. Both of these latter finishes are long-lasting. Frames may be interior- or exterior-glazed [Fig. 3.16(*a*)]. This means that the glass is installed from inside the building or requires the installer to make arrangements to install it from the exterior, respectively. High-rise buildings usually include a window-washing staging system that comes in handy when windows are broken and require replacement (see Fig. 2.35). Doing this from the exterior also prevents interruption of the workplace. Interior glazing, on the other hand, is quicker and more convenient especially during inclement weather. The owner usually has a definite preference concerning this matter. As a general rule, storefronts and

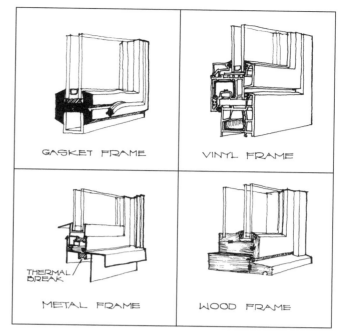

Figure 3.15 Types of window frames categorized by material.

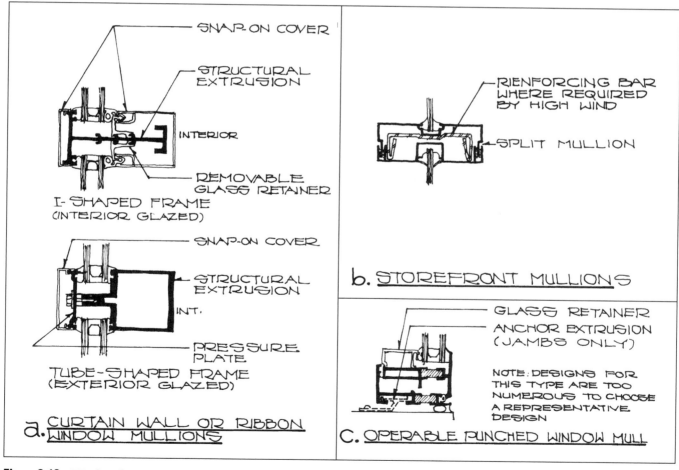

Figure 3.16 Window frame extrusions categorized by window type.

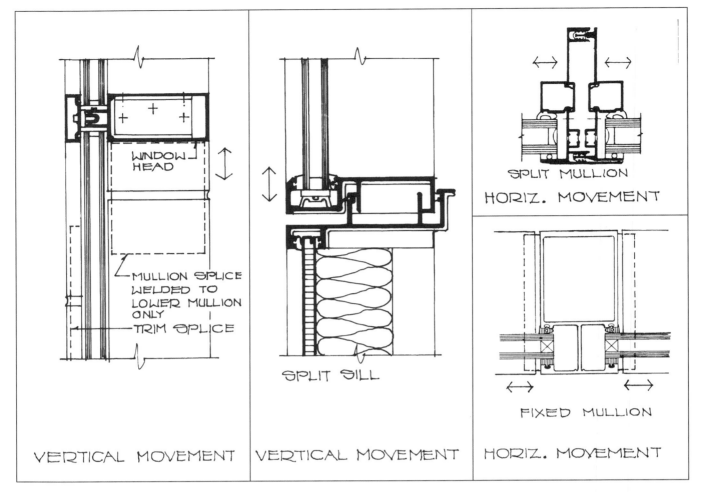

Figure 3.17 Allowance for expansion in curtain wall or strip window framing.

low-rise buildings are glazed from the exterior, while high-rise buildings are installed from the interior during construction and may be reglazed from either side after occupancy depending on mullion design.

Aluminum frames are shaped by extruding the molten metal through special dies. Frame designs vary. They are shaped by many factors including

- *Window types.* Curtain walls and strip windows employ different extrusions from storefronts and punched windows (Fig. 3.16).

- *Method of glazing.* Exterior glazed windows have different profiles from interior glazed ones [Fig. 3.16(a)].

- *Wind resistance capability.* Curtain wall windows span from floor to floor and require mullions with structural stiffness. The usual shapes are tubes and I-beams [Fig. 3.16(a)].

- *Allowance for expansion.* Because aluminum has a high rate of expansion, curtain wall and strip

window mullions are designed with that in mind. One method is to design the mullion as two parts sliding against each other (Fig. 3.17).

- *Method of attaching the glazing.* All aluminum mullions differ from structural silicone and zipper gasket glazing (Fig. 3.18).

- *Energy conservation.* To prevent heat from escaping from the interior and avoid condensation caused by the cold metal, polyurethane is poured in a pocket formed in the extrusion. The back metal is then sawed off to create an interruption in the heat flow. This type of frame is referred to as a *thermally broken* frame. It is usually used with insulating glass to improve the thermal performance of the window (Fig. 1.17).

Figure 3.19 illustrates some of the things that can go wrong with window frames, and Fig. 3.20 shows how to detail the window properly to minimize the possibility of leakage. Frame corners are areas where many leakage problems tend to occur because that is where the joints between the different components are subjected to all the thermal and installation stresses. To minimize the possibility of leakage, sill flashing must end with a dam to catch any water that may enter the frame assembly and convey it to the exterior (Fig. 3.21). Frame corners should be welded, otherwise they must be sealed with a dependable, long-lasting silicone sealant. Frame systems that lack a return can, in most cases, be supplied with a U-shaped receptor to provide the surface needed to receive the sealant and backer rod.

Metal windows may also be assembled from special steel shapes or cold-rolled sheet metal. The use of steel predates that of aluminum. Steel frames were introduced in industrial plants and later used in other building types. Because of rust problems, they were replaced by aluminum frames. Today, manufacturers are producing steel systems with more sophisticated, long-lasting finishes that have corrected the rust problem. Steel window framing systems have a much smaller market share. They are required for windows installed in correctional facilities, fire-rated windows, and prestigious projects including historical restoration. Because steel is stronger than aluminum, smaller sections are required to span large openings. This also influences the choice in certain designs.

Thermal breaks are usually not provided in heavy steel frames due to the fact that steel has a low coefficient of heat transfer as compared to aluminum. Frame assemblies are always welded at the corners, a distinct advantage over unwelded frames. Because steel's melting point is much higher than aluminum, it can withstand higher temperatures without structural failure. For this reason, building codes require fire-rated windows to have steel frames. Figure 3.22 shows typical steel

window frames. Note that hot-rolled steel shapes do not provide a return to receive the sealant and backer rod. The architect must take this into consideration while detailing the system. Other metals such as bronze and stainless steel are also used to manufacture door and window frames for special, high-quality projects.

A common mistake made by some designers during the SD phase is to subdivide a wide window horizontally without providing intermediate vertical mullions to support the dead load of the glass. Dead-load charts (Fig. 3.13) define the maximum length of unsupported horizontal mullions. When in doubt, check with the product representative before finalizing the design to prevent unpleasant surprises and the need for change orders to correct this situation.

STRUCTURAL GLAZING

There are two kinds of structural glazing systems. The first is the all-glass wall where the lites are supported by glass mullions. The second employs structural silicone to perform the dual roles of sealant and structural gluing agent to fasten the glass to support mullions.

The first system is used in prestigious main lobbies (Fig. 3.23) and projects that require an uninterrupted view of an event such as enclosed racetrack stands and football press and reserved viewing boxes. This system utilizes ¾- or 1-in (20 or 25 mm) thick tempered glass fins in lieu of metal mullions to provide lateral support for the glazing. The fins are fastened with metal plates or special bolts (Fig. 3.24) to glass lites that are heat-strengthened or fully tempered. All joints are sealed with a durable silicone sealant. Structural glazing is designed to accommodate either single-thickness or insulating glass. When used in a storefront application with heights limited to 10 to 12 ft (3 to 3.6 m), the sup-

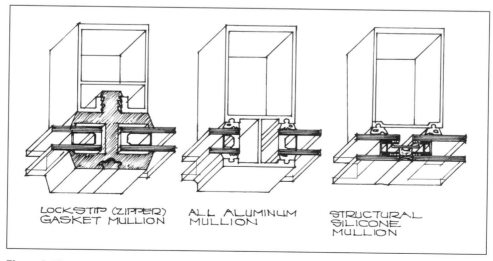

Figure 3.18 Types of frames categorized by glazing method.

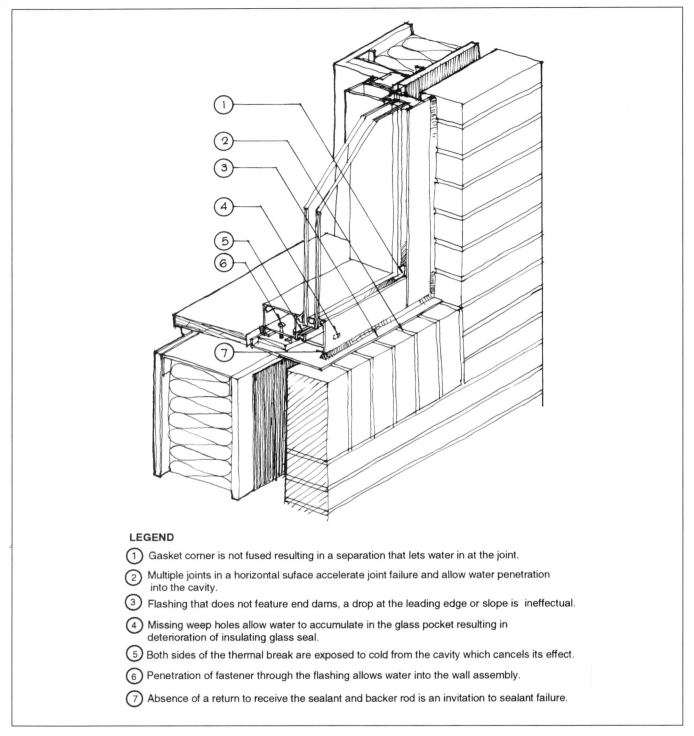

LEGEND

① Gasket corner is not fused resulting in a separation that lets water in at the joint.

② Multiple joints in a horizontal suface accelerate joint failure and allow water penetration into the cavity.

③ Flashing that does not feature end dams, a drop at the leading edge or slope is ineffectual.

④ Missing weep holes allow water to accumulate in the glass pocket resulting in deterioration of insulating glass seal.

⑤ Both sides of the thermal break are exposed to cold from the cavity which cancels its effect.

⑥ Penetration of fastener through the flashing allows water into the wall assembly.

⑦ Absence of a return to receive the sealant and backer rod is an invitation to sealant failure.

Figure 3.19   Some causes of leakage in a window frame.

porting glass mullion may be omitted to present a clean, all-clear glass facade (Fig. 3.11).

Structural silicone glazing costs approximately 10 to 12% more than conventional mullion systems. It can either be applied at the job site or between U-shaped extrusions and the glass during fabrication of the window unit. This extrusion is then engaged to the mullion (Fig. 3.25).

Some experts maintain that silicone glazing is risky if the silicone is field-applied and insist on the shop-

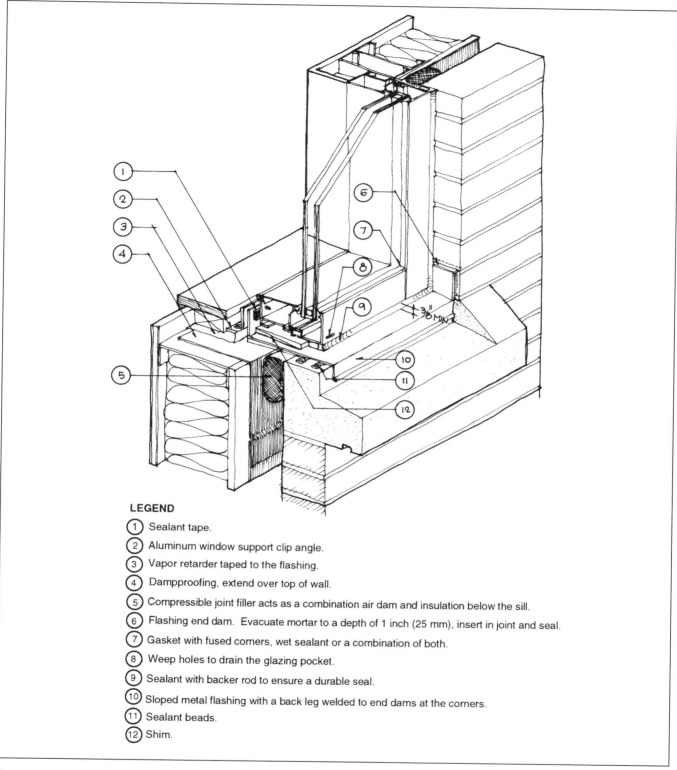

3/8" MIN.

LEGEND

(1) Sealant tape.

(2) Aluminum window support clip angle.

(3) Vapor retarder taped to the flashing.

(4) Dampproofing, extend over top of wall.

(5) Compressible joint filler acts as a combination air dam and insulation below the sill.

(6) Flashing end dam. Evacuate mortar to a depth of 1 inch (25 mm), insert in joint and seal.

(7) Gasket with fused corners, wet sealant or a combination of both.

(8) Weep holes to drain the glazing pocket.

(9) Sealant with backer rod to ensure a durable seal.

(10) Sloped metal flashing with a back leg welded to end dams at the corners.

(11) Sealant beads.

(12) Shim.

Figure 3.20   How to detail the frame properly to minimize the possibility of leakage.

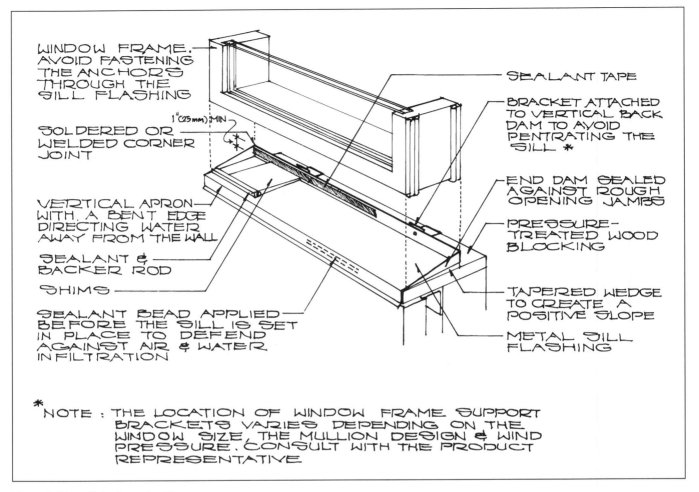

WINDOW FRAME.
AVOID FASTENING
THE ANCHORS
THROUGH THE
SILL FLASHING

SOLDERED OR
WELDED CORNER
JOINT

1" (25 mm) MIN

VERTICAL APRON
WITH A BENT EDGE
DIRECTING WATER
AWAY FROM THE WALL

SEALANT &
BACKER ROD

SHIMS

SEALANT BEAD APPLIED
BEFORE THE SILL IS SET
IN PLACE TO DEFEND
AGAINST AIR & WATER
INFILTRATION

SEALANT TAPE

BRACKET ATTACHED
TO VERTICAL BACK
DAM TO AVOID
PENTRATING THE
SILL *

END DAM SEALED
AGAINST ROUGH
OPENING JAMBS

PRESSURE-
TREATED WOOD
BLOCKING

TAPERED WEDGE
TO CREATE A
POSITIVE SLOPE

METAL SILL
FLASHING

*NOTE : THE LOCATION OF WINDOW FRAME SUPPORT
BRACKETS VARIES DEPENDING ON THE
WINDOW SIZE, THE MULLION DESIGN & WIND
PRESSURE. CONSULT WITH THE PRODUCT
REPRESENTATIVE

Figure 3.21   Sill flashing details.

fabricated preglazed units mentioned above. The AAMA recommends a field test for adhesion after the silicone is fully cured.

RUBBER GASKETS

Lock-strip gaskets were first used in an architectural application in the General Motors technical center in Michigan in 1952. Gaskets can be custom designed for special applications. Standard profiles take the form of an H or a reglet (Fig. 3.26). They must be installed to exacting tolerances by an experienced crew. Ideally, there should be no gap between the glass edge and the gasket and between the gasket and the frame. This, however, makes installation extremely difficult if not impossible. The AAMA recommends a clearance of ⅛ to ³⁄₁₆ in (3 to 5 mm) to ease the assembly. It further recommends that for openings that exceed 100 ft² (9 m²), reinforcing clips should be installed to prevent the glazing from disengaging from the gasket in high winds. Care must be exercised to prevent water from accumulating in the glazing channel especially when insulating

glass is used. Long immersion in water can deteriorate the seal between the glass lite and the spacer causing the glass to delaminate and the system to fail. For that reason, weepholes are a must at the sill extrusion.

In addition to the lockstrip rubber gaskets mentioned in conjunction with aluminum window frames above, gaskets may be used to glaze openings in precast concrete walls. The PCI recommends that the glazing be installed in a reglet or attached to a metal tee bar rather than in a kerf (slot) formed in the concrete (Fig. 3.26) and that the window opening be within the panels to avoid reglet alignment problems.

3.3.3 Glazing

Several types of glass are available to the designer. Each has its own characteristics which are suitable for a specific application. The term *glass types* is used here to describe the basic composition of the glass. It should not be confused with applied treatments such as added chemicals to produce tinted and heat-absorbing glass or metallic coatings to produce reflective and low-e glass.

The following is a description of the types most commonly used in buildings.

SHEET GLASS

This is the least expensive type of glazing. It is produced by melting the raw materials which are mainly sand, lime, and soda in a melting tank. The molten glass is then drawn by inserting a steel bar called a *bait* into the tank and pulling the high-viscosity liquid between rollers in a long oven called a *lehr* that cools the sheet gradually as it moves along toward the end of the oven where it is cut to size.

This type of glass is produced in single strength (SS) with a thickness of ³⁄₃₂ in (2.5 mm) and double strength (DS) ⅛ in (3 mm) thick. Its surfaces are not free from distortion because of the effect of the rollers. It is used mostly in residential construction.

FLOAT GLASS

Float glass is manufactured by floating the glass, as it emerges from the melting tank, on top of molten tin (Fig. 3.27), a process introduced by Pilkington Brothers, Ltd., of England. The dense tin produces a perfectly flat surface free of distortion. This type of glass used to be produced by a costly process involving grinding and polishing the surface by mechanical means to produce plate glass. Today, plate glass is not produced in the United States. Float glass is produced in thicknesses ranging from ⅛ to ⅞ in (3 to 22 mm) and is used for all building types including high-end residential.

HEAT-STRENGTHENED GLASS

Reheating float glass and exposing it to jets of cold air creates stress within the glass between the hot core area and the more rapidly cooling exterior surfaces. This is

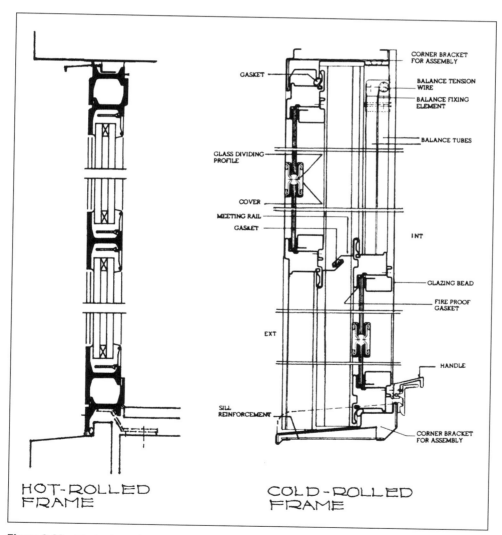

Figure 3.22 Typical steel window frames.

Figure 3.23 Exterior and interior views of the main lobby of the Federal Reserve Bank, Boston. Note the clear view through the structural glazing system. (The Stubbins Associates, Inc., Architects)

similar in principle to strengthening concrete by pre-stressing or posttensioning the reinforcement. Heat-strengthened glass is approximately twice as strong as float glass. It is used to resist heat buildup in spandrel panels (Sec. 3.3.4). This prevents the glass from dissipating solar heat to the building interior. Heat-strengthened glass is also used in deeply recessed windows where part of the glass is exposed to the sun while the rest of the window is cooled by the shadow cast on it. Float glass is more prone to shattering under these conditions. Consultation with the glass manufacturer is necessary to determine which glass type to use in these situations.

TEMPERED GLASS

The tempering process is similar to heat strengthening except that the cooling is done more suddenly. Tempered glass satisfies code requirements for safety glazing subject to sudden impact. It is required by the

Consumer Product Safety Commission to be installed in the following locations to reduce risk of injury where

1. The lowest edge of the glazing material is less than 18 in (460 mm) above any floor or any walking surface.
2. The exposed glazing material in such panels exceeds 9 ft² (0.85 m²).
3. There is a walking surface on both sides, either of which is within 36 in (0.9 m) of such panel, and the horizontal planes of such walking surfaces are within 12 in (300 mm) of each other.
4. Glass panels are located in doors and the side lites adjacent to them.

The contract documents must include reference to these standards and indicate that it is the responsibility of the glazing contractor to conform to their requirements. Glass types included in the window detail sheets must also identify the tempered panels. Incidentally, if a barrier is placed across the panels within a zone 24 to 36 in (610 to 915 mm) above the floor level, regular glass may be used. Check the building code and talk to the glass manufacturer's representative before making the final designations.

Tempered glass is approximately four times as strong as float glass and shatters into small, harmless granules when subjected to sudden impact. One disadvantage of this type of glass is that on relatively rare occasions, some lites will disintegrate spontaneously. Experts attribute this to the presence of impurities such as nickel sulfide (NiS).

In addition to its use in locations where safety glazing is required, tempered glass is used as a component of structural glazing systems and in applications where thermal load differentials occur. It cannot be cut or drilled after fabrication. This means that any holes, notches, or size modifications must be done at the manufacturing plant prior to tempering. It has noticeable optical distortion especially in thicknesses less than ½ in (13 mm). A longer delivery time is required for tempered glass because it is custom-fabricated.

LAMINATED GLASS

This type of glass is composed of two or more layers of glass with a clear vinyl interlayer fusing them into a single sheet. Its use is not common in exterior wall fenestration. Projects that require a high degree of sound isolation such as those adjacent to freeways or located at airports may incorporate this type of glass in an insulating glass window design to provide a sound transmission class (STC) rating as high as 42.

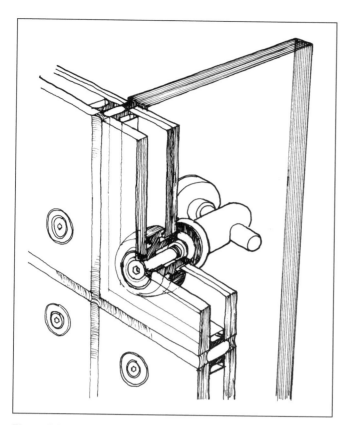

Figure 3.24 The Pilkington bolt anchoring assembly.

Multilayered laminated glass is also required to provide security for jewelry store and drive-through bank teller windows. This latter application requires bullet-resistant glazing composed of at least four layers of glass varying in overall thickness from 1$\frac{3}{16}$ to 2 in (30 to 51 mm). Laminated glass is considered as a safety glass in many applications including skylights and glass installed at an angle.

INSULATING GLASS

Glass is a poor insulator. Window areas represent the bulk of energy loss in exterior walls. To improve the thermal performance of windows, glazing constructed by assembling two or three lites with spacers at the perimeter to create dead-air spaces between them was introduced. These air spaces should not be less than $\frac{3}{16}$ in (5 mm) nor more than $\frac{5}{8}$ in (16 mm) wide to be effective. Gaps wider than $\frac{5}{8}$ in cause convection (the vertical circulation of air between the cold and warm sides) which cancels the insulating effect of this design. The space between the lites is sometimes filled with inert gases such as argon or sulfur hexafluoride to increase the resistance to heat transfer. Insulating glass is effective against heat loss in winter and heat gain in summer.

Double glazing may be fused around the edges [Fig. 3.28(*a*)]. This product is usually used in small lites for residential applications. Lites may also be assembled with a metal spacer containing a desiccant to absorb any moisture present in the air cavity after the glass is

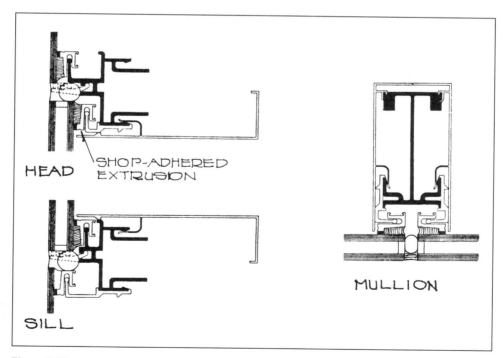

HEAD

SHOP-ADHERED EXTRUSION

SILL

MULLION

Figure 3.25 Shop-fabricated structural silicone glazing using an adhered extrusion. (Bruce Wall Systems)

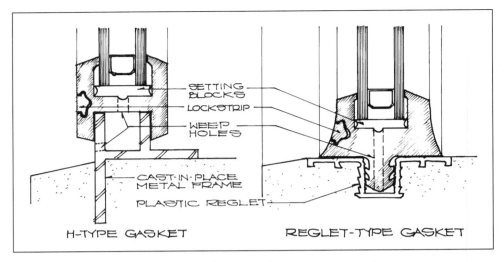

Figure 3.26 Methods of attaching Lock-Strip Gaskets to precast panels.

cemented and sealed to the spacer [Fig. 3.28(b)]. A more recent design provides more insulation without adding to the weight of the window by placing one or two sheets of transparent film to subdivide the air space [Fig. 3.28(c) and (d)]. The film may be coated with reflective or low-e coatings to improve its performance. Insulating glass may incorporate tempered, heat-strengthened, or laminated layers in the assembly. It may also be used in spandrel glass panels.

When evaluating the thermal performance of a window, one must consider the U-value (R = 1/U) of the total assembly, including the frame, rather than the rating at the center of the lite. This makes for a better comparison between different products. To determine glass thickness, the architect must first determine whether the glass is supported on two or four sides (Sec. 3.3.1).

Next, the aspect ratio (the long side divided by the short side) and the maximum wind load (as defined by the code) are calculated. Based on this information, the appropriate thickness can be arrived at by reference to manufacturers' charts in relation to the area of the glass. Figure 3.29 shows a sampling of charts from one manufacturer. Appendix C includes more detailed information for sizing glass.

Glass thickness is also affected by the acceptable rate of breakage for the project. In addition to loading stress, breakage is caused by several factors including lite geometry, support conditions, thermal stress, and surface quality. The charts are usually based on a rate of breakage of 8 lites per thousand. If a lower rate is desired, the manufacturer's representative can usually recommend a modified thickness to achieve that goal at added cost.

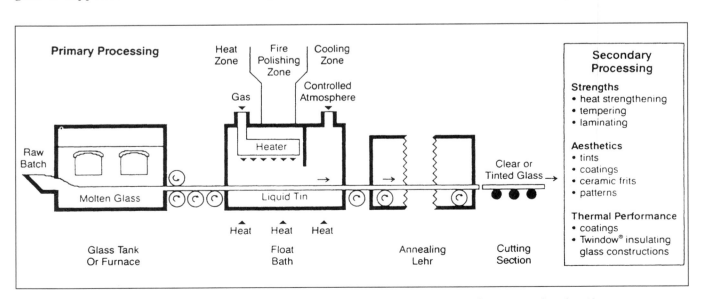

Figure 3.27 The float glass manufacturing process. (Reproduced by permission; PPG Industries, Pittsburgh, PA)

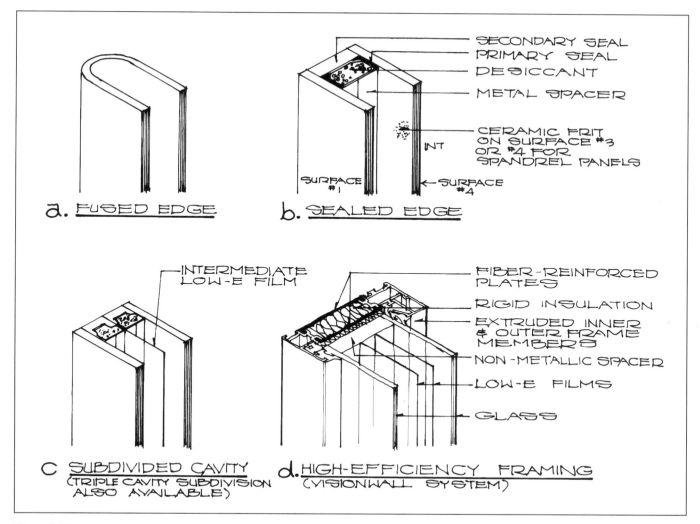

Figure 3.28 Types of insulating glass.

PLASTIC GLAZING

There are two types of thermoplastic products used as window and skylight glazing materials: polycarbonate, which is produced under the trade name Lexan by General Electric as well as by other manufacturers, and acrylic plastic, known by the trade name of Plexiglas produced by Rohm and Haas Company. Both products are combustible. Building codes define the uses and conditions under which these materials may be used. Polycarbonate ignites at 800°F (426°C) and acrylic at 560°F (293°C) when exposed to an ignition source.

Both products are more breakage resistant than glass which makes them suitable for skylights and windows in vandal-prone areas such as correctional facilities and schools. They are bendable, have better sound-loss characteristics than glass, and can be laminated to provide lightweight bullet-resistant lites. Polycarbonate products are much stronger than acrylic and are available in light and dark bronze, opal, and white, while acrylic offers many color choices including mirror. Both products have lesser abrasion resistance than glass, especially uncoated acrylic which is easily scratched by abrasives and sharp tools.

Architects unfamiliar with these products can read manufacturers' product literature to acquaint themselves with the detailing required to frame and seal the edges as well as the code limitations and the advantages they offer over conventional glazing.

3.3.4 Glass Treatments

Clear glass provides undimmed views to the exterior and lets in the maximum amount of light. While these are desirable qualities sought after by designers for most applications, untreated glass also lets in unwanted heat and glare in summer as well as UV rays which cause colors to fade. It also allows heat to escape from the interior in winter. Solar heat hitting a window is divided into three parts. One part is transmitted through the

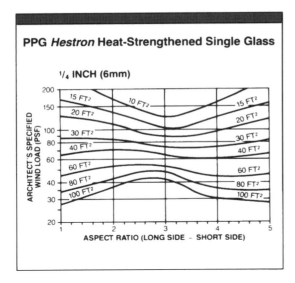

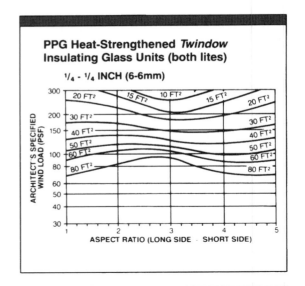

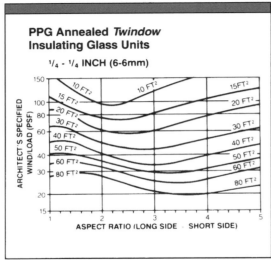

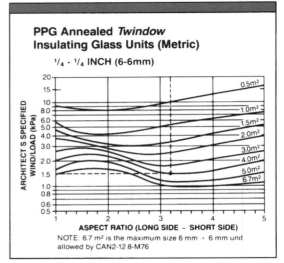

Figure 3.29 Example of charts used in determining the maximum area of a window. (Reproduced by permission; PPG Industries, Pittsburgh, PA)

glass, a second part is reflected to the exterior, and the rest is absorbed by the glass and radiated both to the interior and the exterior. Figure 3.30 shows glass offering the least resistance to solar energy. This type of glass is used to rate the performance of other glass types and thicknesses. Glass can be treated to modify its reflectance, absorption, and heat transmission to minimize energy consumption and add to the comfort and well-being of the building's occupants. To achieve these goals, glass may be heat-absorbing or tinted, reflective, or low-e. These treatments can be used in conjunction with insulating glass to achieve the best results. The conventional way for identifying the surface of the glass where an applied treatment—such as an opacifier—is

located is to call that surface by a number starting with surface No. 1 for the exterior face of the glazing unit and ending with surface No. 4 for an insulating, double-glazed unit. The following is a description of glass treatments.

HEAT-ABSORBING AND TINTED GLASS

Increasing the iron content in glass increases its ability to absorb heat and, by so doing, reduces the heat load on the air-conditioning system. While some of this absorbed heat is reradiated and transmitted by convection to interior and exterior air, a significant percentage is retained in the glass and the overall effect is a reduction in transmitted heat. Heat-absorbing glass may also be tinted to

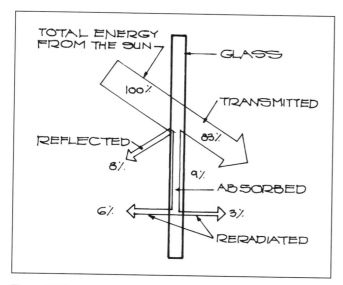

Figure 3.30 Solar heat transmission through glass.

reduce glare as well as increase its absorption. Table 3.1 compares the performance of several types of glass treatment. Clear glass transmits approximately 85% of visible light as opposed to 15 to 70% for the different shades of tinted glass. The shading coefficient is the ratio of solar energy gain through a tinted or reflective glass as compared to transmission through ⅛-in (3 mm) clear glass (Table 3.2). Shading coefficients are used by the mechanical engineer to measure the efficiency of a glass against transmitted heat. The U-value is used to measure the efficiency of a glass against conducted heat. Tinting has no effect on the U-value. In insulating glass, the tinted glass should be the exterior lite.

Shading coefficients are included in manufacturers' literature. Darker colors give the impression of a perpetually overcast sky to the building occupants. The designer should consider using glass with a different shading coefficient for each facade. For instance, for west-facing windows where overheating is to be expected, choose a low shading coefficient glass. High shading coefficient and good energy performance are required for north-facing windows in cold climates.

Spandrel glass used in the area extending between the window head and the sill of the window located in the floor above is usually produced by adding an opacifier to the inboard face of the glass (surface #2) in a monolithic glazing application. This opacifier may be a ceramic frit deposited on the surface of the glass during fabrication. For reflective glass, an opacifier film is adhered to the surface in lieu of the frit. The insulation, in this case, must be placed at least 1 in (25 mm) away from that surface to prevent the opacifier film from delaminating. No such restriction is required if ceramic frit is the medium used. Some manufacturers offer span-

drels with factory-applied foil-faced insulation adhered to the back of these panels providing R-ratings ranging from 5 to 18.

If the design calls for a high degree of uniformity between the spandrel and vision glass panels, the choice of low-light-transmitting (30% or less), highly reflective glass provides the least contrast between the two areas. To reduce the contrast when uncoated, tinted, or low-e glass is used, the designer may opt to use insulating glass to create the illusion of depth in spandrel panels and to use a neutral-colored ceramic frit on surface #3 or #4. Needless to say, choosing to install insulating glass in spandrel areas adds to the cost of the building. A somewhat similar effect can be achieved by creating what is commonly known as a shadow box. In this application, a single, nonopacified lite of a heat-

Glass Type	Direct Transmission	Absorbed Radiation	Total Heat Gain
Regular window glass	85	3	88
Clear glass	74	9	83
Light heat-absorbing glass	20	25	45
Gray glass	30	30	60
Heat-reflecting glass	38	17	55

Table 3.1 Solar gain through some single glass panes, %. (Reproduced by permission; H. J. Cowan, ed., *Handbook of Architectural Technology,* Van Nostrand Reinhold, 1991)

SHADING COEFFICIENTS

GLASS TYPE	NO SHADING	WITH SHADING DEVICE
Single Clear Glass		
1/8"	1.00	0.55–0.70
1/4"–1/2"	0.95	0.55–0.70
Heat-Absorbing Glass (Gray, Bronze, Green-Tinted)		
1/4"	0.70	0.45–0.53
3/8"	0.56	0.40–0.47
1/2"	0.50	0.37–0.40
Single Reflective Coated Glass (Range of Shading Coefficients: 0.25–0.60)	0.25	0.19–0.21
	0.30	0.23–0.24
	0.40	0.30–0.33
	0.50	0.38–0.42
	0.60	0.43–0.50
Clear Insulating Glass	0.83	0.48–0.58
Heat-Absorbing Insulating Glass	0.56	0.39–0.45
(Range of Shading Coefficients: 0.17–0.50)	0.17	0.14–0.16
	0.20	0.17–0.18
	0.30	0.26–0.27
	0.40	0.32–0.37
	0.50	0.40–0.45

Table 3.2 Shading coefficients of some glass types. (Reproduced by permission; Architectural Aluminum Manufacturers Association, *Aluminum Curtain Wall Design Manual,* 1979)

strengthened glass similar in appearance to the type used for the vision lite is backed by dark insulation set back 1 or 2 in (25 or 50 mm). Dirt and staining may develop over time on the surface of the insulation marring its appearance.

Heat-strengthened glass is required in spandrels because heat is prevented from dissipating to the interior as is the case with vision glass. Heat buildup can create stresses that can shatter regular float glass.

REFLECTIVE GLASS

During glass fabrication, a very thin coating of metal or metal oxide can be deposited on the surface to produce reflective glass. This coating may be applied to clear or tinted glass to reflect the sun's rays and reduce the shading coefficient. This is desirable during the summer in hot climates. Shading coefficients for this type of glazing range from approximately 0.30 to 0.70. It should be applied to surface #2 in insulating glass units to achieve the best performance. Both lites should be heat strengthened to reduce the possibility of breakage due to thermal stress.

While reflective glass reduces heat transmittance through the window, it has the following drawbacks:

- It reduces the amount of light passing through the glass.

- It reflects artificial lighting, drastically reducing visibility to the exterior at night.

- Reflected sunlight can bounce into adjacent buildings subjecting their occupants to unwanted glare and heat.

- Reflected sunlight may also bounce into the eyes of drivers on adjacent freeways when the sun is low during the morning or evening rush hours causing accidents.

The designer must realize that no two manufacturers produce the same colors and reflectances. This means that the specifications must cover a range of acceptable colors, reflectances, U-values, and shading coefficients to invite competition. This requires viewing samples of all the alternatives specified and, if possible, seeing examples of buildings where they were installed.

LOW-E GLAZING

Emissivity is the tendency of a surface to give off its absorbed heat. Low emissivity (low-e) coatings applied to a glass surface give the glass the ability to reflect most of the long-wave radiation emitted by interior heat sources back into the building while allowing most of the sun's short-wave heat radiation to pass through to the interior. For colder climates, the low-e coating is deposited on the outer surface of the inner lite in an insulating glass window (surface #3). For hot climates, the coating is deposited on surface number 2. A modified low-e coating is designed for use in this application. It has a much lower shading coefficient.

There are two types of low-e coatings. A *soft coat* is deposited on the glass after fabrication. It is easily damaged by abrasion or moisture and must be located on an inside face of a double-glazed unit or on a film between the two lites. The other type is referred to as a *hard coat*. It is deposited on the surface during manufacture and becomes part of the hard surface. It does not perform as efficiently as the soft coat. There is a correlation between emissivity values and U-values. The lower the emissivity, the lower the U-value. Lower U-values result in higher R-values.

PHASE-CHANGE GLASS

Glass that darkens or lightens its tint depending on the intensity of the sunlight may be used for windows in the near future if it proves to be economically feasible. It is currently used for sunglasses.

Another type of glass uses a low-voltage electric current to achieve similar results or even to make the window opaque. Yet another uses a sandwich panel containing a transparent gel that becomes translucent and reflective when it reaches a certain temperature. It is too early to tell whether any of these research projects will culminate into a product that will compete with the types of glass described in the preceding sections.

The cost of glazing varies widely depending on the type used, glass treatment, and framing selected. Insulating glass may cost as much as 10 times the cost of single glazing. Of course, in the context of overall costs, glazing may represent only 15 to 20% of the cladding system. The energy-efficient glass can effect substantial savings in HVAC equipment costs as well as yearly energy costs.

A full-scale mock-up should be specified to inspect flashing details, troubleshoot any problems, and help the client to visualize the appearance of the final installation. For curtain walls, the mock-up is also used for testing.

3.3.5 Window Treatments

In addition to or in lieu of glass treatments, building interiors can be protected from the heat and glare of the sun by either exterior or interior shading treatments.

EXTERIOR SHADING

This is the most efficient way to protect the interior of a building from the heat of the sun. It is most effective when applied to facades facing the south in the northern hemisphere. This is achieved by providing projecting horizontal planes over the windows. The shadow cast by these projections covers a large area of the glass in summer because of the sun's steep angle. In winter, when the sun is at a lower angle, the warming solar rays penetrate deep into the interior. Architectural Graphic Standards[4] provides ample information about the proper way to implement this approach. A word of caution, glass subjected to partial shading experiences stresses that may cause it to break unless it is heat strengthened. The architect must consult with the glass manufacturer to determine the type of glass to be used to minimize the risk.

INTERIOR SHADING

Shading devices such as mini-blinds, shades, and vertical blinds can cause heat buildup that has the potential for glass breakage when the blind is fully closed. To avoid this problem, a minimum of 1½ in (38 mm) clearance must be maintained between the shading device and two sides of the window opening, either top and bottom or one side and bottom (Fig. 3.31). The same result can be achieved by installing a closure stop to prevent a mini-blind blades from closing more than 60° from horizontal. Other critical dimensions are shown in the figure. Heating and cooling should be directed away from the window to avoid creating different temperature zones in the glass requiring the use of heat-strengthened or tempered glass. If the design calls for the ceiling to be located much lower than the window head creating a pocket where heat can build up, a return-air register should be introduced in this area to prevent that from happening. A rule of thumb is to allow a minimum area for the return-air register of 1 in² (645 mm²) for every inch (25 mm) of window width.

SUMMARY

Exterior walls may be designed as solid load-bearing walls, or they may function as curtain walls supported by a structural frame. Load-bearing walls are used mostly for low-rise industrial and residential buildings, while curtain walls represent the bulk of construction for public buildings. Both types may be constructed as a single-thickness wall or a cavity wall.

Two design philosophies can be applied to exterior cladding. The first is to design the wall as a perfect barrier by sealing all joints and potential leakage points. While today's sealants are dependable and, if chosen correctly and applied without flaws, can last a relatively long time, they will eventually fail and require costly periodic reapplication.

The second design philosophy is to neutralize the force that pushes water into the wall by applying the

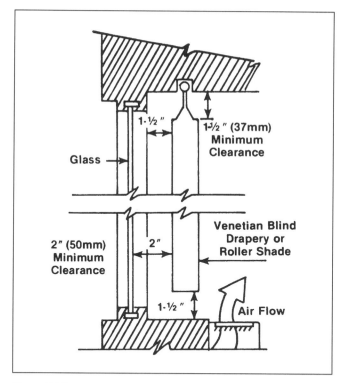

Figure 3.31 Requirements for preventing heat buildup between a window and an opaque blind.

rain screen principle to the design of the wall. This is accomplished by creating a compartmented, vented, and drained cavity behind the exterior skin (rain screen) of the wall. Wind entering the cavity through the vents (which are protected from rain penetration) pressurizes the cavity compartments to provide an equal and opposite force to deter the wind and rain from passing beyond the rain screen.

Cavity compartment sizes are related to wind speed. Where wind is fastest, the compartments are smallest. This zone occurs at the corners and top of the building and should be divided by vertical dividers occurring approximately 4 ft (1.20 m) on center within a zone of approximately 20 ft (6 m) of the corner. The rest of the facade should be subdivided at approximately 30-ft (9 m) intervals both horizontally and vertically.

Rain screen design functions well in rigid, impermeable walls such as all-metal and all-glass cladding systems but can be applied to any type of curtain wall. To qualify as a rain screen pressure-equalized system, the compartments must be capable of substantially impeding the movement of air currents. This design can be applied to a joint between air-impermeable panels, to all-glass curtain wall mullions, or to the full cavity behind a cavity wall.

Windows can be described as punched, strip, storefront, or curtain wall. Window frames may be constructed of aluminum, steel, structural glass, and zipper gasket combined with aluminum frames or lodged in a metal reglet in precast concrete. Wood frames form the bulk of residential and some low-rise commercial construction.

Choosing the right type of glazing requires consultation with a glass representative. The color is determined by the designer to be compatible with surrounding materials. Its intensity is determined by energy conservation and discussion with the mechanical engineer to determine the optimum shading coefficient. Reflective glazing is suitable in hot climates, while low-e glass is designed for use in cold climates. A modified type of low-e glazing is also used in warm climates.

A ¼-in- (6 mm) thick float glass is the type most often used in medium-size and large projects. It may be used as a single-thickness or double-glazed (insulating) lite.

The first is more prevalent in temperate climates, while the latter is a must in colder regions. Tempered glass is used where safety is required such as around entrances. It is four times as strong as float glass and, when broken, shatters into small, harmless pieces. Heat-strengthened glass is required where glazing is subjected to stresses such as unequal shading or in spandrel areas where heat buildup occurs. Tempered glass is sometimes used in these locations also. Laminated glass is composed of two or more layers fused with a transparent vinyl interlayer. It provides safety and superior sound insulation, but because it is more costly, its use is much more limited than the other types in building exteriors.

Exterior and interior shading devices reduce glare and thermal penetration into the building interior. They require careful design to achieve the required results.

CHAPTER 4

Wall Assemblies

4.1 GENERAL

The subject of exterior wall cladding has too wide a scope to cover in a single chapter or even a single book for that matter. It encompasses too many materials, systems, and methods of construction. This chapter provides as much information as possible on the five types of wall assemblies most commonly used in public buildings. Each section starts with a brief historical review of the assembly's early beginnings illustrating points that may be relevant to the reader. It proceeds with a description of the components that form the assembly as well as the ornamental work that can be used to enrich the design. This is followed by axonometric drawings illustrating the system to give an overall picture of the assembly. Each section also includes a description of what can go wrong to help avoid common pitfalls. The reader is strongly advised to read the preceding chapters before referring to the information shown here. Understanding the principles is the best insurance against their misapplication.

Wall section details are usually developed over a period of time through many iterations and brainstorming sessions. For complicated projects such as high-rise buildings and walls constructed with unconventional materials, the architect should seek the advice of cladding consultants and specify that a mock-up be constructed and tested to ensure that the design will perform as intended.

Needless to say, each project presents its unique set of conditions which must be addressed with care and understanding. The person in charge of the project must use good judgment in developing each specific section and detail based on the dictates of the particular design being developed. He or she must refer to the applicable codes, review technical literature, confer with the consultants participating in the project, and seek the input of product representatives.

Because each section covers a totally different subject, it is treated as an independent topic complete with a summary. References and bibliography are included at the end of the book.

4.2 UNIT MASONRY WALLS

4.2.1 Historical Background

Unit masonry is a general term used to represent relatively small building components used to construct walls. It encompasses several materials including clay products such as brick, hollow tile, and terra cotta; CMU (or concrete block as it is commonly known); and glass block. This subsection provides a very brief review of the history of brick, CMU, and glass block.

BRICK

Brick is one of the first materials used by humans to construct shelters. Clay is readily available and, unlike stone, does not require any special tools to quarry. One of the oldest bricks was discovered under the biblical city of Jericho and dates back nearly 10,000 years (Fig. 4.1). Note the thumb imprints which increased the contact between the brick and the clay mortar. Most ancient civilizations including the ancient Egyptian, Mesopotamian, Persian, Greek, Roman, Indian, and Chinese civilizations used brick to construct walls and, in some cases, vaulted roofs. The remains of these structures still stand to this day (Fig. 4.2). The Romans used large 24 × 24 in (600 × 600 mm) kiln-fired bricks to construct some of their structures. Their designs included arches and corbels (Fig. 4.3).

Figure 4.1   Ten-thousand-year-old brick from Jericho. (Reproduced by permission; Richard Rush, "Innovation in Masonry," *Progressive Architecture,* Penton Publishing, February 1979; tracing by author)

Figure 4.2   Example of brick work from ancient Persia: the Sassanian Palace of Ctesiphon.

Conventional, unreinforced load-bearing brick masonry reached its height limit at the completion of the 16-story Monadnock Building built in Chicago in 1891. This building required 6-ft- (1.8 m) thick walls at ground level to carry the load.

Today, modern kilns produce bricks under strict quality controls. They offer a wide selection of colors and textures ranging from white to black and from smooth to rough. The bulk of brick construction is executed as a veneer or cavity wall with metal (or wood) stud or CMU backing.

CMU

The origins of the concrete block industry can be traced back to nineteenth-century England. These early beginnings produced primitive products using crude ingredi-

Figure 4.3   Apartment building at Ostia Antica, Italy.

CONCRETE BLOCK USED ON THE FREEMAN HOUSE LOS ANGELES 1925

BILTMORE HOTEL & COTTAGES 1920

Figure 4.4   Examples of concrete block designed by Frank Lloyd Wright.

Figure 4.5 Decorative CMU screen designed by Edward Durell Stone.

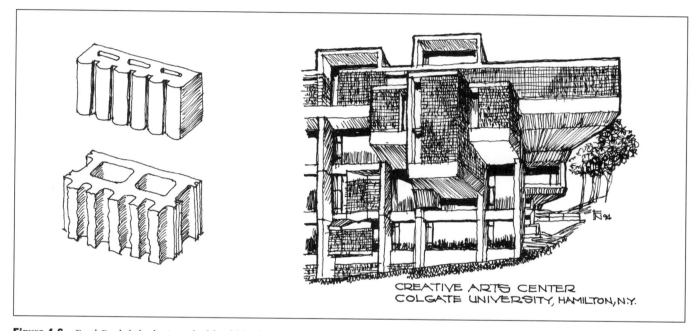

Figure 4.6 Paul Rudolph designed ribbed block to create textured surfaces.

ents. After the invention of Portland cement—also in England—and the establishment of a plant in the United States in 1871, many efforts at making concrete block were attempted. In 1904 Herman Besser, a German immigrant purchased a hand-operated block manufacturing machine. His son Jesse introduced several labor-saving improvements to the machine including automatic loading and power tamping. Today, concrete block is produced all over the world in fully automated plants producing a long-lasting, standardized product at a reasonable cost.

Some of the big names in architecture participated in the design of distinctive concrete block. Examples include decorative and unusual block designed by Frank Lloyd Wright (Fig. 4.4), screens designed by Edward Durell Stone (Fig. 4.5), and ribbed block introduced by Paul Rudolph which has become an industry favorite (Fig. 4.6).

GLASS BLOCK

Glass block, produced in a manner similar to the block used in walls today, was first manufactured in Germany by Deutsche Luxfer Prismen-Gesellschaft in 1902. The Corning-Steuben block was introduced in America in 1935. Pittsburgh Corning, which is currently the sole American manufacturer of glass block and glass brick, was established in 1937 and started manufacturing these products in 1938.

4.2.2 Components
BRICK

Brick is manufactured in several standardized sizes. Modular brick is usually favored by architects because its width and length are based on a 4-in (100 mm) module. This makes it easy to compute dimensions. In addition, the height of three courses including one ⅜-in (10-mm) joint is 8 in (200 mm) which matches the

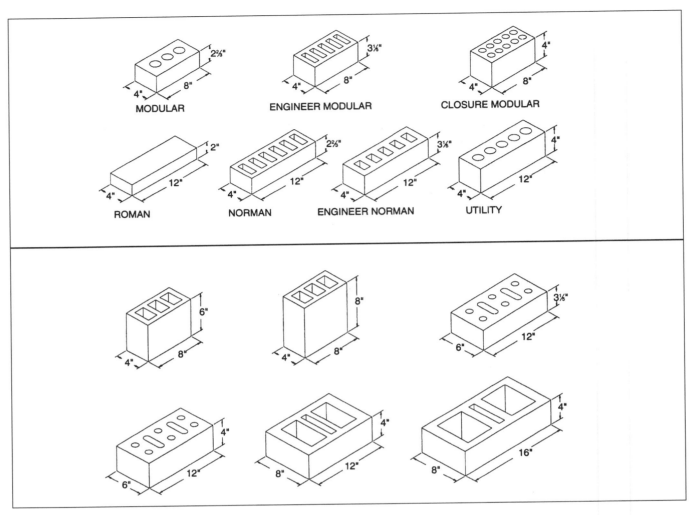

Modular Brick Sizes
(Nominal Dimensions)

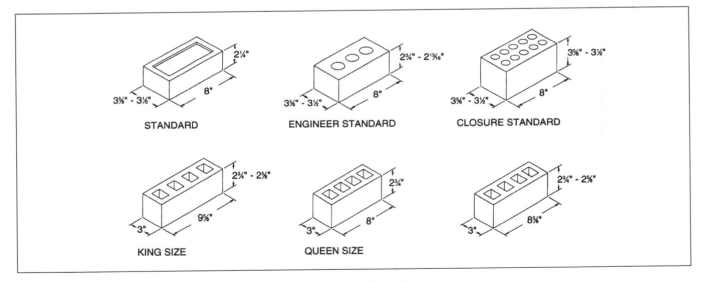

Non-Modular Brick Sizes
(Specified Dimensions)

Figure 4.7 Common brick sizes. (Reproduced by permission; Brick Institute of America, *Tech Note No. 10B,* June 1993)

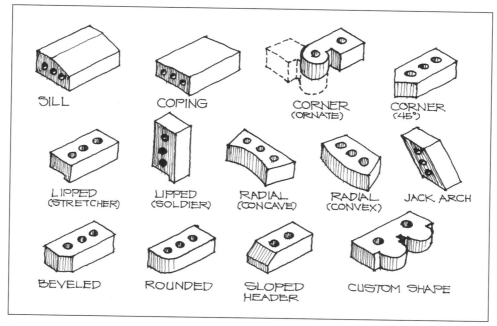

Figure 4.8 Examples of special brick.

Figure 4.9 Color deviation at the corner of this building is caused by the use of special brick.

height of a concrete block. Each manufacturer produces several standard sizes. The larger the brick, the more economical the construction. Figure 4.7 shows a few of the more common sizes. Plan dimensions should represent multiples of whole bricks to avoid excessive and costly cutting in the field.

In addition to standard sizes, brick manufacturers produce some special shapes for particular applications such as sills, copings, cornices, and rounded corners (Fig. 4.8). Special shapes may also be designed by the architect in consultation with the manufacturer to enhance the design. In many cases, the manufacturer uses standard forms modified to produce the special brick. Sometimes the special brick is cut from uncored

standard-size bricks. In either case, there is a color difference between cored and uncored brick when they are exposed to heat in the kiln. Architects must compare samples of the special brick to the standard brick to be used in the project because a light color or texture deviation may occur (Fig. 4.9).

Because the architect does not usually determine which manufacturer will be awarded the contract to supply the brick, the standard practice is to determine an estimated cost for the brick which is referred to as an *allowance* for the contractors to base the bid on. After the contract is awarded, the contractor submits several samples conforming to the specifications for the architect to choose from. The specifications should give the contractor enough information describing the size, grade, and type of brick as well as whether nonstandard or special brick is included. This minimizes cost overruns when the final selection is made. One must be aware that brick size and the inclusion of special brick shapes has an effect on the price. Another method is for the architect to choose acceptable samples from three manufacturers and name them in the specifications for the contractor to base the price on.

Depending on the manufacturing method, brick may be called wire-cut, molded, glazed, sawed, handmade, or sand cast. Each has a distinctive look. Brick is graded as SW for *severe weathering* (the most durable kind), MW (for *mild weather*) which should be used in areas not subject to long-lasting weather extremes, and NW (for *negligible weather*) which should be used for interior applications only. Finally, a brick is identified by its

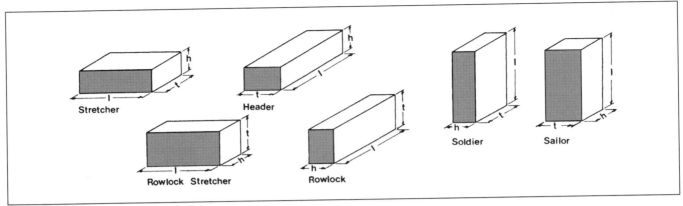

Figure 4.10   Brick positions in a wall. (Reproduced by permission; Brick Institute of America, *Tech Note No. 10B,* June 1993)

position in the wall (Fig. 4.10). The U.L. Directory includes designs for brick with stud wall backup rated for 45-min, 1-h, 1½-h, and 2-h protection. It also includes a 4-h rated design for brick veneer with CMU backup.

Thin brick was introduced in the fifties. This product ranges in thickness from ½ to 1 in (13 to 25 mm). In addition to the flat rectangular brick simulating the look of standard modular brick, thin brick is produced in other shapes to give the appearance of a standard size brick (Fig. 4.11). While it is cheaper and faster to construct as a veneer, it is easier to damage (Fig. 4.12) and does not have the advantages of thermal mass, sound, or fire resistance inherent in conventional brick walls.

CMU

Concrete masonry units are manufactured from Portland cement, graded aggregates, and water. Other ingredients may be added to reduce weight, add color, or act as a water repellent. Units are produced to close tolerances in highly automated plants. There are two kinds of units, hollow and solid. Hollow units are those units in which the net concrete cross-sectional area parallel to the bearing face is less than 75%. The type of aggregate used in manufacturing the unit determines whether it is *normal weight* weighing more than 125 pounds per cubic foot (lb/ft^3) (2002 kg/m^3) or *lightweight* units weighing 105 lb/ft^3 (1682 kg/m^3) or less. In addition to the familiar concrete block units, special shapes are used for special functions. Architects must check availability with local manufacturers before making a choice. Figure 4.13 illustrates some typical units.

Building codes determine minimum wall thickness in relationship to the span. The span is identified as either vertical between supports such as floors, spandrel beams, and bracing elements or horizontal between columns, pilasters, or intersecting walls. The structural engineer usually determines exterior wall thickness, type of fixation, and reinforcement based on code-mandated lateral forces. Tables 4.1 and 4.2 give maximum heights and allowable loading based on conservative assumptions.

As in brick masonry, it is good practice to base plan dimensions on multiples of whole units. In this case, the

Figure 4.11   Thin brick. (Reproduced by permission; Brick Institute of America, *Tech Note No. 28C,* February 1990)

Figure 4.12   Placing thin brick veneer at ground level is an invitation to damage.

Wall height, ft.	Allowable vertical axial load, kips per lin. ft.											
	6 in. wall with No. 4 bars			8 in. wall with No. 5 bars			10 in. wall with No. 6 bars			12 in. wall with No. 7 bars		
	w =10	20	30	10	20	30	10	20	30	10	20	30
8	12.6	9.9	7.3	18.0	16.3	14.5	23.1	21.8	20.5	27.8	26.8	25.8
10	10.4	7.5	2.6	16.6	13.9	11.1	22.1	20.0	18.0	27.1	25.5	23.9
12	7.8	2.7		14.8	11.0	7.2	20.7	17.9	15.0	26.0	23.7	21.5
14	5.0			12.6	7.8	2.9	19.1	15.3	11.5	24.8	21.8	18.8
15	3.6			11.0	5.9		18.0	13.8	9.5	24.0	20.5	17.1
16				10.2	4.4		17.3	12.5	7.7	23.2	19.4	15.5
18				7.7			15.2	9.4	3.7	21.7	16.9	12.2
20				5.1			12.8	6.3		19.5	13.9	8.3
22							10.4	3.2		17.8	11.2	4.7
24							7.9			15.1	8.0	
25							6.7			13.9	6.5	
26										13.2	5.3	
30										8.4		

* Design assumptions: Minimum f'$_m$=1,500 psi, reinforcing bars are centered on wall at 32 in. oc, w = wind load, psf.

Table 4.1 Maximum wall heights for nonreinforced hollow unit concrete masonry walls subjected to concentric loads and wind* (Reproduced by permission; National Concrete Masonry Association, *NCMA Tek 103,* 1978)

modular dimension is 8 in (200 mm) which is the width of a 7⅝-in (194-mm) unit plus half a joint on each side. Special attention must be paid to door and window openings (Fig. 4.14). Ignoring this rule of dimensioning will result in excessive unit cutting in the field and higher costs. Half-height units are usually available for use when the gap between the last full course and the underside of the structure requires that size. Half units are also used at the bottom of the wall as a starter course.

Concrete masonry units are effective in resisting the spread of fire. The U.L. Directory includes CMU wall designs tested to provide 2-, 3-, and 4-h protection which are usually acceptable to code enforcement

Concentric load, plf	Maximum wall heights, ft. **											
	t = 6 in.			8 in.			10 in.			12 in.		
	w =10	20	30	10	20	30	10	20	30	10	20	30
0	10.0	7.1	5.8	12.8	9.0	7.4	16.0	11.3	9.2	19.6	13.9	11.4
500		8.4	6.9	13.3	10.5	8.6	16.7	12.7	10.4	20.0	15.4	12.6
1,000		9.6	7.8		11.9	9.7		14.0	11.4		16.8	13.8
1,500		10.0	8.7		13.0	10.6		15.2	12.4		18.2	14.8
2,000			9.4		13.3	11.5		16.2	13.3		19.3	15.8
2,500			10.0			12.4		16.7	14.1		20.0	16.7
3,000						13.1			14.9			17.6
3,500						13.3			15.6			18.4
4,000									16.3			19.2
4,500									16.7			20.0

*   Design assumptions: Minimum f'$_m$ = 1350 psi; Type S mortar, allowable flexural tensile stress = 23 x 1.33 = 30.6 psi; w = wind load, psf.
** Maximum wall heights limited to 20 times nominal wall thickness (t).

Table 4.2 Allowable vertical axial loads for reinforced hollow unit concrete masonry walls subjected to wind* (Reproduced by permission; National Concrete Masonry Association, *NCMA Tek 103,* 1978)

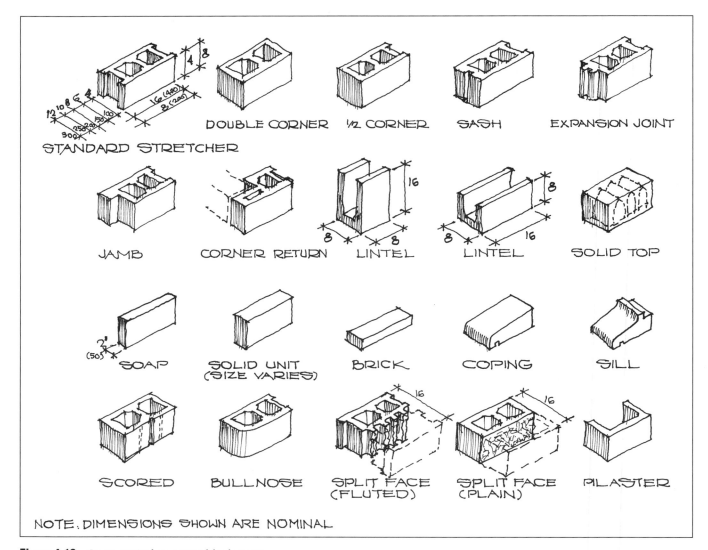

Figure 4.13 Some typical concrete block units.

authorities. Units used in these walls must meet certain classification requirements. Another advantage of CMU walls is their ability to block out sound transmission. Walls built with lightweight 8-in (200 mm) units have a sound transmission class (STC) rating of approximately 48. Normal-weight units having the same thickness have an STC rating of approximately 52. Special attention must be paid to sealing the perimeter of these walls to maintain that rating. Styrofoam inserts improve the STC rating as well as the R-value. Special slotted units are designed to enhance sound absorption in noisy interior spaces such as machine shops (Fig. 4.15).

The linear coefficient of thermal expansion for CMU varies from 0.00021 to 0.00052% depending on the density of the units. Lightweight units fall in the lower end of the range, while the heavier units tend to expand more when exposed to heat. Other factors affecting expansion include color and wall orientation (dark walls and walls facing south experience higher temperatures). While CMU, like any heavy masonry wall, has the advantage of thermal mass (see Sec. 1.4), insulation is required to improve thermal performance. This can be accomplished by one of three methods. The most thermally efficient of these is to attach rigid insulation to the exterior as part of an exterior insulation and finish system (EIFS) assembly. This takes full advantage of the masonry mass. Another method is to fasten the rigid or semirigid insulation to the interior face of the wall and add metal strips to receive the wallboard. The third method provides insulation by pouring perlite or vermiculite granules in the CMU cells or by pouring the granules into the cavity. Providing insulation within the cells whether by pouring granules or adding Styrofoam inserts is the least efficient method because it allows cell partitions to poke through the insulation causing thermal bridging. This deficiency has been corrected in a recently introduced product which isolates the two faces of the block with a zigzagging layer of polystyrene insulation (Fig. 4.16). The manufacturer claims an R-15 to R-24 rating for this product depending on the wall thickness.

A lightweight solid concrete block manufactured from autoclaved cellular concrete (ACC) has long been used in Europe. Production in the United States is being planned by Hebel USA of Roswell, Georgia. The block weighs 30 lb/ft³ (480 kg/m³), has a compressive strength of approximately 500 lb/in² [3447.5 kilopascals (kPA)], an R-value of 13 for an 8-in- (200 mm) thick wall, and can be cut with a handsaw. It is manufactured from a mixture of fly ash (a by-product of the coal industry), lime, Portland cement, aluminum powder, and water and is then autoclaved and cut into blocks or wall panels. It will be interesting to see whether it is priced competitively enough to gain the market acceptance it enjoys in Europe and Japan.

GLASS BLOCK

Glass blocks are manufactured by pouring molten glass into forms to shape the shell of half the hollow block. The glass is permitted to cool, and then the two halves are fused to form one hollow glass block unit. The standard size is a nominal 8 × 8 × 4 in (200 × 200 × 100 mm). Other sizes are also shown in Fig. 4.17.

Units may be slightly tinted, reflective, or sandblasted. A solid, transparent unit, referred to as a *glass brick,* is produced by Pittsburgh Corning. It is vandal-resistant and suitable for use in detention facilities and areas subject to abuse. The standard size is 8 × 8 × 3 in (200 × 200 × 75 mm). Variations to that size are also available. Thickset block is another product manufactured by the same company and is designed to provide an STC rating of 50 as compared to 37 for standard block of the same size.

There are no glass block walls with a fire rating certified in the U.L. Directory. Fire-rated windows, however, do exist. Check the latest U.L. Building Materials Directory, the applicable building code, and authorities having jurisdiction for acceptable products. Rated fixed windows that can be incorporated in a rated wall assembly can reach an area of 120 ft² (11 m²).

Standard glass block may be transparent, semitransparent, patterned to distort the view, or be made translucent by inclusion of a fiberglass insert to reduce glare.

MORTAR AND GROUT

The same types of masonry mortars are used for brick, CMU, and glass block. These types are M, S, N, O, and K. Type K is used for tuck-pointing in restoration projects. It is composed of 1 part Portland cement, 2½ to 4 parts of hydrated lime, and 2¼ to 3 parts sand. Type N

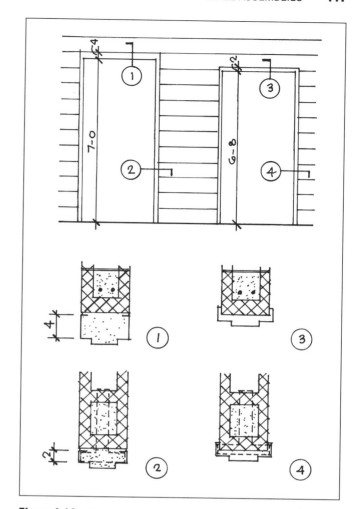

Figure 4.14 Door openings sized to avoid cutting CMU.

is a medium-strength mortar suitable for the majority of applications. To make it easy to remember this designation, one can associate the letter N with the word *normal.* Type S is recommended for reinforced masonry walls two or more stories in height and in locations with high winds. As a general rule, if wind loads exceed 25 lb/ft² (122 kg/m²), use this type of mortar. Associating the letter S with the word *strong* helps in remembering these facts. Type M is a high-strength mortar recommended for use below grade as well as for walls subjected to high compression, severe frost action, or high lateral loads caused by wind or earthquakes. Type O is a low-strength mortar for use in interior partitions and non-load-bearing walls of solid masonry units. Table 4.3 lists these characteristics as well as alternate selections. Building codes usually mandate the type of mortar to be used for most applications based on certain design criteria.

Masonry cements are premixed mortars popular among masons because of their excellent workability. Their strengths vary depending on the manufacturer.

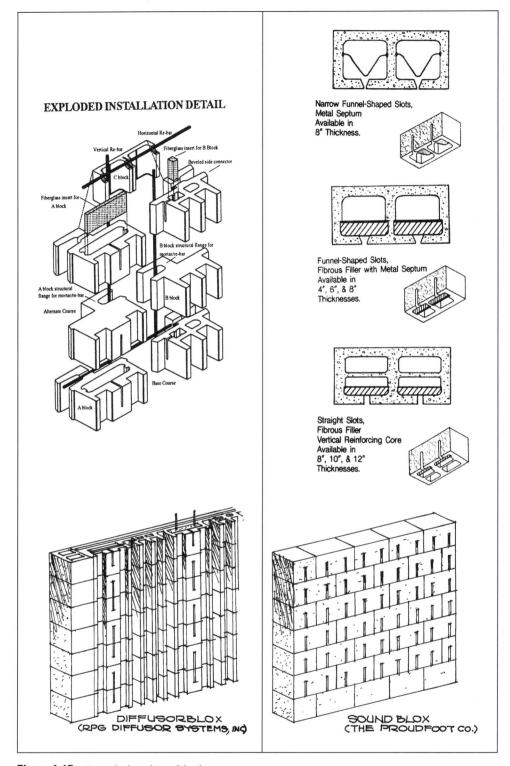

Figure 4.15   Sound-absorbing blocks.

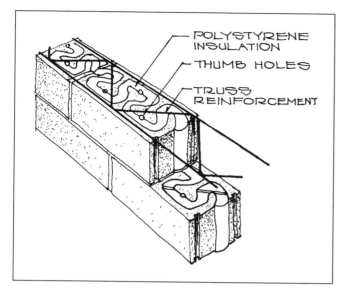

Figure 4.16 Insulated block without thermal bridging. (From Thermalock Products, Inc.)

They may have less strength than job-mixed mortars. Architects should demand that they be tested to prove that their performance is at least equal to the specified mortar. Air entrainment and waterproofing additives are not recommended because they decrease the bond to the masonry units.

Grout is a low slump mixture of either sand and cement (fine grout) or pea gravel, sand, and cement (coarse grout). Table 4.4 shows the conditions under which each of these two types of grout are to be used.

The following recommendations should be observed in regard to mortars:

1. Control sand volume by using a measuring box. Measuring the amount of sand by counting shovelfuls is unacceptable.

2. Mortar sets 2 h after being mixed on hot, dry, and windy days or after 2½ h on humid days. It must not be used after that time. Skilled masons have an instinctive feel for the correct amount of water to add (retemper) to the mortar for good adhesion. Mortar, unlike concrete, is not weakened by the added water. The excess water is either absorbed by the brick or evaporates.

3. Use full mortar beds and head joints. Do not allow bed joint furrowing or head joint slushing. A brick should not be subjected to movement after placement or the bond will be irreparably broken.

4. Absorbent brick or brick heated by the sun should be soaked 2 to 24 h before use depending on the rate of absorption. It should be dry to the touch at the time of use. One crude but convenient test is to draw a circle on the brick using a wax pencil and a quarter as a guide—

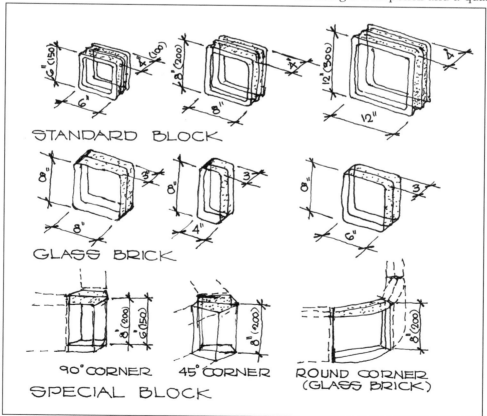

Figure 4.17 Common glass block sizes.

Location	Building Segment	Mortar Type	
		Recommended	Alternative
Exterior, above grade	loadbearing wall non-loadbearing wall parapet wall, chimney and veneer wall	N N N	S or M O[B] or S S
Exterior, at or below grade	foundation wall, retaining wall, manholes, sewers, pavements, walks and patios	M	S[C] or N[C]
Interior	loadbearing wall non-loadbearing partitions	N O	S or M N

[A]This table does not provide for many specialized mortar uses, such as reinforced masonry, acid-resistant mortars and fire box mortar.

[B]Type O mortar is recommended for use where the masonry is unlikely to be frozen when saturated or unlikely to be subjected to high winds or other significant lateral loads. Type N or S mortar should be used in other cases.

[C]Masonry exposed to weather in a nominally horizontal surface is extremely vulnerable to weathering. Mortar for such masonry should be selected with due caution.

Table 4.3   Guide for the selection of masonry mortars (Reproduced by permission; Brick Institute of America, *Tech Note No. 8A, Revised,* Table A1, September 1988)

about 1 in (25 mm) in diameter—and placing 20 drops of water inside the circle using an eyedropper. If the water disappears within 1½ min, the brick needs wetting to prevent it from drawing too much water from the mortar resulting in a weakened bond.

5. At the end of the workday, protect the top of the wall from rain and moisture by attaching a heavy plastic sheet or tarpaulin to the top and extending it at least 2 ft (600 mm) down the exposed side(s) of the wall. This measure helps to prevent efflorescence (Fig. 4.18). This phenomenon will be described more fully in Sec. 4.2.5.

CONTROL JOINTS

Expansion and contraction due to thermal changes must be accommodated in masonry walls. In addition, brick expands when it absorbs moisture and CMU shrinks over time. This shrinkage is referred to as *creep*. If these

Maximum grout pour height, ft.	Specified grout type*	Minimum width of grout space, in.**·†	Minimum grout space dimensions for grouting cells of hollow units, in.†·‡
1	Fine	¾	½ by 2
5	Fine	2	2 by 3
12	Fine	2½	2½ by 3
24	Fine	3	3 by 3
1	Coarse	1½	1½ by 3
5	Coarse	2	2½ by 3
12	Coarse	2½	3 by 3
24	Coarse	3¾	3 by 4

*Fine and coarse grouts and aggregates are defined in ASTM C476 and C404.
**For grouting between wythes.
†Grout space dimension equals grout space width minus horizontal reinforcing bar diameter.
‡Area of vertical reinforcement shall not exceed 6% of the area of the grout space.

Table 4.4   Maximum pour heights and specified grout types with respect to grout space (Reproduced by permission; American Concrete Institute, Table 4.3.3.4 of ACI 530.1/ASCE 6/TMS 602-1992)

changes are not allowed for, the wall will crack or bow. Control joints located approximately 25 ft (7.6 m) apart are usually adequate to accommodate this movement. The spacing of these joints should coincide with offsets and between walls with different heights or loading. Typical details are shown in Fig. 4.19.

The Brick Institute of America (BIA)[18] recommends the use of the following formula to calculate control joint width:

$$W = [0.0005 + 0.000004 \, (T_{max} - T_{min})]L$$

where   0.0005 in/in (0.0005 mm/mm)
   = coefficient of moisture movement
0.000004 in/in per °F (0.000007 mm/mm per °C)
   = coefficient of thermal movement
   W = total expected movement of brick veneer, in (mm)
   T_{max} = maximum mean temperature of brick veneer, °F (°C)
   T_{min} = minimum mean temperature of brick veneer, °F (°C)
   L = length of brick veneer wall, in (mm)

This formula can be applied to the following example: Given $T_{max} = 150°F$ (65.6 °C) and $T_{min} = 32°F$ (0°C), compute the control joint width between two panels 25 ft (7600 mm) long.

$$W = [0.0005 + 0.000004 \, (150 - 32)] \, (25 \times 12)$$
$$= (0.0005 + 0.00047) \, 300 = 0.29 \text{ in}$$

Metric:

$$W = [0.0005 + 0.000007 \, (65.6 - 0)] \, 7600$$
$$= (0.0005 + 0.00046) \, 7600 = 7.3 \text{ mm}$$

The BIA states that "since most sealants are only about 50% efficient, the joints should be sized to accommodate twice the expected movement." This means that for

Figure 4.18   Efflorescence on a wall of a school building.

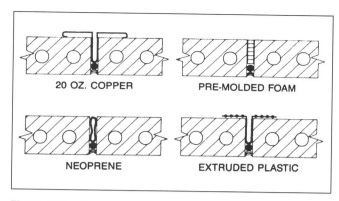

20 OZ. COPPER

PRE-MOLDED FOAM

NEOPRENE

EXTRUDED PLASTIC

Figure 4.19   Expansion joint fillers. (Reproduced by permission; Brick Institute of America, *Tech Note No. 28B, Revision II,* February 1987)

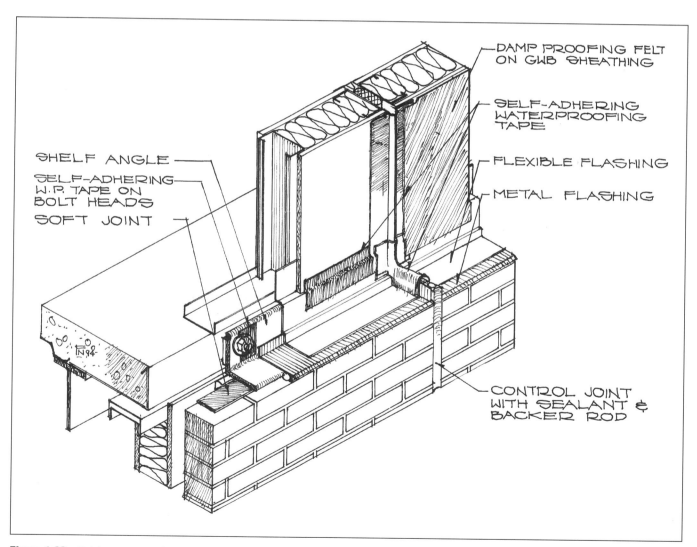

Figure 4.20   Brick masonry detail at the intersection between a control joint and a shelf angle.

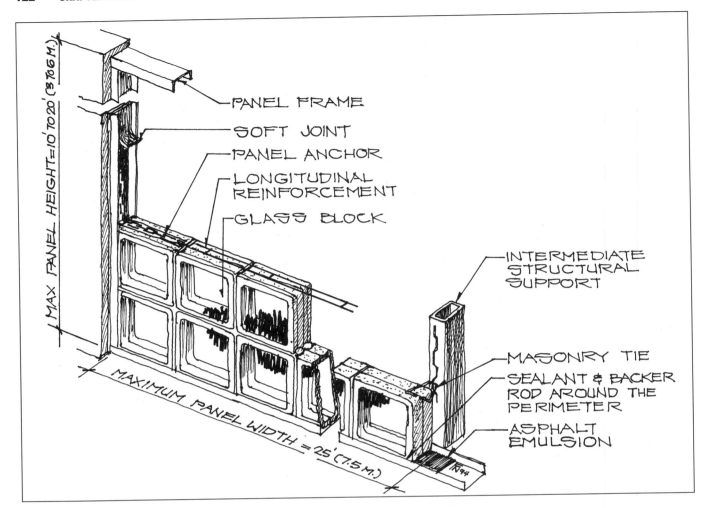

Figure 4.21 Glass block panel details.

this example, the joint width should be between ½ and ⅝ in (13 to 16 mm). Horizontal joints are required at shelf angles also (Fig. 4.20). The same formula should be used to compute the joint width between the bottom of the shelf angle and the brick below it. A simple alternative is to multiply the distance between shelf angles (in inches) by 0.0015. Elastomeric sealants such as polysulfide and polyurethane are used to seal both vertical and horizontal control joints.

For CMU, the ultimate magnitude of creep is assumed to be 2.5×10^{-7} per unit of length per pound per square inch. The coefficient of thermal movement is approximately 0.045% per 100°F (37.8°C). Control joints are recommended to be at the same intervals as in brick masonry and at one side of 6 ft (1.8 m) or both sides of larger openings with offsets for lintel bearings and within 10 ft (3 m) of corners. Joint width is usually determined by the standardized width of the gasket.

The coefficient of thermal expansion for glass block is 47×10^{-7}. This high coefficient restricts the maximum size of glass block panels to approximately 144 ft² (13 m²) and of solid glass brick to 100 ft² (9.25 m²). These sizes may be reduced to resist high wind pressure. Consult product representatives to determine maximum height and width of panels based on the design wind pressure and standard soft joint details between panels. Each panel is isolated from adjacent panels by an expansion joint filler attached to a support member, and the perimeter is sealed (Fig. 4.21).

The Basic Building Officials and Code Administrators International, Inc.[19] (BOCA®, 1993) stipulates under Section 2115.2 that the maximum dimension of a panel shall be 25 ft (635 mm) in length and 20 ft (500 mm) in height between structural supports and expansion joints and the area shall not exceed 144 ft² (13 m²).

MASONRY ANCHORS AND REINFORCEMENT

Two main types of metal restraints are used in masonry construction, unit ties (which may be rigid or flexible), and longitudinal reinforcement. Unit ties (Fig. 4.22) are

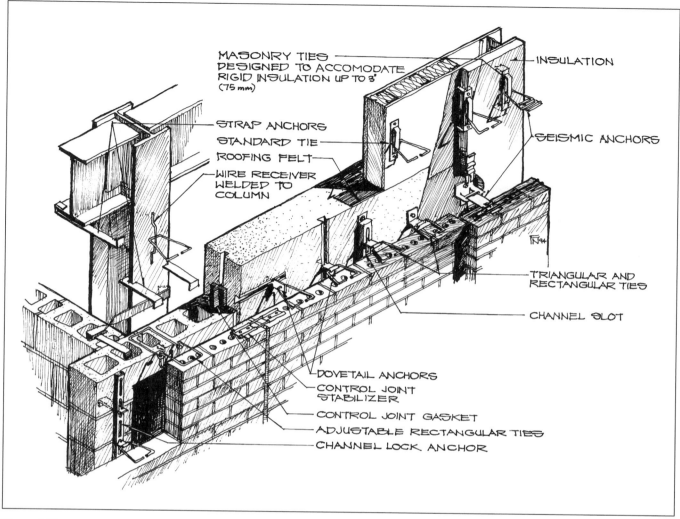

Figure 4.22 Common methods of anchoring brick veneer to various backups using masonry ties.

used to tie one wythe of the wall to the backup. These ties must be manufactured to withstand corrosion, transfer lateral loads to the backup wall with minimal deformation, allow the wall to move longitudinally to accommodate expansion or contraction due to thermal and other forces, and provide height adjustments. The clearance between the tie and its anchor must not exceed certain limits to prevent the veneer from cracking. This clearance is usually referred to as the *mechanical play* which should range between 0.02 and 0.05 in (0.5 and 1.3 mm) (Fig. 4.23). The familiar corrugated ties used in low-rise residential construction are not acceptable for use in public buildings because they allow too much movement in the wall resulting in unacceptable cracking. Wire ties should be a minimum ³⁄₁₆ in (9 mm) in diameter. The BIA recommends a minimum spacing as shown in Table 4.5 and Fig. 4.24. Ties must be placed a maximum 8 in (200 mm) from wall edges including

control joints. Brick panel top edge can experience more loading than the rest of the panel area. For that reason, ties should be placed within two or three courses from the top of the wall panel.

Because the part of the ties located between the veneer and the backup wall is exposed to the atmosphere and inaccessible for inspection and maintenance, the ties must be manufactured from a durable metal such as stainless steel, hot-dipped galvanized steel, copper-clad steel, or fusion-bonded epoxy-coated steel. Each of these can develop problems. Stainless steel, while very durable, can cause corrosion in carbon steel (the metal used in studs) through galvanic action between the stainless-steel screws and the studs. This happens because condensation forms on the screws which are exposed to freezing. All the other types are subject to damage in handling or defects in manufacture. It is essential that they be inspected before use. If studs are to be welded, 18 gauge should be the minimum used to prevent burn through. As a matter of fact, specifying 18 or even 16 gauge as a minimum regardless of whether the studs will be welded or screw-fastened is a good policy because the heavier metal will resist corrosion for a much longer period of time than lighter gauges. The BIA advocates that the studs be zinc-coated to conform to Grade G-90 and that field welding not be permitted. Screws used to attach the sheathing and ties may be cadmium-plated, hot-dipped galvanized, or polymer-coated after being galvanized for added protection since stainless-steel screws cause galvanic action and should not be used. A special self-adhering waterproofing tape placed between the tie and sheathing will seal around the screw penetration and prevent moisture from penetrating into the wall from the exterior (Fig. 4.25). Plastic clips are available to act as a drip, preventing water migration across the reinforcement and into the backup (Fig. 4.26). These clips can also be used as retainers for rigid insulation.

Longitudinal reinforcement (Fig. 4.27) is used to tie both wythes of a masonry cavity wall. It is also used as

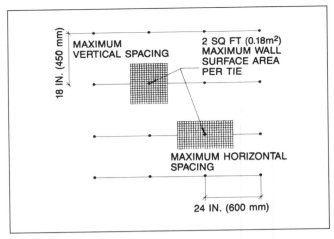

Figure 4.24 Spacing of metal ties. (Reproduced by permission; Brick Institute of America, *Tech Note No. 28B, Revision II,* February 1987)

part of the reinforcement in reinforced load-bearing walls and to control shrinkage in single-wythe walls. Truss-type reinforcement must not be used when insulation is placed in the cavity. This type can cause the wall to bow because it does not allow the heated exterior wythe to move independently of the cooler insulated backup. Use ladder reinforcement instead. Longitudinal reinforcement must be placed so that one longitudinal wire is placed over each face shell of the CMU backup and a third is located over the brick or solid block veneer.

Glass block reinforcement allows the assembly to act as a cohesive panel between restraining supports. In this application, ladder reinforcement is combined with sheet-metal anchors at two course intervals. The anchors tie the panel to the supports (Fig. 4.21).

SHELF ANGLES

Shelf angles (sometimes referred to as relieving angles) are continuous angles tied to the structure to carry the masonry veneer. These angles are sized and detailed by the structural engineer. A minimum two-thirds of the brick width should bear on the angle, and it must be designed for a maximum deflection of $L/600$ or 0.3 in (8 mm). Angles must be interrupted at control joints and detailed with a soft joint underneath to allow the lower wall panel to expand vertically (Fig. 4.28). It is recommended that these angles be placed at each floor if the facade is exposed to high winds to prevent cracking (Fig. 4.29) and that the final adjustment be made by the mason. Designing the stud assembly for a maximum deflection of $L/720$ can reduce the incidence of cracks even if the shelf angles are placed every second floor. For that reason, some codes allow the placement of angles at these locations.

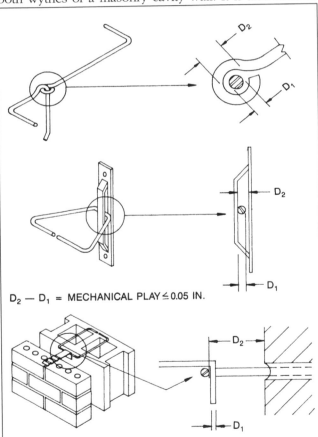

$D_2 - D_1$ = MECHANICAL PLAY ≤ 0.05 IN.

Figure 4.23 Mechanical play in masonry ties. (Reproduced by permission; Brick Institute of America, *Tech Note No. 44B,* September 1988)

Wall Type	Cavity or Air Space Width (in.)	Tie System	Maximum Area Per Tie (sq ft)	Maximum Vertical Spacing (in.)	Maximum Horizontal Spacing (in.)
Cavity	≤ 3½	Unit Tie	4½	24	36
		Std. Joint Reinforcement	—	16	—
		Unit Adj. Double Eye & Pintle	2⅔	24	24
		Unit Adj. Single Eye & Pintle	1¾	16	16
		Adj. Joint Reinforcement	—	16	—
	> 3½ but ≤ 4½	Unit Tie	3	24	36
		Std. Joint Reinforcement	—	16	—
		Unit Adj. Double Eye & Pintle	2	24	24
		Adj. Joint Reinforcement	—	16	—
Veneer/ Wood Stud	1	Corrugated	3¼[3] 2⅔[4]	24 24	24 24
Veneer/ Steel Stud	2 but ≤ 3	Adj. Unit Veneer Ties	2	18	24
Veneer/ Concrete or CMU Backup	≤ 1	Adj. Unit	2⅔	24	24
Multi-Wythe Brick	—	Unit Ties	4½	24	36
		Std. Joint Reinforcement	—	16	—
Brick/Block Composite	—	Unit Ties	4½	24	36
		Std. Joint Reinforcement	—	16	—
Two-Wythe Grouted	—	Unit Ties	2⅔[5]	16	24
		Std. Joint Reinforcement	—	16	—

[1]Based on minimum tie diameters and gages listed in Table 2.
[2]Masonry laid in running bond. Consult applicable building code for special bond patterns such as stack bond.
[3]One and two-family wood frame construction not over 2 stories in height.
[4]Wood frame construction over 2 stories in height.
[5]For high-lift grouted walls. Masonry laid in running bond.

Table 4.5 Tie spacing recommendations.[1,2] (Reproduced by permission; Brick Institute of America, *Tech Note No. 44B*, September 1988)

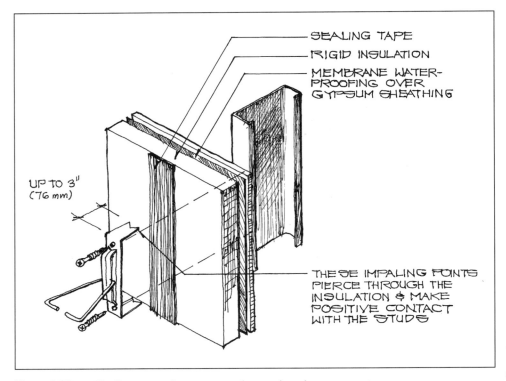

Figure 4.25 Self-adhering sealing tape used to seal anchor penetrations.

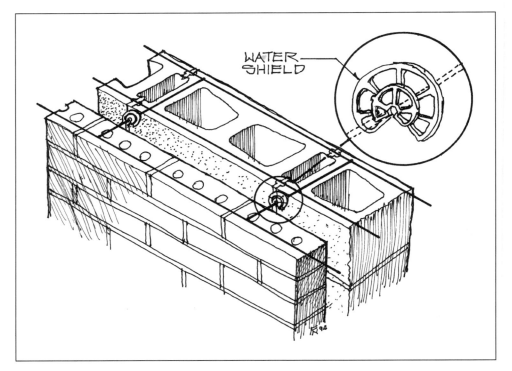

Figure 4.26 A plastic water shield clipped to longitudinal reinforcement to prevent water from traveling along the wire into the backup. The shield is also used as a retainer for rigid insulation placed over the backup.

The torquing of the bolts and/or welding to the supporting structure must, however, be done by the steel fabricator. One way of attaching the shelf angles is for the steel fabricator to bolt it finger-tight to the structure. The mason builds the wall up to the angle and makes the final adjustment to coincide with the coursing and the minimum gap for expansion. The steel fabricator then tightens the bolt to the required torque and spot welds the nut. Section 2.2.3 provides more information about this.

LOOSE LINTELS

Loose lintels are called *loose* because they are not fastened to the wall or the backup structure. They are just placed on the wall to carry masonry over an opening. The minimum size for brick should not be less than 3½ × 3 × ⁵⁄₁₆ in (89 × 75 × 8 mm) with the 3½-inch leg horizontal. Lintels are sized in a schedule included in the specifications or in the structural details sheets. Architects must check to determine that all opening widths are covered. In many cases, this schedule is an office standard not modified from project to project and may cover only openings up to 8-ft (2.4 m) wide for example. If one of the openings is 10-ft (3 m) wide, the architect will have to go to the trouble of issuing a change order to correct the oversight if the drawings are issued for construction without checking this schedule. Loose

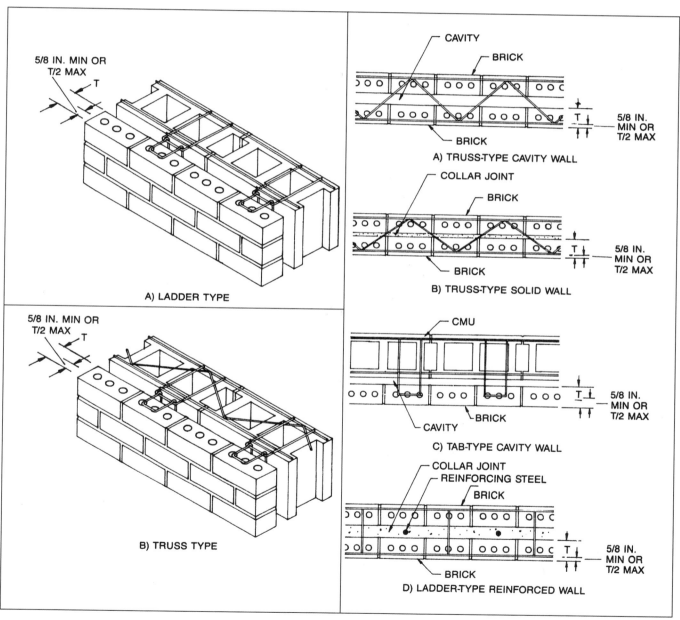

Figure 4.27 Longitudinal masonry reinforcement. (Reproduced by permission; Brick Institute of America, *Tech Note No. 44B*, September 1988)

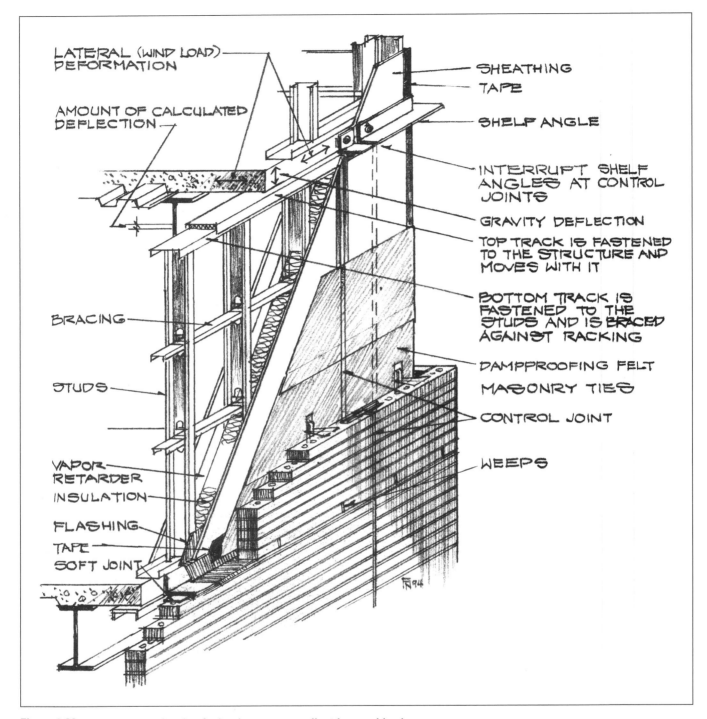

Figure 4.28 Construction details of a brick masonry wall with a stud backup.

lintels may be constructed of other materials such as stone, lintel block, or cast stone (precast) (Fig. 2.27). Section 2.2.4 provides more information on loose lintels.

FLASHING

Flashing is a water-impermeable sheet material designed to direct water to the exterior through weepholes. It is required in all masonry construction at window heads, under sills, at the base of the wall, above shelf angles, and under parapet copings. Base flashing is required even in solid, single-wythe walls to prevent moisture from migrating upward from the grade beam causing dampness in the interior and efflorescence on the exterior face of the brick.

In masonry work, aluminum and lead are not recommended as flashing material because they eventually corrode when they come in contact with salts in the mortar. Table 4.6 evaluates the different types of flashing materials. Some experts consider 16-ounce (oz) (78 kg/m^2) lead-coated copper as a dependable and durable material for flashing. Stainless steel is also acceptable although it is harder to form and solder and is costlier. Flexible flashing products are also extensively used. One of the most popular products in this category is copper-fabric flashing. It is composed of a thin sheet of copper bonded on both sides to asphalt-impregnated fiberglass fabric. EPDM or a self-adhering waterproofing membrane such as Bituthene by W. R. Grace or similar products are preferred in locations other than shelf angles. Because flexible flashing is incapable of forming a drip or adhering to the sealant, it is not recommended for placement above shelf angles. Use metal above shelf angles. Figure 4.30 shows a detail that simplifies fabrication of the metal part while taking advantage of the easy to form flexible flashing.

The following recommendations can go a long way toward ensuring that a wall is flashed properly:

1. Flashing segments must be lapped at least 6 in (150 mm) at joints and sealed with mastic.

2. Extend the metal edge at least ¼ in (6 mm) beyond the face of the wall and bend it downward to form a drip.

3. Detail flashing at control joints in a manner that allows the joints to move without allowing water to seep in, as shown in Figure 4.20 or by other proven methods.

4. If pea gravel is placed over flexible flashing to aid in draining the cavity, adequate support must be provided under it to prevent tears especially at laps and extra protection should be provided over bolt heads. Consider using a drainage panel such as Enkadrain instead.

5. All discontinuous flashings such as those placed above lintels and under sills must have end dams (Fig. 4.31) to prevent water from falling off the ends and spattering onto both the veneer and backup causing noise, efflorescence, and possible leakage problems.

Special attention must be given to complicated configurations associated with multicornered designs. An axonometric drawing is very helpful in explaining what is intended to the masonry contractor. Flashings must extend 6 to 9 in (150 to 230 mm) up the backup wall and be tucked behind the sheathing (stud walls), embedded in a horizontal joint (masonry), or placed in a reglet (concrete) (Fig. 4.32). The preceding information is applicable to brick, CMU, and glass block spandrel areas. It is recommended that the glass block be either mirrored or sandblasted (back face) to prevent the flashing and spandrel beam from showing through.

WEEPHOLES AND VENTS

Moisture accumulation in the cavity is directed to the exterior through weepholes (weeps) in the exterior wythe. These holes may be created by omitting mortar

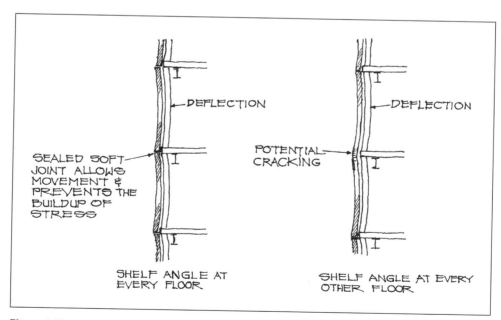

Figure 4.29 Placing a shelf angle at every floor minimizes the incidence of cracks at negative bending locations. (Sketches by author based on material from a seminar given by Simpson, Gumpertz & Heger, Inc., Boston)

Type	Description	Advantages	Disadvantages
Copper	10 to 20 oz. sheet (3 to 6 kg/m^2)	Durable; available in special preformed shapes; is not affected by chemicals present in the mortar unless chloride-based additives are used	Will stain adjacent surfaces*
Plastics	20 to 40 mil (.5 to 1 mm)	Flexible; easy to form; very widely used	Durability varies with the type used; depends on test data for: (a) resistance to UV (b) resistance to alkalis, (c) compatibility with joint sealant
Galvanized Steel	.015 inch minimum (.38 mm)	Low cost (not recommended)	Corrodes in fresh mortar; bending reduces durability
Stainless Steel	Type 304 .01 inch minimum (.25 mm)	Excellent durability	Relatively more expensive
Combination Flashings	Copper laminated to felt or Kraft paper	Easy workability and lower cost	Dependability depends on the product selected; refer to manufacturer's literature
Asphalt-impregnated Felt		None (not recommended)	Easily damaged; turns brittle and decays with time
Aluminum		Durable if not in contact with fresh mortar	Wet mortar corrodes aluminum**
Sheet Lead		None (not recommended)	Like aluminum, it is corroded by the alkalis present in the mortar; galvanic action between the two materials further disintegrates the metal

This table is based on information contained in *Technical Notes 7A Revised,* March 1985 issued by the Brick Institute of America (reproduced by permission).

* Some experts recommend the use of 16 oz. (5 kg/m^2) lead-coated copper to overcome the staining problem.
** Aluminum may be used under window sills if isolated from mortar. It should not be embedded in the brick jambs.

Table 4.6   Flashing materials

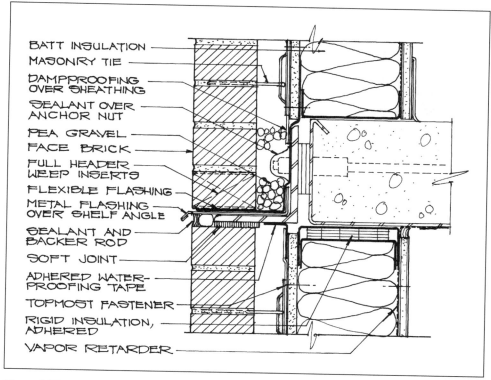

BATT INSULATION
MASONRY TIE
DAMPPROOFING OVER SHEATHING
SEALANT OVER ANCHOR NUT
PEA GRAVEL
FACE BRICK
FULL HEADER WEEP INSERTS
FLEXIBLE FLASHING
METAL FLASHING OVER SHELF ANGLE
SEALANT AND BACKER ROD
SOFT JOINT
ADHERED WATER-PROOFING TAPE
TOPMOST FASTENER
RIGID INSULATION, ADHERED
VAPOR RETARDER

Figure 4.30 Combining metal and flexible flashing at shelf angles.

from a header joint at intervals or by inserting plastic tubes in the joints (Fig. 4.33). Rectangular tubes are not as easily clogged as round ones. Weepholes must be placed directly above the flashing at approximately 2-ft (600-mm) intervals (Fig. 4.34). To prevent insect infestation, glass fiber or stainless-steel wool should be inserted in the weephole. Plastic mesh applied to the back side of the veneer may also be used to act as an insect screen. If rope wicks are used to drain the cavity, they should be placed at 16-in (400-mm) intervals.

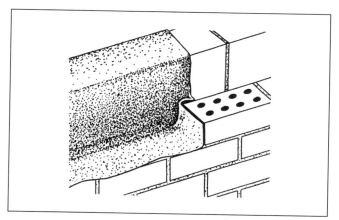

Figure 4.31 Flashing end dam. (Reproduced by permission; Brick Institute of America, *Tech Note No. 7, Revised,* February 1985)

Many of the problems that plague masonry can be traced back to mortar accumulation at the bottom of the cavity. This results in blockage of weepholes causing damp spots in the interior and leaching of salts in the mortar causing efflorescence on the exterior face and in some cases spalling part of the brick due to water freezing just below the brick surface. To avoid these problems, it is essential that the cavity be clear of mortar accumulations during construction. The BIA recommends that the cavity be a minimum of 2 in (50 mm) wide to give the mason better control, that the mortar be beveled toward the cavity to minimize the amount of mortar extruded from the joint after the next course is placed, and flattening the extruded mortar rather than cutting it off. Another method mentioned in the BIA literature is to place a wood strip slightly narrower than the cavity on the ties and raise it, by means of a wire or string attached to it, before the next row of ties is installed. The BIA recommends the placement of graded pea gravel to a height of several inches above the horizontal surface of the flashing to create passages to the weeps even if mortar drops in the cavity. The same solution can be achieved by placing a drainage medium such as the one recently introduced by Mortar Net USA, Ltd. This product is manufactured from high-density polyethylene or nylon strands woven into an open mesh cut in a dovetail pattern to prevent mortar from

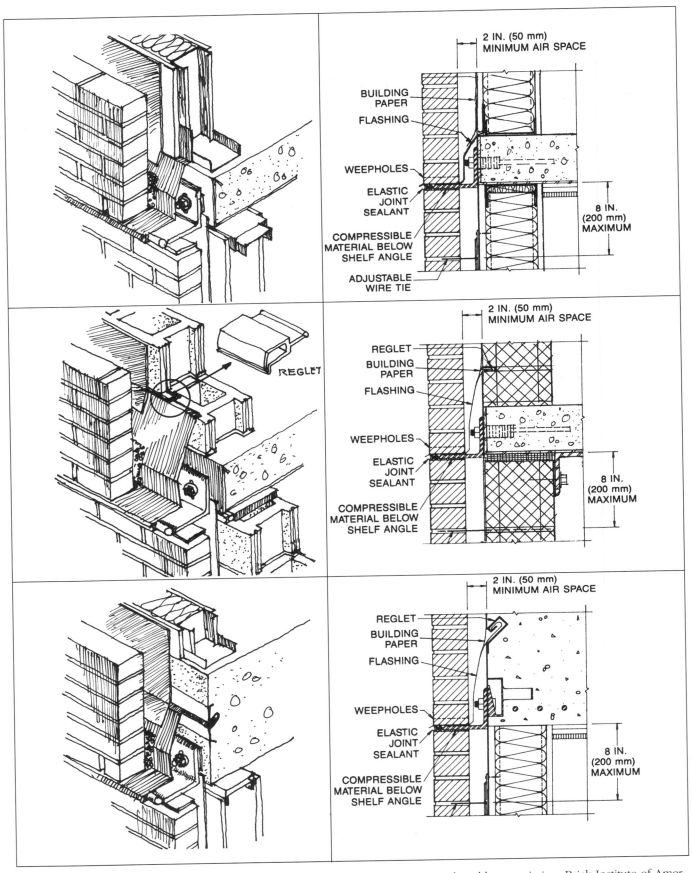

Figure 4.32 Flashing terminations in different backup walls. (Bottom section reproduced by permission. Brick Institute of America; *Tech Note No. 28B, Revision II,* February 1987)

132

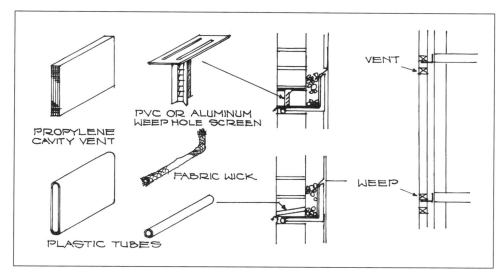

Figure 4.33 Weeps and vents.

damming the cavity. This allows any leakage to proceed unhindered to the weepholes. The product is only 1 in (25 mm) thick and requires a double thickness to fill a 2-in (50-mm) cavity as well as a 16-in (400-mm) high back-flashing to accommodate its height. The cost is much higher than pea gravel, but the benefit may be worth the price. Yet a third method is to dry-set every third stretcher placed on the flashing and shim it into position, build the wall, remove the loose stretchers after the wall is built, clean the cavity of any mortar accumulation, and then butter these bricks and set them into the wall leaving one side without mortar to create the weepholes (Fig. 4.35).

If the wall is designed as a rain screen, special polypropylene inserts (Fig. 4.33) may be spaced at 16-in (600 mm) intervals below shelf angles to act as pressure-equalizing vents. These inserts also act to vent any vapor escaping from the wall assembly especially if the veneer is glazed. Since glazed masonry does not allow vapor to migrate to the exterior, in the absence of vents, vapor may get trapped behind the glazed face, freeze, and cause it to pop off.

COPINGS AND SILLS

The capping component placed at the top of a wall or parapet is referred to as a *coping*. Copings and windowsills may be constructed of brick, stone, or cast stone. Metal may also be used as a coping. As a general rule, the less number of joints introduced in these horizontal surfaces, the less the chance of leakage, mortar failure, and brick spalling. The placement of through-wall flashing under these components is very important. Since cast stone is precast concrete, it may contain salts that can contribute to efflorescence (Sec. 4.2.5).

4.2.3 Ornamentation
BRICK

Brick has a long history of being used for ornamentation. Some decorative elements are functional in nature. Arches (Fig. 4.36) are inherently ornamental, but they perform the function of spanning over openings as well. Arches may be introduced in veneer as well as in solid walls. Regular or special brick may be used in their construction. They must be engineered to resist superimposed and lateral loads, and adjacent walls must be designed to resist their thrust. Check the building code and involve the structural engineer before finalizing the design.

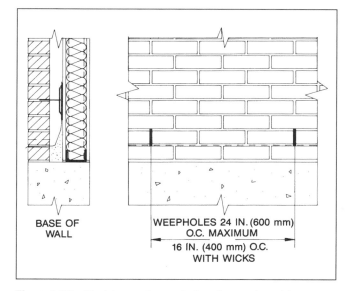

Figure 4.34 Flashing and weepholes. (Reproduced by permission; Brick Institute of America, *Tech Note No. 28B, Revision II,* February 1987)

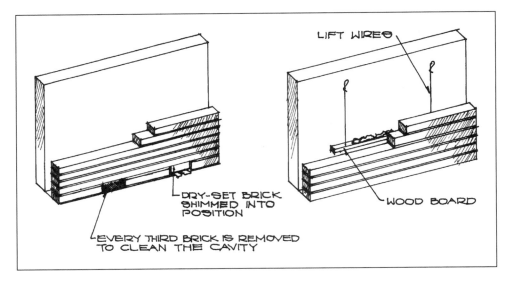

Figure 4.35 Methods of cleaning the cavity.

Corbels are highly decorative and function as cantilevers. At least that was the intent when walls were load-bearing. Today, they are rarely used, and when used, they are backed by a supporting structure constructed from light-gauge steel framework or a unistrut system anchored to concrete (Fig. 4.37).

Brick also creates a pattern depending on the bond chosen by the designer. Many of the bonds shown in Fig. 4.38 are traditionally used in double-wythe walls but can be emulated in cavity walls by either cutting the brick in half to introduce headers or ordering half bricks from the brick fabricator. In either case, this represents an additional cost.

Other elements such as contrasting colors, special banding, patterns, and reliefs serve to embellish the design. Using brick with contrasting or complementary colors, introducing stone, tile, cast stone, or special

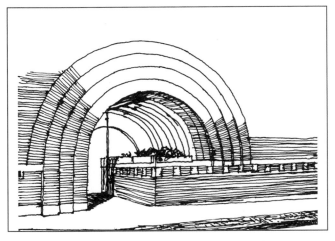

Figure 4.36 V.C. Morris gift shop (currently used as an art gallery), San Francisco (designed by Frank Lloyd Wright).

brick elements is another way of enhancing the design. Figures 4.39 and 4.40 show two examples of what can be done to enrich the design using today's brick vocabulary. Architects should research the rich history of brick architecture for inspiration to create innovative designs using today's materials, technology, and economics.

CMU

Concrete masonry units do not have the rich and long history of clay brick architecture. They do not offer the range of colors and shapes that can be found in brick. Nevertheless, they do offer some opportunities for creating imaginative design. As mentioned at the beginning of this section, architects can custom-design special block to achieve this goal (Figs. 4.4 to 4.6). Standard blocks with special surface treatment include split-face block which is produced by casting an oversize block and shearing it to form two blocks (Figs. 4.13 and 4.41). This product is produced with a plain or fluted face. While fluted blocks give the wall an interesting texture, their horizontal joints are rather difficult to tool properly. Creating vertical grooves either by saw-cutting or using sash block (Fig. 4.42) is another way of introducing interest in the design. Courses with different heights can also be mixed to create a pattern. False joints and colored or glazed units can also be used in that regard (Fig. 4.43). Distinctive block designs can be incorporated in the wall. Check for availability with local suppliers.

GLASS BLOCK

Glass block has its own esthetics based on a simple geometry as well as its transparent or translucent nature. Like CMU, a limited selection of patterns can be intro-

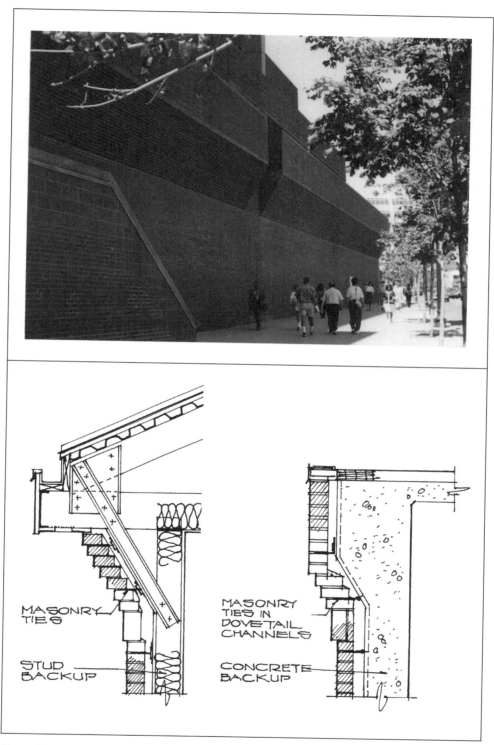

Figure 4.37 Corbel detailing for veneer wall.

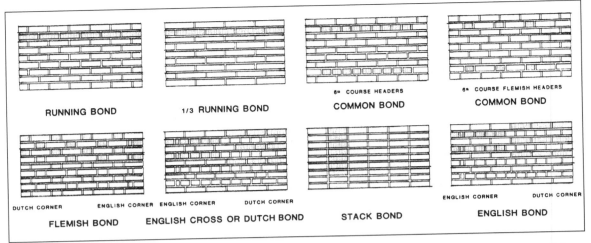

Figure 4.38 Brick bond patterns. (Reproduced by permission; Brick Institute of America, *Tech Note No. 30,* September 1988)

duced in the design. Rounded corners and wall articulation can also be used as design elements (Fig. 4.44).

4.2.4 Assemblies

BRICK

A brick wall may be constructed as a solid load-bearing assembly. Header bricks tying both wythes in this wall type are not recommended in exterior walls because they can act as a conduit for water causing leaks or dampness. Ladder reinforcement is preferred for that purpose. The collar joint between the wythes acts as a water barrier if properly executed. It must be applied to the backup wall at each course as the work progresses. This is referred to as *back parging.* This method is used if the joint is less than 1 in (25 mm) in thickness. Joints that exceed that width are filled by pouring a soupy grout mixture into the gap. It is consolidated by puddling low-lift pours or using a vibrator for high-lift pours. Solid or barrier-type walls can perform satisfactorily if executed properly; however, they do not provide a second line of defense should a leak occur.

Cavity walls may be constructed as a veneer backed by a CMU wall or with a stud backup (Fig. 4.45). Wood studs are usually used in low-rise residential construction, the discussion of which is outside the scope of this book. Steel studs represent the bulk of construction for commercial and other public buildings.

While masonry backup walls are more durable and provide better acoustical insulation and their thermal mass can enhance the wall's energy performance, they tend to cost more, require more time to construct, and are not preferred in seismic zones (see Sec. 1.5). They also require heavier structural support and more elaborate foundations than stud wall backup. Stud wall assemblies must be capable of withstanding lateral

forces without deflecting more than $L/720$ and must be braced with horizontal bridging at regular intervals.

The soft joint between the top of the wall and the shelf angle must be sized to accommodate thermal and moisture expansion as well as structural deflection. The studs in non-load-bearing walls must not be fastened to the top track to prevent the load from being transmitted from the floor to the studs causing them to buckle. A double-track arrangement with a gap in between prevents this from happening. This detail also isolates the studs from the in-plane deformation of the structure (see Fig. 2.9).

Fiberglass-faced sheathing is preferred to the paper-faced type because it is more water resistant. This is especially the case if the sheathing is to be exposed for a length of time during construction delays. It is advisable to protect the sheathing with overlapping 15- or 30-lb felt to act as a dampproofing membrane (Fig. 4.28). If another type of membrane is used, it must have a perm rating of at least five times that of the vapor retarder to prevent condensation from being trapped within the assembly and causing the studs to corrode (see Sec. 1.3.3).

Windows and doors must not be attached to both the veneer and the backup because these wythes experience different movements and can exert pressures on the frame causing glass to break and doors to jam.

Factory-built panelized brick assemblies are a relative newcomer to the brick industry. They are shop-fabricated under quality control procedures and may be constructed as all-brick reinforced panels backed with a few structural members (Fig. 4.46) or as a thin brick facing for precast concrete, GFRC, or cement board.

The all-brick assembly was developed in the early fifties in Europe. Prefabrication started in the United

States in the sixties and is currently well established as an alternative to conventional construction. Panels may be constructed of either standard solid brick (up to 25% cored) or hollow brick (up to 60% cored). This latter (Fig. 4.47) is more economical, is lighter weight than solid brick, and allows more grout to be placed around the vertical rebars. The integral steel backing frame enhances panel strength to accommodate point loads at supports and during hoisting.

Thin brick facers may have a flat back for use with a latex-based adhesive mortar on a cement board fastened to a stud backing. They may also have dovetail depressions at the back to be better integrated with their backup when used to face precast and GFRC panels. When used in this application, they are placed in the form on a liner that controls the width of joints and then the backing is either poured over reinforcement (concrete) or sprayed on (GFRC).

Panelized systems allow the work to proceed without being affected by adverse weather conditions. They enable the contractor to enclose the structure at an early stage to commence interior work and require hoisting cranes instead of scaffolding. These cranes may already be at the site to perform other tasks. The added cost in this case would be minimal. Prefabricated panels also allow the designer to introduce repetitive and complicated configurations which may not be practical if the wall is built conventionally. The reason is that the mason can build the panels in the shop over a single jig rather than construct a complicated form for each one. Each system must be value-engineered to determine the advantages, disadvantages, and cost implications. Some of these panels are designed as a rain screen; others function as a barrier wall. This aspect must also be evaluated to determine whether there is any danger of leakage.

CMU

Concrete masonry unit wall assemblies are similar to the brick walls described above. They use the same components except for the masonry units themselves (Fig. 4.48).

GLASS BLOCK

Glass block walls, by necessity, are single-thickness walls. They require good workmanship to prevent leakage and soft joints around the panels. Figure 4.49 shows a typical assembly.

4.2.5 What Can Go Wrong
EFFLORESCENCE

You may have noticed masonry walls marred by white stains (Fig. 4.18) and wondered about what caused them. Research indicates that this phenomenon which is referred to as *efflorescence* is caused by moisture migrating through the mortar, dissolving salts within it, and leaching to the surface. Efflorescence may also be caused by salts in the brick itself or by the CMU backup in composite walls.

Figure 4.40 Integrating sculpture and lighting elements in a brick wall. Paul J. Gutman Library, Philadelphia. (designed by Shepley, Bulfinch, Richardson and Abbott, Architects). (Photograph by Jean Smith; reproduced by permission)

Figure 4.39 Using contrasting colors to create an interesting pattern: Back Bay Train Station, Boston (designed by Kallmann, McKinnell and Wood, Architects, Inc.).

Figure 4.41 Split-face block.

Figure 4.42 Decorative vertical reveals can create interest in an otherwise ordinary looking CMU wall. They can be introduced either by saw cutting or using sash block.

To avoid this problem, brick must be tested according to ASTM C67 to assess the amount of salts present within it. Walls must also be protected during construction against wetting by rain, and the wall must be designed and detailed as a well-drained cavity wall. A tight vapor retarder also prevents water vapor from escaping from the interior and condensing within the wall adding to the causes of efflorescence. Cement used in the mortar must be specified to contain the least amount of alkali since a high percentage can be one of the causes of this problem. In addition, sand and water must be clean and the joints must be filled and tooled properly to minimize the likelihood of efflorescence.

Should efflorescence occur, it can be removed either by brushing or by a pressurized water spray. It is important, however, to try to ascertain the cause and deal with it first to prevent its recurrence. Preventive measures

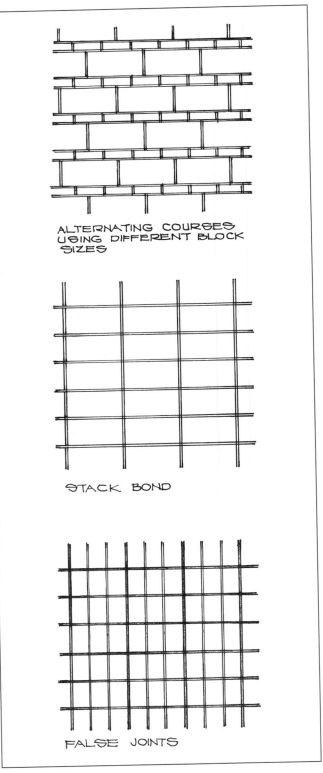

Figure 4.43 Concrete masonry unit coursing to create different scales and patterns.

can be as simple as a visual inspection of flashings, sealants, and vapor retarders during construction to ensure that they are properly executed.

CRACKING

Cracks are the most noticeable and alarming causes for concern in masonry construction. They also act as a conduit for water into the cavity and can further damage the wall if water freezes within them. As the water freezes, it increases in volume and can spall parts of the brick. Cracking can be caused by the following:

1. *Inadequate control joint width or spacing.* As mentioned, they should be located approximately 25 ft (8 m) apart, coinciding with offsets, and near corners and sized according to the formula included in the text. Under no circumstances should the joint width be less than ½ in (13 mm). Horizontal joint reinforcement and shelf angles must be interrupted at control joints.

2. *Structural elements with inadequate stiffness.* Structural elements such as studs in backup walls, shelf angles, and spandrel beams must be stiff enough to limit deflection caused by lateral and gravity loads.

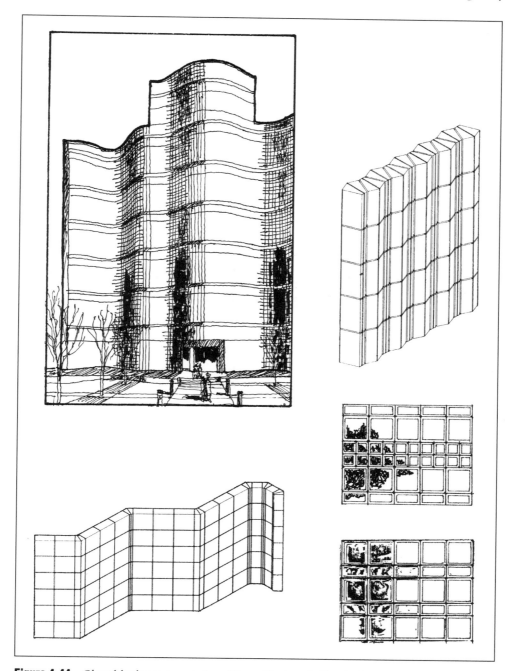

Figure 4.44   Glass block ornamentation. (From Pittsburgh Corning)

3. *Differential movement between dissimilar materials.* Encasing a steel column in brick and mortar is an invitation to cracking. Leave a space around the column and use flexible ties instead. Differential settlement of foundation is also an obvious cause of cracking. Excessive deflection, tying clay and concrete masonry in a manner that does not allow them to move separately, and the omission of a soft joint under shelf angles are all causes for walls to crack or bow and brick to spall.

4. *Parapet cracking.* Because parapets are exposed to thermal expansion on both sides while the wall below them is exposed only on one side, they tend to expand more and can experience bowing and horizontal cracking. To prevent that from occurring, the parapet should

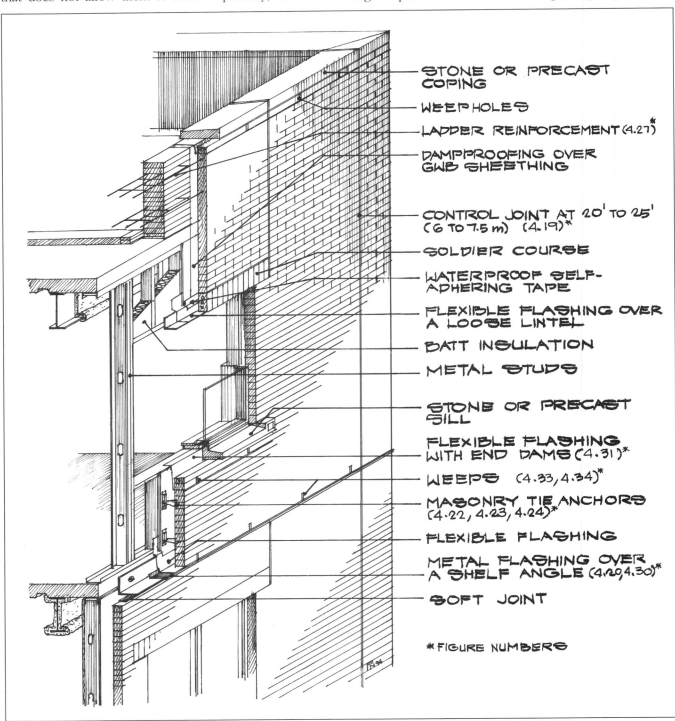

STONE OR PRECAST COPING

WEEPHOLES

LADDER REINFORCEMENT (4.27)*

DAMPPROOFING OVER GWB SHEATHING

CONTROL JOINT AT 20' TO 25' (6 TO 7.5 m) (4.19)*

SOLDIER COURSE

WATERPROOF SELF-ADHERING TAPE

FLEXIBLE FLASHING OVER A LOOSE LINTEL

BATT INSULATION

METAL STUDS

STONE OR PRECAST SILL

FLEXIBLE FLASHING WITH END DAMS (4.31)*

WEEPS (4.33, 4.34)*

MASONRY TIE ANCHORS (4.22, 4.23, 4.24)*

FLEXIBLE FLASHING

METAL FLASHING OVER A SHELF ANGLE (4.20, 4.30)*

SOFT JOINT

* FIGURE NUMBERS

Figure 4.45 Brick veneer with stud backup assembly.

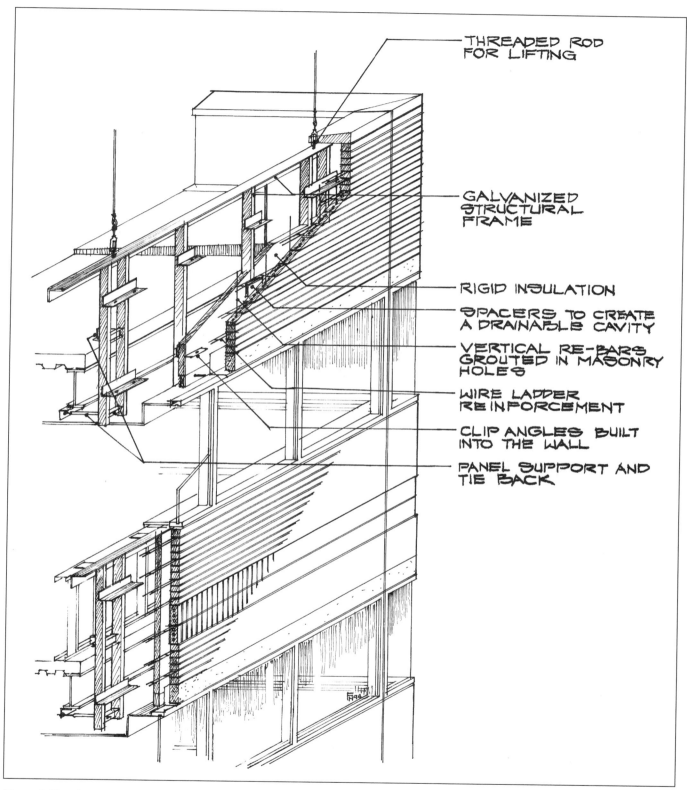

THREADED ROD
FOR LIFTING

GALVANIZED
STRUCTURAL
FRAME

RIGID INSULATION

SPACERS TO CREATE
A DRAINABLE CAVITY

VERTICAL RE-BARS
GROUTED IN MASONRY
HOLES

WIRE LADDER
REINFORCEMENT

CLIP ANGLES BUILT
INTO THE WALL

PANEL SUPPORT AND
TIE BACK

Figure 4.46 Shop-fabricated masonry panels.

be built of the same material front and back, it must be reinforced both vertically and horizontally, and intermediate control joints should be introduced between the joints continuing from the wall below (Fig. 4.50).

5. *Other problems resulting from poor detailing.* Omitting dampproofing can result in sheathing deterioration and water penetration into the wall causing corrosion to the studs, loss of R-value as the insulation becomes wet, and mildew damage to interior finishes. Poor detailing or improper installation of flashing or omitting it from locations that require protection can cause similar problems.

These are a few of the things that can go wrong if the architect is not well versed in the proper design, detailing, and surveillance of unit masonry construction. Implementing the defense measures described in this section can go a long way toward avoiding most of the potentially serious problems that cause deterioration in a brick wall assembly.

Summary

Unit masonry is a term used to describe wall construction where relatively small components are used. Brick,

CMU, and glass block fall into this category. Brick is produced in both modular size based on a 4-in (100 mm) module and nonmodular dimensions. The larger the dimensions, the lower the cost. Plan dimensions should be structured in a way that would avoid excessive cutting of brick. Architects can either include an allowance representing the cost of the brick for the contractors to base their bids on or select samples from three manufacturers and name them in the specifications.

The grades to choose from are SW for severe weathering, MW for mild weathering, and NW for negligible weathering (used in interior walls). Thin brick is used as a facer for precast concrete or is adhered to cement board over studs in a manner similar to tile facing.

Concrete masonry units are produced as hollow or solid units. They can be either normal or lightweight. They are effective as a fire barrier with ratings of 2, 3, and 4 h. Wall thickness is determined by either the horizontal or vertical span and code-mandated loads. These units are effective in blocking sound transmission, and they dampen the highs and lows of heat transmission with their thermal mass especially if insulation is placed on the exterior. Truss reinforcement is not recommended if the backup masonry is insulated.

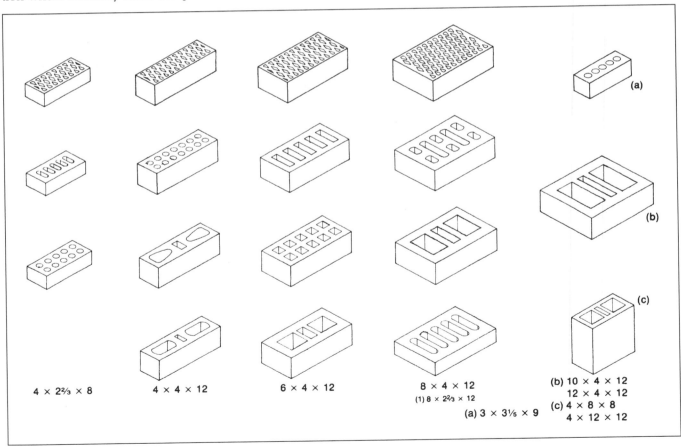

Figure 4.47 Hollow brick. (Reproduced by permission. Brick Institute of America, *Tech Note No. 41, Revised,* September 1988)

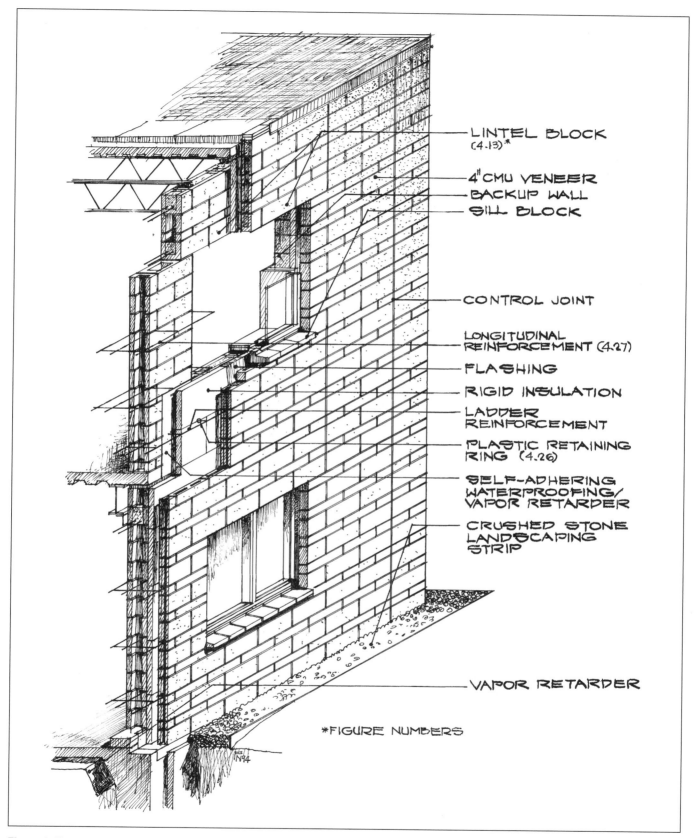

LINTEL BLOCK (4.13)*

4" CMU VENEER

BACKUP WALL

SILL BLOCK

CONTROL JOINT

LONGITUDINAL REINFORCEMENT (4.27)

FLASHING

RIGID INSULATION

LADDER REINFORCEMENT

PLASTIC RETAINING RING (4.26)

SELF-ADHERING WATERPROOFING/ VAPOR RETARDER

CRUSHED STONE LANDSCAPING STRIP

VAPOR RETARDER

*FIGURE NUMBERS

Figure 4.48 Concrete masonry unit assembly.

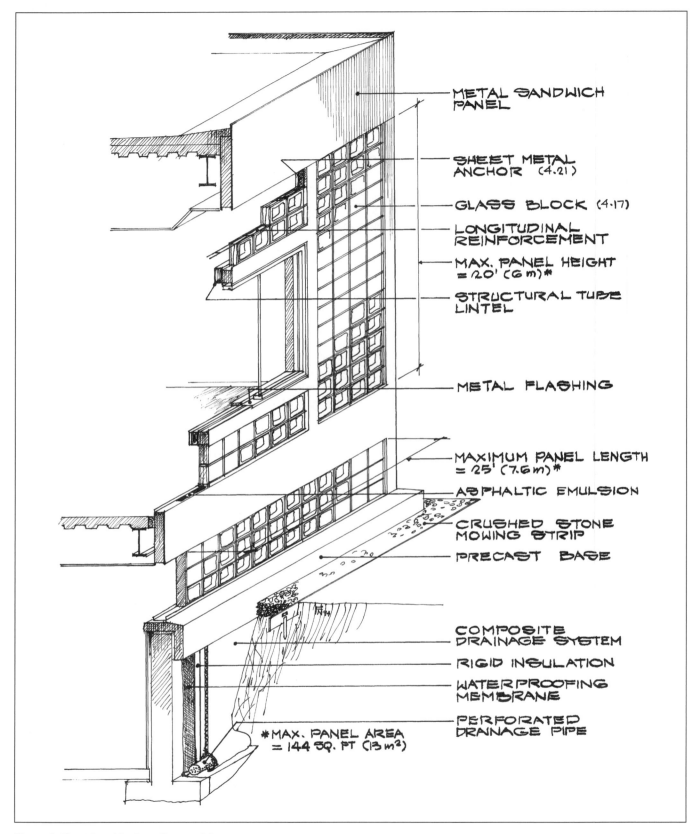

METAL SANDWICH PANEL

SHEET METAL ANCHOR (4.21)

GLASS BLOCK (4.17)

LONGITUDINAL REINFORCEMENT

MAX. PANEL HEIGHT = 20' (6m)*

STRUCTURAL TUBE LINTEL

METAL FLASHING

MAXIMUM PANEL LENGTH = 25' (7.6m)*

ASPHALTIC EMULSION

CRUSHED STONE MOWING STRIP

PRECAST BASE

COMPOSITE DRAINAGE SYSTEM

RIGID INSULATION

WATERPROOFING MEMBRANE

PERFORATED DRAINAGE PIPE

*MAX. PANEL AREA = 144 SQ. FT (13m²)

Figure 4.49   Glass block wall assembly.

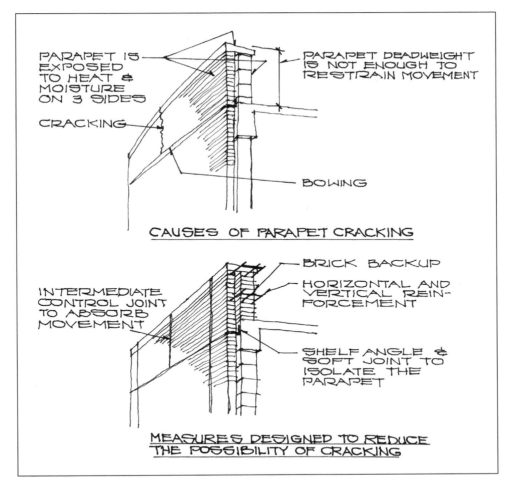

Figure 4.50 Parapet cracking.

Glass block is hollow, while glass brick is solid. Because glass has a relatively high expansion rate, it must be divided into panels not to exceed 144 ft² (13 m²) in area for glass block and 100 ft² (9.25 m²) for glass brick. These panels must be surrounded by soft joints.

The mortar type most commonly used is type N. Type S is recommended for walls two or more stories in height, and type M is used in foundations. Masonry cements are premixed. Their components are proprietary, and their strength must be determined by testing. Grout is a low-slump type of mortar used to fill voids around reinforcement, collar joints, and other locations. It is described as *fine grout* when it is a mixture of sand and cement and as *coarse grout* if it is composed of pea gravel, sand, and cement. Lime is added to the mixture in both cases.

Control joints in unit masonry should be spaced at approximately 25-ft (7.6 m) intervals, at offsets, between elements with different heights, at openings, and near corners. These joints allow the wall to move to accommodate thermal expansion, contraction, and creep.

Metal unit ties anchor the veneer to the backup wall while allowing it to move both vertically and longitudinally. They should be placed as close as possible to the top and bottom of the panel. Longitudinal reinforcement is used in both solid and cavity masonry walls and as part of the reinforcement in load-bearing, reinforced walls.

Shelf angles carry the veneer. They must be designed to a maximum deflection of $L/600$ and to a rotation less than 1/16 in (1.5 mm). Their final adjustment and fixation must be coordinated between the mason and the miscellaneous steel installer. Loose lintels should be sized by the structural engineer. Steel lintel angles should not be less than 3½ × 3 × 3/16 in (90 × 75 × 8 mm) and have a minimum bearing of 4 in (100 mm) at each side of the opening. Stone and cast stone are also used as lintels.

Flashing directs water accumulations in the cavity toward weep holes in the veneer. It protects shelf angles and lintels and is placed under copings and sills and over grade beams. Lead-coated copper and stainless steel are preferred. Flexible flashing may be installed over shelf angles if it is combined with metal flashing.

Figure 4.51   Detail from the Great Hall at the Temple of Karnak, Egypt.

Efflorescence is caused by the passage of water through mortar or brick, dissolving certain salts and depositing them on the exterior face of the wall. Using low-alkali cement, testing the brick, preventing the accumulation of water during construction, and tooling the joints can go a long way toward preventing this problem. Brushing and using a high-pressure water spray can be used to remove efflorescence.

Cracking is caused by many factors including the location and width of vertical and horizontal control joints, structural inadequacies, and differential movements.

Figure 4.52   Dovetail stone ties at the top of a wall. Temple of Edfou, Egypt. (Traced from a photograph; Auguste Choisy, *L'Art de bâtir chez les Égyptiens,* 1904)

4.3   STONE WALLS

4.3.1   Historical Background

Stone masonry was used throughout history to construct important, long-lasting buildings. Its abundance and proven durability made it a natural choice for that purpose around the world. The ancient Egyptians constructed their first mastabas (burial chambers), pyramids, and temples using stone in the third millennium B.C. They developed a distinctive architecture with a structural logic that stands as a testimony to their great culture to this day (Fig. 4.51). They introduced several construction innovations including gypsum mortar and dovetail connections fashioned from lead, copper, stone, or wood to connect stones, a precursor to the masonry ties used today (Fig. 4.52). They engraved a record detailing many of their activities on these temple walls and burial chambers. Unfortunately, these records did not detail their methods of construction for these architectural marvels. The means of hoisting gigantic stones to great heights remain a mystery. To this day, nobody is sure how the pyramids were built.

The Egyptians were followed by the Greeks who introduced the architectural "orders" which form the basis of western classic architecture (Fig. 4.53). Many of these orders were slightly modified by the Romans who constructed many of the significant buildings in Europe,

North Africa, and the Middle East during their long reign. The Romans spanned large openings using the arch, a design credited to the Etruscans whose history is rather obscure. The Romans along with the Greeks before them, used molten lead poured through channels carved in the stone to connect and align the pieces (Fig. 4.54).

Stone reached its top potential for refinement in the Middle Ages. During that time, master builders designed graceful structures with intricate detailing. They introduced flying buttresses to resist the thrust of their vaulted ceilings. Rainwater was channeled into a system of gutters leading to scuppers sculpted into cantilevered grotesque figures known as gargoyles. It is conceivable that LeCorbusier was inspired by these gargoyles when he designed the scuppers for the chapel at Ronchamp (Fig. 4.55). In a similar manner, architects can draw inspiration from the past to introduce innovative designs using today's materials and technology.

Examples of impressive stone buildings can be seen all over the world. The limited space prevents me from elaborating on innovations introduced by Islamic, Asian, and South American civilizations. Load-bearing stone walls are sturdy and durable requiring little maintenance. Thick stone walls have the capacity to dampen the diurnal temperature swings by absorbing solar heat during the day and radiating it back during the night

Figure 4.54 Molten-lead channels in Roman stone masonry used in lieu of mortar. (From Joseph Durm, *Die Baukunst der Römer,* 1905)

(see Sec. 1.4.2). However, they have the following drawbacks:

1. They are heavy and thus require more substantial foundations.

2. Shipping and handling costs more, and they require more time to erect.

3. The side of the wall facing the interior is usually left exposed to view because of stone's aesthetic appeal. This means, however, that the wall is uninsulated and cold to the touch especially in colder climates.

4. Spaces surrounded by this type of wall require more energy to heat and are noisier when crowded because the hard surfaces reflect sound waves.

5. The walls are thicker and occupy more area lessening the habitable space.

All these shortcomings have made this type of wall unsuitable in today's construction scene except on rare occasions. Thin stone veneers, 2 in (50 mm) thick or less, were developed to give the appearance of solid stone walls while avoiding their disadvantages. In most instances, one cannot tell the difference between the two because of the concealed fasteners and supporting structure. As will be explained later in this section, this type of construction must be detailed very carefully to avoid the many problems that can occur during its useful life span.

4.3.2 Components

To detail exterior stone-clad walls properly, architects must become acquainted with the components and support systems currently available. After the decision is made to use stone as the cladding material, the architect should meet with one or two stone fabricators to gather information about the durability, bearing capacity, opti-

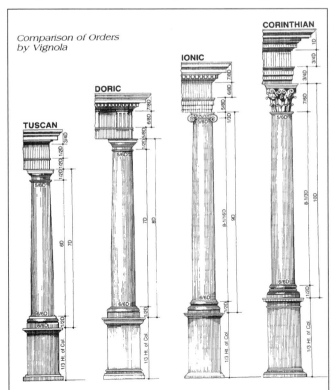

Figure 4.53 Classical architectural orders. (From Hartmann Sanders Co.)

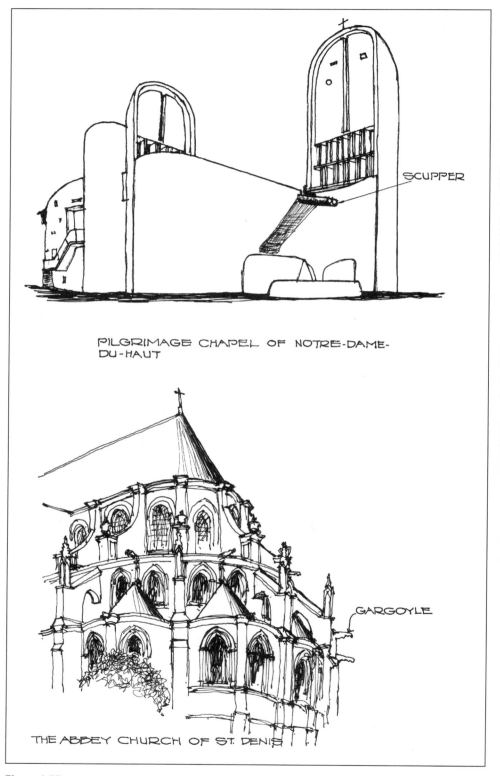

PILGRIMAGE CHAPEL OF NOTRE-DAME-DU-HAUT

SCUPPER

THE ABBEY CHURCH OF ST. DENIS

GARGOYLE

Figure 4.55   Scupper at the chapel at Ronchamp could have been inspired by medieval gargoyles.

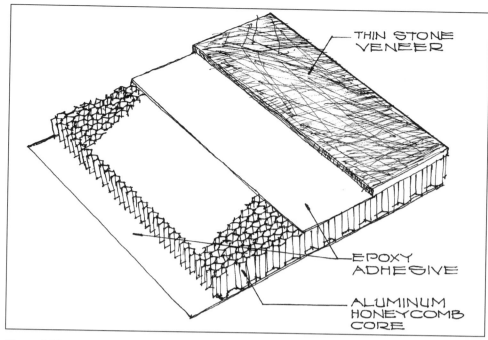

Figure 4.56 Lightweight, composite panels: The SPI system.

mum thickness, and panel sizes. Other information such as cost, the appropriate anchoring hardware and assemblies suitable for the budget, and local practice should also be discussed. Based on that information, the architect sketches typical wall sections and discusses them with the structural engineer to determine points of support, control joints, the effect of structural deformation due to seismic and wind forces, as well as the extent of deflection. Other issues that may affect the design such as the minimum tolerances are also discussed.

This subsection provides information about the various types of stone, their methods of construction, and the miscellaneous hardware used to anchor them. Structural information is included in Chap. 2, joint sealants are described in Sec. 1.3.2, and seismic effects are described in Sec. 1.5.

STONE

There are three types of stone groupings: igneous, sedimentary, and metamorphic. Igneous rock was formed by volcanic action: granite, traprock, and lava rock fall into this group. Sedimentary stone was formed by shell fragment accumulations (limestone), sand (sandstone), and other ingredients which settled as sediment under water. These sediments were incorporated into rock through adhesion by natural cementing agents and compaction. Oolitic limestone, dolomite limestone, and other varieties fall under this group. (Oology is a branch of ornithology dealing with birds' eggs. The structure of oolitic limestone consists of small, round grains resem-

bling fish eggs.) Sandstone can be either coarse, medium-, or fine-grained. Most sandstone used in buildings is medium-grained. Metamorphic stone (stone that has changed form or metamorphosed from another type of stone) was formed from sedimentary rock exposed to tremendous heat and pressure. Marble, slate, schist, gneiss, and quartzite are examples. Marble is subdivided into four groupings: A, B, C, and D. Type A marbles are flawless, type B less so, and so on.

Polishing the stone can darken the color and express the veining more clearly. A shiny finish will not last on polished marble exposed to the weather because of the effect of mild acids in rain.

Stone panel thickness varies depending on the type of stone and the size of the piece. Structurally weaker stones are cut thicker than stronger stone. Likewise, the larger the piece, the thicker it must be to resist the stresses that occur during shipping and handling. The added thickness is also needed to resist the positive and negative wind pressures once it is mounted on the building.

A relative newcomer to the industry are composite thin stone systems created by bonding a thin stone veneer ranging in thickness from 4 to 7 mm (5/32 to 5/16 in) to a steel mesh or an aluminum honeycomb backing to form exterior cladding panels. These panels, which weigh substantially less than conventional stone panels (see Fig. 4.56 for an example), are easily field cut and do not require heavy hoisting equipment resulting in a cost savings over conventional construction. While a

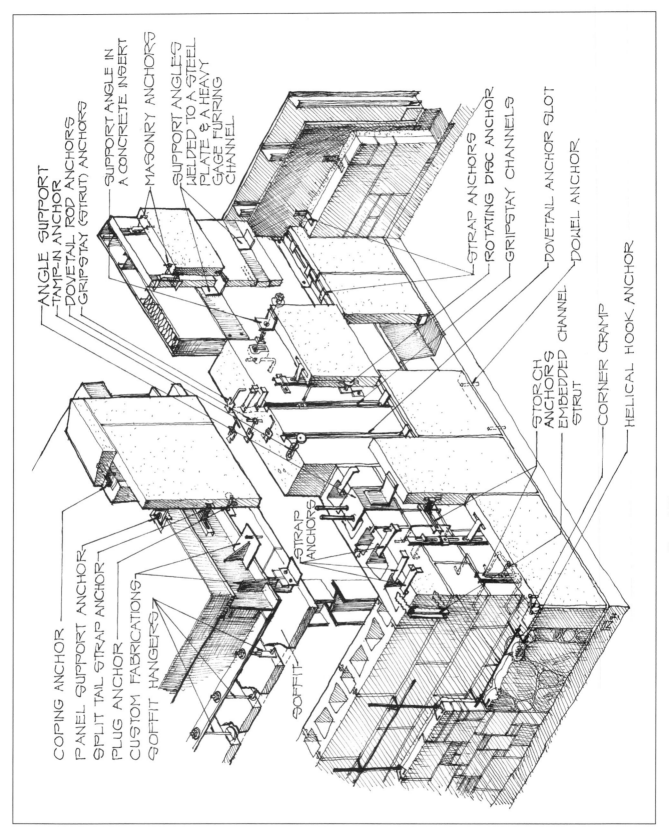

ANGLE SUPPORT
TAMP-IN ANCHOR
DOVETAIL ROD ANCHORS
GRIPSTAY (STRUT) ANCHORS
SUPPORT ANGLE IN A CONCRETE INSERT
MASONRY ANCHORS
SUPPORT ANGLES WELDED TO A STEEL PLATE & A HEAVY GAGE FURRING CHANNEL

STRAP ANCHORS
ROTATING DISC ANCHOR
GRIPSTAY CHANNELS
DOVETAIL ANCHOR SLOT
DOWEL ANCHOR

STORCH ANCHORS
EMBEDDED CHANNEL
STRUT
CORNER CRAMP
HELICAL HOOK ANCHOR

COPING ANCHOR
PANEL SUPPORT ANCHOR
SPLIT TAIL STRAP ANCHOR
PLUG ANCHOR
CUSTOM FABRICATIONS
SOFFIT HANGERS

STRAP ANCHORS

SOFFIT

Figure 4.57 Stone anchors in different backup walls.

Figure 4.58 The Ames Building, Boston (designed by Shepley, Rutan & Coolidge, Architects, 1889).

Figure 4.59 Using different finishes on the same stone to create ornamental patterns.

few high- and medium-rise buildings have used this product, the long-term durability of this system in exterior applications has not been established as yet because of the fact that it has not been on the market long enough. This product, however, is definitely suitable for some applications where weight is critical such as recladding over existing facades in remodeling work and for use in seismically active zones.

The choice between the hand-set method and a panelized system is governed by many factors including the size of the project, the prevalent skill and practices in the locality, project schedule, weather conditions, and cost. For example, a large project located in an area plagued by inclement weather and scheduled for completion in a short time almost mandates the use of a panelized system because the panels can be shop-fabricated in an area protected from the weather, transported to the site, and hoisted to their final positions in

a relatively short time. The opposite is true for a smaller project located in an area with good weather, plentiful skilled labor, and a generous deadline.

ANCHORING HARDWARE

Anchors used to fasten thin stone to a backup must be manufactured from a durable nonstaining metal. Stainless steel is the metal most often used. Stone anchors are manufactured in standard shapes (Fig. 4.57). The stone fabricator is a good source of information about which anchors to use for different conditions. The Marble Institute of America (MIA) recommends the following guideline for locating the anchors:

> Under typical conditions, trade practices provide for a minimum of four anchors per piece of stone up to 12 square feet of surface area, and two for each additional eight square feet. Weight, size, shape, and type of stone may dictate deviations from the foregoing. Stainless steel, bronze, and brass wire and straps, and copper wire are preferred for their non-corrosive qualities.[20]

The MIA further recommends that relieving angles be provided over all openings and at each story height (maximum vertical spacing should not exceed 20 ft) and that studs be a minimum 16 gauge. The wire ties mentioned above are usually used to fasten stone to low-rise buildings or for interior applications.

If studs are used as a backup, the architect should make a tentative layout of the studs superimposed on the elevation, sketch the position of the anchors, and modify the layout as needed based on discussions with the structural engineer and stone fabricators. The construction documents must include the design loads and require that the fabricator provide shop drawings signed and sealed by a structural engineer registered in the state. These drawings must be checked to ensure that they do not conflict with the architectural design intent. They are then passed on to the project engineer to be checked for structural integrity.

4.3.3 Ornamentation

Stone ornamentation can take several forms. Historically, craftspeople carved stone into intricate patterns and moldings (Fig. 4.58). This type of ornamentation has become prohibitively expensive and is currently reserved for preservation work on significant historic buildings. In today's vernacular, ornamentation can be achieved by creating patterns composed of contrasting finishes. A similar effect can be achieved using stone with contrasting colors. Introducing other materials as inserts is another way to embellish the facade. These materials can be metal, ceramic tile, or other durable materials matching the longevity of the stone. Arranging the stone pieces to articulate the facade either horizontally or vertically is another approach.

While ornamentation can enrich the design, the architect should minimize the number of joints between stone pieces. This can be achieved by having one large piece of stone polished, subdividing its surface with false joints, masking parts of the panel, and applying a rough finish to the remaining parts to create the pattern (Fig. 4.59). If the pattern is created by stones with different colors, the different pieces may be preassembled as a veneer with precast, GFRC, or stud backing. In this case, the coefficients of thermal expansion for all the different pieces should be approximately the same.

Too much ornamentation can add substantially to the cost and, unless done tastefully, can become monotonous. Choosing focal points like main entrances, win-

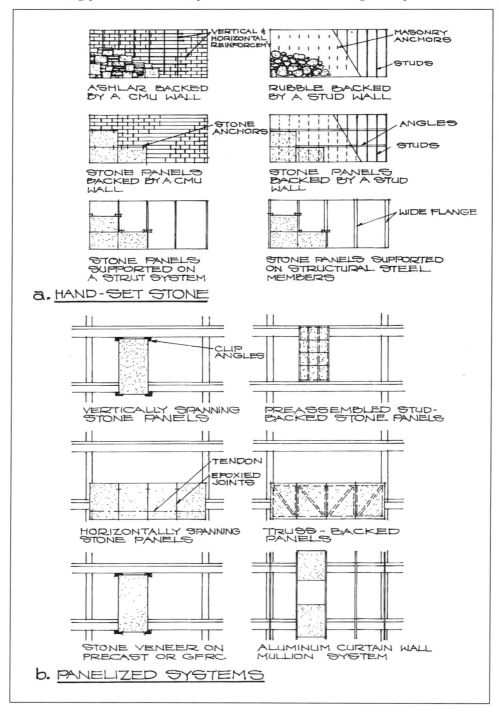

Figure 4.60 Hand-set and panelized stone systems.

Figure 4.61 Common patterns for hand-set stone walls.

dow surrounds, and elevation tops and bottoms to apply the ornamentation and leaving the rest of the elevation plain is a common approach.

4.3.4 Assemblies and Details

Choosing the right kind of stone and the type of assembly suitable for the project depends on many factors. In addition to the obvious issue of color and texture choices addressed by the designer, the stone must be durable, especially if the building is subject to temperature extremes, freeze-thaw cycles, and acid rain or smog. It must also have a good bearing capacity in relationship to the stone thickness bearing on the supports.

The designer must investigate the availability of the stone especially if it is imported. The importance of this

issue was demonstrated in a program series entitled "Skyscraper" aired by PBS (public television). The series monitored the construction of a high-rise building in New York City. In one of the segments, the stone subcontractor failed to deliver the imported stone cladding on time causing the completion date for the multimillion dollar project to be postponed. The developer had to face the possibility of being sued by the major tenant, a prominent law firm, for a breach of contract. Of course, postponing the delivery date meant that the developer could not collect rent to make payments on the construction loan as well. To avoid this dilemma, the architect should secure a written commitment from the quarry stating that the chosen type of stone shall be supplied in the quantities required for the project and deliv-

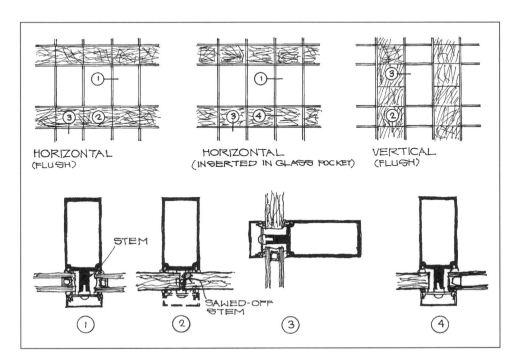

Figure 4.62 Some of the different ways used to integrate stone panels into a curtain wall mullion system.

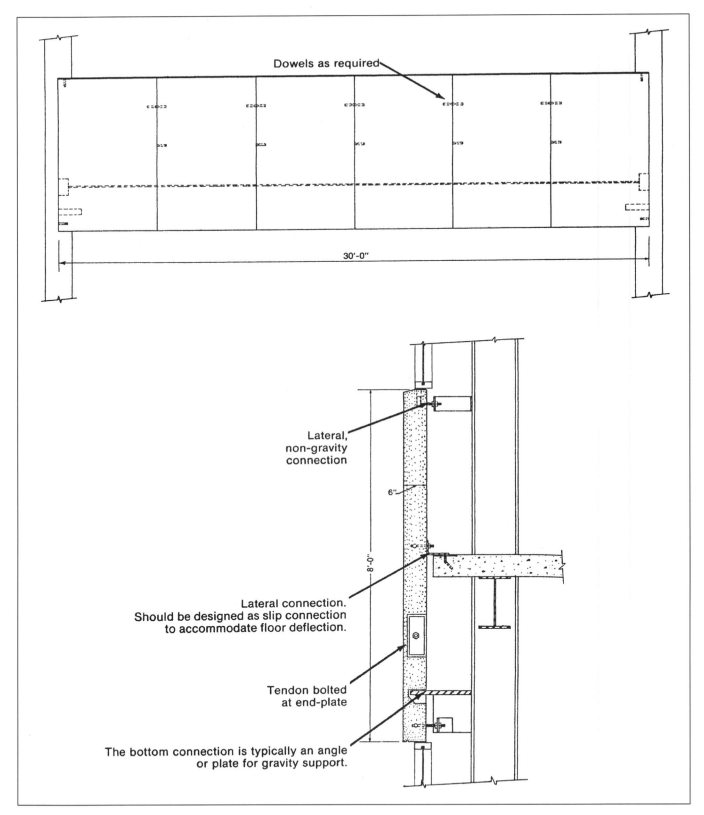

Figure 4.63 Posttensioned, horizontal spanning stone panel. (Reproduced by permission; from Indiana Limestone Institute of America, Inc., *Indiana Limestone Handbook,* 19th ed., 1992)

ered within a certain period of time after the award of contract upon request by the general contractor. Otherwise, the quarry would be assessed a specified penalty. Designating another type of stone as an acceptable alternate to be priced by the bidder and supplied if the first choice does not materialize at a set time may be another avenue to pursue.

HAND-SET SYSTEMS

Setting stone piece by piece is referred to as *hand-set stone*. The individual stones may be light enough to be lifted by hand and laid in the wall in a manner similar to brick masonry [Fig. 4.60(*a*)]. Walls built in this fashion can be coursed or uncoursed as shown in Fig. 4.61. Limestone used in this application is laid in mortar containing more lime than cement. Hand-set stone may also be mechanically hoisted and maneuvered to its final position by hand.

PANELIZED SYSTEMS

Stone may be shop-fabricated and assembled into panels. These panels may be all-stone construction; a stone veneer backed with precast, GFRC, or a metal subframe composed of a steel truss; or a stud assembly. In glass curtain walls, stone panels may be integrated into the mullion system to form spandrel panels [Fig. 4.60(*b*)]. Mullions may be modified to allow the stone to form a continuous surface either horizontally or vertically depending on the design (Fig. 4.62). Horizontally spanning panels are usually attached to columns. An intermediate lateral support may be required to brace the panel against wind pressure or seismic movement. This support must be designed to allow the spandrel beam to deflect independently from the panel (Figs. 2.20 and 4.63).

Choosing the appropriate type of assembly whether it is hand-set or panelized is a decision that requires some research. It depends upon the following factors.

1. *The design of the facade.* Strip windows suggest that the stone be arranged in horizontal panels; punched windows may suggest a whole bay panel or vertical panels. Stone accents in glass curtain walls may require that the stone be installed at the curtain wall installer's shop.

2. *The type of backup.* Ashlar and small stone panels suggest that the stones be hand set with ties to a masonry or stud backup (Fig. 4.57). Larger stone areas with widely spaced joints may suggest large panelized systems used as a veneer either over precast or GFRC or attached to a steel truss or to special subframes [Fig. 4.60(*b*)]. Alternatively, the stone panel itself may span either horizontally between columns or vertically between floors.

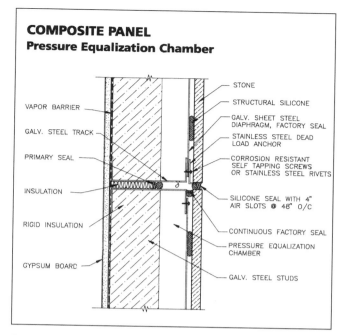

Figure 4.64 Example of a rain screen design. (From Eastern Exterior Wall Systems, Inc.).

3. *Weight.* If the bearing soil is weak or the project is located in a seismically active area, weight can be a critical factor. Lightweight systems such as stone-veneered GFRC or truss-backed stone panels would be preferable to precast or stone-only panels. The lightweight systems achieve savings in the support structure and foundations. Steel truss systems, because of their economies of weight, are suited for spans that exceed 35 ft (11 m).

4. *The defense strategy against leakage.* The decision to construct the cladding as a barrier wall or a rain screen, pressure-equalized system has an impact on which type of construction to select. The rain screen design requires a second line of defense which suggests a compartmented panel design with two-stage vented joints (Fig. 4.64), while the barrier wall can be achieved with any of the systems described above.

These are a few considerations that suggest to the detailers which systems to investigate. Of course, the project budget is the ultimate influence on which system shall be chosen, and, for panelized systems, the distance from the fabricator's shop to the site can, in some cases, also be a cost factor. If it is too far, the cost of transportation and handling can tip the scales in favor of another system or even of another type of cladding.

Figure 4.65 illustrates an assembly clad in marble based on the Zibell anchoring system used by the Georgia Marble Company, Atlanta, which is shown in Fig. 4.66. The system is designed to support ⅞-in (22 mm) or

1¼-in (32 mm) marble; it is relatively lightweight, goes up fast, and provides adequate support for the panels. The position of the kerf (the saw cut in the thickness of the stone to engage the anchor) must be determined very carefully. It is affected by the strength of the stone and the lateral forces that are imposed on it. Strut anchoring systems require scaffolding. This makes them suitable only for low-rise and remodeling projects.

Because the support for this system cannot be integrated in the backup wall, all the defenses against water

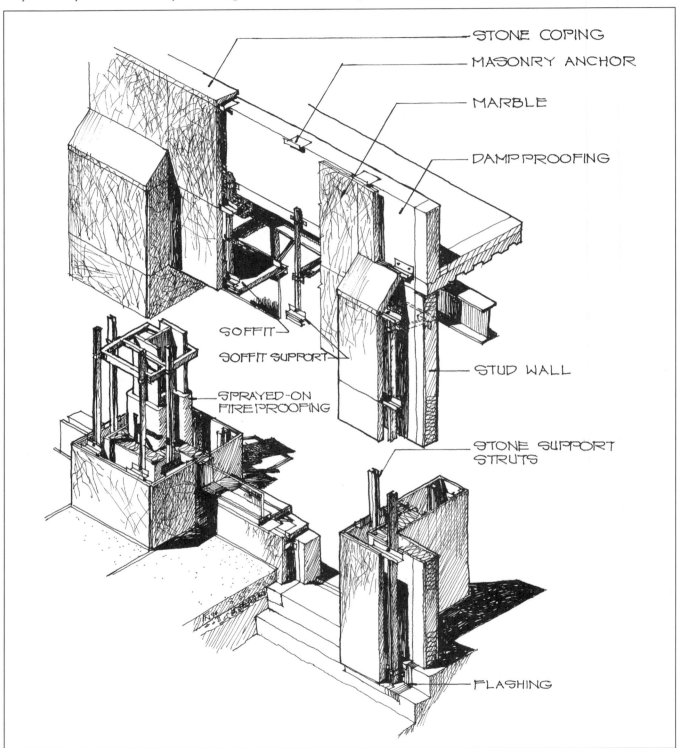

STONE COPING
MASONRY ANCHOR
MARBLE
DAMP PROOFING
SOFFIT
SOFFIT SUPPORT
SPRAYED-ON FIREPROOFING
STUD WALL
STONE SUPPORT STRUTS
FLASHING

Figure 4.65   Isometric drawing of a strut-backed marble assembly.

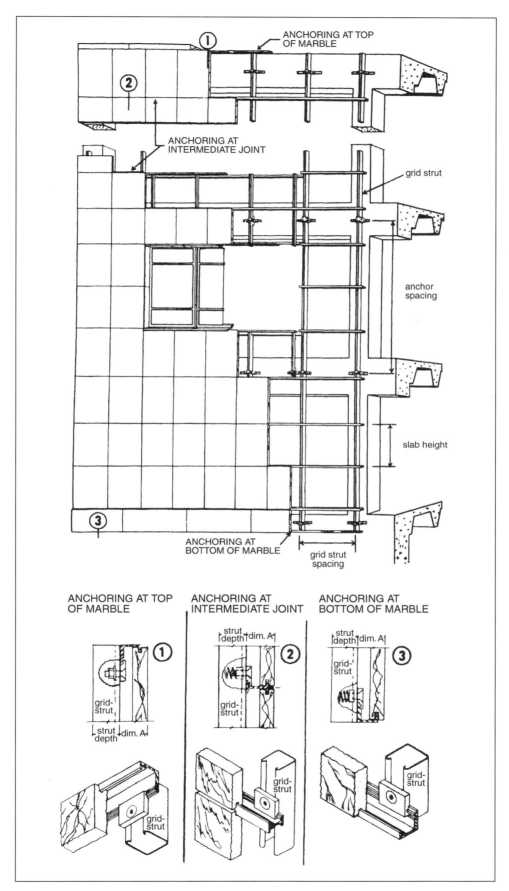

Figure 4.66 The Zibell Anchoring System. (From Georgia Marble Co.)

157

and air infiltration from the exterior and vapor exfiltration from the interior (see Chap. 1) must be provided. Also, isolation between different metals (the struts are galvanized steel while the hardware engaging the stone is aluminum) must be provided to prevent corrosion that is caused by electrolysis (see Sec. 1.6.2). This sys-

tem is a hand-set system.

Figure 4.67 represents an example of heavy construction using limestone backed by a CMU wall. This type of assembly is also suitable for sandstone and granite. It is supported at each floor by a shelf angle. Individual panels are attached to the backup with anchors grouted into

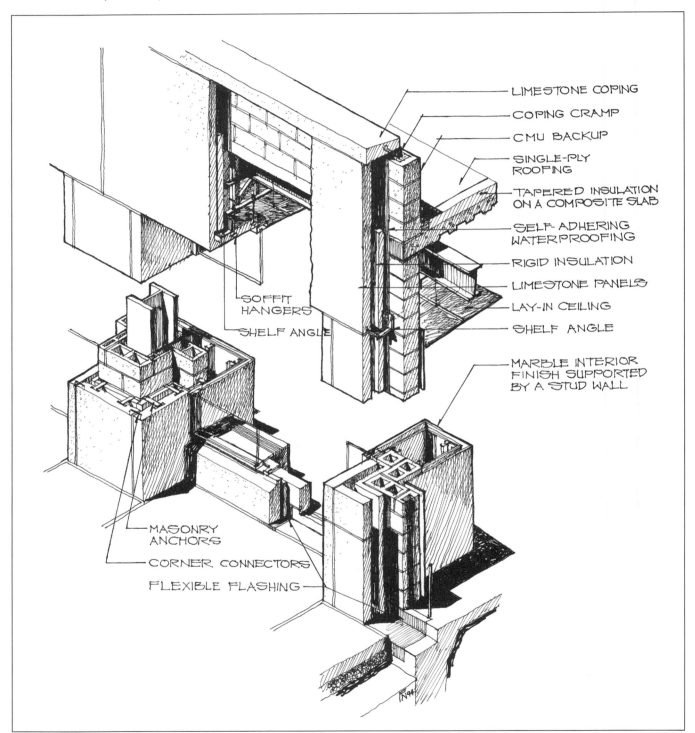

Figure 4.67   Isometric drawing of a CMU-backed limestone assembly.

the CMU cells. Rigid insulation is installed in the cavity over an adhered waterproofing membrane which also acts as a vapor retarder. Alternatively, rigid or semirigid insulation may be installed on the inside using zee furring channels or other methods designed to receive the wallboard. This wall assembly is very durable and provides a good defense against sound and thermal transmission. It is a hand-set system.

Figure 4.68 illustrates a stone assembly using a shop-fabricated system with a welded stud backing. As a gen-

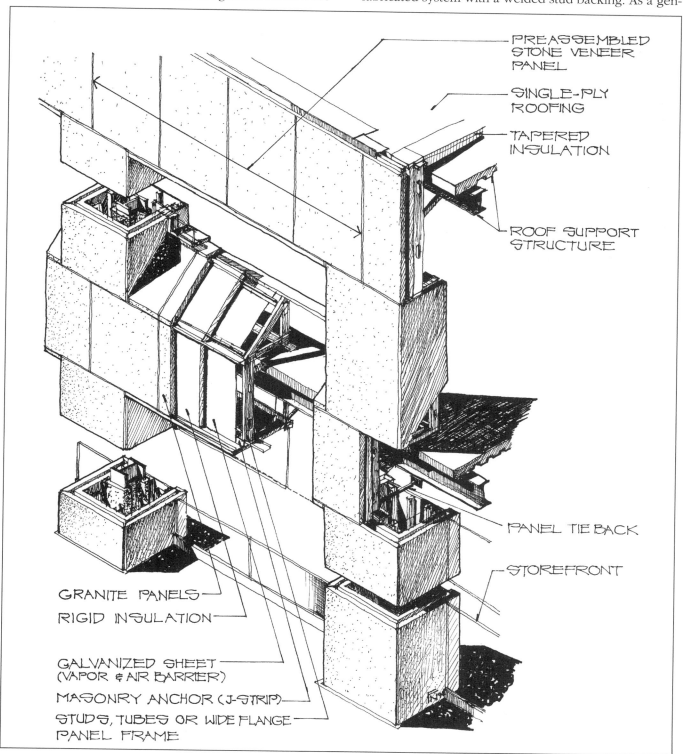

PREASSEMBLED STONE VENEER PANEL

SINGLE-PLY ROOFING

TAPERED INSULATION

ROOF SUPPORT STRUCTURE

PANEL TIE BACK

STOREFRONT

GRANITE PANELS
RIGID INSULATION
GALVANIZED SHEET (VAPOR & AIR BARRIER)
MASONRY ANCHOR (J-STRIP)
STUDS, TUBES OR WIDE FLANGE PANEL FRAME

Figure 4.68   Isometric drawing of a panelized assembly using stud-backed granite.

eral rule, studs supporting a stone veneer should be at least 16 gauge. Panels spanning from column to column require a truss support to resist the substantial lateral and gravity forces. This particular example shows a beam-supported panelized system. The tie backs are located at the bottom of the panel. Flat panels are usually supported at the bottom and tied back at the top (Fig. 4.69). An example of a stud-backed limestone panel is shown in Fig. 4.70.

Granite is a hard and durable stone that can be expressed in many finishes ranging from polished to rough. The assembly shown in this drawing places the insulation at the exterior to avoid thermal bridging. It provides a galvanized sheet to act as a barrier to water, vapor, and air as well as to brace the studs. A means of draining the narrow cavity between the insulation and the granite must be provided.

These illustrations depict a few of the many kinds of stone assemblies available today. Some of the other assemblies are covered in the text.

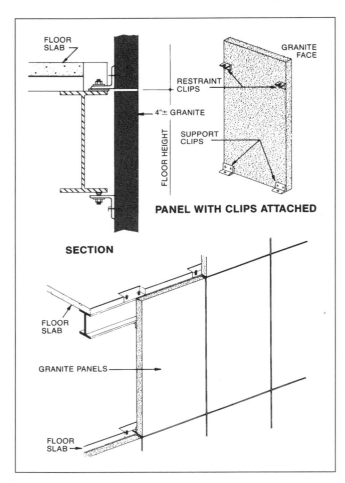

Figure 4.69 Example of vertically spanning stone panels. (From a granite manufacturer's literature.)

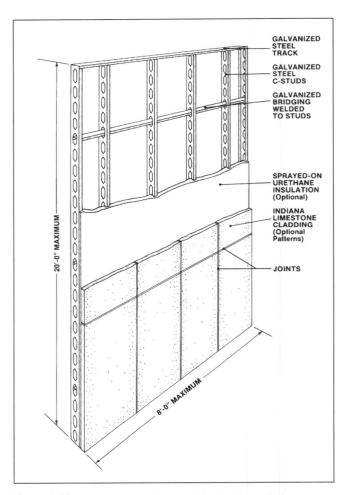

Figure 4.70 Example of a flat, stud-backed panel. (From Harding & Cogswell Corp.)

4.3.5 What Can Go Wrong

Several problems can develop when thin stone cladding is chosen. Acid rain and pollution can cause the surface to erode; certain marbles may bend; anchorages may develop problems; leakage in the system may enter into stone pores causing stains and efflorescence, and, in severe cases, water can freeze in cracks and cause the stone to spall. Even certain finishes can be detrimental to the long-term stability of the stone. A description of some of these problems follows.

HYSTERESIS

Some marbles have a tendency to become bowed into dish shapes if the panel thickness is not adequate to resist the stresses caused by temperature differences between the face exposed to the sun and the back of the panel. These marbles, unlike other types of stone, do not return to their original dimension after the sun sets. This phenomenon is referred to as *hysteresis*. In addition to the dishing effect mentioned above, the stone becomes weaker and more susceptible to attack by pollutants and the freeze-thaw cycle.

Hysteresis can be very costly. For instance, Chicago's 80-story Amoco building was faced with 1¼-in (32 mm) thick Carrara marble cladding in 1974 which had to be replaced recently by 2-in (50 mm) thick granite at a cost of 60 to 80 million dollars because of panel distortion in the original marble.[21]

ANCHORAGE PROBLEMS

Concentrated stresses caused by shims must be avoided. The specifications should state the minimum area of the shims based on calculations by the structural engineer. Temporary shims used in leveling the stone must be removed after the final attachment to avoid stone fracture due to point loads. Panel thickness must not be determined before the support system is engineered and the selected stone's properties are evaluated. These supports must be permitted to move independently from the building structure to allow it to deform without causing stress in the cladding components.

Anchors embedded in stone should be manufactured from 302 or 304 stainless steel isolated from dissimilar metals to prevent electrolysis (galvanic action) from eroding the metal (see Sec. 1.6.2). All kerfs must be sealed with a durable sealer such as silicon to prevent water from accumulating in these troughs, freezing, and spalling the stone. In fact, any part of the stone profile that has the potential for entrapping water must be modified to avoid this potential problem.

LEAKAGE

Wall assemblies must be detailed to minimize leakage. This can be achieved either by designing the cladding as a drained cavity wall or as a rain screen (see Chap. 3). Ian Chin of Wiss, Janney, Elstner (WJE), an architectural

Figure 4.71 Dark areas on granite caused by water accumulation in the cavity.

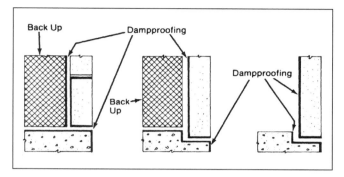

Figure 4.72 Locations of dampproofing in limestone walls.

engineering firm in Chicago with special expertise in stone technology, states that if water gets into the wall through the joints and seeps into the stone from behind, it cannot evaporate easily and may cause dark areas to appear (Fig. 4.71). If it freezes, it may cause the stone to spall off.[22]

Designing the cladding as a drained cavity is always the most prudent course to take. In some cases, architects are so occupied with solving problems associated with support, aesthetics, insulation, joint width, and stone thickness that they forget to specify and locate the weep tubes required to drain the system. An experienced and conscientious stone fabricator usually rectifies this oversight. It is a good policy, however, to indicate their location on the drawings.

EXFOLIATION

Sedimentary stones, especially sandstone, have a tendency to absorb water especially if the thin stone is placed with its bedding plane parallel to the face of the stone (on edge). The *bedding plane* is the horizontal plane that the layers of sediment were formed on. In that position, the thin stone acts as a blotter sucking any moisture accumulation beneath it. If the water freezes and expands within the stone, layers will start spalling off the surface weakening the stone, marring the facade, and posing a danger to pedestrians.

To avoid the possibility of exfoliation, the specifications must stipulate that the stone be cut with its face perpendicular to the bedding plane and that it be allowed to dry out before installation. This type of wall assembly must be detailed carefully to prevent any water accumulation beneath or behind the stone. A drained cavity behind the stone veneer with properly detailed and executed flashing and weeps can go a long way toward mitigating this problem.

According to the Indiana Limestone Institute (ILI), if moisture charged with salts is allowed to permeate the stone from its back or bottom bed, crystal growth can occur below the stone's surface causing stress on pore walls. The result is flaking or exfoliation. The ILI recommends that dampproofing in the form of either waterproof cementitious or bituminous stone backing be applied to the unexposed stone surfaces up to 1 ft above grade (Fig. 4.72). The bituminous coatings are often difficult to apply cleanly and will retard mortar adherence.[23]

DESTRUCTIVE FINISHES

Bushhammering or thermal finishes cause a reduction in the effective thickness of the stone panel. Forrest Wilson, a professor emeritus at Catholic University in Washington, D.C., states,

> A ⅛ inch (3 mm) reduction of a 1¼ inch (32 mm) veneer reduces bending strength by roughly 20 percent and may increase elastic deflection under wind loads by as much as 37 percent. This problem can be further affected by job-site weathering.
>
> Thermal treatment can result in micro-fracturing, particularly of quartz and feldspar. Thermal shock causes fracture along cleavages, and micro-cracks encourage water absorption with consequent degradation due to cyclic freezing.[24]

This information was based on conversations Mr. Wilson had with the scientists at the firm of WJE mentioned above.

Ian Chin suggests that a water blast finish in which the stone is subjected to a thin water jet at pressures as high as 20,000 lb/in² (137.9 MPa) results in a rough texture without microcracking.[17] Architects should consider this type of surface treatment as an alternative to thermal finish.

These are but a few examples of what can go wrong. Thin stone assemblies are, in most cases, dependable if detailed properly. The person entrusted with the details must observe the required tolerances and clearances, choose the right panel thickness (especially when the method of mounting them requires kerfs), design the joints properly, and protect the panel backs from water infiltration. He or she must choose a type of stone that can withstand the weather conditions prevalent in the area of the project, specify a finish that does not detract from its strength, and provide the appropriate backup system. Conversations with stone fabricators and other consultants are essential in that regard.

Summary

Stone has been used in the construction of important buildings and monuments since ancient times. Today, thin stone cladding is used as a veneer or facer to precast or GFRC rather than as a bearing wall. This type of construction may be backed up by CMU or stud walls or assembled into panels spanning vertically between floors or horizontally between columns or metal deck backup panels.

The designer's choice of stone should not be based on aesthetics alone but rather on durability considerations especially if it is subject to acid rain and freeze-thaw cycles. The supplier must provide a guarantee of adequate supply and delivery on time. Choosing the most suitable assembly for the project is influenced by fenestration; the type of backup; weight limitations; and whether the wall is designed as a barrier, cavity, or rain screen. It also depends on local skills, the prevalent type of construction methods used in that locality, and the applicable building code.

Stone thickness is determined by panel size and the type of stone selected for the project. Stone falls under three categories. Igneous stone such as granite is a hard and durable stone formed by volcanic action. Sedimentary stone such as limestone and sandstone was formed by sedimentation of sea shells or sand in water or held together by natural cementing agents and compaction forces. Metamorphic stone such as marble was formed under tremendous heat and pressure.

Building stone may be hand set or assembled into panels. Hand-set stone may have CMU or stud backup or it may be attached to a subframe. Panelized systems may be constructed of stone capable of spanning horizontally or vertically, or it may be backed by studs, a truss system, GFRC, or precast concrete.

Three methods of ornamentation may be employed to enrich the facade. Contrasting finishes may be used to form a decorative pattern. Different colored pieces may be arranged to achieve a similar effect, or engraved designs may be included in the facade. Minimizing the number of joints should be the goal of the designer.

Many problems can plague thin stone construction. Among them are marble hysteresis, weakening of the stone by destructive finishes, leakage, and anchorage problems caused by shimming or deformations in the building structural frame. All anchors must be manufactured of stainless steel or other durable metals.

4.4 CEMENT-BASED SYSTEMS

4.4.1 Historical Background

Cement-based wall systems are those which include Portland cement in their fabrication. Site-cast, precast, and glass fiber reinforced concrete fall into this category. Concrete masonry unit wall systems, which are in a gray area between unit masonry and cement-based wall assemblies, were discussed in Sec. 4.2.

SITE-CAST CONCRETE

Concrete was first introduced by the Romans who used *pozzolana* (a volcanic ash) mixed with slaked lime to form a crude cementitious material which they mixed with stone rubble to form a primitive kind of concrete. This concrete formed the bulk of the massive Roman walls, triumphal arches, and vaulted roofs (Fig. 4.73). The wall facings were built conventionally using dressed stone, brick, or a combination of both. In a similar fashion, the Dutch used *trass,* a light-colored volcanic material to form concrete in the seventeenth and eighteenth centuries. They were followed by Joseph Aspidin, an Englishman who in 1824 patented the process to produce Portland cement in reference to Portland stone, a durable and much used stone in England.

The idea of introducing steel in the cement mixture may have been introduced by several individuals working individually. One of the first patents was granted to William B. Wilkinson for a steel cable reinforced flooring system in 1854. Thirteen years later, Joseph Monier, a Frenchman specializing in garden furniture, intro-

duced wire mesh into concrete to prevent his creations from cracking. The first application of reinforced concrete to architecture was done by his compatriot Auguste Perret in 1903 (Fig. 4.74). He was followed closely and apparently independently by Frank Lloyd Wright who constructed a church using exposed concrete for the walls, roof, and decorative elements. This was quite a break with tradition and the result was impressive (Fig. 4.75).[25]

PRECAST CONCRETE

The first use of precast concrete was also credited to Perret who used precast decorative screens in his design for Notre Dame Du Haut Cathedral finished in 1923. It was Pier Luigi Nervi, however, who raised precast con-

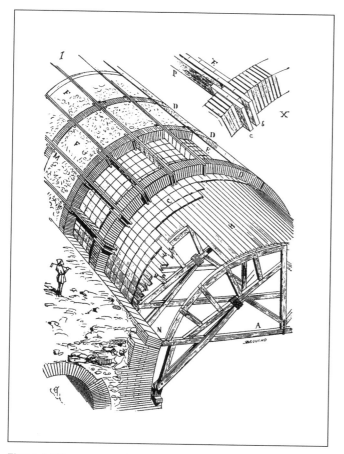

Figure 4.73 Concrete barrel vault and wall core as constructed by the Romans. (From Viollet-le-Duc, "Voûte," *Dictionnaire Raisonné,* Vol. 9, 1858–1868)

Figure 4.74 Apartment building at Rue Franklin, Paris (designed by Auguste Perret, architect, 1903).

crete to a fine art in the design of the many buildings he was entrusted with including the Palazzetto Dello Sport (Fig. 4.76).

GFRC

Glass fiber reinforced concrete is a relatively new product. It was developed in England in the mid-1960s and marketed by Pilkington Brothers Glass Company and its licensees worldwide. Because alkali in the concrete destroys glass fibers, the British developed an alkali-resistant glass. Russian researchers pursued a different approach to the problem. They altered the cement to reduce the amount of alkali affecting the glass. The Pilkington product was introduced in the United States in 1975.

4.4.2   Components

FORMS

While forms are not considered as a part of the final wall, they give the wall its final shape and represent a sizable percentage of the cost. Forms may be constructed of wood boards, plywood, steel, or fiberglass. Round column forms may be manufactured from a disposable, spirally wound fiber tube that can be peeled off and discarded after use. Alternatively, a reusable molded fiberglass tube can be used. Occasionally, precast concrete panels can function as a permanent form for columns and other wall elements (Fig. 4.77).

Forms must be properly braced to withstand the substantial pressure of wet concrete. They must be watertight to prevent the formation of *honeycombs* or *bug holes* and their surrounding dark stains. In addition, if a uniform color is required, as is the case whenever concrete is exposed to view, the form material should be

nonabsorptive ensuring that the form joints will not move or leak. Other potential leakage areas at the bottom of the form and around form ties must be sealed. These ties maintain the two form sides at a constant distance and are usually positioned approximately 2 ft (600 mm) on center in both directions. If the design calls for wider spacing, the forms may be engineered to accommodate this requirement. Figure 4.78 shows an example of a well-executed exposed concrete facade with evenly spaced ties, form joints, and rustications. Because it is difficult, if not impossible, to hide the imprint of form joints on a smooth finish wall, fake joints or rustications (Fig. 4.79) may be necessary. Other measures shown in the figure include:

1. Placing the reinforcement deeper inside the wall by increasing the concrete cover to 2 or 3 in (50 or 75 mm). This includes the tie wires which are often left protruding close to the surface causing rust and eventual spalling. Figure 4.80 shows an example where the cover was grossly inadequate. The exact thickness of the concrete cover depends on the composition of the mix and the size of reinforcement. The structural engineer should be consulted in that regard.

2. Sealing all the joints to prevent water from escaping at these junctures and causing voids and stains in the surface.

3. Providing studs and walers to adequately support the form and prevent it from bulging as a result of the pressure of wet concrete.

Ribbed, corrugated, or striated liners create some of the most popular surfaces imprinted with different rib spacing and depth executed to provide either smooth or

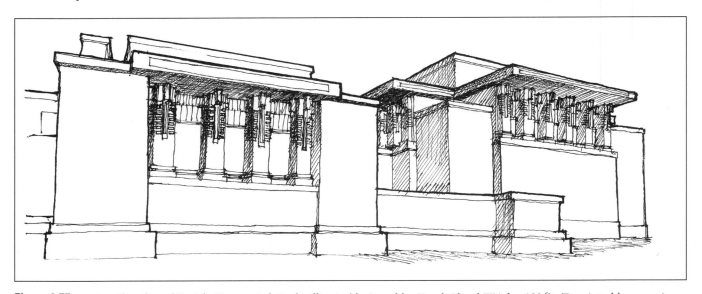

Figure 4.75   Unity Church and Parish House, Oak Park, Illinois (designed by Frank Lloyd Wright, 1906). (Reprinted by permission of Progressive Architecture, Penton Publishing)

Figure 4.76 The Palazzetto Dello Sport (designed by Pier Luigi Nervi, architect).

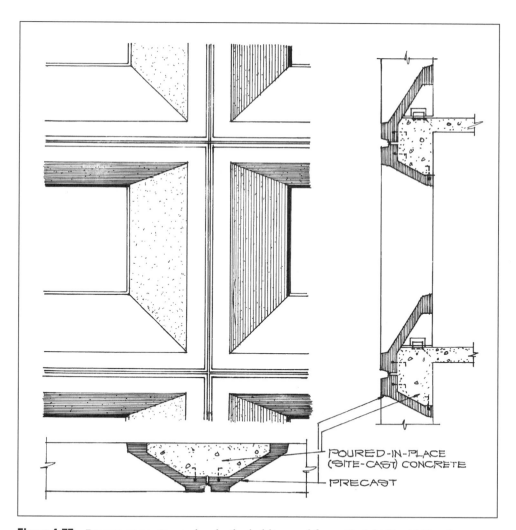

POURED-IN-PLACE
(SITE-CAST) CONCRETE

PRECAST

Figure 4.77 Precast concrete used as both cladding and form. Dwight David Eisenhower
Army Medical Center, Fort Gordon, Georgia. LBC&W, Architects. (Based on drawings and a
photo by Precast/Prestressed Concrete Institute, *Architectural Precast Concrete,* 1989; reproduced by permission)

Figure 4.78 Example of a well-executed exposed concrete facade.

fractured surfaces. Other liners create random parallel reveals, rough-sawn wood, simulated brick, or stone imprints. Heavy sandblasting, chemical etching, and jackhammering are also used to enrich the surface and hide its flaws. Some of these treatments can make the surface rough enough so as not to require rustication at form joints. False joints should, however, be introduced between pours because of the rough juncture and possible color differences at these locations.

Because concrete shrinks over time in a process called *creep*, the designer must include control joints to subdivide the facade into panels not to exceed 20 ft (6 m) in length. The American Concrete Institute recommends[26] that these joints be placed on both sides of the wall to reduce wall thickness by 25% and that horizontal reinforcement be reduced by 50% at the joint to ensure that shrinkage cracking will occur at that location rather than haphazardly. The joint must be sealed to prevent water and air infiltration from occurring at these cracks (Fig. 4.81).

CONCRETE

Concrete is a mixture of Portland cement, a fine aggregate (usually sand), a coarse aggregate (usually gravel or crushed stone), and water. Reinforcing steel bars are placed in forms prior to the concrete pour. A set period of time is required for the concrete to reach its initial set at which time the forms may be removed.

The compressive strength for concrete can reach up to 19,000 lb/in^2 (131 MPa) which is usually expressed as 19 kips per square inch (Ksi). This type of mix is used in the lower columns of some high-rise buildings because of the very high concentrated loads at these locations. The most commonly used mixes vary between 3 and 4 Ksi (20 to 28 MPa). Concrete performance can be modified by adding certain ingredients to the mixing operation. A partial listing of these ingredients or admixtures includes:

1. Air-entraining agents which improve workability and reduce damage due to the freeze-thaw cycles.

2. Accelerators and retarders that modify the setting time to allow the forms to be removed faster or to allow more time for placing the concrete, respectively.

3. Superplasticizers to allow the concrete to flow more readily while reducing the water content. Reduced water adds to the strength of the concrete. These admixtures give the concrete a darker color. Architects must be aware of this fact when the design calls for exposed concrete. If a superplasticizer is specified for the columns and not for other parts of the exterior wall, there will be a very clear difference in color between them.

4. Other admixtures include fly ash, silica fume, corrosion inhibitors, and coloring agents.

Table 4.7 provides more detailed information about admixtures.

Architectural concrete usually requires consolidation by means of hand-held vibrators. Uneven consolidation can result in surface voids or honeycombing. Patching these imperfections is visually unacceptable for concrete intended to be exposed to view.

REINFORCEMENT

Steel reinforcement is usually designed by the structural engineer. The only involvement that architects have in this aspect of wall design is to discuss with the engineer the location of control joints, form ties, and the minimum cover or other measures required to protect the steel from rusting and against possible spalling of the concrete.

SITE-CAST CONCRETE

Exposed architectural concrete requires a more thoughtful approach than regular structural concrete. A specifi-

TYPE OF ADMIXTURE	EFFECT ON CONCRETE	INGREDIENTS GENERALLY USED	METHOD OF ADDING	ADVANTAGES	DISADVANTAGES	MAJOR USE IN CONCRETE
Accelerators	Speeds hydration of cement	Calcium chloride	Maximum 2 lb./ 94-lb. bag of cement	Speeds setting time; develops strength earlier; lowers freezing point of water by 3°F; increases heat due to hydration	Increases expansion and contraction; reduces resistance to sulfates; increases efflorescence and the corrosion of high-tension steels	In cold weather, speeds setting time and strength and shortens protection time
Air-entraining agents	Introduces minute air bubbles throughout concrete	Rosin, beef tallow, stearates, vinsol resin, lauryl sodium sulfate, foaming agents	Usually 1/4 to 1 1/2 oz./100 lb. cement	Increases plasticity and cohesiveness; reduces bleeding; greatly increases resistance to freezing and thawing	Requires careful control; may require more frequent slump tests; causes some loss of strength	For all concrete exposed to freezing, thawing, and salt application
Latex (non-reemulsifiable bonding type)	Improves adhesion and increases both tensile and flexural strength	Organic polymer-type latex and air-detraining agents (do not use air-entraining cements)	Generally 4 gal./ 94-lb. bag of cement	Increases water retention, adhesion to substrates, tensile strength, and resistance to freezing and thawing	More difficult to finish; a steel-troweled finish should be avoided	Flash coats, toppings, course leveling, and patching
Inert, finely divided powders	Corrects gradation of aggregates deficient in fines	Powdered glass, sand (silica), slate flour, stone dust, lime	As per manufacturer's directions	Corrects deficiency in fines for coarse aggregates; improves workability	Increases water requirements and drying shrinkage; decreases strength in rich mixes	Improves workability
Water reducing or plasticizing agents	Lowers water-cement ratio; lubricates solid particles in mix (aggregates)	Polyhydroxylated polymers, lignosulfonates, or hydroxylated carboxylic acids with calcium chloride or another accelerator in another formulation	As per manufacturer's directions	Reduces water content; increases workability and plasticity	Decreases early strength; may slow hydration	Improves workability and plasticity
Pozzolanic, finely divided powder	Reacts with free lime during hydration of cement to form cementitious materials	Volcanic ash, fly ash (residue from burning coal), calcined shale and clay, siliceous materials, natural cements, some slags	As per manufacturer's directions	Controls alkali-aggregates reaction; improves workability; reduces heat generation, expansion, and contraction; increases strength after 28 days; increases resistance to sulfate attack; may increase permeability	May cause excessive drying shrinkage; reduces durability; reduces early strength	Controls alkali-aggregate reaction; increases resistance to sulfate attack
Retarders	Slows hydration of cement	Zinc oxide, calcium lignosulfonate, derivatives of adipic acid	As per manufacturer's directions	Slows setting; reduces heat due to hydration; reduces expansion and contraction	Some loss of early strength; requires careful control; may require more frequent slump tests	For very hot weather and massive concrete

Table 4.7 A guide to concrete admixtures (Reproduced by permission; Hornbostel, Caleb, *Construction Materials,* 2d ed., Wiley, New York, 1991)

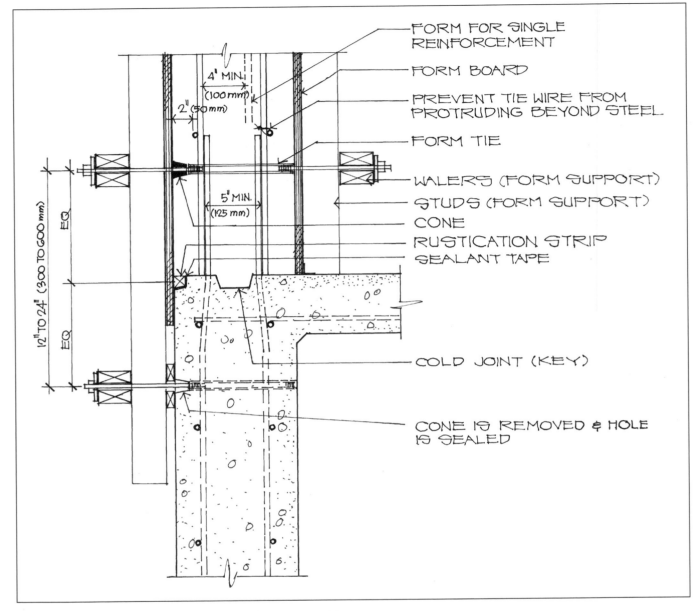

FORM FOR SINGLE REINFORCEMENT

FORM BOARD

PREVENT TIE WIRE FROM PROTRUDING BEYOND STEEL

FORM TIE

WALERS (FORM SUPPORT)

STUDS (FORM SUPPORT)

CONE

RUSTICATION STRIP

SEALANT TAPE

COLD JOINT (KEY)

CONE IS REMOVED & HOLE IS SEALED

4" MIN. (100 mm)

2" (50 mm)

5" MIN. (125 mm)

12" TO 24" (300 TO 600 mm)

EQ

EQ

Figure 4.79   Measures taken to avoid exposed concrete problems.

cation that may be perfectly acceptable for this latter will, in most cases, be unsatisfactory for concrete that is meant to be exposed to view. Special attention to the way the forms are constructed is required: more exacting tolerances controlling wall plumbness are needed; deviations from grade levels, linear alignments, and other dimensional requirements must be specified; and special admixtures to improve its performance may be necessary.

A properly detailed set of drawings combined with expertly written specifications, strict field supervision, and the choice of a contractor experienced in the production of architectural concrete improve the chances of good execution. In spite of all these precautions, pro-

ducing a flawless final result at a competitive price is not a sure thing. A full-scale preconstruction mock-up must be erected using materials and methods of construction identical to those planned for the job. It should include repair patches matching the color and texture of the original pour. The ingredients and techniques used in executing these patches are later applied to correct surface blemishes in the actual work later on. If the mockup is acceptable, a written approval is given to the contractor to proceed with the actual work. Because of the complexity and uncertainty associated with site-cast architectural concrete, architects tend to opt for precast concrete cladding over exposed site-cast concrete when the design calls for a concrete facade.

Figure 4.80 Inadequate concrete cover over reinforcement caused rebars to rust and spall off the thin layer of concrete.

PRECAST PANELS

Unlike site-cast concrete, precast concrete panels are shop-fabricated by experienced technicians under controlled conditions. The choice of finishes can be predetermined by sample selection. A full-size mock-up (Fig. 4.82) can be constructed and tested for leakage or appearance problems. Should a problem be detected during the testing, corrections can be made before full production is initiated. Each panel is completed in one pour, thus avoiding the need for concealment of construction joints (joints between pours), and, in many cases, the panels are prestressed to minimize hairline cracks, resist bowing, and reduce deflection.

In addition to these advantages, precast panels are durable and structurally adequate to resist lateral forces while spanning between floors or between columns. Panels may be used as a load-bearing wall element to combine both appearance and function (Fig. 4.83), and as mentioned under the Forms subsection, they can also be used in lieu of concrete forms in a manner that harks back to Roman construction (Figs. 4.73 and 4.77). Figure 4.84 shows, in schematic form, the different ways in which panels may be configured. Figure 4.85 shows typical panel supports.

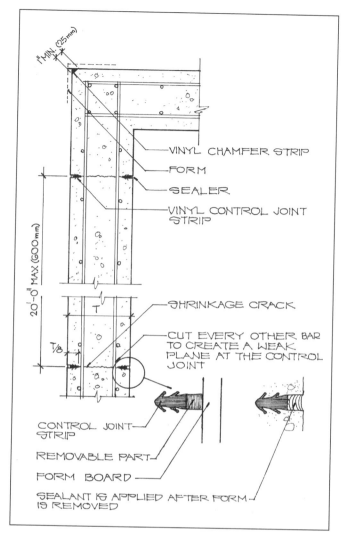

Figure 4.81 Control joints.

Because the mold used in casting the panels represents a sizable percentage of the overall cost, the designer should make every effort to minimize the number of molds. This does not necessarily mean that the design should degenerate into monotonously repetitious elements. Some variations can be introduced by adding blockouts to the form. The designer should discuss ways to reduce the number of molds with one or two precasters before finalizing the design. If at all possible, the drawings should provide acceptable alternate panel sizes. This allows precasters with different capabilities to compete for the job and may result in lower bids.

Construction drawings must define each precast panel (plan, elevation, and section) by type and dimensions. Some designers opt not to include these details in the belief that shop drawings will fill that function and that they can catch any deviations from the design intent when these drawings are presented. In theory, this can work. In real life, however, by the time shop drawings

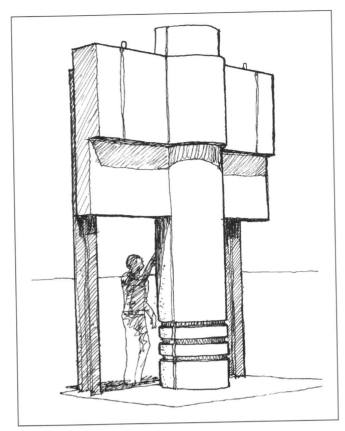

Figure 4.82 Example of a precast mock-up. (Traced by permission from a photograph; Precast/Prestressed Concrete Institute, *Architectural Precast Concrete,* 1989)

Figure 4.83 A building under construction demonstrating load-bearing precast walls, columns, and beams. (Traced by permission from a photograph; Precast/Prestressed Concrete Institute, *Architectural Precast Concrete,* 1989)

are presented for review, the person most familiar with this part of the project may be engaged in another project or may have accepted a position in another office, and the general contractor is sending several other submittals at the same time that require quick responses. In any case, it is much easier and faster to catch discrepancies between shop drawings and a detailed set of panel drawings than to check against panels drawn on the elevations. In addition, detailed drawings enable each bidder to price the job based on the same assumptions.

Attention to detail, familiarity with trade practices, and transportation and handling limitations can go a long way toward avoiding potential problems. Panel size limitations are usually determined by truck dimensions (Fig. 4.86). A *lo-boy* truck with a low bed may allow panels to exceed the dimensions shown. Weight is another factor to consider. Because each truck is capable of hauling 20 to 22 tons without requiring a special permit, the designer should size the panels with that in mind. A panel weighing 12 tons is not economical compared to one weighing 10 tons because the truck will not be carrying a full load. To estimate the weight, allow 150 lb/ft^3 (2403 kg/m^3). Table 4.8 provides guidelines for panel thickness relative

to size. Use it only for design development. A discussion with fabricators can shed some light on this issue. Hoisting the panels also requires some planning because it impacts the project's cost. While this issue is usually handled by the contractor or a construction management firm, it should be considered during the schematic design phase. Buildings with low wings adjacent to a multistory wing are especially problematic because of the complicated hoisting operations (Fig. 4.87).

Form design can also have an effect on panel detailing. As a general rule, forms constructed with integral sides (sides that are not removed after each pour) are required to have rounded or chamfered corners and a minimum 1 in 12 inches (25 in 300 mm) draft to enable the fabricator to extract the precast piece from the mold without damaging the surfaces or corners. A more pronounced draft of 1 in 8 inches (25 in 200 mm) is preferable especially for thin or delicate pieces. The designer should be aware of this requirement particularly if panels have deep fins. An axonometric drawing may be

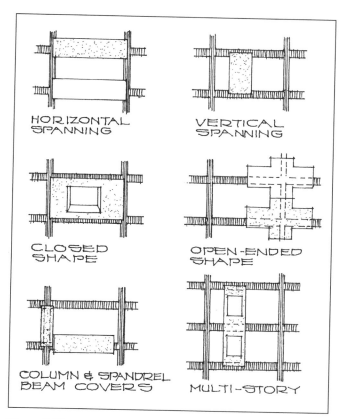

Figure 4.84   Panel shapes.

HORIZONTAL SPANNING

VERTICAL SPANNING

CLOSED SHAPE

OPEN-ENDED SHAPE

COLUMN & SPANDREL BEAM COVERS

MULTI-STORY

necessary to define complicated pieces to avoid misinterpretation of intent (Fig. 4.88).

The clearances between panel and support structure must be adequate to accommodate structural frame and panel tolerances (see Table 2.1). Tolerances are the allowable deviations from perfectly executed construc-

tion, a condition that is usually unattainable in the field (see Sec. 2.2.5).

A conference between the architect, the general contractor, and the precaster should be convened to resolve any conflict between the contract documents and shop drawings to simplify the process. The following are a few technical tips recommended by Sidney Freedman, director of architectural precast services at the PCI:[27]

1. Panel connections should be protected by one of the following methods, presented in order of increasing cost:

    a. Paint with shop primer

    b. Coating with zinc-rich paint, zinc metalizing

    c. Cadmium plating

    d. Hot-dip galvanizing

    e. Use of stainless steel

    Fully exposed connections subject to regular inspection and maintenance need only protective painting.

2. If the steel frame supporting the panels is required to be fire-rated, the panel connections should have the same rating.

3. Good design utilizes standardized products and enough clearance to allow workers to provide reasonable tolerances and to access connections comfortably to make field adjustments.

Chapter 2 contains more information relating to structural issues concerning panel support and support frame deformation.

Panel Dimensions**	8'	10'	12'	16'	20'	24'	28'	32'
4'	3"	4"	4"	5"	5"	6"	6"	7"
6'	3"	4"	4"	5"	6"	6"	6"	7"
8'	4"	5"	5"	6"	6"	7"	7"	8"
10'	5"	5	6"	6"	7"	7"	8"	8"

*   This table should not be used for panel thickness selection.
**   This table represents a relationship between overall flat panel dimensions and thickness below which suggested bowing and warpage tolerances should be reviewed and possibly increased. For ribbed panels, the equivalent thickness should be the overall thickness of such ribs if continuous from one end of the panel to the other.

Table 4.8   Guidelines for panel thickness for overall panel stiffness consistent with suggested normal panel bowing and warping tolerances* (Reproduced by permission; Precast/Prestressed Concrete Institute, *Architectural Precast Concrete,* 1989)

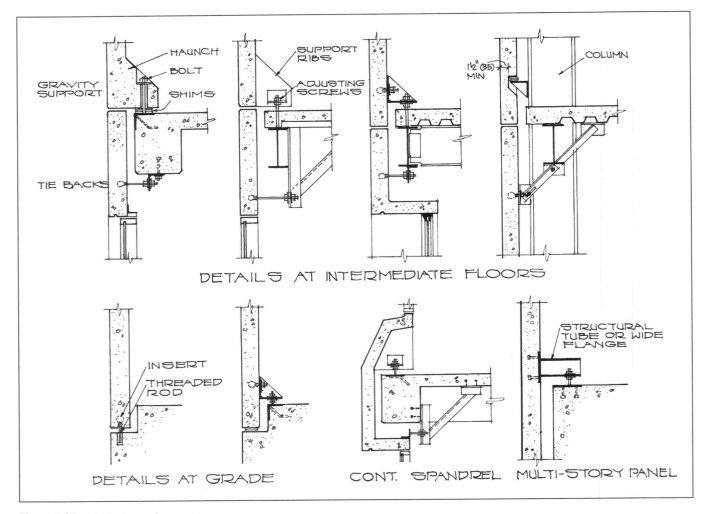

DETAILS AT INTERMEDIATE FLOORS

DETAILS AT GRADE   CONT. SPANDREL   MULTI-STORY PANEL

Figure 4.85 Typical panel supports.

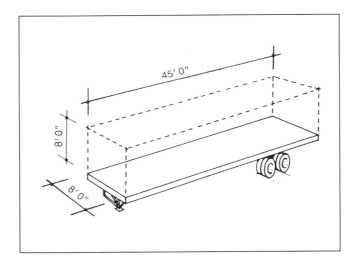

Figure 4.86 Staying within typical truck dimensions should be considered in the early design stages. (Reproduced by permission; Precast/Prestressed Concrete Institute, *Architectural Precast Concrete,* 1989)

GFRC PANELS

Glass fiber reinforced concrete wall panels are fabricated from a mixture of alkali-resistant glass fibers and a slurry comprised of Portland cement and sand. The glass fibers are combined with the slurry at the discharging nozzle of a spray gun (Fig. 4.89) and compacted with a hand roller to a thickness varying from ½ to ⅝ in (13 to 16 mm). Water vapor permeability of GFRC ranges from 5 to 11 perm-in [7.3 to 16 × 10⁻⁹ g/(Pa · s · m)] for water-to-cement ratios at 0.25 and 0.35, respectively. This allows any vapor that may pass through the vapor retarder to escape to the exterior (see Sec. 1.3.2).

Glass fiber reinforced concrete panels are backed by framing systems constructed with structural studs (Fig. 4.90) or structural shapes (usually tubes). Integral GFRC-covered Styrofoam ribs fused to the back face of the panel may also be used as panel stiffeners if the shapes are complex or stud corrosion is an issue. Stud framing is the most frequently used support method because of its speed of assembly and low cost. Sandwich panels may be constructed with several types of

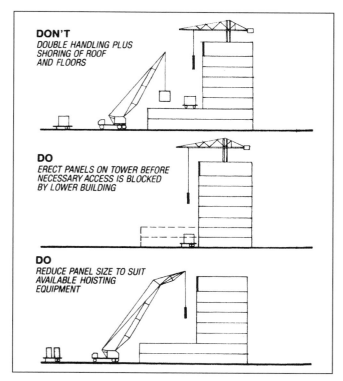

Figure 4.87 Access for trucks and hoisting equipment. (Reproduced by permission; *Architectural Precast Concrete,* Precast/Prestressed Concrete Institute, 1989)

cores incorporating hidden ribs and be mounted without a metal structural backing. If the core is made up of rigid insulation, the panel may tend to bow because the outer skin is exposed to heat while the back skin is not. Specific design guidelines for this type of panel have not been developed at this time.

Glass fiber reinforced concrete panels were successfully manufactured for up to 30 ft (9 m) in length with ½-in (13 mm) skin thickness. Panels exceeding 20 ft (6 m) in length require an intermediate control joint to limit shrinkage. The distance from panel edges to the anchors should be equal and short to minimize warping (Fig. 4.91).

Fire-rating can be achieved by integrating certain measures in panel design. The PCI states that GFRC made with an acrylic thermoplastic copolymer dispersion for curing purposes will meet the requirements for the National Fire Protection Association's (NFPA) Class A and Uniform Building Code (UBC) Class I when tested according to ASTM E84, resulting in a 0 Flame Spread Rating and in a smoke density of less than 5. Fire tests conducted according to ASTM E119 are shown in Table 4.9.

Glass fiber reinforced concrete panels are indistinguishable from precast panels because they are faced with the same finishes, form liners, or applied

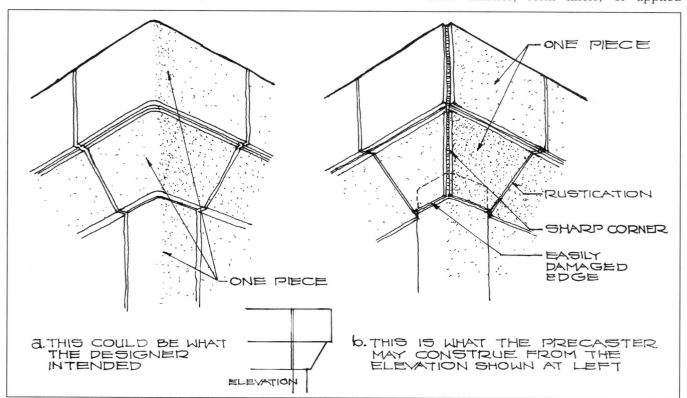

Figure 4.88 An example of deviation from design intent caused by insufficient detailing. An isometric drawing like the one shown in part (a) would prevent this from occurring. (Reproduced by permission; traced from illustrations in Precast/Prestressed Concrete Institute, *Architectural Precast Concrete,* 1989)

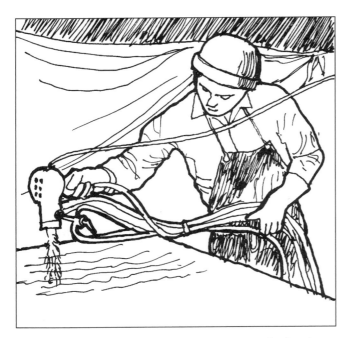

Figure 4.89 Worker spraying GFRC onto a panel. The glass fiber is added to the cement/sand slurry at the nozzle. (Traced from a photograph by Cem-Fil)

veneers. They are usually fabricated by precasters and cost about the same as precast panels but have the advantage of weighing on average 14 lb/ft^2 (68 kg/m^2). This is a fraction of the weight of the average precast panel. Lighter panels mean that more panels can be loaded on a truck and shipped longer distances for the same cost. Should GFRC be listed as an alternate to precast concrete in the construction documents, fabricators from a wider area will be in a position to compete for the job because of this weight advantage. The lighter weight also means that smaller cranes or forklifts can be used to place them on the building. This translates into savings on the cost of equipment leasing. Weight advantage also means savings on the building frame and foundations. This makes the choice more advantageous in areas prone to seismic activity.

Because panels must be aligned from the exterior, the stud backing may be slightly out of plumb or misaligned. For that reason, the wallboard should be attached to horizontal furring channels that can be shimmed to correct these deviations. Panel dimensional tolerances are shown in Fig. 4.92.

PANEL SUPPORTS

The structural consultant in charge of the project must determine the location of panel support points to enable the precaster's engineer to design panel reinforcement and supporting hardware. The contract documents should include all loads and their points of application. While the architect does not get involved in the actual design of the panel connector and its anchorage, he or she must allow for the tolerances required for the supporting structure's imperfections and the adjustment movement required for positioning the panels. Figure 2.23 illustrates 10 basic design principles for cladding panel connectors. Panel supports should not be shown on architectural drawings because there are no standard supports used by the industry. Each fabricator develops proprietary or off-the-shelf hardware suited to production and erection procedures peculiar to that particular fabricator.

Glass fiber reinforced concrete panels are attached to the stud or tube frame by means of anchor rods that are designed to absorb shrinkage and thermal movements (Fig. 4.93). The frame itself is supported on or attached to the slab edge. The PCI recommends that the studs be a minimum of 16-gauge material if the connections are to be welded, the studs must be either painted or galvanized, and that hot-dip galvanizing after fabrication is not necessary. Under normal circumstances, structural steel members equal to or greater than $^3/_{16}$ in (5 mm) in thickness do not require corrosion protection. Anchors embedded in the panel, however, should be protected against corrosion, and a gap of between $^1/_8$ and $^3/_8$ in (3 and 10 mm) must be left between the foot of the anchor and the body of the panel before the GFRC cover is applied to prevent the anchor from being perceptible at that location (Fig. 4.93). Panels are supported on clip angles and restrained with rod tie backs in a manner similar to precast concrete panels (Fig. 4.90).

Clearances recommended by the PCI are as follows:

A good rule of thumb is that at least 1 inch (25 mm) clearance be required between GFRC panels and precast concrete members with 1½ inch (38 mm) preferred; 1½ inch (38 mm) is the minimum clearance between the GFRC panels and cast-in-place concrete with 2 inch (51 mm) preferred. For steel structures, 1 inch (25 mm) is the minimum clearance between the back of the GFRC panel frame and the surface of the fireproofing with 1½ inch (38 mm) preferred. If there is no fireproofing required on the steel, 1½ to 2 inch (38 to 51 mm) clearance should be allowed in tall, irregular structures regardless of the structural framing materials. The minimum clearance between a column cover and the column should be 2 inches (51 mm), with 3 inch (76 mm) preferred because of the possibility of columns being out of plumb or a column dimension interfering with the completion of the connection

All connections should be designed with the maximum adjustability in all directions that is structurally and architecturally feasible. To accommodate any misalignment of the building frame, connections should provide for vertical, horizontal, and lateral adjustments of at least 1 inch (25 mm). Tolerance of hardware items cast into, or fastened to the structure should be ±¼ inch (±6 mm) in all directions. Connection details should consider the possibility of bearing surfaces being sloped or warped from the desired plane.

The minimum shim space between various connection elements should be ¾ inch (19 mm) for steel structures or 1 inch (25 mm) for cast-in-place concrete structures with 1½ inch (38 mm) preferred.[28]

Ideally, panel support hardware should be readily accessible for periodic inspection. This, however, is not standard practice. The hardware is usually not exposed to

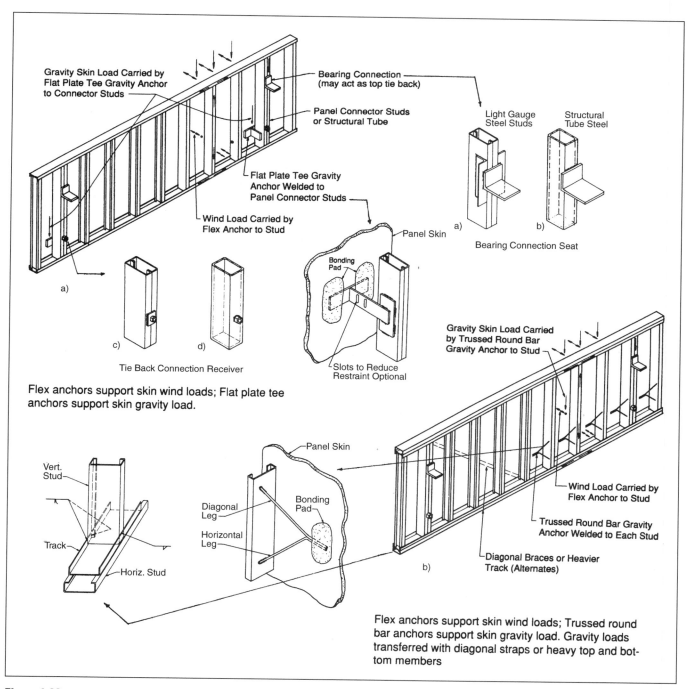

Figure 4.90 Glass fiber reinforced concrete stud backing details. (Based on several drawings from Precast-Prestressed Concrete Institute, *Recommended Practice for Glass Fiber Reinforced Panels*, GFRC, 3d ed., 1993; reproduced by permission)

excessive wetting and, in most cases, is galvanized. On the rare occasion that a problem develops, a relatively small opening in the backup wall can be cut to enable the inspector to examine the connection. After the problem is fixed, the opening would be patched. One issue that must be observed is that panel connections must have the same fire rating as the structural frame. In addition to panel supports and tie backs, alignment connections may be used between individual panels to prevent misalignments similar to those shown in Fig. 4.94.

INSULATION

Insulating site-cast or precast concrete walls can be achieved by adding rigid insulation to the exterior or interior face of the wall. If applied to the interior face,

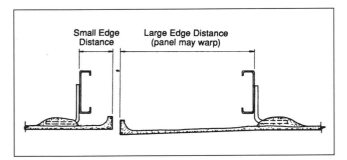

Figure 4.91 Effect of edge distance on bowing or warping of panel. (Reproduced by permission; Precast/Prestressed Concrete Institute, *Recommended Practice for Glass Fiber Reinforced Panels,* 3d ed., 1993)

the insulation can be placed between metal zee strips that serve to hold the insulation in place as well as provide a metal strip for fastening the wallboard to. Semi-rigid insulation can also be attached to the wall in that location. If the exterior of site-cast walls is not intended to be exposed, Styrofoam boards can be attached to that face as part of an EIFS assembly (Sec. 4.6).

Precast panels are insulated by attaching rigid insulation to the interior surface or by placing the insulation between two concrete pours to form a sandwich panel (Fig. 4.95). An air cavity may also be introduced in an assembly designed as a rain screen (see Sec. 3.2.2).

Sandwich panels may be designed as composite or noncomposite. In a noncomposite panel, the two precast wythes are connected with flexible ties. This allows the wythe facing the exterior to expand and contract without transferring stresses to the interior wythe. In a composite panel, the wythes are attached with rigid ties or continuous ribs. This can create internal stresses that can cause the panel to bow unless the two wythes are prestressed and a slight camber is introduced in the panel to counteract the bowing.

A conventional stud and batt insulation arrangement can be rather risky because it is impractical to place a protective layer of sheathing on the exterior face of the studs to protect the stud assembly (including the insulation) from moisture infiltrating from the exterior. This, however, is the usual method of insulating GFRC panels. Because leakage through the panel itself is highly improbable in GFRC panels due to the absence of microcracking (dense matrix and fiber reinforcement),

Fire Endurance	Outside Wythe	Steel Studs or GFRC Ribs		Insulation	Inside Wythe	Overall Thickness
		Type	Maximum Spacing			
2 hr*	3/8 in. GFRC; 6 in. Returns	5 in. Ribs	24 in. (nominal)	5 in. TFB	5/8 in. GWB-C	7-3/8 in.
2 hr	1/2 in. GFRC; 1-1/2 in. Returns	4 in. Studs	16 in. (nominal)	5 in. TFB	1/2 in. + 1/2 in. GWB-C	6-1/2 in.
2 hr	1/2 in. GFRC;** 1-1/2 in. Returns	6 in. Studs	24 in. (nominal)	5 in. TFB	1/2 in. + 1/2 in. GWB-X	9 in.
1 hr	1/2 in. GFRC; 5 in. Returns	4 in. Studs	16 in. (nominal)	5 in. TFB	5/8 in. GWB-C	6-1/8 in.

* Surface of inside wythe exposed to fire.

** Contained 5 percent acrylic thermoplastic copolymer by volume of GFRC.

Explanation of Symbols and Terms

GFRC = glass fiber reinforced concrete

GWB-X = Type X gypsum wallboard

GWB-C = Sheetrock brand Firecode C gypsum wall panels produced by United States Gypsum Co.

TFB = Thermafiber CW 40 batts produced by United States Gypsum Co.

Table 4.9 Description of wall panel assemblies fire-tested in the United States. (Reproduced by permission; Precast/Prestressed Concrete Institute, *Recommended Practice for Glass Fiber Reinforced Panels,* 3d ed., 1993)

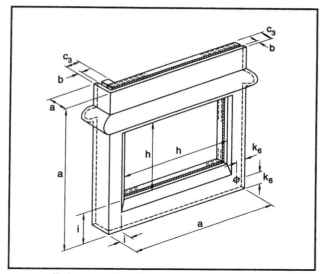

Tolerance locations.

a. Overall height and width of units measured at the face adjacent to the mold:
   1. 10 ft (3 m) or under .... ± 1/8 in. (± 3 mm)
   2. 10 ft (3 m) and over .... ± 1/8 in. per 10 ft (± 3 mm per 3 m); 1/4 in. (6 mm) maximum

b. Edge return ..... +1/2 in., - 0 in. (+13 mm, - 0 mm)

c. Thickness:
   1. Architectural facing thickness .... ±1/8 in. (±3 mm)
   2. GFRC backing .... +1/4 in., - 0 in. (+ 6 mm, - 0 mm)
   3. Panel depth from face of skin to back of panel frame or integral rib .... + 3/8 in., -1/4 in. (+ 10 mm, - 6 mm)

d. Angular variation of plane of side mold .... ± 1/32 in. per 3 in. (± 1 mm per 75 mm) depth or ± 1/16 in. (± 1.5 mm) total, whichever is greater.

e. Variation from square or designated skew (difference in length of two diagonal measurements) .... 1/8 in. per 6 ft (3 mm per 2 m) or 1/4 in. (6 mm) total, whichever is greater.

f. Local smoothness .... 1/4 in. per 10 ft (6 mm per 3 m)

g. Bowing: Bowing shall not exceed L/240 unless it can be shown that the member can meet erection tolerances using connection adjustments.

h. Length and width of blockouts and openings within one unit .... ± 1/4 in. (± 6 mm)

i. Location of window opening within panel ....± 1/4 in. (± 6 mm)

j. Warpage: Maximum permissible warpage of one corner out of the plane of the other three shall be 1/16 in. per ft (5 mm per m) distance from the nearest adjacent corner, unless it can be shown that the member can meet erection tolerances using connection adjustments. This requirement is illustrated in Fig. 38.

k. Position of integral items
   1. Stud frame and track .... ± 1/4 in. (6 mm)
   2. Flashing reglets at edge of panel .... ± 1/4 in. (± 3 mm)
   3. Inserts .... ± 1/2 in. (± 12 mm)
   4. Special handling devices ..... ± 3 in. (± 75 mm)
   5. Location of bearing devices . ± 1/4 in. (± 6 mm)
   6. Blockouts .... ± 3/8 in. (± 10 mm)

l. Stud frames shall be fabricated within the following tolerances shown in Fig. 42.

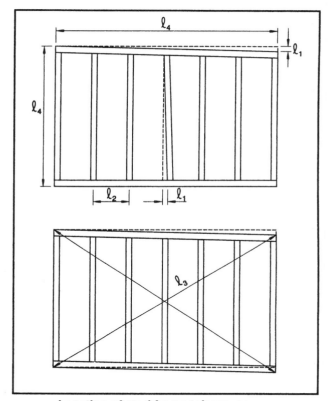

Location of stud frame tolerances.

1. Vertical and horizontal alignment .. 1/4 in. in 10 ft. (6 mm in 3 m)
2. Spacing of framing members .... ± 3/8 in. (± 10 mm)
3. Squareness of frame (difference in diagonals) .... 3/8 in. (10 mm)
4. Overall size of frame .... ± 3/8 in. (± 10 mm)

Figure 4.92 Tolerances for GFRC panels and their stud backup. (Reproduced by permission; Precast/Prestressed Concrete Institute, *Recommended Practice for Glass Fiber Reinforced Panels,* 3d ed., 1993)

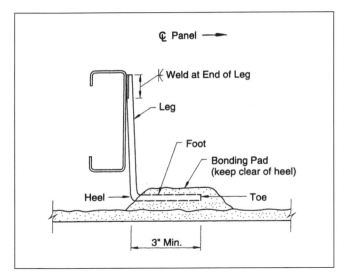

Figure 4.93 Typical flex anchor. (Reproduced by permission; Precast/Prestressed Concrete Institute, *Recommended Practice for Glass Fiber Reinforced Panels,* 3d ed., 1993)

Figure 4.94 Example of protruding, misaligned panels. Flaws exaggerated by lighting conditions.

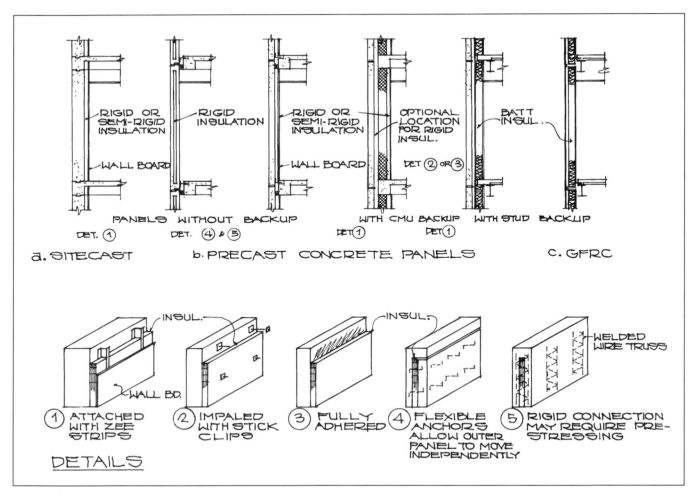

Figure 4.95 Common methods of insulating cement-based cladding systems.

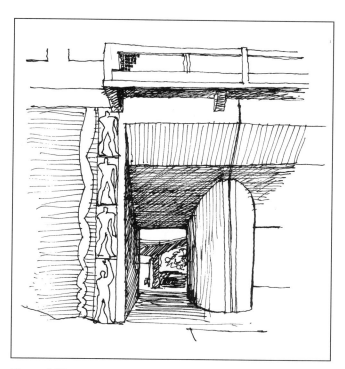

Figure 4.96 Sculptured depressions in site-cast concrete (a design by Le Corbusier).

the danger of leakage is concentrated in the joints. For long-term, trouble-free performance, a two-stage joint (see Sec. 1.3.2) should be used. To achieve this, the panel return at the joint should be approximately 4 or 5 in (100 to 125 mm) long.

To calculate joint width using the formula included in Sec. 4.2.2, one must be aware that the panel face temperature is usually higher than the ambient air temperature at the site. For instance, panels can be 20 to 80°F (7 to 62°C) greater due to solar heat gain.

4.4.3 Ornamentation

Site-cast walls can be articulated by attaching a fiberglass liner simulating any of several profiles and textures to the forms. Surface treatments which include exposing the aggregate by means of a retarder, sandblasting, or adding a coloring agent to the mix to give the wall a warmer tone are also available. As mentioned before, the architect may also integrate the rustications that mask joints between panels and between different pours in the design and combine them with the sunk cones that are part of the form ties to create a rhythm and human scale in the facade. Another method of ornamentation is to create sculptured depressions in the surface by attaching inserts to the form prior to pouring the concrete (Fig. 4.96). Manipulating the surface itself to give the building a sculptured look (Fig. 4.97) is the ultimate form of ornamentation.

Precast and GFRC panels may be embellished by color, texture, and veneers.

COLOR AND TEXTURE

By using aggregates of varying colors and adding color to the matrix, the fabricator can offer a wide palette of colors ranging from white to black. These colors can be

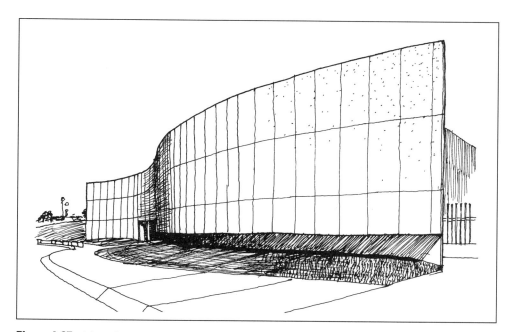

Figure 4.97 The plastic nature of site-cast concrete is demonstrated in buildings like Century High School in Santa Ana, CA (designed by Ralph Allen & Partners, Architects).

affected by surface texture. Rough or striated surfaces make colors seem darker and can mask flaws. White cement gives the most consistent color results at a relatively small percentage of panel cost, while regular cement may produce some color variations between panels. The PCI states that shades of red, orange, yellow, brown, and gray are the least costly colors; blue is expensive; black has a tendency to fade to gray; and dark colors show efflorescence more readily than lighter tones.[29]

Panelized systems can be decorated by using the same methods described under the section titled "Forms" on page 168. The PCI lists four factors that should be considered in choosing a texture:

1. *Subdividing the panel area by means of rustication (false joints).* This tends to deemphasize any variations in texture.

2. *Size of aggregate.* The viewing distance is a factor in deciding aggregate size. The greater the distance, the larger the aggregate.

3. *Wall orientation.* This determines the amount of light falling on the surface and how the panel will weather.

4. *Aggregate particle shape and surface.* Particles may be rounded, irregular, angular, or flat. Their surface may be glossy, smooth, granular, crystalline, pitted, or porous. These characteristics determine how the surface will weather and reflect light.

VENEERS

Panels may be faced with another material. Brick, tile, and natural stone are often used to cover the whole surface or provide an accent. The back side of thin bricks should be profiled in a key or dovetail configuration to develop an adequate bond to precast panels.

There are certain advantages to facing a precast panel with brick over building the brick veneer conventionally. These include:

■ Saving the cost of scaffolding

■ Avoidance of interruptions caused by inclement weather (panels are shop-fabricated)

■ Reduction in the incidence of efflorescence

■ Reduction in the possibility of cracking and the leakage associated with it

Thin bricks are usually used in that method. They are placed in the form over a liner shaped in a way that gauges the joint to a precise width and depth. The reinforcement is then placed over the brick, and concrete is poured over it. Glass fiber reinforced concrete panels faced with thin brick or tile must be designed to resist the bowing caused by the different properties of the

two materials. This may require using an elastomeric joint sealant instead of mortar in the joints to absorb the expansion of the clay facing. It would be prudent to check with the PCI for advice before deciding on using this type of facing. Bonding tile directly to the concrete during the casting operation is preferable to applying it after the concrete has hardened.

Typical anchor details for stone veneer are shown in Fig. 4.98. The bond breaker shown in these details allows differential movement between the two materials. The anchor holes should be sealed with silicone sealer to eliminate intrusion of water into the holes. Some designers prefer to use epoxy instead of silicone to increase the shear capacity and rigidity of the anchors. In that case, ½-in (13 mm) elastomeric sleeves should be placed on the anchors next to the back surface of the stone to accommodate the differential movement. A properly graded silica sand in the GFRC slurry reduces the possibility of bowing.

4.4.4 Assemblies

Figures 4.99 and 4.100 are axonometric drawings of precast and GFRC assemblies. These illustrations provide in graphic form some of the information included in the text to give an overall picture of these assemblies. Of course, each project has its own unique set of circumstances and code requirements that determine its details. These factors may differ from the drawings shown here.

4.4.5 What Can Go Wrong
SITE-CAST CONCRETE

After a period of high popularity in the sixties and seventies, interest in exposed concrete has waned. This is partly due to changing architectural trends and partly to the unpredictability of the quality of the final product. Architects have to pay much more attention to the construction process to ensure that the results match their expectations. The design of the form, the placement of the steel reinforcement, the water-to-cement ratio, the concrete mix, and the type of finish are important factors that affect the final result.

Forms must be rigid and braced against deformation. Their joints must be properly braced to prevent them from opening up under the pressure of the fluid concrete mix.

Reinforcing steel should be placed at a depth of approximately 2 in (50 mm) from the face of the form to provide adequate cover. Insufficient reinforcement cover can result in stress cracking and rusting of the steel which can cause the concrete to eventually spall off (Fig. 4.80). Rust can occupy up to four times the volume of steel and can exert tremendous pressure causing

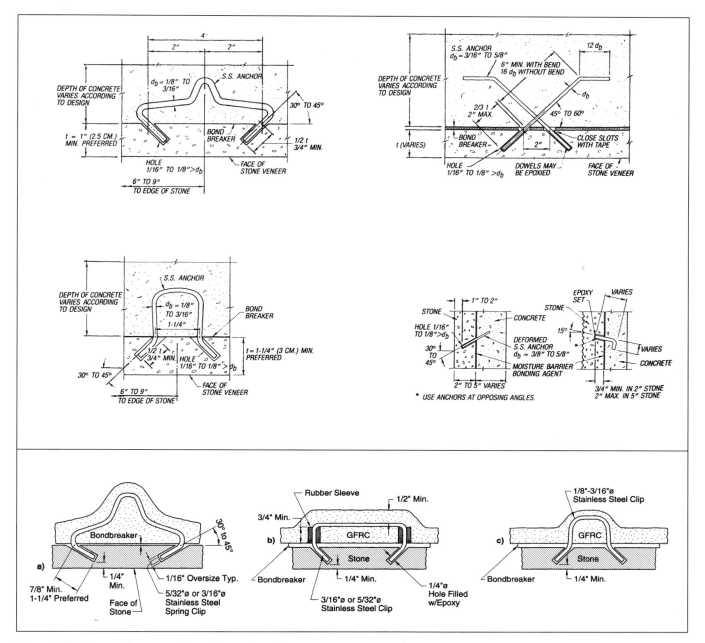

Figure 4.98 Types of stone anchors. (Reproduced by permission; Precast/Prestressed Concrete Institute, *Recommended Practice for Glass Fiber Reinforced Panels,* 3d ed., 1993, and *Architectural Precast Concrete,* 2d ed., 1989)

the initial hairline cracks parallel to these rebars as well as rust staining. Rustication and reveals between different pours must not reduce the concrete cover mentioned above.

The concrete mix must be designed properly and monitored carefully. If the water-to-cement ratio is too high, it can result in rapid crack formation as the water evaporates. A high quality mix with a water-to-cement ratio of 50% or less can help avoid this condition. Admixtures such as accelerators used to permit early removal of the forms can cause shrinkage cracks, dis-

coloration, and corrosion in steel rebars. If accelerators must be used, they should meet ASTM C494 requirements and should not exceed 2% by weight of cement. Chloride levels in mixing water and sand should also be monitored to avoid a similar effect on the steel. Air-entraining admixtures enhance the cohesiveness of the mix, improve workability, and reduce bleeding (water rising to the surface). These admixtures form microscopic bubbles throughout the mix that can accommodate the expansion of ice crystals when infiltrated water freezes. The freeze-thaw cycle can play havoc with exposed concrete causing it to spall and deteriorate especially if air-entraining agents are not used.

PRECAST CONCRETE

Architectural precast concrete is produced under strict quality control by fabricators specializing in that type of construction. Examples of failure are extremely rare except for the effect of major earthquakes which can cause cracking especially at corner panels attached to both corner elevations. A properly constructed precast panel with support points designed to accommodate thermal movements, deflection, and supporting struc-

ture deformations due to lateral loads is one of the most dependable wall systems.

There are, however, a few design decisions that can affect the optimal performance of the system. The following is a partial listing.

Deflection. If the panels are supported on a spandrel beam, their vertical joints may experience some distortion due to deflection. Cantilever deflection can also cause panels to rotate (see Chap. 2). To reduce the effect of these movements, beams and cantilevers should be designed to experience minimum deflection. Supporting the panels directly on the column is a better

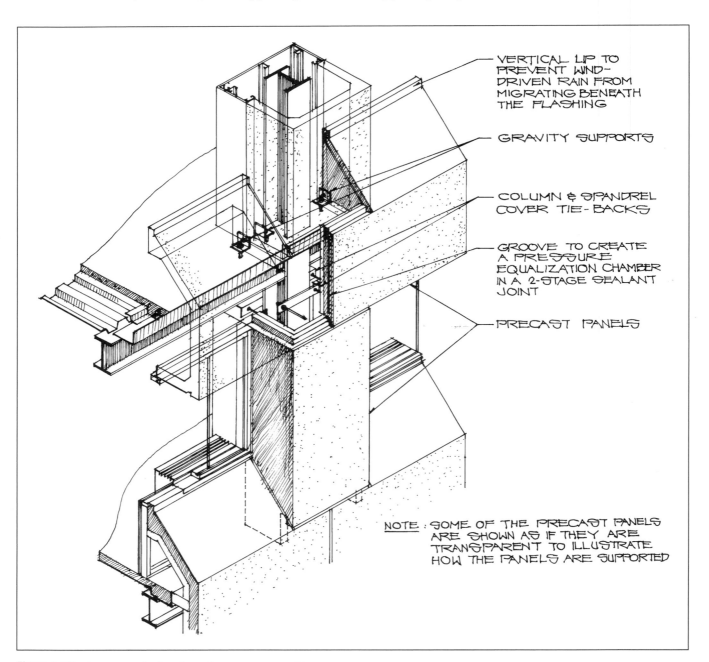

Figure 4.99 Axonometric drawing of a precast assembly.

solution (Figs. 2.3 and 4.101). If vertical joints are required by the designer, rustication may be added to simulate the look of individual panels.

Bowing. Brick expands over time, while concrete shrinks. This can cause brick-faced panels to bow. Several measures can be used to mitigate this phenomenon; panel thickness may be increased, stiffening ribs may be added to the back, or a double layer of reinforcing steel may be used. Other measures include prestressing the steel (flat panels only) or introducing a slight camber [1

in in 40 ft (25 mm in 12 m)] into the panel to offset the expected bowing. As mentioned elsewhere, bowing may also occur when stone veneers are used or with certain types of sandwich panels (Fig. 4.102) unless certain measures are taken.

Structural frame shortening. On high-rise concrete frame buildings, columns may shorten by as much as 5 to 6 in (127 to 152 mm) in 40 stories due to creep. As a result, connecting hardware may not match up with the concrete inserts in the frame. Joint widths and panel height

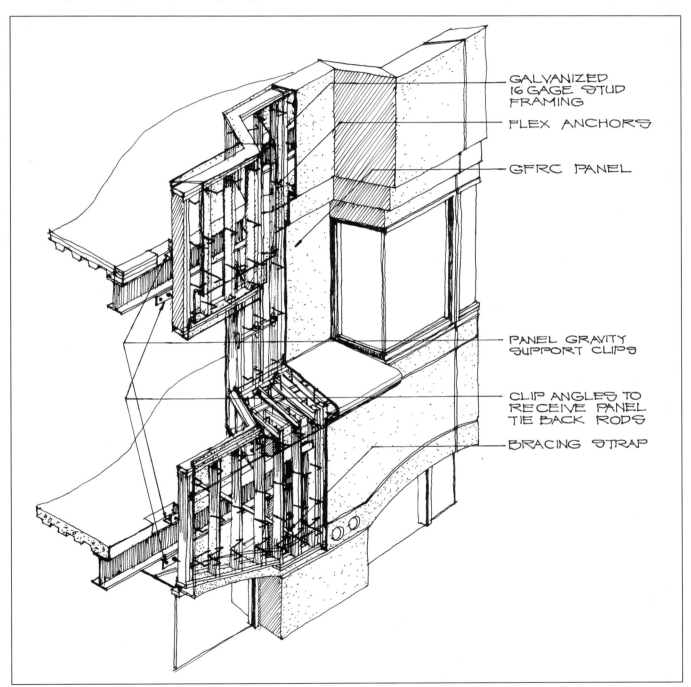

Figure 4.100   Axonometric drawing of a GFRC assembly.

Figure 4.101   Precast panels supported directly on the columns.

Figure 4.102   Bowing of precast panels. Note the false joint in the middle of the panels.

must be calculated to accommodate this difference.

Staining and streaking. Panel surfaces can be marred by water runoff. Rain collects the accumulated dirt on the facade and stains panel surfaces at lower levels. To minimize this problem, the PCI recommends[30] the following measures:

- Use rough-textured surface treatment and darker colors.
- Cant the panels either inward or outward (Fig. 4.103).
- Include drips in the soffits to reduce streaking.
- Break up large blank surfaces with horizontal projections.
- Create vertical grooves below mullions and fins to channel the stain.
- Use rounded or splayed corners to reduce the concentration of rain at these locations.

Architects should also take note of the orientation of the building. If the building is oriented in a manner that lets the sun shine parallel to the facade, smooth flat panels should be avoided as much as possible to avoid the condition shown in Fig. 4.94 where flaws are exaggerated.

GFRC

Many of the items listed above apply to GFRC panels. Despite the identical appearance of the two systems, GFRC experiences a higher rate of shrinkage and possible warpage due to the high cement content in the mixture (80% as opposed to 50%). To mitigate this problem, forms for large panels must be lengthened by an amount equal to the calculated shrinkage in the panel and supports must be designed to accommodate the

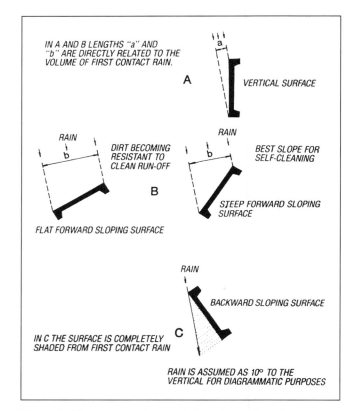

Figure 4.103   Volume of rain likely to hit wall surfaces. (Reproduced by permission; Precast/Prestressed Concrete Institute, *Architectural Precast Concrete,* 2d ed., 1989)

shrinkage movement in addition to the other movements mentioned in the text. Heavier-gauge studs should also be used to resist panel bowing.

Discoloration. Panels can develop discoloration during production. This results in uneven color distribution.

Staining the panels by using a light-colored stain has been very successful as a remedy. Efflorescence caused by leaching of salts can result in chalky patterns especially on darker panels. This can be remedied by the use of a sealer, exposed aggregate, or ribbed surfaces.

Cracking. The following is a partial list of locations where cracking can occur.

1. At areas where nuts for attachments such as clip angles are overtightened

2. At large or sharp changes in section thickness

3. At window frame shims and corners

4. At support hardware if prevented from free in-plane movement caused by temperature or creep

Hardware should be detailed to prevent panel supports from binding. Corrosion must not be allowed to become a factor. One technique to avoid a corrosion-fused connection is the use of plastic or fiber washers.

Summary

Concrete walls may be made of site-cast, precast, or glass fiber reinforced concrete. Exposed site-cast concrete walls must be executed according to a stricter specification and detailing than structural concrete to avoid unsightly blemishes. Special attention must be paid to form construction to prevent leaks, bowing, honeycombs, and staining. Control joints to limit shrinkage cracking and reveals between pours must be included in the design. The designer can arrange rustication located at panel joints and tie cones into an orderly design composition in conjunction with one of the many textures that can be created by form liner suppliers.

Precast panels can be produced as curtain or load-bearing walls. They may also be designed to perform the dual function of form and finish. Cast stone is a form of precast for small elements used as lintels, sills, or trim in masonry walls.

Precast concrete panels should be detailed individually to avoid misunderstanding by the bidders. The most economical designs use flat panels and repetitive sizes. If the design calls for panels that require complicated forms, try to use the least number of panel types because these forms represent a sizable part of the overall cost. The maximum size of the panel is usually dictated by the maximum size allowed to be trucked on the road and by crane capacity. Panel weight should not exceed 20 tons and should preferably be under 10 tons. [To compute the weight, allow 150 lb/ft³ (2403 kg/m³).] Industry standard clearances and tolerances must be observed to avoid misalignments and problems in the field. Panels should be detailed to minimize the effect of dirt. This can be accomplished by manipulating the panel angle, using darker or rough textures, or using panels surfaced with polished stone. Subdividing large plane surfaces by introducing horizontal cornices and vertical rustication under mullions are measures that should be considered.

Glass fiber reinforced concrete gives the same appearance as precast concrete and costs approximately the same. Its ingredients are a combination of cement and sand slurry mixed with a low-alkali fiberglass to a thickness of ½ to ⅝ in (4.5 to 16 mm) backed by a structural stud or steel tube framing system, and, in some cases, the panels are stiffened with integral GFRC ribs. Because of its lighter weight, GFRC is well suited to applications where weight is crucial. Examples include restoration work, seismically active locations, and buildings located on soils with a poor bearing capacity.

4.5 METAL CLADDING

4.5.1 Historical Background

Compared to conventional materials like stone and brick, metal cladding systems are in their infancy. While stone was used to build monuments like the pyramids almost 5000 years ago, the first substantial architectural application of metal was in the Crystal Palace in London in 1851. The building skeleton was constructed of prefabricated cast-iron components. It covered 18 acres [7 hectares (ha)] and was finished in 4 months, a remarkably short time for the construction of such a large building. During that period, conventionally constructed buildings of comparable size required years to finish. Lower Manhattan boasts one of the largest collections of buildings with cast-iron exterior walls. Some of them even incorporate cast-iron supporting structure. Figure 4.104 shows an example of a cast-iron facade in Boston.

Until a relatively short time ago, metal cladding used to be associated with industrial or utilitarian buildings like warehouses and industrial plants. During World War II, curved corrugated metal panels attached to a metal subframe were used extensively to provide shelter for storage; other uses included a chapel designed by Bruce Goff (Fig. 4.105). Metal was also used on the exterior of gas stations in the twenties and thirties in the United States. The rectangular panels were preformed into pan-shaped units attached to masonry walls in a manner almost identical to some of the systems in use today.

Aluminum was first used as cladding around 1930. One of the earliest examples is the penthouse on the roof of the Federal Reserve Bank of Pittsburgh (Fig. 4.106). Today, steel and aluminum curtain walls are quite common. They offer a wide choice of finishes, colors, panel construction, and joint detailing. While these metals rep-

Figure 4.104   Cast-iron facade on a building in Boston.

resent the vast majority of applications, other metals such as stainless steel, bronze, and copper are also used occasionally for projects that require a special image.

4.5.2 Components

Like all exterior systems, metal cladding comprises three main components:

Figure 4.106   Federal Reserve Bank of Pittsburgh. Constructed in the early 1930s. (Traced from a photo published in American Architectural Manufacturers Association, *Aluminum Curtain Wall Design Guide Manual,* 1979)

- Panels
- A supporting structure
- Joints between panels

PANELS

It is hard to categorize panels into neat, well-defined types because each system has its own distinctive features which make generalization difficult. Most systems, however, fall into one of four main categories:

1. Siding panels
2. Insulated sandwich panels
3. Honeycomb core panels
4. Sheet-metal and composite panels

Figure 4.105   Chapel constructed from standard metal components used in military buildings during World War II (designed by Bruce Goff, architect).

Siding Panels. While the term *siding* may not be universally used to refer to these panels, it is used here for ease of reference. Siding panels are used mostly to construct curtain walls for industrial buildings which include manufacturing plants, warehouses, utility buildings, and mechanical penthouses. These panels may be manufactured from steel or aluminum to a maximum length of 45 ft (14 m). Longer panels are available on special order. Panels are produced in flush or fluted profiles (Fig. 4.107). As can be readily perceived, fluted panels are more rigid than flat ones. This allows them to span longer distances. Panels that face the exterior are referred to as *face panels*. Those that face the interior, if used, are called *liner panels*. Their function is to provide interior finish, conceal the insulation, and add rigidity to the assembly.

Metal panels used in this system are manufactured in different profiles, width, depth, length, and gauge depending on the manufacturer. They may be field-assembled or preassembled into panels at the factory to expedite and simplify the erection process. Preassem-

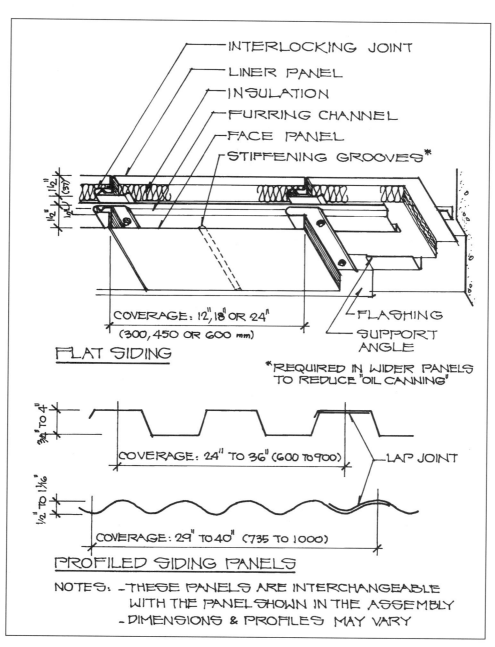

Figure 4.107 Flat and profiled siding.

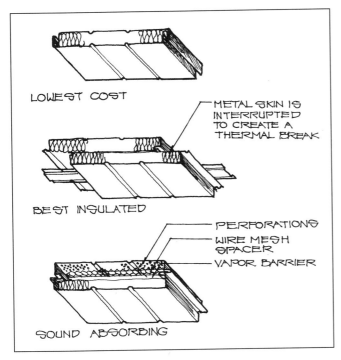

Figure 4.108 Factory-assembled siding.

bled panels (Fig. 4.108) are faster to install. They are especially useful in the construction of manufacturing plants because they are relatively easy to detach and reinstall to accommodate building expansion. As can be seen from the figure, there is a choice between an energy-efficient thermally broken panel and panels with interlocking sides that can act as thermal bridges conducting heat to the exterior. The former must be protected from wetting prior to installation since part of the insulation is exposed. Panel width represents the exposed face not counting side laps. It varies from 12 in (300 mm) for flat-faced and special profile panels to 40 in (1.0 m) for corrugated or 36 in (0.9 m) for fluted panels. Panel depth varies from ½ to 4½ in (13 to 115 mm) depending on the profile with 1½ in (38 mm) being widely used. Adjacent panels may be interlocking or lapped. The latter are joined to the supporting structure (girts or subgirts) with exposed fasteners. Liner panels may be perforated to absorb sound. Usual gauges for both exterior and liner panel profiles are 18, 20, 22, and 24 for steel and 0.032, 0.04, and 0.05 for aluminum.

Insulated Sandwich Panels. Insulated foam-core panels are 24, 30, and, in some cases, 36 in (600, 765, and 900 mm) wide and have a maximum length of 30 ft (9 m) (Fig. 4.109). Custom panels varying in width from 12 to 36 in (300 to 900 mm) are also available. Panels are manufactured in a continuous process from steel coils forming the exposed inner and outer faces of the panel at the same time that a plastic foam is injected to form

the core. Standard panel thickness is 2 in (50 mm) with thicknesses up to 5 in (127 mm) available from some manufacturers. Smooth-faced panels with lapped joints are most commonly used for public buildings. A second type with raised sides and striations is available for use on more utilitarian buildings.

Honeycomb Core Panels. These panels are produced from either steel or aluminum laminated to an aluminum or Kraft paper honeycomb core to form a rigid, flat panel (Fig. 4.110). Widths vary from 24 to 42 in (600 mm to 1.05 m). Custom widths from 6 to 54 in (150 mm to 1.4 m) are also available from some manufacturers. This panel type is manufactured in shorter lengths than foam-core panels. Standard thickness varies from ½ to 4 in (13 to 102 mm) with 2 in (51 mm) being the most widely used. In addition to use as exterior cladding, honeycomb panels are used for signage and sunscreens.

While it is acceptable for the back side of these panels to be exposed to view in industrial buildings, it is customary in commercial and public buildings to furr out the wall for the following reasons:

- Horizontal panels require vertical supports at intervals that may not coincide with the location of partitions.

- The relatively shiny finish with exposed joints is usually not appropriate or compatible with other interior finishes.

- Electric outlets and piping are sometimes required at exterior walls. Furring can accommodate these utilities.

- Window frames are usually deeper than the panel thickness and require clip angles or other method of attachment which would be unsightly if left exposed.

- The energy code may require a higher R-value than that provided by the standard 2-in foam-core panel. Placing insulation batts within the furring can raise the value to the required level. A means to vent water vapor must be provided in this assembly since metal panels act as a vapor barrier.

- The clearance gap between the slab edge and the cladding as well as panel support structure usually require concealment within the furred area.

Half-inch-thick panels fall into a gray area between honeycomb core and composite panels. Because their core is constructed from nonflammable aluminum, they were introduced to compete with the thermoplastic core panels described under sheet-metal and composite panels. Thermoplastic, like all plastics, is flammable.

Sheet-Metal and Composite Panels. This type of panel is not manufactured in standard sizes. It is custom-

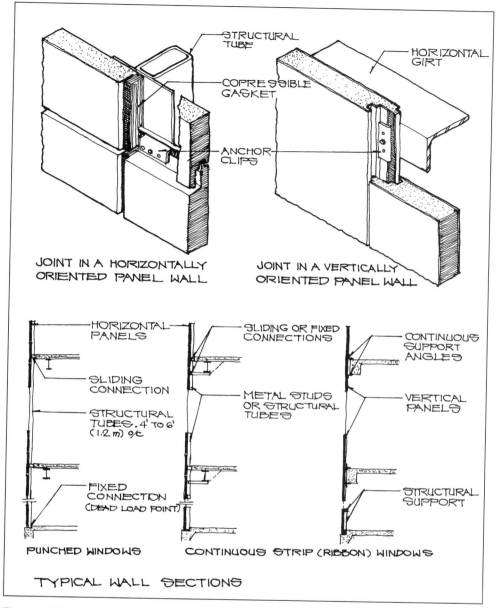

STRUCTURAL TUBE

COPRESSIBLE GASKET

ANCHOR CLIPS

HORIZONTAL GIRT

JOINT IN A HORIZONTALLY ORIENTED PANEL WALL

JOINT IN A VERTICALLY ORIENTED PANEL WALL

HORIZONTAL PANELS

SLIDING CONNECTION

STRUCTURAL TUBES. 4' TO 6' (1.2 m) o/c

FIXED CONNECTION (DEAD LOAD POINT)

PUNCHED WINDOWS

SLIDING OR FIXED CONNECTIONS

METAL STUDS OR STRUCTURAL TUBES

CONTINUOUS STRIP (RIBBON) WINDOWS

CONTINUOUS SUPPORT ANGLES

VERTICAL PANELS

STRUCTURAL SUPPORT

TYPICAL WALL SECTIONS

Figure 4.109 Foam-core panels.

fabricated for each project limited only by standard sheet-metal widths. Sheet-metal panels may be manufactured from any metal, while composite panels are manufactured from two 0.02-in (0.50 mm) sheets of aluminum sandwiching a core of extruded thermoplastic to form a perfectly flat surface (Fig. 4.111). Total thicknesses are available in 4 and 6 mm (⅛ and ¼ in) for exterior applications. Composite panels are also manufactured with cores formed from corrugated or honeycomb aluminum, PVC, mineral fiberboard, hardboard, or other materials as an alternative to thermoplastic which is flammable. This does not necessarily mean that panels with thermoplastic cores should not be used in applications requiring walls to be constructed of noncombustible materials. It only means that architects should demand that the manufacturer provide proof that the panel is acceptable to the authority having jurisdiction over the approvals for the project.

Because sheet-metal and composite panels are too thin to provide space for a backer rod, panel edges must be bent to provide the needed depth (Fig. 4.112). Aluminum sheet-metal panel thickness is ⅛ in (3 mm) in most cases. Large panels may require thicker metal or reinforcing angles fastened to the back. Steel panels are usually formed from a 28- or 24-gauge sheet formed in the same manner as aluminum.

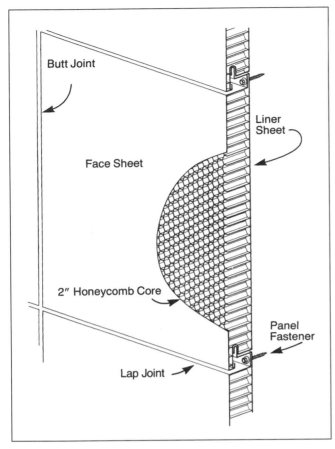

Figure 4.110 Honeycomb core panels. (Procon, a product manufactured by Construction Products, Inc.)

Other core materials used on composite panels include polystyrene, polyisocyanurate, perlite, phenolic material, and exterior plywood. This type of panel is usually thick enough to accommodate the sealant and backer rod. The most prevalent thickness using this type of core is 1 in (25 mm). Panels with sealed metal edges are suitable for use within a glass framing system in lieu of glass spandrels. Many of the panel types described above can be fabricated to provide a curved surface. Check with the manufacturer before finalizing the design radii.

SUPPORTING STRUCTURE

Siding Systems. Liner panels span vertically between an angle fastened to a concrete curb and a horizontal structural member called a *girt*. Subgirts in the form of hat furring channels may be screwed directly to liner panels or to zee-clips if a thicker insulation is required (Fig. 4.113). Face panels are then screwed to the subgirts. Two subgirts are required when gypsum wallboard is added to create a fire-rated assembly (Fig. 4.114). In locations where a danger of explosion is present, building codes mandate that wall panels be designed to allow the explosive force to vent to the exterior to reduce the possibility of structural damage to the building resulting in its collapse. Panel manufacturers offer several designs based on fasteners, clips, or washers that will fail when subjected to a specific pressure. Restraining cables fastened to the structure prevent these panels from acting like projectiles causing injury or damage to other property or personnel (Fig. 4.115).

Sandwich Panel Systems. Foam- or honeycomb-core panels 2 in (51 mm) or more in thickness are capable of spanning between floors or horizontally between vertical structural members placed at intervals ranging from 8 to 14 ft (2.4 to 4.3 m) or more depending on panel construction, wind intensity, the number of spans the panel covers, and panel thickness. Manufacturers provide span tables defining maximum allowable spans relative to wind intensity. Panels are fastened to the supporting structure with concealed fasteners placed within each joint (Fig. 4.116).

A dialogue between the architect and more than one panel manufacturer is essential during the design development phase of the project to determine the most appropriate method of support. Figure 4.109 shows one manufacturer's way of supporting its product.

Sheet-Metal and Composite Systems. These systems depend on a backup wall to provide structural support. The method of attachment depends on the cladding system selected and the makeup of the backup wall. In most cases, the distance between the face of the wall and the backup ranges between 1 and 3 in (25 and 75 mm). Figure 4.117 illustrates a method of attachment using extrusions to engage a composite panel using gaskets to seal the joint. Shims are used to align the panels. An important factor in evaluating these systems is the ease of removing each panel without disturbing the rest of the cladding (Fig. 4.118). This feature allows the owner to replace damaged panels or investigate an area of the backup wall for leakage without having to remove large segments of the cladding system, an expensive and time-consuming proposition. One feature to look for in that regard is the accessibility to fasteners from the exterior. As can be seen in the figure, the swivel retainer clips can be rotated to allow the panels to be disengaged.

JOINTS

Joints between panels are the only weak element in the defense against leaks. Systems that depend on the barrier wall approach using sealants are the least sophisticated. Those that utilize the rain screen principle with pressure equalization stand a better chance of performing faultlessly over a long period of time.

Siding Systems. Field-assembled panels may be interlocking or lapped (Fig. 4.107). Factory-assembled pan-

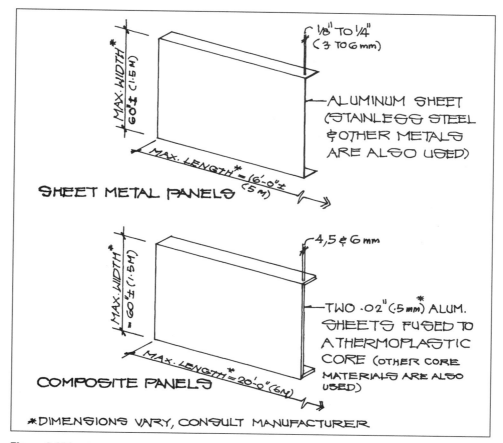

Figure 4.111 Composite and sheet-metal aluminum panels.

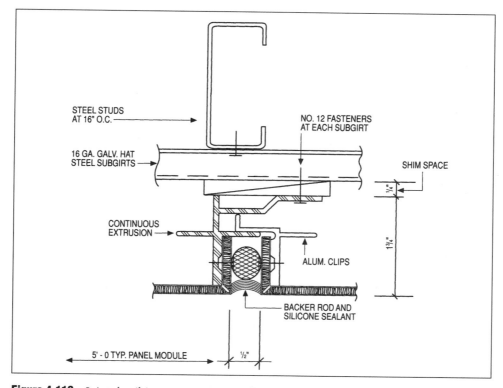

Figure 4.112 Joint detail in a composite panel assembly showing bent edges to receive the sealant and backer rod. (From Reynolds Metals Company)

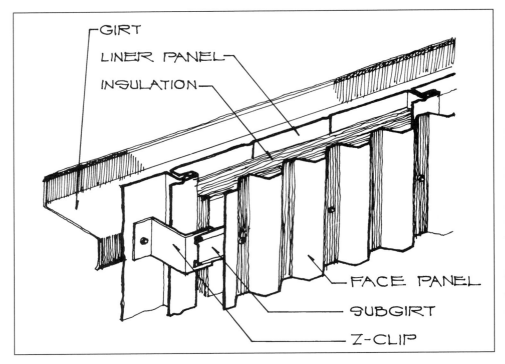

Figure 4.113 Including a zee-clip in the assembly allows insulation thickness to be increased. Zee-clip depth may be increased to allow any required insulation thickness. (Traced from a drawing by ASC Pacific, Inc.)

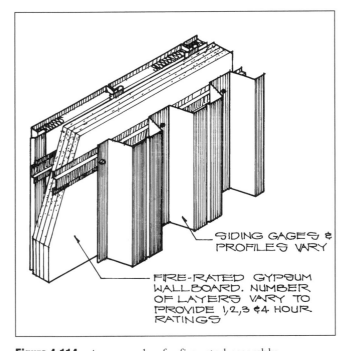

Figure 4.114 An example of a fire-rated assembly.

els are usually detailed with a tongue-and-groove or interlocking profile (Fig. 4.108).

Sandwich Panel Systems. The best foam-core panel systems are manufactured with lapped, interlocking, and thermally broken joints preformed at the factory along their long sides. While the long side of the panels is formed in the factory in that manner, the short side is cut to length and must be detailed by the architect. This can be done either by bending the face metal part way at the plant or by placing an extrusion in the joint (Figs. 4.119 and 4.120). If the system is designed as a rain screen and installed properly, the optional factory-applied sealant placed toward the exterior may not be necessary. Honeycomb-core panel systems are detailed in a similar fashion. If at all possible, architects should avoid less sophisticated systems depending entirely on wet-sealed joints because they require costly periodic maintenance and may eventually leak.

Sheet-Metal and Composite Systems. Virtually every type of joint is available for these systems. A sampling is shown in Figs. 4.112, 4.117, and 4.118. Many manufacturers' representatives will claim that theirs is a rain screen system. As explained in Chap. 3, *rain screen* is a loose term used to describe either a drained cavity wall or a pressure-equalized system. This latter has the advantage of preventing water from entering the cavity. This requires that the space between the panels and the

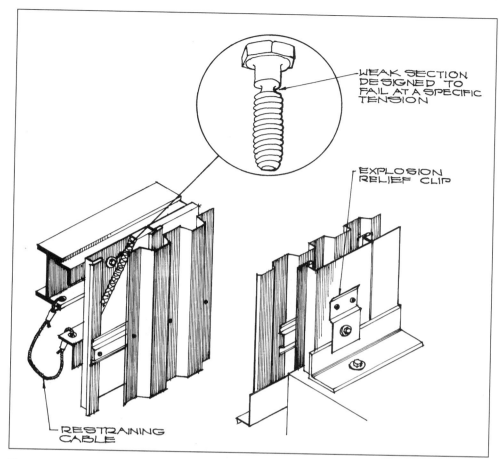

WEAK SECTION DESIGNED TO FAIL AT A SPECIFIC TENSION

EXPLOSION RELIEF CLIP

RESTRAINING CABLE

Figure 4.115 Measures used to allow the panels to detach in an explosion.

backup wall be subdivided to prevent air from migrating between the compartments. While many sheet-metal and composite panel systems seem to comply with this requirement, panel returns, which can act as partitions, are shimmed. The gap between the panel return and the backup wall allows air currents to migrate between panels, unless these gaps are sealed in some fashion or the backup wall is constructed in a manner that obviates the need for shims. These systems do not qualify as pressure-equalized systems and must depend on sealants or gaskets as their sole defense against leakage. If one of these systems is used, the wall should be designed as a cavity wall with sheathing and dampproofing. In addition to partitioning, the system must resist the forces that move water. These are described in Sec. 1.3.1 and apply to all wall systems. Theoretically, dampproofing is not required for the pressure-equalized system, but it is advisable to protect the backup with dampproofing such as roofing felt to provide an added measure of defense.

Architects should evaluate the systems under consideration for conformance to the principles described in Chap. 1 by constructing a comparison matrix as described in Sec. 2.4.3.

4.5.3 Ornamentation

Metal cladding is the embodiment of the high-tech approach to design. Its smooth surfaces and clean, uncluttered look contrast with the detailing usually used with traditional materials. Designers have several tools at their disposal to provide variety in their designs. These include various types of articulations and finishes.

ARTICULATION

Curved panels can be introduced at building corners. Minimum radii are set by each manufacturer. Even corrugated and fluted systems can be bent to radius by crimping. Sharp bends can create depth (Fig. 4.121). Recessed windows, if combined with drips, can provide protection to prevent streaking on glass surfaces as well as reduce the possibility of leakage.

Another tool at the designer's disposal is to introduce special extrusions or provide a flush or recessed strip with a different color to enliven an otherwise monotonous facade (Fig. 4.122). Extrusions can also be used as flashing between vertically oriented panels (Fig. 4.120).

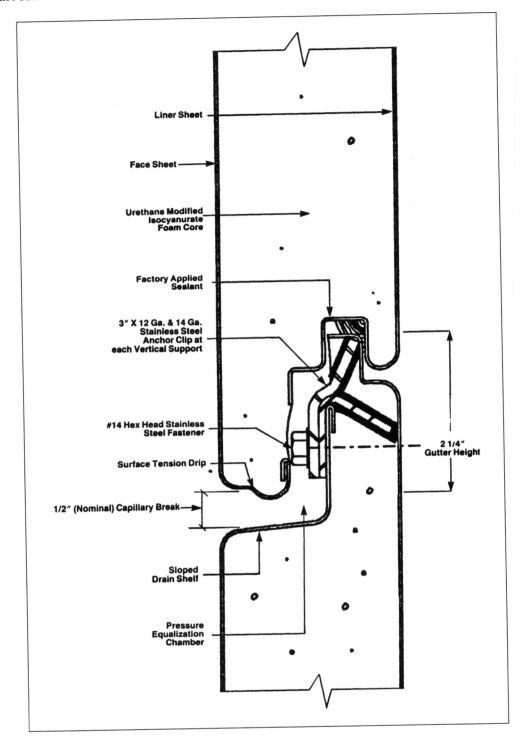

Liner Sheet

Face Sheet

Urethane Modified
Isocyanurate
Foam Core

Factory Applied
Sealant

3" X 12 Ga. & 14 Ga.
Stainless Steel
Anchor Clip at
each Vertical Support

#14 Hex Head Stainless
Steel Fastener

Surface Tension Drip

1/2" (Nominal) Capillary Break

Sloped
Drain Shelf

Pressure
Equalization
Chamber

2 1/4"
Gutter Height

Figure 4.116 Concealed fasteners in a 2-in (50-mm) sandwich panel system. (From H.H. Robertson Company)

FINISHES

Many finish options are available for use on aluminum and steel. The purpose of a finish is to protect the metal from environmental deterioration as well as to enhance its appearance. Finishes can take the form of an applied material covering the surface to prevent damaging elements from attacking it. Paint provides this kind of protection. Another form of protection is provided by oxidization of the metal itself to form a patina on the surface to isolate the metal from further deterioration.

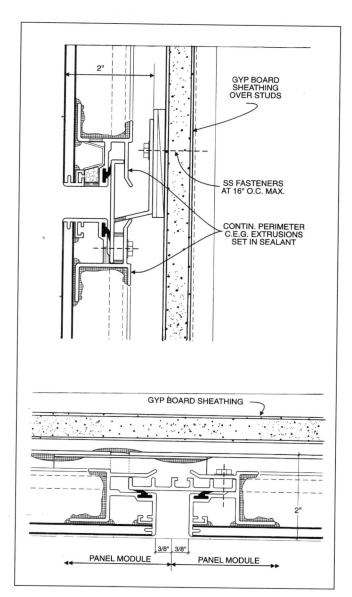

Figure 4.117 Method of attachment for a composite panel using extrusions. If the shims are specified to be continuous and sealed at their junctions, the system could qualify as a pressure-equalized cladding. (From Reynolds Metals Company)

Paints. The most durable paint options are fluorocarbon-based paints and porcelain enamels. Fluorocarbons are called by several proprietary names, most notably Kynar 500 (a trademark of Pennwalt Corp.), one of the most durable finishes on the market. It has excellent color retention over a relatively long period of time as well as minimal surface erosion and outstanding resistance to fading.

Porcelain enamel finish consists of specially formulated glass applied to the precleaned and pretreated metal surface and fired to an approximate temperature of 1500°F (815°C) in a two-coat application. This process is very durable and color-fast; however, it costs more than other coatings. The metal must not be bent or impacted after the coating is applied since any stress applied to the surface can cause crazing.

Powder coatings were introduced more recently. This type of paint is applied in the form of a dry powder containing no solvents. An electrostatic process is used to distribute the powder on the surface of the metal and is then oven-cured. Fluorocarbon paint consisting of polyvinylidine fluoride resin may be applied in this fashion to provide a durable finish without harming the ozone layer through the release of volatile organic compounds (VOC) as is the case with spray-applied paints.

Acrylic and polyester paints are not as durable as those mentioned above. They will experience a certain amount of chalking and fading with the passage of time. Because they cost less, they are appropriate for use on projects with lower budgets where longevity of the finish beyond 20 years is not important. Using lighter colors is recommended when using these types of paints. Other paints are available. Check with manufacturers when you are faced with special project conditions requiring unusual finishes. Choosing a paint to resist corrosive atmospheres is one example. All solvent-based paints may be applied either by a coil-coating process at the plant or by spraying at the fabricator's shop. They are used on both steel and aluminum. The architect must specify that the paint conforms to ASTM tests for hardness, adhesion, chalking, accelerated weathering, abrasion, and other desired qualities.

Oxidization. Aluminum, when exposed to the atmosphere, forms a hard patina through surface oxidization. This patina prevents further deterioration of the surface. Anodization, which is an electrolytic process, accelerates oxidization and produces a much thicker patina or film that offers better protection than the natural process. Anodized aluminum is rated according to the thickness of that film. The American Architectural Manufacturers[31] Association designates the film suitable for use in exterior applications as Architectural Class I with a thickness of 0.7 mils and over. While anodized aluminum is more susceptible to attack by acid-laden environments than some good quality paints, it is easily recyclable without incurring the expense of stripping the paint first. Perfect match between panels is difficult to achieve. Some designers find this aspect to be objectionable, while others value it because it provides subtle variations similar to color variations between individual stones or brick.

Steel can be protected in a similar fashion. A special high-strength low-alloy steel referred to as *weathering steel* can be left exposed and allowed to form a permanent layer of rust that protects the steel from further

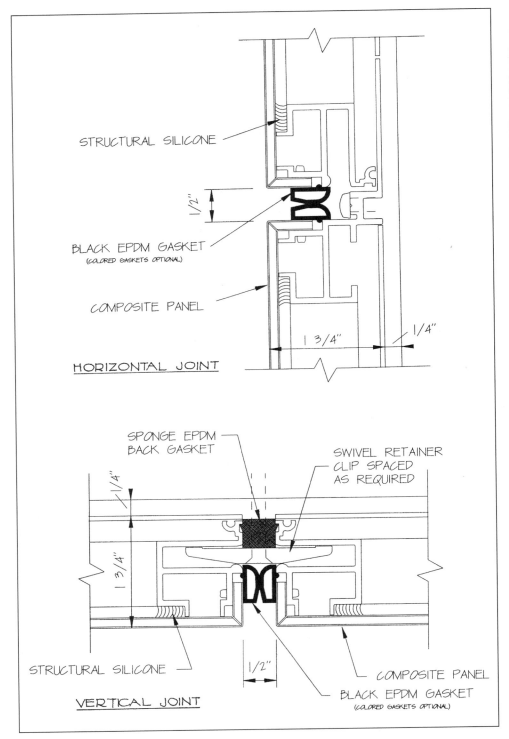

STRUCTURAL SILICONE

1/2"

BLACK EPDM GASKET
(COLORED GASKETS OPTIONAL)

COMPOSITE PANEL

1 3/4"

1/4"

HORIZONTAL JOINT

SPONGE EPDM
BACK GASKET

SWIVEL RETAINER
CLIP SPACED
AS REQUIRED

1/4"

1 3/4"

STRUCTURAL SILICONE

1/2"

COMPOSITE PANEL

BLACK EPDM GASKET
(COLORED GASKETS OPTIONAL)

VERTICAL JOINT

Figure 4.118 A design that allows panels to be easily removed. (From LIN-EL System 2000 series)

corrosion. It was introduced by Eero Saarinen in his design for the Deere & Company Headquarters Office Building in 1964. He used Cor-Ten Steel a trademark name of United States Steel (USS). Many designers use that name instead of the generic term of weathering steel. Since that initial use, several major buildings including the USS Headquarters in Pittsburgh, the Ford Foundation Building in New York, and the Knights of Columbus Headquarters in New Haven, Connecticut were constructed with weathering steel cladding (see Fig. 2.31). Special detailing is required to prevent rust from staining adjacent surfaces during its initial forma-

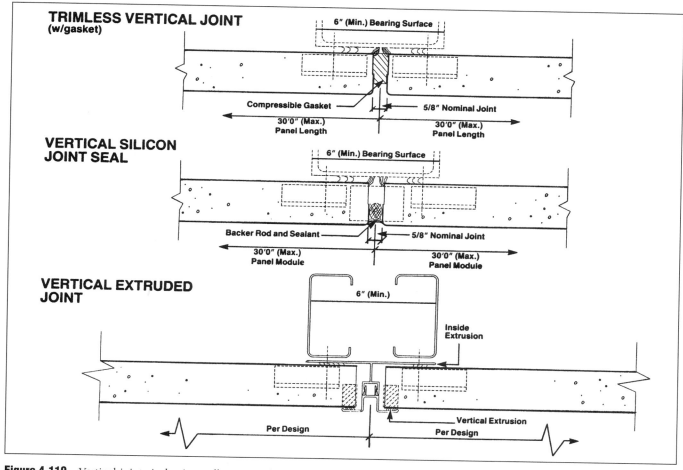

Figure 4.119   Vertical joints in horizontally oriented sandwich panels. (From H.H. Robertson Company)

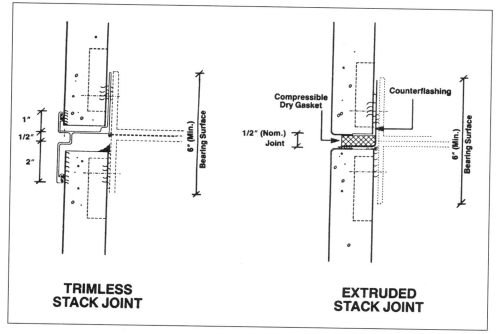

Figure 4.120   Horizontal joints in vertically oriented sandwich panels. (From H.H. Robertson Company)

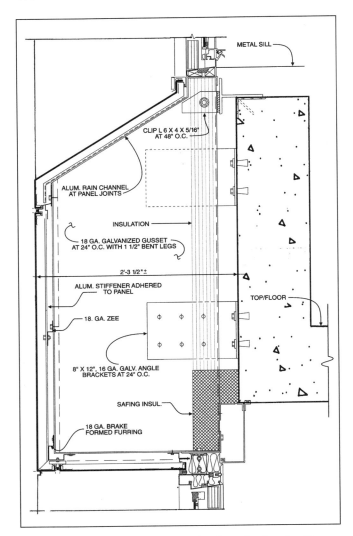

Figure 4.121 Bent panels create depth in the facade. (From Reynolds Metals Company)

tive stage. In spite of its durability and rich warm color, weathering steel seems to have fallen out of favor although it is still being used to construct highway bridges. Other metals such as copper or brass can also be left to weather naturally.

Stainless Steel. Using stainless steel adds 12 to 15% to cladding costs as compared to carbon steel or aluminum. While this amount appears to be sizable, one must consider it in the context of the total cost of the project and its life-cycle costs because stainless steel is extremely durable. Other factors such as the image and prestige that this material bestows on the building should also be considered. Image can attract higher rents and create its own financial dynamics.

Stainless steels are iron-based alloys containing 10.5% or more chromium. There are over 50 stainless-steel alloys classified according to their metallurgical structure as austenitic, ferritic, and martensitic. Austenitic is the classification used for architectural applications.

Type 304 is the alloy most widely used. It has a nominal composition of 18% chromium and 8% nickel. The Specialty Steel Industry of the United States publishes several informative pamphlets. It is a good source of information on stainless-steel alloys with special formulations and finishes. Standard finishes are described in Table 4.10. It should be noted that the shade and reflectivity of panels can vary if the ore is mined at different locations giving an effect similar to the variations in anodized aluminum panels. If uniformity is required by the designer, the raw materials should be procured from the same source. Table 4.11 provides information about standard dimensions of stainless-steel products. The types most often used in the production of fasteners are 302, 304, and 305. For highly corrosive atmospheres, type 316 should be used.[10] Consult panel manufacturers before making a final choice especially in the choice of fasteners connecting different metals, including carbon steel, that have the potential of corroding due to electrolysis (see Fig. 1.38).

4.5.4 Assemblies
SIDING SYSTEMS

This is the cheapest and least sophisticated metal panel system. It is mainly used to enclose industrial and utilitarian buildings. The most prevalent type is field-assembled from liner panels attached to horizontal structural members. Insulation is then placed within these panels, and a subgirt is next screwed to the panel at approximately 4-ft (1.2 m) intervals on which to fasten the exterior face panel (Fig. 4.123). Panels are usually placed vertically although, occasionally, you will find a design that places them horizontally. The detail at the top of the wall depends on its interface with the roof. It may be metal coping, a flashed gutter, or a sloped fluted or corrugated roof panel crimp-curved to connect with the wall panels. Flashing is placed at the bottom of the metal panels to direct any leakage or condensation to the exterior. The fabricator will readily fax information relative to gauge, maximum allowable spans, and standard details applicable to the project at hand upon request. Wall assemblies can provide 1-, 2-, 3-, and 4-h fire protection by including a number of fire-rated gypsum wallboards between the face and liner panels.

Perforated liner panels may be used to reduce noise by absorbing sound. A vapor retarder must be placed between this panel and the insulation to prevent water vapor from passing through the perforations, soaking the insulation, reducing its R-value, and condensing within the assembly causing the metal to corrode (if steel panels are used).

Panels with deep flutes can span longer distances between supporting girts. This makes them more economical in certain cases.

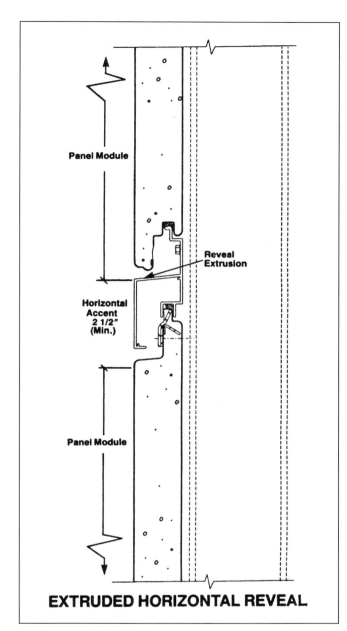

Figure 4.122 Extruded strips to introduce color or a depressed reveal in a flat facade. (From H.H. Robertson Company)

SANDWICH PANEL SYSTEMS

Wall assemblies using foam- or honeycomb-core panels are shown in Fig. 4.124. Major manufacturers offer a complete cladding system including fenestration. This is referred to as *single sourcing* and has the advantage of focusing the responsibility into a single entity capable of correcting any condition that causes a leak. This is a definite advantage over the conventional method of having separate subcontractors for the wall and window components. If a leak occurs, each would place the blame on the other, and it becomes almost impossible to prove

where the responsibility lies. Architects must be careful, however, in specifying a single-source system, because this may narrow the competition and result in higher costs. In addition, for government work, some states require *filed sub-bids.* This means that the general contractor cannot execute certain parts of the project using his or her own labor force but must entrust these parts to an independent subcontractor. Windows may fall under this category, and, in some cases, the client may not approve a single-source system. Architects must research these issues and take an appropriate course of action. In some cases, it is advantageous to specify another window system as an alternate and include a few details to be priced competitively and evaluate the prices of the alternate against each contractor's base bid. Like other panelized systems, sandwich panel assemblies require that a mock-up be constructed and tested to prove that the system will perform as designed. While this test performs an important function if the design is unusual or unique, it is unnecessary if standard systems are used. Most experts recommend that a field test be conducted on several locations to test the erected system against air and water leakage.

SHEET-METAL AND COMPOSITE SYSTEMS

These systems are lightweight. In most cases, they have very limited spanning capability. This means that an insulated masonry or stud backup wall (Fig. 4.125) is needed to support the panels. Composite panels are extremely flat with joint details ranging from simple bends to complex extrusions. The figure shows a slope on horizontal surfaces and weep or vent holes to vent any vapor escaping from the interior. This is important since the metal surface is impervious to vapor and can trap water inside the wall assembly. While, theoretically, no dampproofing is required on the backup wall, it is always a good policy to cover it with 15-lb felt to provide insurance against improper field execution.

Uninsulated metal systems are imminently suited for remodeling old, outdated facades because they impose very little extra load on the building. As an added benefit, they provide protection against the leaks inherent in many of these buildings.

4.5.5 What Can Go Wrong
LEAKAGE

The most vulnerable elements of a metal wall assembly are the joints between panels. Wet-sealed joints can fail causing leaks. Likewise, dry seals (gaskets) can let in water during violent rainstorms especially at the junction between vertical and horizontal joints. Systems that are designed with more than one defense mechanism fare better. If one defense fails, the backup prevents leakage

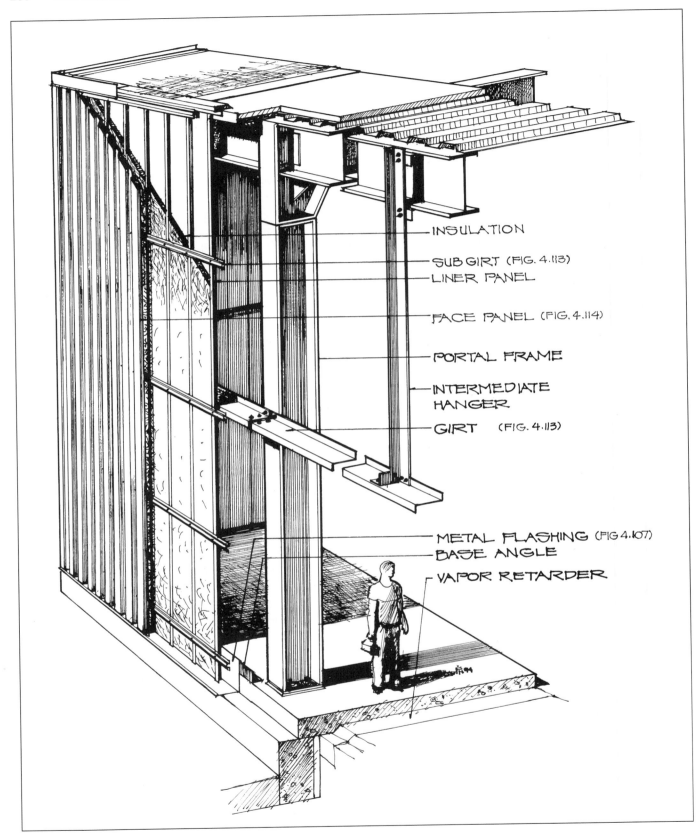

INSULATION

SUB GIRT (FIG. 4.113)
LINER PANEL

FACE PANEL (FIG. 4.114)

PORTAL FRAME

INTERMEDIATE
HANGER

GIRT   (FIG. 4.113)

METAL FLASHING (FIG 4.107)
BASE ANGLE

VAPOR RETARDER

Figure 4.123 Metal siding assembly.

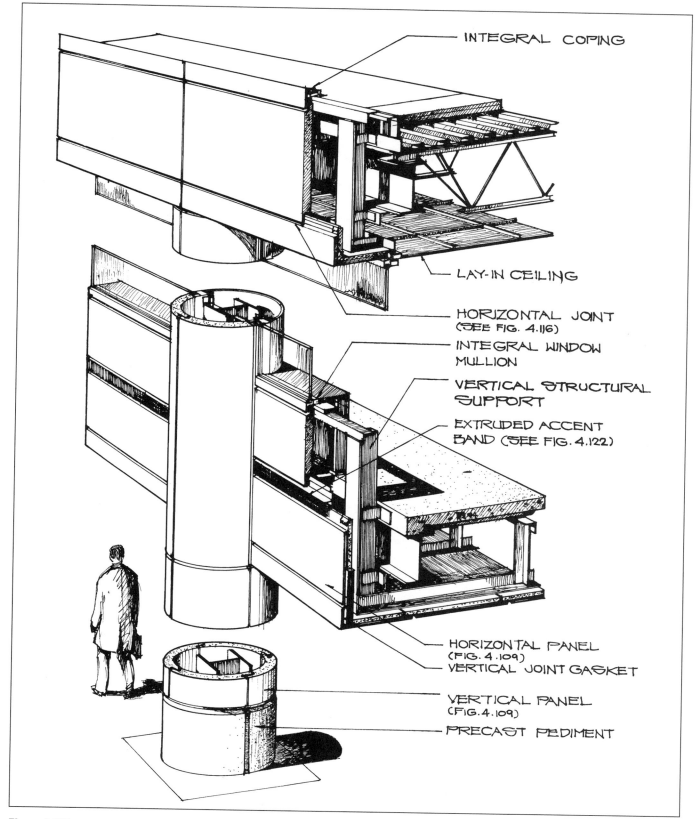

INTEGRAL COPING

LAY-IN CEILING

HORIZONTAL JOINT
(SEE FIG. 4.116)

INTEGRAL WINDOW
MULLION

VERTICAL STRUCTURAL
SUPPORT

EXTRUDED ACCENT
BAND (SEE FIG. 4.122)

HORIZONTAL PANEL
(FIG. 4.109)

VERTICAL JOINT GASKET

VERTICAL PANEL
(FIG. 4.109)

PRECAST PEDIMENT

Figure 4.124   Metal sandwich panel assembly.

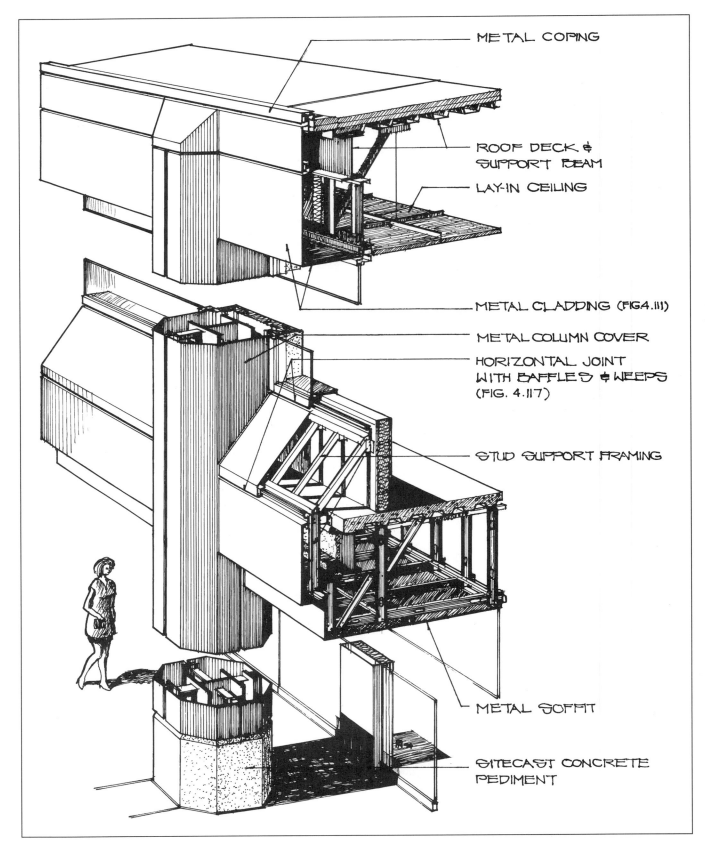

METAL COPING

ROOF DECK &
SUPPORT BEAM

LAY-IN CEILING

METAL CLADDING (FIG 4.III)

METAL COLUMN COVER

HORIZONTAL JOINT
WITH BAFFLES & WEEPS
(FIG. 4.II7)

STUD SUPPORT FRAMING

METAL SOFFIT

SITECAST CONCRETE
PEDIMENT

Figure 4.125   Composite or sheet-metal panel assembly.

STANDARD MECHANICAL SHEET FINISHES

Unpolished or Rolled Finishes:

No. 1 A rough, dull surface which results from hot rolling to the specified thickness followed by annealing and descaling.

No. 2D A dull finish which results from cold rolling followed by annealing and descaling, and may perhaps get a final light roll pass through unpolished rolls. A 2D finish is used where appearance is of no concern.

No. 2B A bright, cold-rolled finish resulting in the same manner as No. 2D finish, except that the annealed and descaled sheet receives a final light roll pass through polished rolls. This is the general-purpose cold-rolled finish that can be used as is, or as a preliminary step to polishing.

Polished Finishes;

No. 3 An intermediate polish surface obtained by finishing with a 100-grit abrasive. Generally used where a semifinished polished surface is required. A No. 3 finish usually receives additional polishing during fabrication.

No. 4 A polished surface obtained by finishing with a 120-150 mesh abrasive, following initial grinding with coarser abrasives. This is a general-purpose bright finish with a visible "grain" which prevents mirror reflection.

No. 6 A dull satin finish having lower reflectivity than No. 4 finish. It is produced by Tampico brushing the No. 4 finish in a medium of abrasive and oil. It is used for architectural applications and ornamentation where a high luster is undesirable, and to contrast with brighter finishes.

No. 7 A highly reflective finish that is obtained by buffing finely ground surfaces but not to the extent of completely removing the "grit" lines. It is used chiefly for architectural and ornamental purposes.

No. 8 The most reflective surface; which is obtained by polishing with successively finer abrasives and buffing extensively until all grit lines from preliminary grinding operations are removed. It is used for applications such as mirrors and reflectors.

Table 4.10 Standard finishes for stainless steel (Reproduced by permission from Specialty Steel Industry)

to the interior long enough to allow repairs to be made. An example is shown in Fig. 4.126. The suggested details published by the manufacturer omit the dampproofing and sheathing shown in the figure, but because this system is a barrier wall system (see Sec. 3.2.2) depending on a wet-applied sealant that will eventually fail, it would be prudent to add this extra line of defense Architects must pay special attention to panel corners and review the way panel returns are sealed (welded corners perform best), how horizontal joints are detailed in their juncture with vertical joints, and how the system conforms to the principles described in Sec. 1.3.1.

IMPACT DAMAGE

Metal panels, especially low-gauge sheet aluminum and thin composites are highly susceptible to impact damage. This usually occurs at ground level where traffic or vandalism can cause dings or crushing of the surface (Fig. 4.127). One way to prevent this from occurring is to construct the bottom of the wall with a more solid material such as concrete or masonry and start the metal at a higher elevation out of harm's way. Another solution is to use a thicker gauge in that area or plant shrubs adjacent to the wall. Placing bumpers or bollards where impact by vehicles is likely is also advisable.

OIL CANNING

Honeycomb and foam-core panels as well as composite panels are perfectly flat and give the facade a solid appearance. This is not necessarily the case with light-gauge sheet-metal panels. Oil canning is the waviness associated with some metal siding and large 24-gauge aluminum panels. These panels impart a cheap and

flimsy look to the building. To avoid this, a heavier gauge than the minimum should be chosen. In addition, an embossed texture or striations should be used to stiffen the panels, reduce their shininess, and help mitigate this flaw. Using ⅛-in (3 mm) aluminum panels folded 90° or fused to an extrusion around the perimeter is recommended. Large panels should be reinforced at the back at intervals to stiffen them.

Architects should consult manufacturer's technical personnel or a cladding consultant to get advice on these and other issues such as foam-core panel delamination and the type of fasteners to use to fasten the panel to a different metal before making final decisions. Visiting projects where the panel being proposed was used can shed some light on what to use and what to avoid.

Summary

In terms of exterior wall materials, metal cladding is a new development. There are four main categories of metal cladding. Metal siding is field-assembled or partially assembled at the factory and field-erected. It is used for industrial and utilitarian buildings in most cases. Foam- or honeycomb-core panels 2 in (50 mm) or more in thickness are capable of spanning between floors or vertical structural members such as studs or steel tubes. They may be faced with either aluminum or steel sheet metal. Foam-core panels are also manufactured in thicknesses ranging from 1 to 5 in (25 to 127 mm) with 2-in (50 mm) steel-faced foam-core panels being the most widely used. Honeycomb-core panels are extremely flat and available in wider panels. Some manufacturers offer total cladding responsibility by including windows in the system. This can be advanta-

CLASSIFICATION OF STAINLESS STEEL PRODUCT FORMS

Item	Description	Dimensions		
		Thickness	**Width**	**Diameter or Size**
Sheet	Coils and cut lengths: Mill finishes Nos. 1, 2D & 2B Pol. finishes Nos. 3, 4, 6, 7 & 8	under $^3/_{16}$" (4.76 mm) " " "	24" (609.6 mm) & over all widths	—
Strip	Cold finished, coils or cut lengths Pol. finishes Nos. 3, 4, 6, 7 & 8	under $^3/_{16}$" (4.76 mm) " " "	under 24" (609.6 mm) all widths	—
Plate	Flat rolled or forged	$^3/_{16}$" (4.76 mm) & over	over 10" (254 mm)	—
Bar	Hot finished rounds, squares, octagons and hexagons Hot finished flats	— $^1/_8$" (3.18 mm) to 8" (203 mm) incl.	— $^1/_4$" (6.35 mm) to 10" (254 mm) incl.	$^1/_4$" (6.35 mm) & over —
	Cold finished rounds, squares, octagons and hexagons Cold finished flats	— $^1/_8$" (3.18 mm) to 4$^1/_2$" (114 mm)	— $^3/_8$" (9.53 mm) to 4$^1/_2$" (114 mm)	over $^1/_8$" (3.18 mm) —
Wire	Cold finishes only: (in coil) Round, square, octagon, hexagon, and flat wire	under $^3/_{16}$" (4.76 mm)	under $^3/_8$" (9.53 mm)	—
Pipe & Tubing	Several different classifications, with differing specifications, are available. For information on standard sizes consult your local Steel Service Center or the SSIUS.			
Extrusions	Not considered "standard" shapes, but of potentially wide interest. Currently limited in size to approximately 6$^1/_2$" (165.1 mm) diameter, or structurals.			

Table 4.11 Classification of stainless-steel product forms (Reproduced by permission from Specialty Steel Industry)

geous to the client if a leak occurs. On the other hand, it may limit competition or it may be unacceptable in government work. Panels are produced in standard and custom sizes. The designer must be aware of panel width constraints during the schematic design phase.

Sheet-metal and composite panel systems are custom-fabricated for each project. Panel size is limited only by metal coil width. Composite panels are composed of two very thin sheets of aluminum laminated to any of several types of cores. Thermoplastic is one of the most prevalent. However, because this material, like all plastic is flammable, several nonflammable materials were introduced to compete with it. Panel thickness for exterior use is usually 4, 5, or 6 mm. They are usually bent at 90° around the perimeter and attached to a structural backup.

Each system features a different type of joint. Wet joints using sealants need periodic maintenance. Gasketed systems may leak unless combined with a backup defense mechanism. The most successful systems use a well baffled rain screen with a pressure-equalized cavity or open, baffled joints with a properly dampproofed backup.

Ornamentation can take the form of crimping fluted panels to execute curves, creating depth in the facade by executing sharp bends in the panels, vacuum-forming aluminum panels, or adding special extrusions

to provide reveals with or without a different color.

Finishes provide protection as well as enhance the appearance of the metal. It can take the form of an applied finish like paint or oxidization produced by the metal itself. The best paints are fluorocarbons, applied either by spraying or powder coating, and porcelain enamel. Oxidization takes the form of anodization for aluminum or a special kind of stable rust formed on a high-strength low-alloy weathering steel. Other metals such as copper also form a protective patina to weather naturally.

Stainless-steel alloys contain chromium and nickel. Type 304 is the most widely used alloy in architectural applications. Types 302, 304, and 305 are used in fasteners. Type 316 is used for areas with corrosive atmospheres.

Metal cladding is more easily damaged than conventional masonry construction. Unseemly dents and dings marring its appearance are caused by vehicles or vandals. Providing bollards or bumpers at driveways and planting shrubs can reduce this danger. Constructing the lower part of the wall from other materials is also an effective solution. Choosing a system designed for a relatively easy way of replacing damaged panels is advisable. It has the added effect of simplifying inspection procedures should a leak or a problem in the backup

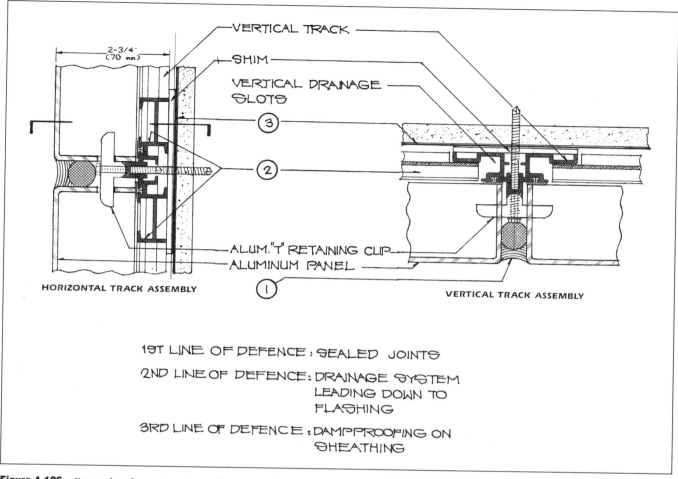

Figure 4.126 Example of a system that offers several lines of defense. (From Tech Wall, a product of Alply, Inc.)

occur. This is especially important where metal cladding is used to reclad older buildings. Oil canning is a term used to describe waviness in the metal surface occurring in systems using thin sheets. It can be mitigated by using a thicker gauge, texturing or striating the metal, or using composite panels.

4.6 STUD-BACKED WALLS

This type of backup wall represents a large percentage of modern wall construction. The bulk of nonresidential projects, where masonry or concrete is not used, utilizes steel studs as the backup for several types of cladding. The reason is that steel studs are lightweight, fast to erect, economical, noncombustible, and are not susceptible to rot or infestation. They do, however, have their shortcomings. They corrode when exposed to continuous moisture, they deflect more than masonry, and they act as thermal bridges conducting heat to or from the exterior. This section explores these systems starting with a brief history of the origin of studs.

4.6.1 Historical Background

Throughout history, lumber was produced by roughly squaring timber with hand tools. The introduction of the water-powered sawmill at the beginning of the nine-

Figure 4.127 Damage to a composite panel at ground level.

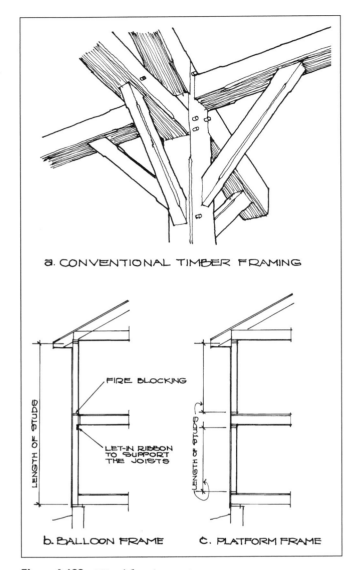

Figure 4.128 Wood framing systems.

teenth century revolutionized the lumber industry, and, eventually, standardized lumber sizes were established.

Modern stud framing was introduced in 1832 by George Washington Snow, a Chicago builder. Prior to that time, all wood structures were constructed from heavy timber post and beam frames assembled by craftsmen who fashioned intricate tongue-and-groove joinery [Fig. 4.128(*a*)]. A relatively large work force was required to erect these frames. Mr. Snow designed an easier and faster method that could be assembled by only two people. It was given the name *balloon frame* by its detractors to denote its flimsiness [Fig. 4.128(*b*)].

The balloon frame had a serious flaw. Unlike heavy timber which has the ability to resist a serious fire, this type of light framing with studs extending the full height of a two-story building, provided a ready path for fire to travel between floors. The space between the studs acted as a chimney flue, conducting fire and smoke to the upper story very rapidly. In addition, the length of the studs made them difficult to handle during construction. To correct these shortcomings, the *platform* framing system was introduced [Fig. 4.128(*c*)]. It provided a firestop of sorts between floors.

Steel studs were introduced shortly after World War II to compete with wood and to absorb some of the excess manufacturing capacity of the steel industry resulting from the cessation of hostilities. Stud dimensions are similar to those of wood, and the design of the assembly is almost identical. The only significant difference is in the way the pieces are fastened together and the open-sided profiles of the parts in contrast to the solid wood components. While wood is fastened by nailing, steel members are attached either by self-tapping screws or by welding. This system gained wide acceptance for public and commercial buildings.

4.6.2 Components

Exterior stud walls are constructed by fastening studs to horizontal members called tracks or runners. They are located at both ends of the vertical studs. Exterior sheathing and interior wallboard are then fastened to this framing to form surfaces ready to support the exterior finish. These boards also perform an important structural function by acting as a diaphragm adding lateral strength to the assembly. Since this book does not address residential or similar small buildings, this section will not cover wood components.

STUDS

Steel studs are cold-formed, C-shaped vertical framing members. They are prepunched to allow pipes and wiring to be installed within the wall cavity. These holes are also used to accommodate bridging. When used to accommodate utilities, punched web holes are sometimes fitted with insulating plastic grommets to speed installation and prevent damage to the wiring and pipes being threaded through them.

Exterior wall stud gauges vary from 20 gauge (thin) to 14 gauge (thick). The gauge most often used in welded assemblies is 18 gauge because it can withstand the intense heat generated by gas metal arc welding (GMAW) or stick welding [also known as shielded metal arc welding or (SMAW)] without burn through. For lighter gauges, metal-inert gas (MIG) welding is used. Stud sizes vary from 1⅝ to 6 in (40 to 150 mm). This latter is the most often used in exterior walls because it

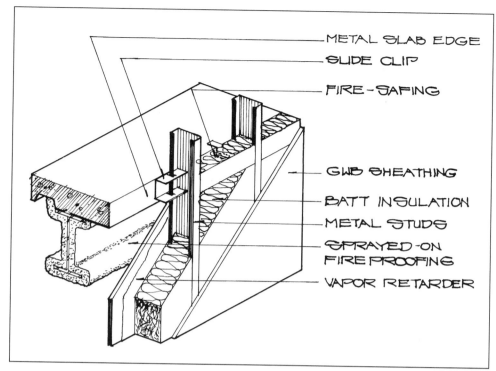

Figure 4.129 Stud attachment to allow deflection movement.

allows for the placement of an adequate thickness of batt insulation and reduces deflection caused by lateral (wind) forces. Lengths up to 40 ft (12 m) are available. Longer studs are used in curtain walls to span more than one floor. They are fastened to the slab edge in a way that allows the structure to deflect without transferring the load to the studs (Fig. 4.129). Because this condition (where studs are attached to the slab edge) is, in essence, a balloon frame arrangement, a fire-stopping material must be installed between the studs to prevent fire from traveling between floors. This material is referred to as a *firestop* and is manufactured from a dense form of mineral fiber. It is manufactured from natural rock heated to its melting point at temperatures in excess of 2000°F (1100°C) and converted into a fibrous material using a production method similar to that used in manufacturing fiberglass.

The standard spacing for studs in exterior walls is 16 in (400 mm). Shorter spacing is usual at building corners and upper floors of multistory construction where accelerated wind velocities exert added pressure or suction. As mentioned in Chap. 2, there are two ways to design an exterior wall stud system, by assigning the task to the structural consultant or by writing a performance specification requiring the contractor to present shop drawings signed and sealed by an engineer registered in the state. For important projects such as high-rise buildings

or for locations subject to unusual wind conditions, a wind tunnel test subjecting a model of the building and its surroundings to air velocities similar to those expected at the site and monitoring the pressure (or suction) at a grid of points in the area of the elevation by means of sensors is advisable. Based on this data, the design wind loads are determined and written in the specifications. For smaller projects, wind loads are determined by the code.

Stud assemblies may be stick-built. This means that the studs are fastened individually at the site or may be preassembled into panels on or off the site and raised by hand or hoisted to their final location where they are attached to the structure.

TRACKS

Top and bottom tracks or runners are U-shaped. They are sized to fit snugly on both sides of the studs. In load-bearing construction, both the top and bottom tracks are fastened to the studs. In curtain wall construction, beam deflection is accommodated by constructing a double track at the top of the assembly. One track featuring deeper legs is fastened to the slab edge or beam, while the second one is welded to the studs and placed within the upper track. A gap is left between the two (see Fig. 2.3(c)] to allow the structure to move independently of the stud assembly. Sheathing must not be fas-

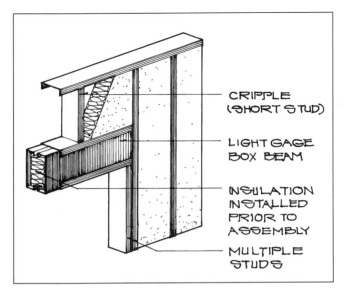

Figure 4.130 Light-gauge box beam at window head (wide window openings).

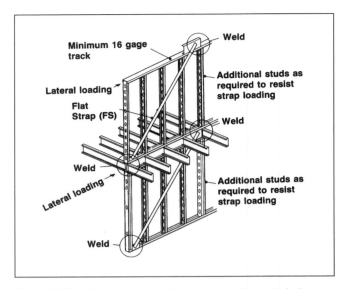

Figure 4.131 Bracing at building corners. (From Dale/Incor Industries)

tened to the top track lest it impede the movement. The dampproofing membrane is lapped so that it may not be damaged by the movement.

HEADERS

A header is a relatively short, simply supported beam transferring loads from above to the jambs of an opening in a manner similar to a masonry lintel. This term is also used to describe a similar member which transfers loads from floor joist to beams located at both sides of an opening in a floor assembly. Window and door headers are supported by a single, double, or triple studs at the jambs. The number of studs is determined by the width of the opening and the superimposed loads.

For narrow openings, headers may be constructed from a track that receives short lengths of studs which are referred to as *cripples*. Wider openings or openings that are required to transfer floor loads usually require a box beam arrangement constructed from joists and tracks welded together (Fig. 4.130). A similar type of construction may be required at the sill to transfer gravity and wind loads. Insulation must be placed in the box beam before final assembly.

BRACING AND BRIDGING

To prevent bearing stud walls from racking (the deformation caused by lateral forces) diagonal braces constructed from steel straps are screwed or welded to one or both faces of the studs at the corners of the building (Fig. 4.131). Curtain or infill walls do not require bracing if the studs span from floor to floor. Stud assemblies that span from window head to the sill of the window

above in curtain walls featuring strip windows usually require bracing back to the floor system (Fig. 4.132).

Bridging provides resistance against the tendency of studs to rotate or bend as a result of lateral or gravity loading. It takes the form of straps placed on both sides of the studs or 1½-in (40 mm) cold-rolled channels placed in the web punched holes at a maximum interval of 4 ft (1.2 m). Strap bridging may be combined with a track under certain conditions (Fig. 4.133).

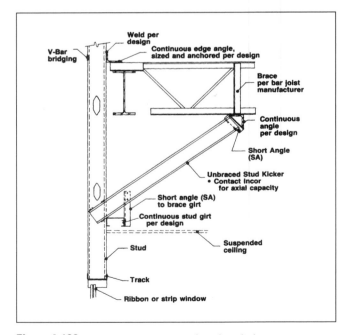

Figure 4.132 Bracing at strip window head. (From Dale/Incor Industries)

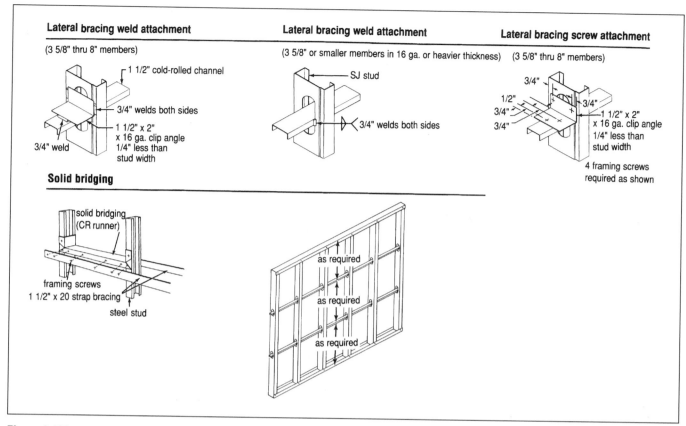

Figure 4.133   Examples of bridging. (From Unimast Incorporated)

SHEATHING

Boards fastened to the exterior face of the studs are referred to as sheathing. They function as an exterior skin enclosing the structure as well as a base to attach dampproofing to. Several materials are employed as sheathing. The type most often used is the ½-in (13-mm) gypsum sheathing. Because the paper facer on these boards has been known to deteriorate if the exterior finish (brick, metal, etc.) is delayed for a length of time leaving the sheathing exposed to the weather, sheathing with a fiberglass facer was introduced and is rapidly gaining acceptance. This type is more durable and more suitable as a substrate for adhered cladding such as EIFS assemblies. Board width for both types is 4 ft (1.2 m); standard lengths are 8, 9, and 10 ft (2.4, 2.7, and 3 m). Type X is ⅝ in (16 mm) thick and is used in fire-rated assemblies. Gypsum sheathing is also produced in 2 × 8 ft (0.6 × 2.4 m) panels with V-shaped tongue and groove edges. This type is more commonly used in multistory buildings.

Cement board is another durable sheathing material used in exterior walls. Panel measurements vary between different manufacturers. They are fabricated from an aggregated Portland cement slurry reinforced with polymer-coated fiberglass mesh embedded in both surfaces. Exterior-grade cement board should be specified for exterior walls. It is different from the cement board used to back tile in bathrooms.

Joints between sheathing panels may be sealed with a special troweled sealant or a 2-in- (50-mm) wide fiberglass self-adhering tape sealed with acrylic latex caulk. Metal deck and other board types are used as sheathing in certain panelized systems.

FINISHES AND VENEERS

Several materials may be used to provide the exterior cladding for stud systems. In preceding sections, we have reviewed brick cavity wall assemblies (Sec. 4.2), stone (Sec. 4.3), and metal (Sec. 4.5). Other materials are also used to face stud assemblies. They include wood, stucco, EIFS, and tile.

Wood Siding. Some multifamily residential buildings as well as public buildings designed to blend with a residential neighborhood may be clad in wood siding. Sheathing, in that case, may be one of the materials described above, or it may be a wood product such as plywood, wafer board, fiberboard, or oriented-strand board.

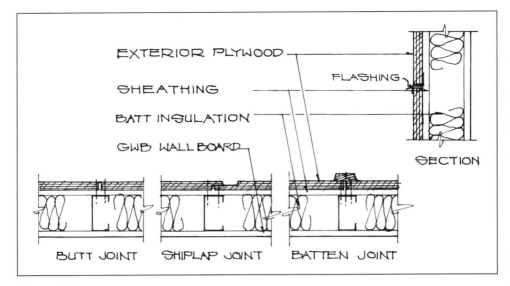

Figure 4.134 Plywood joints.

Plywood siding may be redwood, cedar, fir, or pine. Panels may be plain-faced or grooved to simulate the solid board look. Joints may be butted, battened, or ship-lapped (Fig. 4.134).

Solid wood boards are produced from redwood, cedar, cypress, pine, spruce, and hemlock. The first three are the most costly. They have a natural resistance to water penetration, warping, rotting, and attack by insects. They may be left untreated to weather naturally or stained for added protection. Clapboards are installed horizontally with each board cut in a tapered profile and overlapping the one below it. Vertical siding may have tongue-and-groove joints, or the joints may be covered by battens (Fig. 4.135). Boards may also be installed diagonally or horizontally.

Stucco. Stucco is a type of finish applied like plaster on exterior walls. It is a mixture of sand, Portland cement, lime, and water. When applied to rough surfaces, metal lath is sometimes omitted and a stiff straw brush is used to splatter a dash coat onto the surface to increase its roughness and improve its bond with the next coat. It is not as dependable as attaching metal or wire lath to the surface. This application should be allowed to set before the brown coat is applied. The final coat is the finish coat which is mixed with the required color and troweled smooth or given a choice of textures. A two-coat application is also used.

Stucco may be applied to one of several wall support systems. In addition to the masonry substrate described above, it may be applied to metal lath attached to gypsum or cement board sheathing or supported by closely spaced wires attached to the studs

(Fig. 4.136). The latter is usually used in residential projects. Metal lath on sheathing is the method most often used on stud wall backup. Self-furring diamond mesh 3.4 lb/yd^2 (1.8 kg/m^2) is usually chosen for stucco applications. It leaves a ¼-in (6-mm) gap between it and the sheathing to allow the scratch coat to penetrate into the lath openings and provide a mechanical bond. It also allows any accumulated moisture to drain or vent to the exterior. Flat rib lath with ⅛-in (3-mm) ribs is also used as an alternative to diamond mesh. Figure 4.137 shows two different types of lath and their applications.

A three-coat application is the conventional method of applying stucco. The scratch coat, so called because it is scratched after application to provide a mechanical bond with the next coat, is pressed into the lath with a trowel. It is formulated from one part of quick- or hydrated-lime, three to six parts of sand, and one part Portland cement. Premixed masonry cement is also used. The scratch coat provides a rough uneven surface approximately ⅜ in (10 mm) thick measured from the backup surface.

Before the second coat, which is referred to as the brown coat, is applied, the scratch coat must be dampened and fully cured. This coat is mixed from one part cement, three parts sand, and lime putty measured at 15 to 25% of the cement volume. It is applied either by a trowel or sprayed from a hose. The surface is leveled with a straight edge moved over control joints or edge- and corner-beads installed for that purpose. The brown coat must not be less than ⅜ in (10 mm) thick.

The final coat is the finish coat. It incorporates the desired color and can be either smooth or textured. The

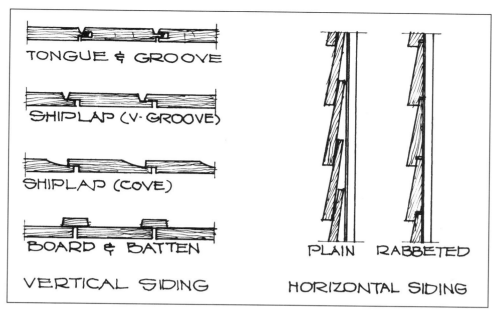

Figure 4.135 Wood siding joints.

same mix used in formulating the brown coat is used on this coat. This is a very thin coat measuring approximately ⅛ in (3 mm) thick. It brings the total thickness to ¾ or ⅞ in (20 or 22 mm).

A three-coat application requires a relatively long time to finish. The scratch coat takes from 4 days to 1 week to harden sufficiently to apply the brown coat. The second coat takes a week or more to be ready for the finish coat which, in turn, requires at least 4 days to set. The conventional, three-coat stucco is labor-intensive and dependent on weather conditions. However, if control joints are positioned at recommended locations, the mixes are properly done, the intervals for setting are observed, and the substrate is stable, it can give long years of dependable service. A more recent development is executed by applying polymer-modified Portland cement base coat to cement boards fastened to the studs over a water barrier. A polymer-based stucco finish completes the job. This type of stucco is more suitable to the fast-paced construction used today because it can be finished the same day.

To control cracking, control joints should be spaced a maximum of 18 ft (5.5 m) in either the vertical or horizontal dimension. Each area must not exceed 150 ft² (14 m²). Self-furring metal lath combined with a drip screed allows the system to drain and improves the bond between the first coat and the lath.

Choosing the appropriate cement is crucial for the success of a stucco application. Air-entraining cements

resist damage caused by freezing as well as improve workability, and truer colors can be obtained by using white cement. Premixed cements formulated expressly for use in stucco simplify and expedite execution as well as control quality.

Like all wall assemblies, stucco components must allow vapor to exit the wall without hindrance (see Sec. 1.3.2).

Exterior Insulation and Finish System (EIFS) Assemblies. As the name implies, an EIFS assembly incorporates rigid insulation with synthetic stucco. Like stucco, it can be applied to both masonry and a sheathed stud backup and offers a choice of textures and colors. This system was first introduced in Germany in 1955 and used successfully in Europe for several years before being introduced in the United States in the 1960s. It differs from stucco in several important ways including the following:

1. It incorporates a layer of uninterrupted rigid insulation that sheathes the building without gaps or thermal bridges. In addition to energy conservation this arrangement protects the wall structure from the thermal fluctuations that cause cracks.

2. Most EIFS assemblies use one or two resilient fiberglass mesh layers to reinforce thin layers of specially formulated (synthetic) stucco.

3. By manipulating the thickness of the insulation, special three-dimensional design articulations can be introduced in the facade.

4. Unlike stucco, EIFS insulation is combustible.

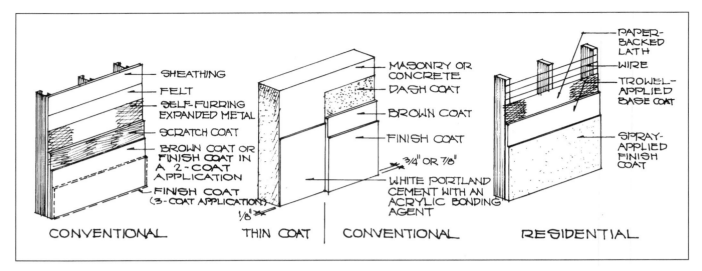

Figure 4.136 Some common stucco systems

An EIFS assembly may be field-applied or shop-fabricated as a panelized system. In both cases, the method of applying the synthetic stucco is the same. The polymer-modified Portland cement used in the EIFS assembly gives the thin coats a certain toughness, better adhesion, reduced water permeability, and improved flexibility. This means that it makes it smoother and easier to apply with a lower cement-to-water ratio than conventional stucco.

The rigid insulation backing may be adhered or mechanically fastened (Fig. 4.138). Alternatively, both adhesive and fasteners are used. It is recommended that walls exposed to high winds be mechanically fastened. At high-impact areas, usually at the lower part of the wall, a double fiberglass mesh or an expanded metal-reinforced system with a ⅜-in- (10 mm) thick two-coat application should be considered.

The Exterior Insulation Manufacturer's Association (EIMA) classifies EIFS under two categories:

1. *PB.* An acrylic polymer-based synthetic stucco finish coat applied over glass cloth embedded in a base coat adhered to rigid insulation. The insulation most commonly used is expanded or extruded polystyrene. Polyurethane and isocyanurate are sometimes used as alternatives to polystyrene. If extruded polystyrene is used, it should be mechanically fastened because its surface is not suitable for adhered applications. Insulation thickness varies depending on the desired R-value. Most applications use 1- to 4-in- (25- to 100-mm) thick boards either adhered or mechanically fastened to sheathing or masonry. PB systems are usually referred to as *thin* or *soft coat* products because of the flexibility inherent in the acrylic polymers used. This flexibility

allows for wider spacing of caulked joints than is required in the PM system described below. Typically joints are mandated at abutting dissimilar materials, at changes in planes, and at joints in the substate.

2. *PM.* A polymer-modified system using a finish coat consisting of a mixture of Portland cement and an acrylic polymer for both the base and finish coat. This system is referred to as a *thick* or *hard coat* product because its components are designed to resist abuse. The finish coat is harder and thicker than that used in the PB system. The reinforcement is either composed of two layers of fiberglass mesh embedded in two base coats, or, in many instances, expanded metal is used

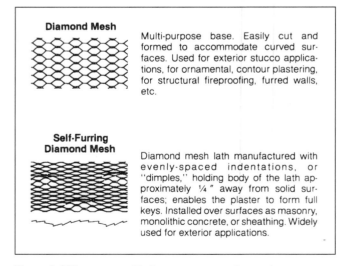

Figure 4.137 Types of lath most commonly used in exterior walls. [Reproduced by permission from the National Association of Architectural Metal Manufacturers (NAAMM)]

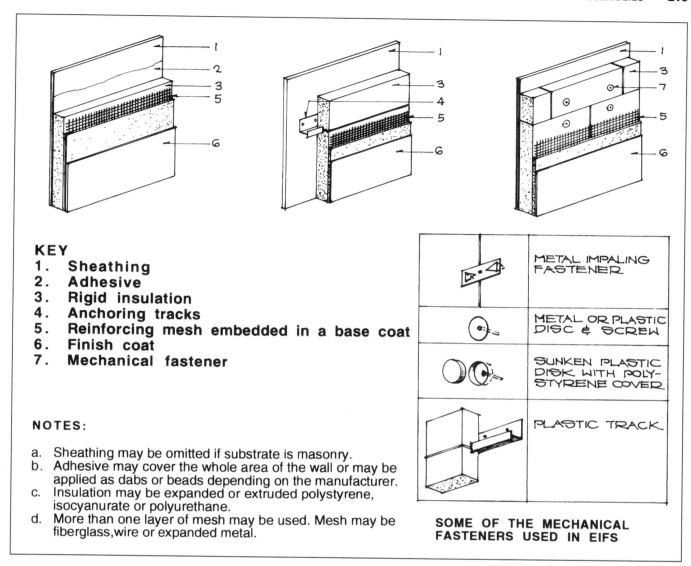

KEY
1. **Sheathing**
2. **Adhesive**
3. **Rigid insulation**
4. **Anchoring tracks**
5. **Reinforcing mesh embedded in a base coat**
6. **Finish coat**
7. **Mechanical fastener**

NOTES:

a. Sheathing may be omitted if substrate is masonry.
b. Adhesive may cover the whole area of the wall or may be applied as dabs or beads depending on the manufacturer.
c. Insulation may be expanded or extruded polystyrene, isocyanurate or polyurethane.
d. More than one layer of mesh may be used. Mesh may be fiberglass, wire or expanded metal.

	METAL IMPALING FASTENER
	METAL OR PLASTIC DISC & SCREW
	SUNKEN PLASTIC DISK WITH POLY-STYRENE COVER
	PLASTIC TRACK

SOME OF THE MECHANICAL FASTENERS USED IN EIFS

Figure 4.138   Common EIFS methods of attachment.

and the insulation board is manufactured from high-density extruded polystyrene. This system is usually mechanically fastened either to masonry or to a denser sheathing such as cement board instead of GWB sheathing. Because of the cement content in the finish coat, more frequent control joints are required to control the shrinkage. Panel length and area should not exceed 30 ft (9 m) and 150 ft² (14 m²), respectively. While this system can withstand a certain amount of abuse, it will crack if subjected to severe impact.

Careful detailing of sealed control joints is a must to avoid problems. Most system failures originate at these locations. Joint sides must be executed carefully. The embedded mesh must be wrapped around the insulation board and extended a minimum 2½ in on the back [Fig. 4.139(a)]. Alternatively, a PVC or galvanized track

would provide the substrate at these locations [Fig. 4.139(b)]. While PVC tracks may perform satisfactorily if covered with a base coat of adequate thickness, metal tracks may crack because of their different rate of expansion.

Polyurethane sealants are used most often. However, manufacturers may recommend other sealants that may be more compatible with their substrate. Check with their representatives before specifying a sealant. A drained two-stage sealant arrangement works best [Fig. 4.139(c)]. A closed-cell backer rod avoids the problem of water saturation which causes joints to fail.

False joints or rustications should not reduce board thickness to less than ¾ in (20 mm). Rounded or squared profiles are preferable to a V-shaped joint because they are less prone to cracking. Both control

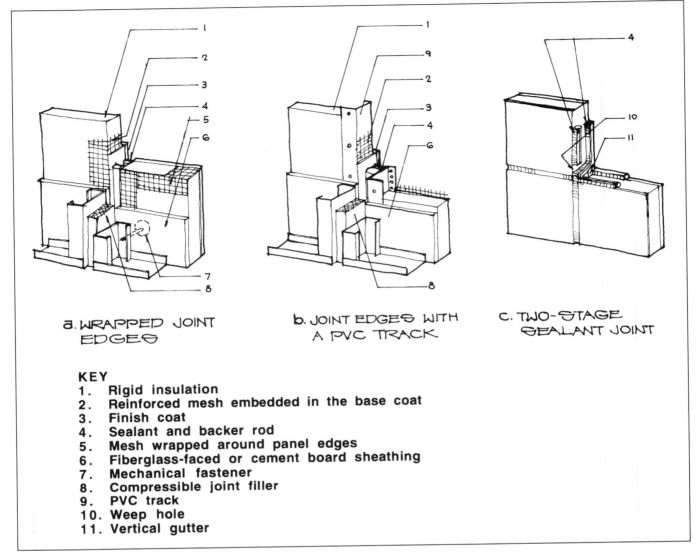

a. WRAPPED JOINT EDGES

b. JOINT EDGES WITH A PVC TRACK

c. TWO-STAGE SEALANT JOINT

KEY
1. **Rigid insulation**
2. **Reinforced mesh embedded in the base coat**
3. **Finish coat**
4. **Sealant and backer rod**
5. **Mesh wrapped around panel edges**
6. **Fiberglass-faced or cement board sheathing**
7. **Mechanical fastener**
8. **Compressible joint filler**
9. **PVC track**
10. **Weep hole**
11. **Vertical gutter**

Figure 4.139   Control joint details for an EIFS assembly.

and false joints must not coincide with joints in the sheathing for the same reason.

Thin-coat (PB) applications perform satisfactorily in most cases. They are more flexible than hard-coat (PM) EIFS assemblies and thus accommodate building frame deflections and deformations with less possibility of cracking. It is recommended that the insulation boards be mechanically fastened and adhered to a stable substrate such as fiberglass-faced GWB or cement board sheathing. Plain GWB sheathing should be avoided or, if used, should be protected by felt or an air barrier or damp-proofing membrane such as Tyvek. A hard coat should be considered for use in areas subject to impact or vandalism. A control joint should separate the two systems.

The EIFS assembly designed according to the rain screen (pressure equalized) principle was introduced in 1993 by Dryvit under the trademark Infinity. The system features a grid of subdivided cavities formed by the joints between the insulation boards (Fig. 4.140). It also features drainage grooved at the back of these boards discharging into a vent or drainage channel. The sheathing is fiberglass-faced GWB. These measures are designed to prevent most of the problems associated with EIFS assemblies. There is a substantial cost increase over a conventional EIFS assembly which makes it almost comparable to the cost of a brick cavity wall at this writing. It has the potential, however, for allowing any seepage to drain without causing major damage and will minimize that seepage because of the pressure-equalization feature. While its design is based on sound principles and its materials are chosen for durability, its introduction is too recent to evaluate its long-term performance.

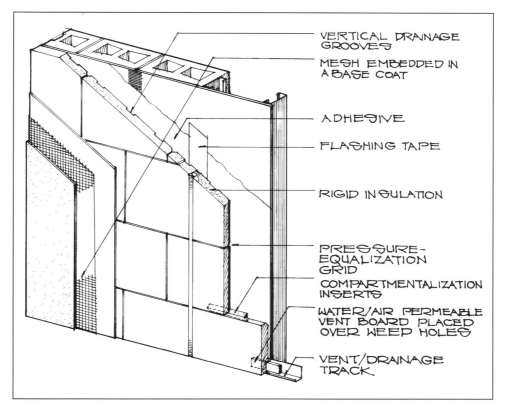

VERTICAL DRAINAGE GROOVES

MESH EMBEDDED IN A BASE COAT

ADHESIVE

FLASHING TAPE

RIGID INSULATION

PRESSURE-EQUALIZATION GRID

COMPARTMENTALIZATION INSERTS

WATER/AIR PERMEABLE VENT BOARD PLACED OVER WEEP HOLES

VENT/DRAINAGE TRACK

Figure 4.140 Components of an EIFS rain screen (pressure equalized) design.

Tile Veneer. Not all tile is suitable for use in exterior walls. The tile chosen for that application must be able to withstand temperature extremes and be impervious to water penetration. Two methods are used to manufacture tile. The first employs a moist clay extruded through a die, while the second uses a relatively dry clay formed under tremendous pressure in a process called *dust-pressing.* This latter method produces a denser tile. After extrusion or dust-pressing, the tile is fired in a kiln. The architect must consult with the tile fabricator to ascertain that the chosen tile is suitable for exterior application before the final selection is made. Thin stone cut to a thickness of ¼ or ⅜ in (6 to 10 mm) is also available for use in the same manner as ceramic tile.

There are several ways to adhere tile to exterior walls. The conventional method sets the tile in a ¾- to 1-in- (20 to 25 mm) thick bed of Portland cement mortar reinforced with metal lath backed with roofing felt and supported by masonry [Fig. 4.141(b)]. This is the same method (with the exception of the wires) used to adhere tiles to masonry. Because it is time-consuming and labor-intensive, it is rarely used in exterior stud wall construction today. Tile used in this thick-set method is required to be wetted before application. Thin-set tile is the predominant method of attachment. Thin-set mortars are used in one layer as thin as 3/32 in (2 mm) troweled over cement board sheathing attached to the studs. A damp-proofing membrane such as roofing felt is usually placed between the studs and the board [Fig. 4.141(a)]. There are two kinds of mortars in this category, dry-set and latex–Portland cement. The first type is formulated from Portland cement, sand, and water-retentive additives. It is available in premixed bags. It does not require the tile to be wetted. Latex-cement mortar is similar but less rigid than dry-set. Silicone adhesive, while not a mortar, is also used to attach ceramic tile to exterior walls. The backup in this application is usually a galvanized metal deck [Fig. 4.141(c)]. A bond-breaker tape behind each joint ensures two-sided adhesion to prevent the joints from failing. Other methods employing different components are also used in tile veneered assemblies.

Because tile is impervious, a method for venting any vapor that may find its way into the cavities between the studs is advisable if the grout is also impervious to the passage of water vapor such as the silicone-adhered assembly described above.

4.6.3 Ornamentation

Architectural treatment of exterior sheathing whether the material is wood, wood derivative, stucco, EIFS, or

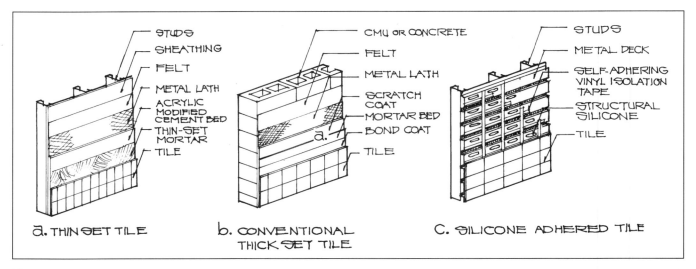

a. THIN SET TILE
b. CONVENTIONAL THICK SET TILE
c. SILICONE ADHERED TILE

Figure 4.141   Common methods of adhering tile to exterior walls.

tile can create an infinite variety of interesting designs. Other materials used in cavity or rain screen wall designs have been addressed in previous sections.

WOOD

Wood structures have a rich heritage of ornamentation. The pleasing wood texture and detailing have graced many historic structures in many parts of the world. In the United States, a large percentage of wood construction is residential. However, some large industrial and some low-rise buildings are executed in wood. This is especially true on the west coast.

Most modern wood buildings use clean lines and interesting massing in lieu of carving as a means of ornamentation. Natural finish represented by staining to accentuate the color and grain of the natural wood is the prevalent architectural treatment. An example of this approach is shown in Fig. 4.142.

STUCCO AND EIFS

While both these materials have the same appearance, an EIFS assembly can be manipulated to give a sculptured three-dimensional appearance to the wall (Fig. 4.143). Both materials can be divided into areas with different colors bordered by reveals and combined with other materials such as tile to introduce points of interest.

Figure 4.142   Redwood plywood used to sheath a public library. (From California Redwood Association)

*NUMBER OF RIGID INSULATION LAYERS

Figure 4.143 Three-dimensional ornamentation made possible by multilayered insulation panels.

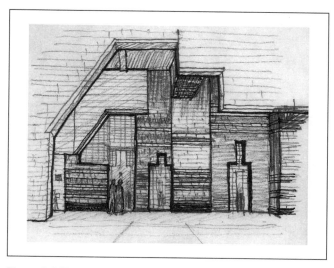

Figure 4.144 Tile ornamentation. (From The Ministry of Foreign Affairs Building, Kuwait; designed by Reima Pietila, architect)

CERAMIC TILE

This material is a very durable, color-fast, and easy to maintain wall finish. On the down side, it is brittle and thin and, unless adhered with a potent mortar, may spall or detach from the wall. For this reason, it should not be used in areas subject to impact or abuse.

Manipulating tile to introduce interesting patterns of contrasting color is one of the main reasons for using this material (Fig. 4.144). Introducing a monochromatic vividly colored area to draw attention to an entrance is another approach. Cladding a whole building in this material should be considered after careful comparison with other alternatives to evaluate relative cost, durability, resistance to corrosive atmospheres, and the construction time factor. A shop-fabricated panelized system is the proper approach for any sizable project. These systems are fabricated under controlled conditions improving quality and speeding construction.

4.6.4 Assemblies

Metal stud assemblies weigh 2 lb/ft² (9 kg/m²) on average. Adding a finish like stucco, tile, or EIFS increases the total weight of the cladding to between 6 and 18 lb/ft² (29 to 58 kg/m³). This is approximately 75% lower than precast or masonry construction.

Stud assemblies may be erected on the site (stick built), shop-fabricated and hoisted to their final posi-tions, and finished using scaffolding (shop-site method) or prefinished either in the shop or on the slab of each floor (prefabricated panels). Each method has its advantages and disadvantages.

STICK BUILT

This method requires minimal hoisting time. The studs required for each floor can be hoisted in one or two lifts in most cases. Minor adjustments to accommodate structural frame imperfections can be made, and transportation costs are minimized. Stick built construction is the most affected by weather conditions at the site and requires scaffolding to apply the finish.

SHOP-SITE METHOD

The stud assembly is shop-fabricated into panels, transported to the site, and hoisted into place. While shop fabrication of the panels reduces weather delays and increases efficiency by utilizing jig operations, mass production methods, and quality control, it causes increases in transportation costs and imposes size limitations on the panels. In addition, it increases hoisting costs and still requires the added costs of scaffolding and is still affected by weather during the application of the finish.

PREFABRICATED PANELS

Total prefabrication has many advantages. It drastically reduces weather as a delaying factor. It allows the contractor to enclose the structure quickly so that interior work can proceed at an early stage. In addition, it does not require scaffolding if windows can be installed from inside the building. In most cases, the sealant and

Figure 4.145 Stucco cracking.

touch-up work can be done from a work platform lowered from the roof or from a "cherry picker."

While prefabricated panelization is advantageous and efficient, it is not necessarily trouble-free. Extra care must be observed to prevent damage to the finish during transit and hoisting. The building frame must be executed to more exacting tolerances to prevent discrepancies in joint widths. In many cases, one panel is left out in each facade for later fabrication based on exact field measurements.

On the whole, this is the method most favored for multistory or complicated profile facades. It is fast, accurate, and requires less construction operations. Stud assemblies are shown in Figs. 4.28, 4.45, 4.68, 4.100, 4.131, and 4.133.

4.6.5 What Can Go Wrong
STUDS

Stud systems are subject to more flexural movement than masonry or concrete wall systems. They are more prone to damage caused by water or moisture penetrating behind the sheathing or interior finish. This incipient deterioration (rot or termite damage in wood studs and corrosion in steel studs) can continue for a relatively long time before detection. By that time, the structural stability of the stud system may have reached a point where the whole system has to be replaced at a cost that could reach as much as three times the original cost of construction. For this reason, it is imperative that the details be developed with full understanding of the various defenses against water penetration. The vapor retarders (see Sec. 1.3.2) must be detailed properly especially at wall edges and penetrations. Head, jamb, and sill details at window and door openings must be drawn at a large enough scale to show the termination and sealing of the edges of the retarder, dampproofing or water-

proofing membranes, as well as air barriers (see Secs. 1.2.2 and 1.3.2). Of course, this does not guarantee that the work will be executed correctly. The architect must conduct a preconstruction conference to stress the importance of executing the details and the rationale behind each as well as answer any questions the contractor or subcontractors may have. Frequent site visits to spot check execution and provide guidance are also very important to prevent bad execution. Other factors that should be considered include fire hazard (see Sec. 1.6.1), electrolysis (see Sec. 1.6.2), and insect infestation (see Sec. 1.6.4).

VENEERS

Wood. Wood siding requires periodic maintenance. Wood stain lasts longer than paint. The difference between the two is that a stain penetrates through the wood fibers while paint is a film that adheres to the surface. Using wood that has a natural resistance to the effects of heat, wind, and rain is advisable in exterior applications. Redwood, cedar, and cypress are recommended if the budget permits. Providing generous overhangs, drips, and flashing also helps to protect the wall.

Stucco. Stucco is a hardy and durable finish if executed properly. It has a tendency to develop cracks if the supporting studs are not stiff enough, have wider spacing than usual, or lack frequent control joints (Fig. 4.145).

EIFS. Delamination can be a major problem for adhered EIFS assemblies. Impact resistance must be considered in areas subject to abuse. Moisture buildup, whether caused by vapor migration from the interior or leaky joints can cause paper-faced sheathing to delaminate and panels to detach from the wall. Depressed rustications where two pieces of rigid insulation abut are of special concern because hairline cracks can occur at these locations. This is especially true if the rustication is V-shaped. If that type of design feature is required, the depression should occur within the same insulation panel rather than over a joint between two panels. Moisture accumulation behind the insulation board caused by sealant failure or hairline cracks within the field of the panel is the bane of these systems. Gypsum sheathing is not suitable for use as a backup for an EIFS assembly especially if the system is adhered. A masonry wall, cement board, or fiberglass-faced GWB sheathing fastened to metal studs should be the substrate for this application.

To minimize EIFS assembly problems, the following measures should be taken:

1. A properly designed and installed vapor retarder must be located at the warm side of the *insulation* (not of the wall assembly).

2. A stable substrate that does not deteriorate if exposed to moisture should be chosen. Examples include masonry, cement board, sheet metal, and stucco. Stud systems should be designed for a maximum deflection of L/240. If cost implications mandate that a gypsum sheathing be used, choose a fiberglass-faced board to avoid the possibility of delamination.

3. Select a PM system in areas prone to damage caused by impact. The EIFS must stop at least 8 in above grade.

4. Use a mildew-resistant finish coat which includes chemicals specially formulated to resist the formation of stains caused by mildew organisms especially in humid climates.

5. Provide flashing and positive slopes at all horizontal surfaces.

Tile. Because tile is impervious to water, it provides one of the better defenses against water penetration from the exterior. It is, however, susceptible to attack by water vapor migrating from the interior of the building. This vapor can accumulate behind the tile, freeze, and cause it to spall. To lessen that possibility, a well-executed and nearly impervious vapor retarder is essential. In addition, vents should be introduced into the assembly to provide a route to the exterior for the small amount of vapor that will pass through imperfections in the retarder.

Tile expansion and contraction should be compatible with the movement of the substrate to which it is adhered to prevent thermal cracking. Control joints should be spaced according to the manufacturer's recommendations and at building expansion and differential settlement joints.

These are a few of the recommendations designed to avoid potential problems. It is recommended that the designer contact the representatives of several manufacturers of the product selected and its equivalents to gather as much information as possible to base the design on the most appropriate system.

Summary

Stud systems are used to construct a sizable percentage of exterior walls. Most commercial and residential construction utilize studs as the supporting structure for cladding. Steel studs were introduced shortly after World War II to compete with wood. Their dimensions were based on lumber dimensions. Components for the steel system parallel closely those used in wood construction; only the method of fastening these components differs.

In addition to the studs and their top and bottom tracks (plates and sills in a wood system), headers, bridging, and bracing, there is exterior sheathing which may be constructed from several materials, including GWB, cement board, stucco on felt and wire support, or plywood and other wood product boards used mostly in wood stud framing. The interior finish board most commonly used is GWB. It may be fire-rated to provide extra protection, or it may be finished with a thin coat of plaster.

Exterior veneers supported by stud systems include wood products such as plywood, clapboards, tongue-and-groove boards oriented vertically, horizontally, or diagonally. Vinyl and aluminum clapboards are used in this application as substitutes for wood. Stucco and EIFS assemblies as well as tile systems are used to finish both wood and steel framing. Cavity walls utilizing brick, stone, or metal may also be backed by studs.

Stud systems are less hardy than heavier support systems such as masonry. The designer must detail them with more care to ensure that water does not enter into the area of the studs causing rot (wood) or corrosion (metal). Studs must be sized to minimize deflection especially when the veneer is brittle, and the veneer itself should be sealed properly and backed by effective dampproofing or designed as a pressure-equalized rain screen assembly.

Stud-backed assemblies are popular because they are economical, they go up fast, and lend themselves readily to panelization. In addition, they are lightweight resulting in savings in transportation and hoisting costs as well as the cost of the supporting structure and foundations.

CHAPTER 5

Drawing the Wall Section

5.1 GENERAL

The person entrusted with the challenging task of drawing and detailing exterior walls must know how to communicate the information described in the preceding chapters to the contractor. This should be done in a clear and unambiguous way without repetition, conflicts, mistakes, or omissions.

The location of each section cut must be chosen carefully. The intent is to cover all different conditions while avoiding repetitious information. In the majority of multistory projects, the area of the wall section enclosing the typical floors does not change too much from wall section to wall section. To avoid repeating the same information over and over, only the first section should be drawn and fully covered by notations. Subsequent sections would cover the new conditions fully and show the repeated area in outline only. A note referring to the first section written next to the outline is all that is needed. This applies only to the labor-intensive manual drafting. This recommendation, and others like it occurring in subsequent sections of this chapter, do not apply to CADD because notes are easily duplicated by the computer, although this duplication also entails the expenditure of time, especially if the operator is not fully trained.

During the course of the project, dimensions may change and notations may be modified. If this information is repeated in building sections, wall sections, and section details, the corrections will have to be done in many drawings wasting time and possibly resulting in missed corrections.

One goal worthy of striving for is to use the same sections drawn for the design development phase in the construction drawing set. To achieve this, the notations should be separated from the drawing because they

inevitably change from phase to phase. This can be accomplished by reproducing them on sticky-back paper that can be removed if necessary or placing them on a separate CADD layer. This chapter provides the means by which the information covering wall construction can be conveyed to the contractor in a concise and well-organized manner.

5.2 POINTS TO CONSIDER

Proper detailing of a wall system can spell the difference between a long-lasting, trouble-free wall and a leaky, drafty, short-lived one. The person entrusted with developing the details must balance durability with construction cost (see Sec. 2.4.1); allow enough tolerances between different assemblies (see Sec. 2.2.5); and make certain that adjacent materials are compatible, adjacent metals are not subject to electrolysis (see Sec. 1.6.2), and the detail is keyed back to its source. Normally, building section locations are shown on the plan, wall section cuts are shown on the elevations, section details are referred back to circled areas on the building section, and window frame details are referred back to circled areas on the section details.

After the detail is sketched, one must make a scenario based on a step-by-step construction sequence to prove its constructibility. This may not be the way the general contractor will build the assembly, but at least it will ensure that the detail is buildable. It is very easy to fall into the trap of developing an intricate detail only to discover that it is unbuildable because another part of the assembly is in the way.

Ensuring that the detail can be constructed as drawn requires that the designer pretend that he or she is entrusted with actually building it. I call this process "wearing the hard hat." The example shown in Fig. 2.18 depicts a detail that looks perfectly buildable until you attempt to screw the top 24 in (600 mm) of the gypsum board panels to the back of the steel studs and discover that the clearance between the fireproofed beam and the boards is not enough to allow an electric screwdriver to be used. For this detail to be buildable, the edge of the beam flange must be placed approximately 12 in (30 mm) away from the face of the wall or the studs must be assembled horizontally, the GWB fastened to them, and the assembled panel hoisted into position. If this latter method is adopted, enough clearance must be provided to seal the vapor retarder against the underside of the slab edge plate. One way of achieving this is to tape the retarder to the deck, making sure that there is enough slack to accommodate deflection.

5.2.1 Sources of Information

CONSULTANT INPUT

Structural elements such as shelf angles, lintels, spandrel beams, and columns are sized by the structural engineer. The location of the structural frame in relation to the exterior face of the wall must be determined in consultations between the architect and the engineer. In a similar fashion, discussions about perimeter heating or cooling must be conducted with the mechanical engineer to determine whether baseboard heating or other mechanical or electrical elements will have an effect on the detailing of the exterior walls. The structural engineer's input, however, has the most impact on exterior wall design and detailing. Valuable information concerning tolerances, deflection, deformation, expansion joints, sequencing, adjustments, frequency of support elements, etc., can be obtained from that individual.

Other sources of information include manufacturer's representatives especially window and wall cladding representatives. One should get information from the most dependable source. In many cases, this means contacting the technical person at the company's home office. Many companies have a toll-free number for that purpose. Before contacting that person, make a list of all the questions and issues to be discussed so that you may get all the answers in one call. If possible, contact more than one source of information to weed out inaccurate feedback. Of course, if the project is large enough to engage the services of a wall cladding consultant, contacting representatives can become less important.

COORDINATION WITH SPECIFICATIONS

Nomenclature used in detail notations must conform to the language used in the specifications. The designer usually photocopies manufacturers' product literature (cut sheets) for products chosen for inclusion in the project during the design development phase and transmits these copies to the specification writer for inclusion in the specifications. During the conference with that individual, an agreement should be reached about the generic terms to be used in both the specifications and details. The project architect should instruct all team members to photocopy all materials used in the details to convey to the specification writer.

Many offices use either the Con-Doc system of notations tied to the specifications or standard keynotes. These are described later in the chapter. One cannot overemphasize the importance of avoiding conflict between the drawings and specifications. Misunderstandings and the resultant costly change orders can be easily avoided if a little time is spent on this step.

INDUSTRY STANDARDS

Almost every manufacturer belongs to an institute or association that issues handbooks, industry standards, and other informative and authoritative literature (App. B). Architects involved in detailing must read this material as early in their careers as possible to get acquainted with the principles and standards as well as the pitfalls to avoid. Every office should include many of these standards in their reference library. This should be combined with the information included in the building code to form the basis for detail development.

5.2.2 Wall Defenses

As we have seen in Chap. 1, many elements attack exterior walls. Water in all its forms [liquid, solid (ice), or gaseous (vapor)] and moving air are the elements that mandate the inclusion of dampproofing membranes, vapor retarders, and air barriers in wall design. Fireproofing of certain wall components or of the whole assembly may also be required by code. A conscious effort must be exerted to see to it that wall detailing clarifies the terminations of these defensive barriers rather than depending solely on the specifications and the judgment of the person in the field to ensure proper execution. The following is a summary of these issues.

DAMPPROOFING

This is the second line of defense in a cavity wall. (The first line of defense is the thickness of the exterior wythe which acts as a rain screen.) Its terminations at shelf angles (see Fig. 4.30), control joints (see Fig. 4.20), and window frame details (Figs. 3.20 and 5.1) must be sealed and clearly shown in the details. Laps at joints in the flashing must be dimensioned, and penetrations through it must be considered and addressed either in the specifications or details. Isometric drawings are useful in clarifying complicated assemblies (Fig. 5.2).

VAPOR RETARDER

The location of the vapor retarder on the warm side is usually known to the designer in the area of the firm's practice. Projects located in other states may require consultation with a local architect, mechanical engineer, or a curtain wall consultant if weather conditions are substantially different. The vapor retarder should be combined with an air barrier to resist both positive and negative air pressures. In cold regions, where the vapor retarder is generally located directly below the wallboard facing the interior, both the vapor retarder and the wallboard (if it is acting as an air barrier) must extend all the way to the structure and be sealed against it. This can be accomplished by an adhesive tape (metal slab edge) or a compatible sealant bead (concrete slab). The vapor retarder ending at window head, jamb, and sill must be shown clearly to avoid gaps. As was mentioned in Chap. 1, a vapor retarder must have at least one-fifth the perm rating of any material located beyond it toward the cold side (Fig. 1.13).

AIR BARRIER

An air barrier must be impervious to wind penetration. It can be located anywhere in the wall assembly. Metal cladding can function as an air barrier, and, because it is a vapor retarder, the area behind the metal must be vented to allow the vapor to exit the assembly. As mentioned above, wallboard can also function as an air barrier if extended all the way to the structure. Like dampproofing and vapor retarders, air barriers must be carefully detailed to ensure that no gaps occur at the edges or at fenestration and other penetrations in the wall to prevent uncomfortable, energy-wasting drafts from occurring.

FIREPROOFING

The code review for the project determines the required hour rating of the fireproofing for the column, beam, and floor slab (see Table 1.6). The floor assembly is required to provide protection to prevent fire from migrating from one floor to the floors above or below it. This means that the gap between the edge of the slab and the cladding must be filled with materials having the same fire rating as the floor. The U.L. *Fire-Resistance Directory* provides rated designs containing rock wool insulation (usually referred to by the generic name *firesafing*) with a special sealant to prevent smoke migration between levels. This is shown in the U-900 series section. The codes also require that flammable types of insulation such as polystyrene must be covered with fire-rated gypsum wallboard all the way to the floor slab above when placed in a location facing the interior of the building.

In some cases, exterior walls (including fenestration) must also be fire-rated. This is usually required when the space between buildings is less than a certain distance defined by the code. Acceptably rated wall assemblies can be found either in the code or the U.L. Directory. Windows are required to be protected by constructing the frames from steel and installing wire glass or a more expensive specially formulated flame-resistant glass instead of conventional glass. Another method of protection is to install sprinkler heads that are activated when the temperature reaches a certain level. These heads are required to be installed on one or both sides of the window depending on their location (see also Sec. 1.6.1).

5.3 DRAFTING GUIDELINES

Since the task of drawing wall sections is so important and requires a wealth of background information, it must be assigned to the most experienced member of the project team. The team leader should provide that person with a set of plans showing the locations of the section cuts, building sections, and elevations as well as relevant parts of the specifications (if available). Ideally, an experienced office-wide technical person should set the standards for

- Drawing hierarchies
- Critical dimensions
- Wall defenses

Drawing or sketching a typical wall section is the best way to convey this information. This sets the basis upon which all the other wall sections can be developed. After the sections are finished, they must be checked to ensure that no unforeseen problems have developed. This section elaborates on each of the standards listed above.

5.3.1 Drawing Hierarchies

Because one drawing cannot contain all the detailed information necessary to build a wall assembly, architects arrange the drawings into a hierarchy drawn at different scales. These drawings include the building section, wall sections, section details, and window frame details. Each of these drawings zooms in on segments of the preceding one to convey information that is too small and indistinct in the smaller scale. Architects should avoid repetition of information provided in one scale in larger-scale drawings. The goal here is to write the information only once so that if a change occurs, the written information needs to be corrected only in one place. The following subsections describe in detail how this applies to scales, notations, and dimensions.

HIERARCHY OF SCALES

Wall sections form the most important component of a family of vertical sections that are drawn at different scales. A rough equivalent of metric scales is shown in parentheses. These sections start with the building section drawn at ⅛ = 1 ft (1:100) or smaller and continue, at ever larger scales, to the window frame details drawn at 3 in = 1 ft (1:5). Each section conveys a different kind of information to the contractor. The building section depicts an overall picture of the building. The wall section goes into more detail about the materials in the assembly and the general dimensioning. Depending on the size of the project, it may be drawn at anywhere between ¼ in = 1 ft (1:50) and ¾ in = 1 ft (1:15). The conventionally accepted scale for wall sections in the United States is ¾ in = 1 ft. This author has used both ½ in = 1 ft (1:25) and ¼ in = 1 ft (1:50) scales successfully and feels that they save both time and effort if combined with enough enlarged details. Wall sections, in turn, act as a reference to still larger details drawn at 1½ in = 1 ft (1:10) showing special features such as shelf angles, flashing, slab edges, and copings. The largest scale is reserved for window frame details. The scale most often used is 3 in = 1 ft (1:5).

The window frame may be photocopied from a manufacturer's brochure [Fig. 5.1(*a*)] or drawn as a simple, generic outline [Fig. 5.1(*b*)]. The second method simplifies and expedites the drafting of window details and does not favor a particular manufacturer. The profile should be representative of the products of all the frames named in the specifications.

The alternative approach entails making multiple photocopies of the head, jamb, and sill drawings of one manufacturer favored by the designer and using them in the details. Scanning them for CADD accomplishes the same goal. A general note stating that the details are based on the frames produced by that particular manufacturer to show the design intent and that other acceptable manufacturers are listed in the specifications should be included.

Both methods are acceptable in most cases. The first approach, while giving the drawings a more polished look, may be objectionable to some government entities because it gives the appearance of favoring the manufacturer whose product is represented, although this is clearly not the case. The drawings show the interface with adjacent materials more clearly than the generic method.

While window details are directed mainly at the window subcontractor, other elements of the details are handled by the general contractor or other subcontractors. These include the sealants, dampproofing, and vapor retarder. The location of the sealant for curtain walls must be drawn so as not to interfere with the weep holes placed at the bottoms of the sill (Fig. 5.3). This location must be the same around the perimeter of the frame.

Window details must clarify the profile of flashing, the end of the vapor retarder, the air barrier, sheathing, dampproofing, and sealants as well as the many components of the window system. Most leakage problems occur because the architect did not show these details clearly and the intent was misunderstood by the contractor, the person checking the shop drawings, and the field supervisor.

HIERARCHY OF NOTATIONS

There are basically three methods used to identify materials drawn in wall sections and section details (Fig. 5.4). These methods are listed on page 226.

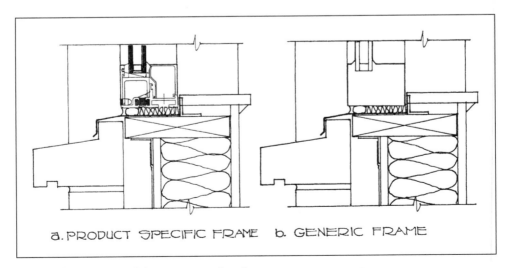

Figure 5.1   Methods of drawing a window frame.

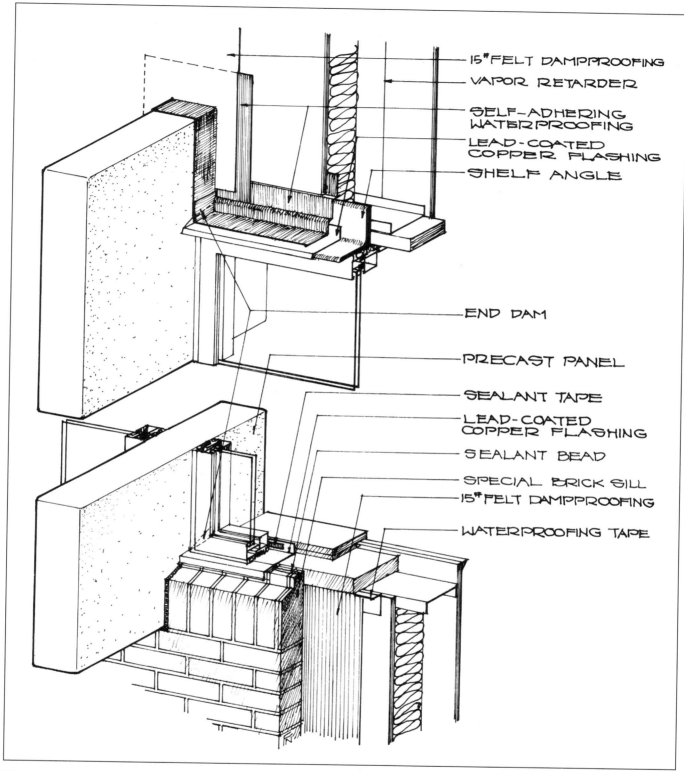

15#FELT DAMPPROOFING
VAPOR RETARDER
SELF-ADHERING WATERPROOFING
LEAD-COATED COPPER FLASHING
SHELF ANGLE

END DAM

PRECAST PANEL

SEALANT TAPE
LEAD-COATED COPPER FLASHING
SEALANT BEAD
SPECIAL BRICK SILL
15#FELT DAMPPROOFING
WATERPROOFING TAPE

Figure 5.2   An example of an axonometric drawing clarifying the locations of wall defenses against water and air penetration.

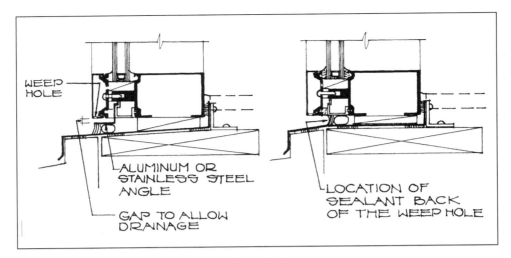

Figure 5.3 Location of sealant must avoid weepholes.

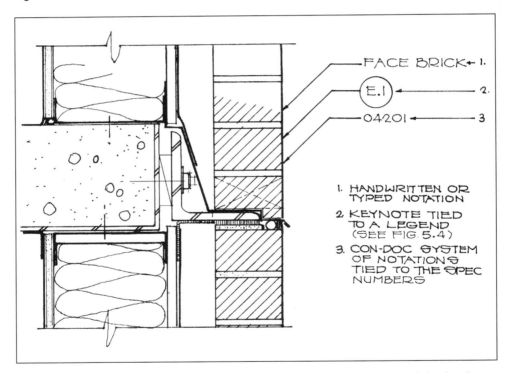

Figure 5.4 The three methods used to identify materials in wall sections and the details associated with them.

1. Hand lettering or typing a description connected to the material with an arrow. This is the method used from time immemorial. It is still used by many firms.

2. Identifying each material by a circled number. Keynotes, placed in the sheet title block, describe what each number represents.

3. The Con-Doc method identifies each material by the specification section number used to describe it. This method eliminates the need to include keynotes in the construction drawings. It was introduced in an article written by Onkal K. (Duke) Guzey in the fall

1985 issue of *Architectural Technology* magazine.[32] The AIA sponsors seminars conducted by Mr. Guzey and James N. Freehof on the subject.

The first method takes more time to do than the other two. In most cases, each notation occurs many times in the group of wall sections and section details. Every time a change in a note occurs, it has to be tracked down and corrected in all the drawings. Written notations, however, are much easier to check at a glance. Any discrepancy or conflict can be readily caught and corrected by the project manager without having to refer to either keynotes in the margin or a description in the specifications.

Using the second method saves time because the notes have to be typed only once. Copies are reproduced on sticky-back paper and attached to each sheet to identify the materials. If corrections have to be made, they will be done only once on new sticky-back paper that replace the ones done before. This method is practical because it comes closest to CADD, it is fast, and the drawings are easily salvageable from phase to phase. While it is not as easy to make a final check of the drawings as in the first method, it is not difficult for the person performing that task to get accustomed to this method. The keynote legend should use nomenclature used in the specifications. This nomenclature should be established by the office to be used on all projects (with additions, if required). Figure 5.5 shows a list I developed for one of the offices I worked at. The advantages of an alphanumeric keynote system are

1. The numbering system allows the user to add materials to the list under each category without having to change the numbers as must be done in a numbers-only system.

2. An established list prevents the user from using a different number for the same material used in a different group of drawings. For example, if one team member is drawing the building wall sections and another is drawing the section and window frame details, each may establish a different numbering system causing confusion.

3. Identifying the materials with letters makes it easier for the user to find the description. For example, if the material is insulation, the search focuses on the B grouping instead of on the whole list which would be the case in a numbers-only system.

The third method has the advantage of tying the material directly to the description in the specifications. It ensures that every material is covered by the specifications and obviates the need for using a keynote legend that may change during the course of the project. It requires the specification writer to be involved early in the process to provide the appropriate numbers. It is, however, well suited to CADD and can be very efficient if used properly. It is well worth investigating and implementing.

Notes should not be repeated between the different components of the hierarchy of drawings. Building sections do not require any material notes. Their purpose is to convey an overall picture of the building—exterior outline, interior organization of spaces, vertical conveying systems, and any unusual features. The location of building section cuts on the plan should be selected

with that purpose in mind. These cuts may shift several times rather than follow a straight line to cover all the main features of the interior. Avoid going into too much detail. Instead of showing the slab and beams and other structural features, show the architectural outline indicating the top of the slab and ceiling with a blank space between them.

The purpose of drawing wall sections is to show all the main elements of the cladding and their supporting structure. These sections must cover all the different conditions around the building resulting from different section profiles, materials, and/or fenestration. Avoid writing notes for areas that are circled to be blown up and included in an enlarged section or window detail. Add notes only if parts of the section are not covered by enlarged details.

For large projects, include a key plan indicating all the wall section cuts in each wall section sheet and key these cuts to the elevations because sections relate more to elevations than to plans.

Enlarged wall section and window details describe all the components of the wall assembly. The bulk of notations occurs here. Both types of details are drawn on sheets subdivided as shown in Fig. 5.6. The subdivision is based on fractions of a standard 8½ × 11 in (215 × 280 mm) sheet. Rectangles may be combined to accommodate any detail size. Other standardized subdivisions work just as well for wall section details. Experiment until you develop a size that works best for you. Window detail sheets include window types and window frame details (head, jamb, and sill details). Window types are elevations of each window in the project showing mullions, glass type (identified as float, tempered, heat strengthened, spandrel, etc.), and whether the window is fixed or operable. Dimensions are added to complete the sheet. Figure 5.7 illustrates the hierarchy of notations.

HIERARCHY OF DIMENSIONS

Building sections should show only the floor-to-floor heights and floor elevations. Wall sections should subdivide the floor-to-floor dimension to show the rough opening dimension. Section and window frame details should include every other missing dimension (Fig. 5.8). Dimensions for all members of the section hierarchy—building section, wall section, and section detail—must be tied to a fixed reference point. In this case, the floor elevation performs this function. Window detail dimensions are usually tied to the nearest rough opening edge.

The following are a few guidelines:

- The floor height at the top of the building should be tied to the top of the structure (top of steel and top of slab) only if the roof is dead flat. If the struc-

EXTERIOR WALL MATERIALS:
E.1 Face Brick
E.2 Precast Concrete
E.3 Glass Fiber Reinforced Concrete (CFRC)
E.4 Preformed Metal Panels
E.5 Stucco on Metal Lath
E.6 Exterior Insulation and Finish System (EIFS)
E.7 Quarry Tile
E.8 Metal Sandwich Panels
E.9 CMU
E.10 Grout
E.11 Stone
E.12 Concrete
E.13 Air Barrier
E.14 3/4" Exterior Plywood

THERMAL & SOUND INSULATION:
T.1 R-____Batt Insulation
T.2 R-____Rigid Insulation
T.3 R-____semi-Rigid Insulation
T.4 Tapered Insulation
T.5 Sound-Attenuation Blankets
T.6 Fire-Safing Insulation
T.7 Sprayed-on Fireproofing

WATERPROOFING:
W.1 Waterproofing Membrane
W.2 Protection Board
W.3 Water Stop
W.4 Subsurface Drainage Matting
W.5 Perforated Drain
W.6 Mud Slab
W.7 Flashing Membrane
W.8 Filter Fabric
W.9 Sealant with Backer Rod
W.10 Self-Adhering Waterproof Tape

DAMPPROOFING:
D.1 GWB Sheathing
D.2 15# Felt
D.3 Metal Flashing
D.4 Flexible Flashing
D.5 Dampproofing
D.6 Weeps
D.7 Vapor Retarder

INTERIOR MATERIALS:
I.1 ____" GWB
I.2 ____" Type 'X' GWB
I.3 Metal Closure
I.4 Guardrail
I.5 Furring Channel
I.6 Zee Strip
I.7 Wood Trim

FENESTRATION (DOORS & WINDOWS):
F.1 Aluminum Curtain Wall
F.2 Fixed Window
F.3 Storefront
F.4 Structural Glazing System
F.5 Structural Silicone System
F.6 Double-Hung Window
F.7 Single-Hung Window
F.8 Casement Window
F.9 Hopper Window
F.10 Awning Window
F.11 Insulating Glass
F.12 Float Glass
F.13 Low 'E' Glass
F.14 Tempered Glass
F.15 Laminated Glass
F.16 Wired Glass
F.17 Window Stool
F.18 Metal Trim
F.19 Steel Frame
F.20 H.M. Door
F.21 Roll-up Door
F.22 Sectional Door
F.23 Aluminum Door
F.24 Revolving Door
F.25 Glass Block
F.26 Aluminum Threshold
F.27 Wood Blocking
F.28 Shim
F.29 Blinds

ROOFING:
R.1 Single-ply Roofing
R.2 Built-up Roofing
R.3 Flashing Membrane
R.4 Metal Counterflashing
R.5 Standing Seam Roof
R.6 Gutter
R.7 Downspout
R.8 Roof Drain
R.9 Overflow Drain
R.10 Roof Scupper
R.11 Traffic Pads
R.12 Skylight
R.13 Awning
R.14 Insulated Curb
R.15 Metal Coping
R.16 Precast Coping
R.17 Stone Coping
R.18 Metal Reglet
R.19 Metal Facia
R.20 Cont. Cleat
R.21 Counterflashing
R.22 Roof Ballast
R.23 Pedestal Pavers

See T.4 for Tapered Insulation

STRUCTURAL*:
S.1 Reinforced Concrete
S.2 Structural Steel
S.3 Shelf Angle
S.4 Loose Lintel
S.5 Lintel Block
S.6 Bracing
S.7 Metal Studs
S.8 Expansion Bolt
S.9 Masonry Anchor
S.10 Ladder Reinforcement
S.11 Anchors
S.12 Metal Deck
S.13 Pour Stop
S.14 Bridging

HVAC:
H.1 Metal Grille
H.2 Fin Tube
H.3 Return Air Register

LANDSCAPING:
L.1 Concrete Paving with Broomed Finish
L.2 Concrete Paving with Exposed Aggregate
L.3 Brick Pavers
L.4 Sand Bed
L.5 Asphalt
L.6 Bollard

MISCELLANEOUS:
M.1 Expansion Joint Cover
M.2 Control Joint
M.3 Reveal
M.4 Quirk
M.5 Louver
M.6 Light Sconce
M.7 Soft Joint
M.8 Metal Grating

NOTES:
1. This list is used on all projects. It includes some items not used on this project.

*2. For all structural member sizes, see structural drawings.

Figure 5.5 An example of a standard notations list used in conjunction with keynotes.

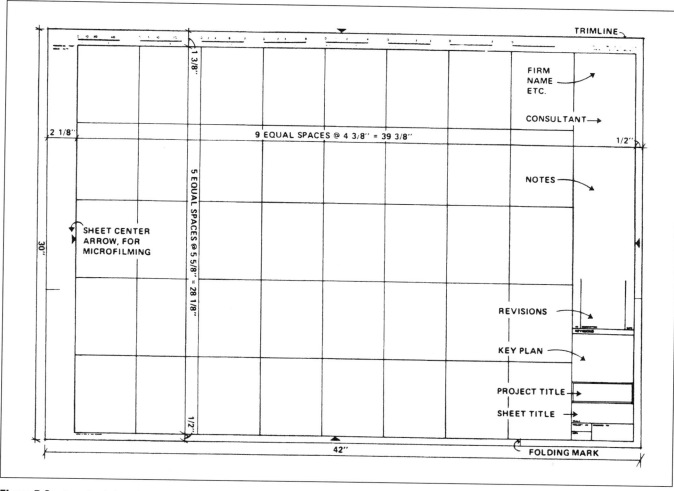

Figure 5.6 Standard detail sheet layout for a 42 × 30 in (1 m × 0.75 m) sheet. This format was recommended by the California chapter of the AIA (since 1981, known as AIA, San Francisco).

ture is sloped toward the drains, carry the dimension string to the top of the wall. Tying the dimension to the top of the roof and identifying it as *variable* serves no purpose. The structural drawings will set the top of structure elevation based on information supplied by the architect.

■ The rough window opening is the dimension of the opening before the window manufacturer installs the window. This is usually the height from the top of the sill blocking to the bottom of the head blocking in masonry construction (studs and tracks if blocking is not used).

■ Floor elevations should start at the entry level which is indicated as ±0. A general note equates this ±0 to the actual elevation taken from the survey. For example, ±0 = 276.33 ft.

■ In masonry construction, dimensions should include the number of courses. The joints must be taken into consideration when the dimension of

these courses is added up. Special attention must be given to joint width at lintels and shelf angles and to the decision to use modular or nonmodular brick.

■ Wall sections should include detailed horizontal dimensions between a known datum such as a column centerline and the exterior face of the wall.

5.3.2 Critical Dimensions

For most wall sections, there are two critical dimensions to be determined at the start of the design development phase. The first is the distance between the column centerline and the face of the wall. The second is the final floor-to-floor height.

COLUMN CENTERLINE LOCATION

This dimension requires some research. It entails getting the maximum column size from the structural engineer. The nominal dimension for a steel column can differ by as much as 2 in from the actual dimension. Ask the engi-

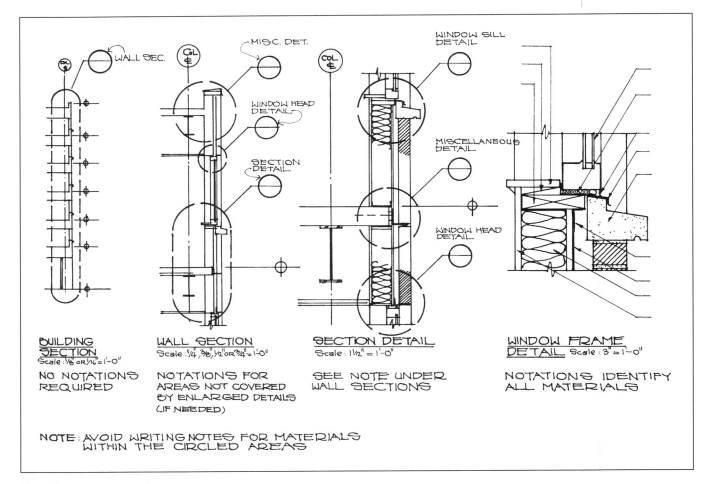

Figure 5.7 Hierarchy of notations.

neer to give a specific actual size. Instead of a 12 × 12 steel column, a W12 × 53 designation would define the size more clearly. This level of detail is usually unavailable at this early stage because the structural design has not been finalized as yet. In many cases, however, the engineer can determine an upper limit beyond which the column size is unlikely to be greater. Next determine the thickness of the fireproofing, if required (see Sec. 1.6.1). The final items to be determined are the thickness of the cladding and the tolerance to be allowed (Fig. 5.9).

FLOOR-TO-FLOOR HEIGHT

This dimension is affected by architectural spatial requirement, minimum room height requirements as defined by the building code, and minimum dimension between ceiling and underside of slab. This last dimension requires input from the structural engineer to determine maximum beam depth and slab thickness. It also requires input from the mechanical-electrical-plumbing (MEP) consultant to determine duct size, ceiling and lighting allowance, and, where a sprinkler system is used, the diameter of the main sprinkler pipe (if it crosses the duct

path) (Fig. 5.10). In some cases, when the ceiling plenum is not deep enough to accommodate all these components, the architect may decide to explore the possibility of creating openings in the beams to allow the ducts or the main sprinkler pipes to pass through. A conference between all the disciplines involved is usually convened to determine what changes need to be made. The structural engineer determines the maximum size of the holes and their locations, and the mechanical engineer determines what size changes can be done to the ducts. Minimizing the ceiling to slab dimension reduces the area of the costly exterior cladding.

5.3.3 Step-By-Step Procedure
SHEET ORGANIZATION

As stated earlier, the conventional way of drawing a wall section is to draw it at a ¾-in scale and write most of the notations and dimensions on that drawing. A few selected areas requiring more detail are enlarged to a 1½-in scale, and window details (head, jamb, and sill) are enlarged to a 3-in scale. This approach works perfectly for low-rise buildings.

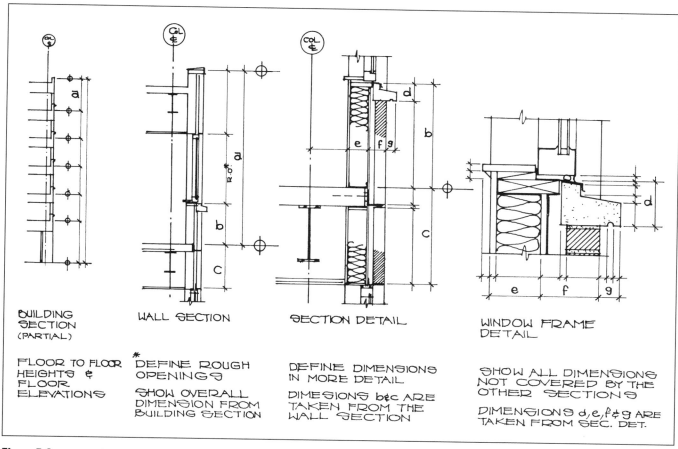

Figure 5.8 Hierarchy of dimensions.

Another way of conveying the information is to treat the wall section as a reference drawing for the enlarged details in a manner similar to a floor plan. The wall section is drawn at a smaller scale such as ⅜ or ¼ in. The major dimensions are shown on this drawing. Areas to be enlarged are circled and keyed to other sheets. This approach has the following advantages:

1. Duplication of information is avoided.

2. In many cases, the wall section is not foreshortened giving a truer picture of what the area surrounding the detail looks like.

3. The details are drawn at a larger scale giving more detailed information.

For tall buildings such as high-rise towers, the sections can be drawn parallel to the long side of the sheet. Each segment width is determined by its three components: the wall section profile, the dimension strings, and the notations. It is recommended that these last two be positioned on opposite sides of the section. Figure 5.11 shows suggested dimensions to determine segment width. Isolating these segments with a vertical

line gives the sheet a more organized look and helps isolate the information for each section while allowing the sections to be placed closer together. It is customary to draw all wall sections facing in the same direction. This allows each segment to be organized in a similar fashion.

Title block may be widened to include the keynotes comfortably. Alternatively, a consecrated band adjacent to the title block can be introduced to accommodate the keynotes. Of course, with Con-Doc or written notations, no space is required for keynotes.

DRAWING THE WALL SECTION

Most experienced persons who undertake the task of drawing wall sections follow a set procedure that gives an organized look to the sheet. The location of wall section cuts should be selected carefully. The goal should be to cover all different conditions while avoiding repetition. A blank wall without openings or articulation should be drawn to show the location of shelf angles, flashing, condition at the column, or other information. This drawing can either be a wall section or a section detail keyed back to the elevation.

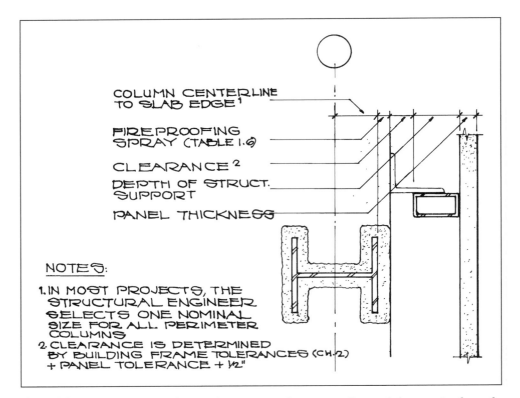

COLUMN CENTERLINE
TO SLAB EDGE[1]

FIREPROOFING
SPRAY (TABLE 1.6)

CLEARANCE[2]

DEPTH OF STRUCT.
SUPPORT

PANEL THICKNESS

NOTES:

1. IN MOST PROJECTS, THE
STRUCTURAL ENGINEER
SELECTS ONE NOMINAL
SIZE FOR ALL PERIMETER
COLUMNS
2. CLEARANCE IS DETERMINED
BY BUILDING FRAME TOLERANCES (CH.2)
+ PANEL TOLERANCE + ½"

Figure 5.9 Determining the distance between a column centerline and the exterior face of the wall.

A step-by-step procedure for drawing wall sections is shown in Fig. 5.12. It is assumed that the wall sections will fit vertically in a 42 × 30 in (1.00 × 0.76 m) sheet and that a keynoting system is used.

The wall section group of drawings provides vital information to the specification writer, the cost estimator, and the contractor. These drawings should be detailed and dimensioned clearly to convey that information in a concise and unambiguous way. Drawing the wall sections and the details associated with them properly can prevent mistakes and omissions in the specifications and cost estimate as well as problems in execution that may cause leakage and deterioration of wall components.

CADD

Computer-aided design and drafting, like pin-registered drafting which preceded it, is very efficient when applied to plans and repetitive tasks. Wall sections, while not as imminently suited to CADD as plans, incorporate many repetitive elements which include:

1. Structural elements such as floor slabs, beams, masonry coursing, and window frames

2. Overall dimensions, detailed dimensions, and floor elevations

3. Notations

Projects that have too many deviations in floor elevations and window heights may not have enough repetitious information to warrant the use of CADD, in which case it may be faster to hand draw and keynote the plans. Computer-aided design and drafting, however, has the advantage of allowing the designer to zoom in on areas that require detailing such as slab or roof edge details and window details. Storing standard generic window frame profiles for curtain wall, punched windows, and storefronts is a real time saver. Each area is enlarged on the screen, further information and detailing are added, and the detail is combined with other details to finish a new sheet in a shorter time than could be done by hand. Modifying repetitious notations is also easier on CADD. This enables the architect to salvage design development drawings and use them for the construction drawing phase.

In a conversation with Evan Shu, AIA, a sole practitioner in Boston serving as codirector of the Boston Society of Architect's Datacad group, he stated that he sketches wall sections freehand and to scale. He then tapes a photocopy reproduced on acetate to the screen and uses it as a guide to develop the section and details. He also stated that a digitizer can be used to achieve the same result without going through the trouble of copying or the mess of taping to the screen.

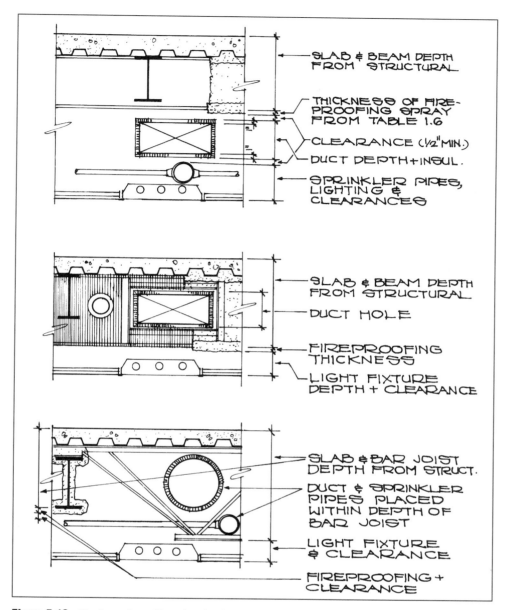

SLAB & BEAM DEPTH FROM STRUCTURAL

THICKNESS OF FIRE-PROOFING SPRAY FROM TABLE 1.6

CLEARANCE (½" MIN.)

DUCT DEPTH + INSUL.

SPRINKLER PIPES, LIGHTING & CLEARANCES

SLAB & BEAM DEPTH FROM STRUCTURAL

DUCT HOLE

FIREPROOFING THICKNESS

LIGHT FIXTURE DEPTH + CLEARANCE

SLAB & BAR JOIST DEPTH FROM STRUCT.

DUCT & SPRINKLER PIPES PLACED WITHIN DEPTH OF BAR JOIST

LIGHT FIXTURE & CLEARANCE

FIREPROOFING + CLEARANCE

Figure 5.10 Designs that affect the depth of a ceiling plenum.

While CADD can be a great asset in the hands of a skilled and knowledgeable operator, it can cause delays and result in uninformative drawings if placed in the hands of an unskilled draftsperson. Delays, caused by having to wait for a plotter to be available in a busy office, can result in frustration and missed deadlines.

Part I of this book contains the technical background needed to draw the wall section properly. The person assigned to draw the wall sections would do well to read that part before tackling this task. Keeping abreast of new developments by attending seminars and reading technical books related to this complicated subject is very important in today's fast developing technologies.

SUMMARY

Designing the exterior cladding requires a wealth of information to develop the drawings detailing exterior walls. If the means to deliver this information do not match the research that went into the design, the result can be disappointing. This chapter explains the most prevalent techniques used to organize this information in a coherent, nonrepetitive, properly notated and dimensioned set of drawings.

Drawing the wall sections and details associated with them properly can prevent mistakes and omissions in the specifications and cost estimate as well as problems in execution that may cause leakage and deterioration

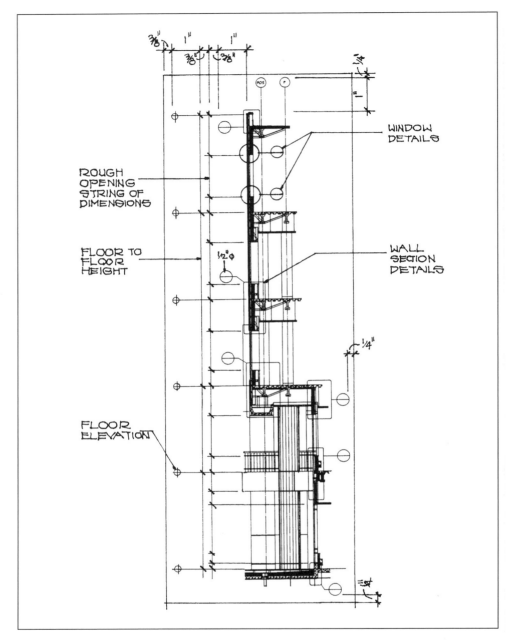

ROUGH
OPENING
STRING OF
DIMENSIONS

FLOOR TO
FLOOR
HEIGHT

FLOOR
ELEVATION

WINDOW
DETAILS

WALL
SECTION
DETAILS

Figure 5.11   Determining the width of a wall section segment. (Computer-drafted wall section by Steve Ng, Shepley, Bulfinch, Richardson & Abbott, Boston.)

of wall components. Special considerations should be given to the position of window frames in relation to all wall defensive elements such as the dampproofing membrane, the vapor retarder, and air barrier to prevent potential leakage points.

Critical dimensions must be determined early in the project. These include the column centerline to face of wall and the floor-to-floor height dimensions. Both require research and discussion with the consultants. As in notations, architects should refrain from repeating the same dimensions in every succeeding enlargement.

Details must not repeat information already shown on

the wall sections. Notations must use uniform nomenclature indicated in the specifications and dimensions must be tied to known reference points such as a finish floor elevation or a column centerline. In addition, elements in the elevation must be included in the dimensioning. This is especially important in unit masonry construction where the number of courses should be shown next to each dimension.

Drawing a wall section usually follows a set procedure that produces a group of sections of uniform organization. Wall sections should face in the same direction, and all floor levels should be aligned from

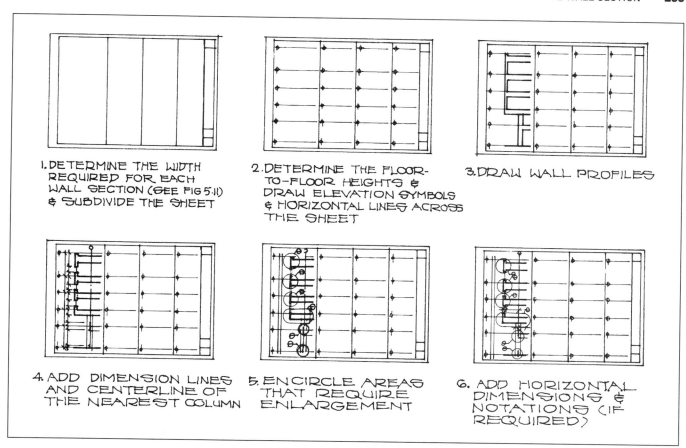

Figure 5.12 Step-by-step procedure to draw a wall section.

section to section. Each material is identified by either a notation or a keynote tied to a legend or, in the case of the Con-Doc system, directly to the specifications. The project architect would do well to keep abreast of new developments by attending seminars and reading up-to-date technical books relating to this important subject.

Computer-aided design and drafting is advantageous for repetitive tasks. For wall sections, it handles repetitive dimensions, notations, window frames, and supportive structures well. It is also very useful for zooming in on parts of the wall section to develop enlarged details. In large offices, a plotter used by too many people can cause delays that lessen the advantages mentioned above.

Conclusion

This book addressed the subject of exterior walls in a comprehensive way to shed some light on this complex and important subject. Because of the introduction of many and varied wall systems, developing trouble-free detailing for exterior walls is becoming more difficult. The incidence of leaks and deterioration in these walls is beginning to outpace the traditional cause for client dissatisfaction, namely roof leaks, now that more dependable roofing systems are becoming more common.

Understanding the forces of nature that cause these problems and the mechanisms devised to counter them and reviewing examples of what can go wrong are the best ways to avoid costly litigation and produce trouble-free details. Developing a feel—a sixth sense, if you will—for structural behavior and cost implications is also essential in the practice of architecture.

The task of developing wall sections requires the person entrusted with this challenging task to be constantly on the lookout for the latest information concerning the system selected by the designer. During my career as a consultant conducting the final check on architectural drawings for major projects, I have encountered quite a few examples of detailing that indicated that the person entrusted with that task spent most of the time refining design aesthetics—the enjoyable part—and too little time developing the details that make the design successful.

While it is important that a knowledgeable person be entrusted with developing the detailing required for exterior cladding, it is no less important that a procedure for checking the final set of drawings be established by the office. Unfortunately, this is not commonly practiced. To do this task properly, an experienced person who was not involved in the drawings should be assigned to perform the checking. An adequate time and budget should be set aside for this activity. This task should be divided into checking the exterior cladding (the subject of this book), and performing a coordination check within the architectural set and between that set and the other disciplines. An experienced checker should be able to finish checking a major project in 3 to 4 weeks. While this may add to the cost of producing the drawings, it saves time spent on issuing addenda and change orders. It also helps preserve the reputation of the firm and has the potential of attracting repeat work from satisfied clients.

An attempt has been made here to provide as wide a spectrum of information as possible in as concentrated a form as is feasible within the limited space and time allocated for this endeavor. Needless to say, to cover this subject thoroughly would require several volumes which, in this day and age, nobody has the time to read. The intent is to provide an overall view of the background information required to avoid the obvious pitfalls. This should be only a first step. Project architects should attend technical seminars, even if they are not subsidized by their offices, and buy relevant books like those listed in the bibliography to acquire more in-depth knowledge of the subject.

While exterior walls are the most visible element of a building, other elements of the built environment are of no lesser importance. One must not lose sight of urban and environmental issues. While most architects are usually not in control of where certain buildings are to be located, they can play a role in influencing the decision makers to prevent the location of environmentally hazardous buildings in close proximity to schools, hospitals, or residential neighborhood. Unfortunately, this is not always observed.

Much has been accomplished in the recent past to conserve energy and reduce the need for polluting power plants. Increased levels of insulation and more efficient HVAC systems have been introduced, tighter building envelopes have become the norm, and more energy-efficient fenestration is being constantly introduced. Alternative sources of energy will eventually replace the current ones and, hopefully, diminish the global levels of pollution.

The architectural profession should strive to find sources of funding to conduct research aimed at creating systems that can be recycled and have an afterlife. Instead of the current practice of demolishing buildings that have reached the end of their useful life, buildings would be planned to be disassembled and their components incorporated into new construction. This would require the creation of special, standardized connecting elements between wall components as well as between elements of the structural frame. A prime example is the components used in space frames. Applying these methods to concrete and masonry would go a long way toward reducing the volume of debris choking landfills as well as eliminating wasteful practices. This is recycling on a grand scale.

Universities should lead the way in that effort because they are uniquely equipped to create cooperation between different disciplines. Other research aimed at emulating nature should also be conducted. Exterior walls based on the function of plant and animal skins is conceivable. Wouldn't it be marvelous if buildings could be designed with a healing mechanism that can stop leaks in a rainstorm? The possibilities for research are limitless if we but keep an open mind, identify the problems, and study parallels in nature to create solutions. Architects, in collaboration with engineers trained in bionics research, can create new products and systems using similar methods to those used by engineers to incorporate features of bird wings in the design of airplane wings. While great progress has been achieved in this century, we must be prepared to meet the challenges of the twenty-first century.

Glossary

Many of the terms explained in the text are not included in this list of definitions. The bulk of this glossary is devoted to masonry construction.

Admixtures: Materials added to a concrete mix to modify its characteristics.

Aggregate: Inert material used with a cementing agent to form concrete or mortar.

Anchor: Metal tie used to secure masonry to a backup wall.

Anodizing: To subject aluminum to electrolytic action as the anode of a cell in order to coat it with a protective film.

Architrave: Member of an entablature resting on the capitals of columns and supporting the frieze.

Arris: Angle, corner, or edge produced by the meeting of two surfaces.

Ashlar Masonry: Masonry composed of rectangular units of shale, or stone, or burned clay. It is generally larger in size than brick and properly bonded; has sawed, dressed, or squared beds.

> **Coursed Ashlar:** Ashlar set to form continuous horizontal joints.

> **Random Ashlar:** Ashlar set with stones of varying length and height so that neither vertical nor horizontal joints are continuous.

> **Stacked Ashlar:** Ashlar set to form continuous vertical joints.

Backer Rod: Compressible rod of plastic foam inserted in a joint to gauge the depth of a sealant. Also known as a *backup rod*.

Backup: That part of a masonry wall located behind the exterior facing.

Baluster: Miniature column or other form of upright which, in series, supports a handrail, as in a balustrade.

Balustrade: Railing or parapet consisting of a handrail and balusters, sometimes on a base member and sometimes interrupted by piers.

Base Course: Lowest course in a masonry wall or pier.

Bat: Piece of brick used to fill an odd dimension.

Batter: Recessing of sloping masonry back in successive courses; the opposite of *corbel*.

Bead: Narrow strip of weld metal or sealant. A metal edge or corner used in conjunction with plaster or GWB as an accessory.

Bed Joint: Horizontal joint between stones, usually filled with mortar, lead, or sealant. Also a horizontal joint between brick courses.

Belt Course: Narrow horizontal course of masonry, sometimes slightly projected such as windowsills which are made continuous. Sometimes called *string course* or *sill course*.

Bent: Frame with rigid corners sometimes referred to as a *portal*.

Bevel: Angle that one surface or line makes with another when they are not at right angles.

Bleeding: Excess water rising to the surface of newly cast concrete.

Blocking: Pieces of wood forming a subframe for windows. Also used to provide a nailing or screwing strip to attach finish materials to.

Bluestone: Gray or blue-gray sandstone that is easy to split into slabs.

Bond: Arrangement of masonry units. Bond may be common, running, stack, Flemish, English, or Dutch (see Fig. 4.38).

Bond Beam: Course or courses of a masonry wall grouted and usually reinforced in the horizontal direction. Serves as a horizontal tie of a wall, as a bearing course for structural members, or as a flexural member.

Bond Breaker: Material used to prevent a sealant from adhering to a backup material.

Bond Stone: Stones projecting laterally into the backup wall used to tie the wall together.

Brake Metal: Sheet metal bent to a desired profile on a power or manual brake machine.

Brownstone: Reddish-brown sandstone containing iron oxide.

Bugged Finish: Smooth finish produced by grinding with power sanders.

Building Brick: Brick for building purposes not especially treated for texture or color. Formerly called *common brick*.

Bulkhead: Base of a sidelight in an entrance frame.

Bull Nose: Convex rounding of a member, such as the front edge of a stair tread or windowsill.

Buttering: Placing mortar on a masonry unit with a trowel.

Buttress: Projecting structure designed to resist the thrust of an arch, vault, or other forces perpendicular to an exterior wall.

Calcite Streaks: Description of a white or milky streak occurring in stone. It is a joint plane usually wider than a glass seam which has been recemented by deposition of calcite in the crack. It is structurally sound.

Camber: Curvature in the bottom of a long span beam designed to compensate for deflection.

Cantilever: Horizontal structural member extending beyond its point of support.

Capillary Action: Force of adhesion between water and a solid. Water can be impelled by capillary attraction from a wet to a dry side of a wall.

Capital: Column cap often carved with geometric shapes.

Carving: Cutting of ornamental shapes, figures, etc., from models or details, which are too intricate to produce from patterns.

Cell or Core: Interior voids in a concrete masonry unit (CMU).

Centering: Temporary form work for the support of masonry arches or lintels during construction.

Chamfer: Bevel to prevent damage to a corner.

Chat-Sawed: Description of a textured stone finish, obtained by using chat sand in the gang sawing process.

Closer: Last masonry unit laid in a course. It may be a whole unit or a portion of one.

Closure: Supplementary or short-length units used at corners or jambs to maintain bond patterns.

CMU: Concrete masonry unit.

Cold-Rolled Steel: Steel shaped by rollers at a temperature at which it is no longer plastic.

Collar Joint: Vertical, longitudinal joint between wythes of masonry in a cavity wall.

Composite Metal Panel: Panel with a metal facing on one or both sides of another material. Panels faced on both sides are also referred to as *sandwich panels*.

Composite Wall: Masonry wall incorporating more than one type of masonry unit. Most often, a brick veneer is used with a CMU backup in this application.

Coping: Material or masonry units forming a cap or finish on top of a wall, pier, pilaster, chimney, etc. It protects the wall from penetration of water from above.

Corbel: A cantilever formed by projecting successive courses of masonry out from the face of the wall.

Cornice: Molded projecting stone at the top of an entablature.

Counterflashing: Flashing turned down over a base flashing to protect its edge from water infiltration.

Course: One of the continuous horizontal layers of units, bonded with mortar in masonry.

Crazing: Fine hairline cracks in the surface of a hard material such as concrete or porcelain.

Creep: Slow change of dimension in cement-based materials due to shrinkage.

Crowfoot: Dark gray to black zig-zag marking occurring in stone. Usually structurally sound.

Culls: Masonry units which do not meet the standards or specifications and have been rejected.

Curing: Process of keeping concrete moist after placement to ensure proper hydration for a set period of time.

Cut Stone: Finished stone fabricated to specific dimensions.

Cutting: Handwork required to finish a stone which cannot be done by machine.

Damp Course: Course or layer of impervious material which prevents capillary entrance of moisture from the ground or a lower course. Often called a *damp check.*

Dampproofing: One or more coatings of a compound that is impervious to water. It is usually applied onto the back of stone or the back of a wall.

Dimensioned Stone: Stone precut and shaped to specified sizes.

Dentil Course: Mold course immediately below the cornice having small uniformly spaced blocks resembling teeth. From the French word *dent* meaning tooth.

Dog's Tooth: Brick laid with their corners projecting from the wall face.

Dressed Stone: Square or rectangular stone cut by hand.

Drip: 1. Projecting course, shaped to throw off water and prevent its running down the face of a wall or other surface. 2. Slot cut in the bottom of a projected stone to interrupt the flow of rainwater adhering to the underside of the course.

Dry Seam: Unhealed fracture which is a plane of weakness in stone.

Economy Brick: Brick whose nominal dimensions are 4 × 4 × 8 in.

Efflorescence: Powder or stain sometimes found on the surface of masonry, resulting from deposition of water-soluble salts.

Engineered Brick: Brick whose nominal dimensions are 4 × 2⅔ × 8 in.

Entablature: Consists of an architrave, frieze, and cornice.

Entasis: Curve resulting from the gradual diminishing of the diameter of the upper two-thirds of a column.

EPDM: Etylene propylene diene monomer, a sheet membrane usually used in single-ply roofing and waterproofing.

Epoxy Resin: Flexible usually thermal setting resin made by polymerization of an epoxide and used as an adhesive.

Expansion Anchor: Metal expandable unit inserted into a drilled hole that grips masonry or concrete by expansion.

Extrusion: Linear product manufactured by forcing a material through an opening to produce a linear shape.

Facade: Exterior face of a building (an elevation).

Facing Brick: Brick made especially for facing purposes, often treated to produce surface texture. They are made of selected clays, or are treated, to produce desired color.

Fat Mortar: Mortar containing a high percentage of cementitious components. It is a sticky mortar which adheres to a trowel.

Felt: Sheet material fabricated from thick, dampproofed building paper or fiberglass fabric. It is used to dampproof walls and as a component in built-up roofing.

Field: Expanse of wall between openings, corners, etc., principally composed of stretchers.

Fieldstone: Rough building stone gathered from riverbeds and fields.

Flashing: Thin, impervious material placed in mortar joints and through air spaces in masonry to prevent water penetration and/or provide water drainage.

Freestone: Fine-grained sedimentary rock that has no planes or cleavage along which it is likely to split.

Frieze: Flat member of the entablature occurring above the architrave and below the cornice.

Frit: Ground-up colored glass fused to spandrel glass to make it opaque.

Frog: Depression in the bed surface of a brick. Sometimes called a *panel.*

Gang Saw: Machine with multiple blades used to saw rough quarry blocks into slabs.

Girt: Beam designed to resist lateral forces in wall construction.

Glass Seam: Vein fillings of coarse crystalline calcite. The vein does not necessarily decrease the strength of stone.

Grounds: Nailing strips placed in masonry walls as a means of attaching trim or furring.

Grout: Mixture of cementitious material and aggregate to which sufficient water is added to produce pouring consistency without segregation of the constituents.

High-Lift Grouting: Technique of grouting masonry in lifts up to 12 ft.

Low-Lift Grouting: Technique of grouting as the wall is constructed.

Gypsum Board: Interior wall finish panel composed of a gypsum core faced with cardboard on both sides. Also known as *wallboard, dry wall,* or *plasterboard.*

Head Joint: Vertical mortar joint between ends of masonry units.

Header: Masonry unit which overlaps two or more adjacent wythes of masonry to tie them together. Often called *bonder.*

Blind Header: Concealed brick header in the interior of a wall, not showing on the faces.

Clipped Header: Bat placed to look like a header for purposes of establishing a pattern. Also called *false header.*

Flare Header: Header of darker color than the field of the wall.

Heading Course: Continuous bonding course of header brick. Also called *header course.*

High-Strength Adhesive: Bonding agent of high ultimate strength used to join individual pieces of stone into pre-assembled units.

Hollow Brick: Masonry unit of clay or shale whose net cross-sectional area in any plane parallel to the bearing surface is not less than 60% of its gross cross-sectional area measured in the same plane.

Hollow Masonry Unit: One whose net cross-sectional area in any plane parallel to the bearing surface is less than 75% of the gross.

Hydrated Lime: Quicklime (calcium oxide) allowed to combine chemically with water and used as an ingredient in masonry mortar.

Igneous Rock: Rock formed by the solidification of volcanic magma.

Incise: To cut inwardly or engrave, as in an inscription.

Inscription: Lettering cut in stone.

Ironworker: Skilled person engaged in the erection of steel frames or reinforcing steel in concrete construction.

Jack Arch: One having horizontal or nearly horizontal upper and lower surfaces. Also called *flat* or *straight arch.*

Joint: Space between masonry units, usually filled with mortar, joint sealant, or epoxy.

Jumbo Brick: Generic term indicating a brick larger in size than the standard. Some producers use this term to describe oversize brick of specific dimensions that they manufacture.

Kerf: Slot cut into stone thickness to be engaged by strap anchors.

Keystone: Wedge-shaped stone placed at the top center of an arch.

King Closer: Brick cut diagonally to have one 2-in end and one full-width end.

Labyrinth: Joint design featuring interlocking baffles to prevent water from penetrating to the interior.

Laitance: Weak layer rising to the surface of concrete due to bleeding.

Lateral Force: Horizontal force such as wind, earthquake movement, or soil pressure on retaining walls.

Lewis Bolt: Tapered head wedged in a tapered recess in stone for hanging soffit stones.

Box Lewis: Tapered metal box wedged in the top of columns or other heavy stones for hoisting.

Lewis Holes: Sinkages in the top beds of stone to engage Lewis pins for hoisting.

Lime Putty: Hydrated lime in plastic form ready for addition to mortar.

Limestone: Sedimentary stone consisting of calcium carbonate, magnesium carbonate, or both.

Lintel: Beam placed over an opening in a wall.

Lockstrip Gasket: Synthetic rubber gasket featuring a strip inserted in a groove to tighten the gasket's hold on the glass. A lockstrip is also referred to as a *zipper.*

Marble: Metamorphic stone formed naturally from sedimentary rock by heat and pressure.

Masonry: Brick, stone, concrete, etc., bonded with mortar.

Modular Masonry Unit: One whose nominal dimensions are based on the 4-in module.

Mastic: Doughlike material used as an adhesive or sealant.

Metamorphic Rock: Rock created by the action of heat and pressure on sedimentary rock.

Miter: Junction of two units at an angle. The junction line usually bisects on a 45° angle.

Moment: Twisting force causing a part of a structure to rotate.

Mortar: Plastic mixture of cementitious materials, fine aggregate, and water.

Natural Bed: Horizontal stratification of stone as it was formed in the deposit.

Noise Reduction Coefficient (NRC): Index of the proportion of incident sound that is absorbed by a surface.

Nominal Dimension: Dimension greater than a specified masonry dimension by the thickness of a mortar joint, but not more than ½ in.

Norman Brick: Brick whose nominal dimensions are 4 × 2⅔ × 12 in.

O.C.: Abbreviation for *on center,* meaning that the dimension is measured between centerlines.

Overhand Work: Laying brick from inside a wall by having workers stand on a floor or on a scaffold.

Parapet: Part of an exterior wall projecting above the roof.

Parging: Process of applying a dampproofing coat of cement mortar to masonry. Sometimes referred to as *pargeting.*

Perm: Unit of vapor permeability used to gauge the rate at which vapor passes through a material.

Pier: Isolated brick column.

Pilaster: Wall portion projecting from either one or both wall faces and serving as a vertical column to stiffen the wall.

Plenum: Space between the ceiling and the floor slab above.

Pointing: 1. Final filling and finishing of mortar joints that have been raked out. 2. Troweling mortar into a joint after masonry units are laid.

Posttensioning: Stretching of tendons used to reinforce concrete after the concrete is poured. The reinforcing strands are placed in a steel or plastic sheath to prevent them from bonding to the concrete.

Preassembled Units: Two or more stones combined into a single unit by the use of epoxy resins, steel framing, or concrete backing.

Precast Concrete: Prefabricated concrete cast at a location other than the site.

Prefabricated Brick Masonry: Masonry construction fabricated in a location other than its final location in the structure. Also known as *preassembled, panelized,* and *sectionalized* brick masonry.

Pressure-Relieving Joint: Joint located at each floor or at a maximum of 15 ft (4.5 m) apart to prevent weight from being transferred between floors. A nonstaining sealant is applied to the joint to seal it.

Prestressed Concrete: Reinforced concrete cast after or before the reinforcement is stretched (prestressed or posttensioned).

Pretensioning: Stretching of tendons used to reinforce concrete prior to pouring the concrete.

Quarry: Location of an operation where a natural deposit of stone is removed from the ground.

Queen Closer: Cut brick having a nominal 2-in horizontal face dimension.

Quoins: Stones at the corners of a wall emphasized by size, projection, rustication, or by a different finish. Also applies to projecting brick corner coursing.

Racking: 1. Method entailing stepping back successive courses of masonry. 2. Forcing a structure to become out of plumb. Also spelled *wracking.*

Raggle: Groove in a joint or special unit that is to receive roofing or flashing. Also referred to as a *reglet.*

Range: Stone equivalent of a course in brick masonry. Range heights need not be the same.

Reglet: Recess that is to receive and secure metal flashing.

Reinforced Masonry: Masonry units, reinforcing steel, grout, and/or mortar combined to act together in resisting forces.

Relief or **Relieve:** Projection of ornamentation.

Reprise: Inside corner of a stone member with a profile other than a flat plane.

Return or **Return Head:** Stone facing with the finish appearing on both the face and the edge of the same stone—as on the corner of a building.

Reveal: Exposed portion of a stone between its outer face and a window or door set in an opening.

Roman Brick: Brick whose nominal dimensions are 4 × 2 × 12 in.

Rowlock: Brick laid on its face edge so that the normal header face is visible in the wall face. Frequently spelled *rolok*.

Rubble: Unsquared stones.

Rustication: Recessed surface cut around or across the face of a stone to produce an accent shadow. Also refers to chamfers and dressed perimeters of individual stones.

Sandstone: Sedimentary stone formed from sand.

Scotia: Concave molding.

Sculpture: Work of a sculptor in three-dimensional form by cutting from a solid block of stone.

Seam: Crack or fissure in a rough quarry block.

Sedimentary Stone: Stone formed from materials such as sand or sea shells deposited as sediments combined with natural cementing agents under high pressure.

Shale: Stone formed from the consolidation of clay or silt.

Shot Sawn: Description of a finish obtained by using steel shot in the gang-sawing process to produce random markings for a rough surface texture.

Shoved Joints: Vertical joints filled by shoving a brick against the next brick when it is being laid in a bed of mortar.

Slab: Slice of stone cut from a large quarry block.

Slate: Metamorphic form of clay easily split into thin sheets.

Slip Joint: Connection which permits vertical or horizontal movement of the cladding with respect to the structural frame.

Slurry Wall: Reinforced concrete retaining wall constructed entirely from the ground surface without the use of a form. It entails the use of specialized excavation equipment and a specially formulated mud (bentonite clay slurry) to prevent the sides from collapsing.

Slushed Joints: Vertical joints filled, after units are laid, by "throwing" mortar in with the edge of a trowel. (Generally, not recommended.)

Smooth Finish: Finish of minimum textural quality, presenting the least interruption of surface. Smooth finish may be applied to any surface, flat or molded. It is produced by a variety of machines.

Soap: Masonry unit of normal face dimensions having a nominal 2-in thickness.

Soffit: Finished underside of a lintel, arch, or portico.

Soft-Burned: Clay products which have been fired at low temperature ranges, producing relatively high absorptions and low compressive strengths.

Soldier: Stretcher set on end with the face showing on the wall surface.

Solid Masonry Unit: One whose net cross-sectional area in every plane parallel to the bearing surface is 75% or more of the gross.

Spall: Small fragment removed from the face of a masonry unit by a blow or by action of the elements.

Spandrel: Stone panel between the windowsill and the window head below it.

Splay: Beveled or slanted surface.

Statue: Sculpture of a human or animal figure.

Story Pole: Marked pole for measuring masonry coursing during construction.

Stretcher: Masonry unit laid with its greatest dimension horizontal and its face parallel to the wall face.

Stringing Mortar: Procedure of spreading enough mortar on a bed to lay several masonry units.

Struck Joint: Any mortar joint which has been finished with a trowel.

Surround: Enframement.

Temper: To moisten and mix clay, plaster, or mortar to a proper consistency.

Template: Pattern used in the fabrication operation.

Terra Cotta: Custom-made, hard-burned, glazed, or unglazed clay building units, plain or ornamental, that are machine-extruded or hand-molded.

Thin Stone: Stone veneer less than 2 in (50 mm) thick.

Throat: Undercut of a projected molding to form a drip.

Tie: Any unit of material which connects masonry to masonry or other materials. See *Wall Tie*.

Tolerance: Acceptable dimensional allowance, under or over sizes called for by the design.

Tooling: Compressing and shaping the face of a mortar joint with a special tool other than a trowel. For stone, a tooled finish customarily has four, six, or eight parallel concave grooves to the inch (25 mm).

Toothing: Constructing the temporary end of a wall with the end stretcher of every alternate course projecting. Projecting units are *toothers*.

Tracery: Curved mullion of a stone window, as in Gothic architecture.

Travertine: Veined marblelike form of limestone with occasional fissures forming a rich pattern.

Trim: Stone used as sills, copings, enframements, etc. with the facing of another material.

Tuck-Pointing: Filling in cut-out or defective mortar joints with fresh mortar.

Undercut: Stone cut or molded so as to present an overhanging part, as a drip mold.

Veneer: 1. Layer of facing material used to cover a wall. 2. Single wythe of masonry for facing purposes, not structurally bonded.

Wall, Bearing: Wall supporting a vertical load in addition to its own weight.

Wall, Cavity: Wall in which the inner and outer wythes are separated by an air space but tied together with metal ties.

Wall, Composite: Wall in which the facing and backing materials are bonded together.

Wall Plate: Horizontal member anchored to a masonry wall to which other structural elements may be attached. Also called *head plate*.

Wall Tie, Cavity: Rigid, corrosion-resistant metal tie which bonds two wythes of a cavity wall. It is usually steel, ³⁄₁₆ inch in diameter, and formed in a zee shape or a rectangle.

Wall Tie, Veneer: Strap or piece of metal used to tie a facing veneer to the backing.

Water Table: Projection of lower masonry on the outside of the wall slightly above the ground. Often a damp course is placed at the level of the water table to prevent upward penetration of groundwater.

Waterproofing: See *Dampproofing*.

Waxing: Filling of voids in marble slabs.

Weepholes: Drainage openings usually inserted at the base of a stone unit to release moisture accumulating between the stone and backup.

Wind (wined): Warp in a semifinished stone slab to be removed by further fabrication.

Wythe: 1. Each continuous vertical section of masonry one unit in thickness. 2. Thickness of masonry separating flues in a chimney. Also called *withe* or *tier*.

Appendix A

METRIC CONVERSIONS

Conversion to International System of Units (SI)

To convert from	to	multiply by
Length		
inch (in.)	millimeter (mm)	25.4
inch (in.)	meter (m)	0.0254
foot (ft)	meter (m)	0.3048
yard (yd)	meter (m)	0.9144
Area		
square foot (sq ft)	square meter (sq m)	0.09290
square inch (sq in.)	square millimeter (sq mm)	645.2
square in (sq in.)	square meter (sq m)	0.0006452
square yard (sq yd)	square meter (sq m)	0.8361
Volume		
cubic inch (cu in.)	cubic meter (cu m)	0.00001639
cubic foot (cu ft)	cubic meter (cu m)	0.02832
cubic yard (cu yd)	cubic meter (cu m)	0.7646
gallon (gal) Can. liquid*	liter	4.546
gallon (gal) Can. liquid*	cubic meter (cu m)	0.004546
gallon (gal) U.S. liquid*	liter	3.785
gallon (gal) U.S. liquid*	cubic meter (cu m)	0.003785
Force		
pound (lb)	kilogram (kgf)	0.4536
pound (lb)	newton (N)	4.448
Pressure or Stress		
pound/square foot (psf)	kilopascal (kPa)**	0.04788
pound/square inch (psi)	kilopascal (kPa)**	6.895
pound/square inch (psi)	megapascal (MPa)**	0.006895
pound/square foot (psf)	kilogram/square meter (kgf/sq m)	4.882
Mass		
pound (avdp)	kilogram (kg)	0.4536
ton (short, 2000 lb)	kilogram (kg)	907.2
ton (short, 2000 lb)	tonne (t)	0.9072
Mass (weight) per Length		
pound/linear foot (plf)	kilogram/meter (kg/m)	1.488
pound/linear foot (plf)	newton/meter (N/m)	14.593
Mass per volume (density)		
pound/cubic foot (pcf)	kilogram/cubic meter (kg/cu m)	16.02
pound/cubic yard (pcy)	kilogram/cubic meter (kg/cu m)	0.5933
Bending Moment or Torque		
inch-pound (in.-lb)	newton-meter	0.1130
foot-pound (ft-lb)	newton-meter	1.356
Temperature		
degree Fahrenheit (deg. F)	degree Celsius (C)	$t_C = (t_F - 32)/1.8$
Energy		
British thermal unit (Btu)	joule (j)	1056
Other		
Coefficient of heat transfer (Btu/ft²/h/°F)	W/m²/°C	5.678
Modulus of elasticity (psi)	MPa	0.006895
Thermal conductivity (Btu-in./ft²/h/°F)	Wm/m²/°C	0.1442
Thermal expansion in./in./°F	mm/mm/°C	1.800
Area/length (in.²/ft)	mm²/m	2116.80
ounces/square foot	kilogram/square meter	0.305
ounces/cubic yard	kilogram/cubic meter (kg/cu m)	0.0371

*One U.S. gallon equals 0.8321 Canadian gallon.   **A pascal equals one newton/square meter.

Material	Thickness, mm	Permeance, ng/(s·m²·Pa)	Resistance[h], TPa·m²·s/kg	Permeability, ng/(s·m·Pa)	Resistance/m[h], TPa·m·s/kg
Construction Materials					
Concrete (1:2:4 mix)				4.7	0.21
Brick masonry	100	46[f]	0.022		
Concrete block (cored, limestone aggregate)	200	137[f]	0.0073		
Tile masonry, glazed	100	6.9[f]	0.14		
Asbestos cement board	3	229–458[d]	0.0017–0.0035		
With oil-base finishes		17–29[d]	0.0035–0.052		
Plaster on metal lath	19	860[f]	0.0012		
Plaster on wood lath		630[e]	0.0016		
Plaster on plain gypsum lath (with studs)		1140[f]	0.00088		
Gypsum wall board (plain)	9.5	2860[f]	0.00035		
Gypsum sheathing (asphalt impregnated)	13	29[d]		0.038	
Structural insulating board (sheathing quality)				29–73[f]	0.038–0.014
Structural insulating board (interior, uncoated)	13	2860–5150[f]	0.00035–0.00019		
Hardboard (standard)	3.2	630[f]	0.0016		
Hardboard (tempered)	3.2	290[f]	0.0034		
Built-up roofing (hot mopped)		0.0	∞		
Wood, sugar pine				0.58–7.8[f,b]	172.0–131
Plywood (douglas fir, exterior glue)	6.4	40[f]	0.025		
Plywood (douglas fir, interior glue)	6.4	109[f]	0.0092		
Acrylic, glass fiber reinforced sheet	1.4	6.9[d]	0.145		
Polyester, glass fiber reinforced sheet	1.2	2.9[d]	0.345		
Thermal Insulations					
Air (still)				174[f]	0.0057
Cellular glass				0.0[d]	∞
Corkboard				3.0–3.8[d]	0.33–0.26
				14[e]	0.076
Mineral wool (unprotected)				245[e]	0.0059
Expanded polyurethane (R-11 blown) board stock				0.58–2.3[d]	1.72–0.43
Expanded polystyrene—extruded				1.7[d]	0.57
Expanded polystyrene—bead				2.9–8.4[d]	0.34–0.12
Phenolic foam (covering removed)				38	0.026
Unicellular synthetic flexible rubber foam				0.029[d]	34–4.61
Plastic and Metal Foils and Films[c]					
Aluminum foil	0.025	0.0[d]	∞		
Aluminum foil	0.009	2.9[d]	0.345		
Polyethylene	0.051	9.1[d]	0.110		2133
Polyethylene	0.1	4.6[d]	0.217		2133
Polyethylene	0.15	3.4[d]	0.294		2133
Polyethylene	0.2	2.3[d]	0.435		2133
Polyethylene	0.25	1.7[d]	0.588		2133
Polyvinylchloride, unplasticized	0.051	39[d]	0.026		
Polyvinylchloride plasticized	0.1	46–80[d]	0.032		
Polyester	0.025	42[d]	0.042		
Polyester	0.09	13[d]	0.075		
Polyester	0.19	4.6[d]	0.22		
Cellulose acetate	0.25	263[d]	0.0035		
Cellulose acetate	3.2	18[d]	0.054		

Metric equivalents for Table 1.3.

Material	Unit Mass, kg/m²	Permeance, ng/(s·m²·Pa)			Resistance[h], TPa·m²·s/kg		
		Dry-Cup	Wet-Cup	Other	Dry-Cup	Wet-Cup	Other
Building Paper, Felts, Roofing Papers[g]							
Duplex sheet, asphalt laminated, aluminum foil one side	0.42	0.1	10		10	0.1	
Saturated and coated roll roofing	3.18	2.9	14		0.34	0.071	
Kraft paper and asphalt laminated, reinforced 30-120-30	0.33	17	103		0.059	0.0097	
Blanket thermal insulation backup paper, asphalt coated	0.30	23	34–240		0.043	0.029–0.0042	
Asphalt-saturated and coated vapor retarder paper	0.42	11–17	34		0.091–0.059	0.029	
Asphalt-saturated, but not coated, sheathing paper	0.21	190	1160		0.0053	0.00086	
0.73 kg/m² asphalt felt	0.68	57	320		0.017	0.0031	
0.73 kg/m² tar felt	0.68	230	1040		0.0043	0.00096	
Single-kraft, double	0.16	1170	2400		0.00056	0.00042	
Liquid-Applied Coating Materials	Thickness, μm						
Commercial latex paints (dry film thickness)[i]							
Vapor retarder paint	70			26			0.038
Primer-sealer	30			360			0.0028
Vinyl acetate/acrylic primer	50			424			0.0024
Vinyl-acrylic primer	40			491			0.0020
Semi-gloss vinyl-acrylic enamel	60			378			0.0026
Exterior acrylic house and trim	40			313			0.0032
Paint-2 coats							
Asphalt paint on plywood			23			0.043	
Aluminum varnish on wood		17–29			0.059–0.034		
Enamels on smooth plaster				29–86			0.034–0.012
Primers and sealers on interior insulation board				51–20			0.020–.0083
Various primers plus 1 coat flat oil paint on plaster				91–172			0.011–0.0058
Flat paint on interior insulation board				229			0.0044
Water emulsion on interior insulation board				1716–4863			0.00058–0.00021
Paint-3 coats	Unit Mass, kg/m²						
Exterior paint, white lead and oil on wood siding		17–57			0.0059–0.017		
Exterior paint, white lead-zinc oxide and oil on wood		51			0.020		
Styrene-butadiene latex coating	0.6	629			0.0016		
Polyvinyl acetate latex coating	1.2	315			0.0032		
Chlorosulfonated polyethylene mastic	1.1	97			0.010		
	2.2	3.4			0.29		
Asphalt cutback mastic, 1.6 mm, dry		8.0			0.125		
4.8 mm, dry		0			∞		
Hot melt asphalt	0.6	29			0.034		
	1.1	5.7			0.175		

[a]This table permits comparisons of materials; but in the selection of vapor retarder materials, exact values for permeance or permeability should be obtained from the manufacturer or from laboratory tests. The values shown indicate variations among mean values for materials that are similar but of different density, orientation, lot, or source. The values should not be used as design or specification data. Values from dry-cup and wet-cup methods were usually obtained from investigations using ASTM E96 and C355; values shown under others were obtained by two-temperature, special cell, and air velocity methods.
[b]Depending on construction and direction of vapor flow.
[c]Usually installed as vapor retarders, although sometimes used as exterior finish and elsewhere near cold side, where special considerations are then required for warm side barrier effectiveness.
[d]Dry-cup method.
[e]Wet-cup method.
[f]Other than dry- or wet-cup method.
[g]Low permeance sheets used as vapor retarders. High permeance used elsewhere in construction.
[h]Resistance values have been calculated as the reciprocal of the permeance and permeability values.
[i]Cast at 0.25 mm wet film thickness.

Metric equivalents for Table 1.3 (*Cont.*).

		Surface Emittance, ϵ					
		Non-reflective $\epsilon = 0.90$		Reflective			
				$\epsilon = 0.20$		$\epsilon = 0.05$	
Position of Surface	Direction of Heat Flow	h_i	R	h_i	R	h_i	R
STILL AIR							
Horizontal	Upward	9.26	0.11	5.17	0.19	4.32	0.23
Sloping—45°	Upward	9.09	0.11	5.00	0.20	4.15	0.24
Vertical	Horizontal	8.29	0.12	4.20	0.24	3.35	0.30
Sloping—45°	Downward	7.50	0.13	3.41	0.29	2.56	0.39
Horizontal	Downward	6.13	0.16	2.10	0.48	1.25	0.80
MOVING AIR (Any position)		h_o	R	h_o	R	h_o	R
Wind (for winter) 6.7 m/s (24 km/h)	Any	34.0	0.030	—	—	—	—
Wind (for summer) 3.4 m/s (12 km/h)	Any	22.7	0.044	—	—	—	—

Notes:
1. Surface conductance h_i and h_o measured in $W/(m^2 \cdot K)$ resistance R in $m^2 \cdot K/W$.
2. No surface has both an air space resistance value and a surface resistance value.
3. For ventilated attics or spaces above ceilings under summer conditions (heat flow down), see Table 5.
4. Conductances are for surfaces of the stated emittance facing virtual blackbody surroundings at the same temperature as the ambient air. Values are based on a surface-air temperature difference of 5.5°C and for surface temperatures of 21°C.
5. See Chapter 3 for more detailed information, especially Tables 5 and 6, and see Figure 1 for additional data.
6. Condensate can have a significant impact on surface emittance (see Table 3).

Metric equivalents for Table 1.4.

Appendix B

TRADE ASSOCIATIONS

AAMA   American Architectural Manufacturers
          Assoc.
        1540 E. Dundee Road, Suite 310
        Palatine, IL 60067
        (708) 202-1350

ACI   American Concrete Institute
        P.O. Box 19150
        Detroit, MI 48219
        (313) 532-2600

AFPA   American Forest and Paper Assoc.
        (American Wood Council of the)
        1111 19th St., NW, Suite 800
        Washington, DC 20036
        (202) 463-2700

AISC   American Institute of Steel Construction
        One East Wacker Dr., Suite 3100
        Chicago, IL 60601-2001
        (312) 670-2400

AISI   American Iron and Steel Institute
        1101 17th St., NW
        Washington, DC 20036-4700
        (202) 452-7100

AITC   American Institute of Timber Construction
        11818 SE Mill Plain Blvd., Suite 407
        Vancouver, WA 98684-5092
        (206) 254-9132

ALSC   American Lumber Standards Committee
        P.O. Box 210
        Germantown, MD 20875
        (301) 972-1700

APA   American Plywood Assoc.
        P.O. Box 11700
        Tacoma, WA 98411
        (206) 565-6600

ASC   Adhesive and Sealant Council
        1627 K St., NW, Suite 1000
        Washington, DC 20006-1707
        (202) 452-1500

ASHRAE American Society of Heating, Refrigerating
          and Air-Conditioning Engineers
        1791 Tullie Circle, NE
        Atlanta, GA 30329
        (404) 636-8400

ASTM   American Society for Testing and Materials
        1916 Race St.
        Philadelphia, PA 19103-1187
        (215) 299-5400

AWCMA   American Window Covering Manufacturers
          Assoc.
        355 Lexington Ave., 17th Floor
        New York, NY 10017
        (212) 661-4261

AWPA   American Wood Preservers' Assoc.
        P.O. Box 286
        Woodstock, MD 21163-0286
        (410) 465-3169

AWS   American Welding Society
        550 LeJeune Road, NW
        P.O. Box 351040
        Miami, FL 33135
        (305) 443-9353

BANC   Brick Association of North Carolina
P.O. Box 13290
Greensboro, NC 27415-3290
(919) 273-5566

BHMA   Builders' Hardware Manufacturers Assoc.
355 Lexington Ave., 17th Floor
New York, NY 10017
(212) 661-4261

BIA   Brick Institute of America
11490 Commerce Park Dr.
Reston, VA 22091
(703) 620-0010

CDA   Copper Development Assoc.
260 Madison Av., 16th Floor
New York, NY 10016
(212) 251-7200

CTI   Ceramic Tile Institute of America
28720 Roadside Dr., Suite 300
Agora Hills, CA 91301-3321
(213) 660-1911
(818) 889-8453

EIMA   Exterior Insulation Manufacturers Assoc.
2759 State Road 580, Suite 112
Clearwater, FL 34621
(813) 726-6477

EJMA   Expansion Joint Manufacturers Assoc.
25 N. Broadway
Tarrytown, NY 10591
(914) 332-0040

FGMA   Flat Glass Marketing Assoc.
White Lakes Professional Bldg.
3310 S.W. Harrison St.
Topeka, KS 66611-2279
(913) 266-7013

FM   Factory Mutual Research Organization
1151 Boston-Providence Turnpike
P.O. Box 9102
Norwood, MA 02062
(617) 762-4300

FTI   Facing Tile Institute
P.O. Box 8880
Canton, OH 44711
(216) 488-1211

GA   Gypsum Association
810 First St., NE, Suite 510
Washington, DC 20002
(202) 289-5440

HMA   Hardwood Manufacturers Assoc.
400 Penn Center Blvd.
Pittsburgh, PA 15235
(412) 829-0770

HPVA   Hardwood Plywood and Veneer Assoc.
1825 Michael Farraday Dr.
P.O. Box 2789
Reston, VA 22090
(703) 435-2900

IGCC   Insulating Glass Certification Council
c/o ETL Testing Laboratories, Inc.
P.O. Box 2040
Route 11, Industrial Park
Cortland, NY 13045
(607) 753-6711

ILI   Indiana Limestone Institute of America
Stone City Bank Building, Suite 400
Bedford, IN 47421
(812) 275-4426

MBMA   Metal Building Manufacturer's Assoc.
c/o Thomas Associates, Inc.
1300 Sumner Ave.
Cleveland, OH 44115-2851
(216) 241-7333

MIA   Marble Institute of America
33505 State St.
Farmington, MI 48335
(313) 476-5558

ML/SFA   Metal Lath/Steel Framing Assoc.
(A Division of the National Association of
    Architectural Metal Manufacturers)
600 S. Federal St., Suite 400
Chicago, IL 60605
(312) 922-6222

NAAMM   National Association of Architectural Metal
    Manufacturers
600 S. Federal St., Suite 400
Chicago, IL 60605
(312) 922-6222

NAIMA   North American Insulation Manufacturers
    Assoc.
44 Canal Center Plaza, Suite 310
Alexandria, VA 22314
(703) 684-0084

NBGQA   National Building Granite Quarries Assoc.
P.O. Box 482
Barre, VT 05641
(802) 476-3115

NCMA   National Concrete Masonry Assoc.
2302 Horse Pen Rd.
Herndon, VA 22071-3406
(703) 435-1900

NFPA   National Fire Protection Assoc.
One Batterymarch Park
P.O. Box 9101
Quincy, MA 02269-9101
(617) 770-3000
(800) 344-3555

N.F.P.A. National Forest Products Assoc.
(See AFPA. Now known as the American
Wood Council of the American Forest
and Paper Assoc.)

NHLA   National Hardwood Lumber Assoc.
P.O. Box 34518
Memphis, TN 38184-0518
(901) 377-1818

NLGA   National Lumber Grades Authority
1055 W. Hastings St., Suite 260
Vancouver, British Columbia
Canada V6E 2E9
(604) 687-2171

NPA   National Particleboard Assoc.
18928 Premiere Court
Gaithersburg, MD 20879
(301) 670-0604

NPCA   National Paint and Coatings Assoc.
1500 Rhode Island Ave., NW
Washington, DC 20005
(202) 462-6272

NWWDA   National Wood Window and Door Assoc.
1400 E. Touhy Ave., #G54
Des Plaines, IL 60018
(708) 299-5200
(800) 223-2301

PCA   Portland Cement Assoc.
5420 Old Orchard Road
Skokie, IL 60077
(708) 966-6200

PCI   Precast/Prestressed Concrete Institute
175 W. Jackson Blvd.
Chicago, IL 60604
(312) 786-0300

RIS   Redwood Inspection Service
405 Enfrente Dr., Suite 200
Novato, CA 94949
(415) 382-0662

SGCC   Safety Glazing Certification Council
c/o ETL Testing Laboratories
Route 11, Industrial Park
Cortland, NY 13045
(607) 753-6711

SHLMA   Southern Hardwood Lumber Manufacturers
Assoc.
(See HMA. Now known as the Hardwood
Manufacturers Assoc.)

SIGMA   Sealed Insulating Glass Manufacturers
Assoc.
401 N. Michigan Ave.
Chicago, IL 60611
(312) 644-6610

SJI   Steel Joist Institute
1205 48th Avenue North, Suite A
Myrtle Beach, SC 29577
(803) 449-0487

SMA   Screen Manufacturers Assoc.
3950 Lake Shore Dr., Suite 502-A
Chicago, IL 60613-3431
(312) 525-2644

SMACNA Sheet Metal and Air Conditioning Contractors National Assoc.
4201 Lafayette Center Dr.
Chantilly, VA 22021
(703) 803-2980

SPIB   Southern Pine Inspection Bureau
4709 Scenic Highway
Pensacola, FL 32504
(904) 434-2611

SSPC   Steel Structures Painting Council
4400 Fifth Ave.
Pittsburgh, PA 15213-2683
(412) 268-3327

SWI   Steel Window Institute
c/o Thomas Associates, Inc.
1300 Sumner Ave.
Cleveland, OH 44115-2851
(216) 241-7333

TCA   Tile Council of America
P.O. Box 326
Princeton, NJ 08542-0326
(609) 921-7050

UL   Underwriters Laboratories
333 Pfingsten Rd.
Northbrook, IL 60062
(708) 272-8800

WLPDIA Western Lath, Plaster, Drywall Industries Assoc.
(Formerly California Lath & Plaster Assoc.)
8635 Navajo Rd.
San Diego, CA 92119
(619) 466-9070

WWPA Western Wood Products Assoc.
Yeon Building
522 SW 5th Ave.
Portland, OR 97204-2122
(503) 224-3930

GOVERNMENT AGENCIES

EPA Environmental Protection Agency
401 M St., SW
Washington, DC 20460
(202) 382-2090

FAA Federal Aviation Administration
(U.S. Department of Transportation)
800 Independence Ave., SW
Washington, DC 20590
(202) 366-4000

FHA Federal Housing Administration
(U.S. Department of Housing and Urban
Development)
451 Seventh St., SW
Washington, DC 20201
(202) 708-1422

FS Federal Specification (from GSA)
Specifications Unit (WFSIS)
7th and D St., SW
Washington, DC 20407
(202) 708-9205

GSA General Services Administration
F St. and 18th St., NW
Washington, DC 20405
(202) 708-5082

MIL Military Standardization Documents
(U.S. Department of Defense)
Naval Publications and Forms Center
5801 Tabor Ave.
Philadelphia, PA 19120

NIST National Institute of Standards and
Technology
(U.S. Department of Commerce)
Gaithersburg, MD 20899
(301) 975-2000

OSHA Occupational Safety and Health
Administration
(U.S. Department of Labor)
200 Constitution Ave., NW
Washington, DC 20210
(202) 219-6091

Appendix C

WINDLOADS ON COMPONENTS AND CLADDING FOR BUILDINGS LESS THAN 90 FEET TALL

The material presented in this publication has been prepared to simplify the determination of structural wind load requirements per ASCE 7-88. It should be noted that ASCE 7-88 may not have local precedence. The resulting wind load tables may or may not agree with local codes.*

The design wind load tables are based on ASCE 7-88 with the following assumptions:

- Wind load tables are based on Exposure C.
- The tributary area of the structural element is less than or equal to 10 ft.^{2}.
- Does not apply to roof areas.
- The slope of the roof is greater than 10°.
- Building is less than 90 feet tall. For buildings over 90 feet tall, ASCE 7-88 should be consulted.
- The building is completely enclosed and all cladding, windows and doors are designed to withstand the full wind load.
- Applicable to components and cladding.

If the tributary area is greater than 10 ft.^{2} or if the roof slope is less than 10°, the design wind loads from the tables may be conservative. However, if the building has openings in the elevation which may allow wind to pass through, the design values in the tables may be too low. For these cases, ASCE 7-88 should be consulted.

NOTE: Windows and doors designed to resist the wind loading are not considered openings.

INSTRUCTIONS:

1. Determine the Basic Wind Speed (V) in mph from Figure 1 based on the location of the building.

2. Determine the Roof Height (h) of the building in feet. This is the mean height of the roof above the lowest grade adjacent to the building. Eave height may be used for roof slope θ of less than 10°.

3. Determine least width (B) of the building in feet. This is defined as the shortest distance between two parallel lines which contain the entire building floor plan.

4. Determine high pressure outside corner loading zones (a) in feet from Figure 2.

    a = (0.10) x (B) or
    a = (0.4) x (h), whichever is smaller.
    but not less than either (0.04) x (B) or 3 feet.

5. Determine design wind loads from Table 1: "Design Wind Load Tables" which follow.

6. All design pressure values are assumed for buildings with an Importance Factor Category of I and at least 100 miles inland from a hurricane oceanline. See Table 2 for the definition of other categories.

7. If category II, III or IV is more appropriate and/or if the building is located within 100 miles of a hurricane oceanline, then multiply the design pressure by the corresponding factor in Table 3.

TABLE 1: DESIGN WIND LOAD TABLES (psf)

Mean Roof Height (ft.)	Positive Pressure All Areas	Negative Pressure	
		Area 4	Area 5
BASIC WIND SPEED - 70 MPH			
15	16.6	-17.6	-22.6
20	18.0	-19.1	-24.6
25	19.2	-20.4	-26.2
30	20.3	-21.5	-27.7
40	21.9	-23.3	-29.9
50	23.4	-24.8	-31.9
60	24.6	-26.1	-33.6
70	25.7	-27.2	-35.0
80	26.7	-28.3	-36.4
90	27.7	-29.4	-37.8
BASIC WIND SPEED - 80 MPH			
15	21.6	-22.9	-29.5
20	23.5	-24.9	-32.1
25	25.1	-26.7	-34.3
30	26.5	-28.1	-36.1
40	28.7	-30.4	-39.1
50	30.5	-32.4	-41.7
60	32.2	-34.1	-43.9
70	33.5	-35.6	-45.7
80	34.9	-37.0	-47.6
90	36.2	-38.4	-49.4
BASIC WIND SPEED - 90 MPH			
15	27.4	-29.0	-37.3
20	29.8	-31.6	-40.6
25	31.8	-33.7	-43.4
30	33.5	-35.6	-45.7
40	36.3	-38.5	-49.5
50	38.7	-41.0	-52.7
60	40.7	-43.2	-55.5
70	42.4	-45.0	-57.9
80	44.1	-46.8	-60.2
90	45.8	-48.6	-62.5
BASIC WIND SPEED - 100 MPH			
15	33.8	-35.8	-46.1
20	36.7	-39.0	-50.1
25	39.3	-41.7	-53.6
30	41.4	-43.9	-56.5
40	44.8	-47.5	-61.1
50	47.7	-50.6	-65.1
60	50.3	-53.3	-68.5
70	52.4	-55.6	-71.4
80	54.5	-57.8	-74.3
90	56.6	-60.0	-77.2
BASIC WIND SPEED - 110 MPH			
15	40.9	-43.4	-55.8
20	44.5	-47.2	-60.6
25	47.5	-50.4	-64.8
30	50.1	-53.1	-68.3
40	54.2	-57.5	-73.9
50	57.8	-61.3	-78.8
60	60.8	-64.5	-82.9
70	63.4	-67.2	-86.4
80	65.9	-69.9	-89.9
90	68.5	-72.6	-93.4

*ASCE 7-88 (formally ANSI A58.1) "Minimum Design Loads for Building and Other Structures." ASCE, 345 East 47th Street, New York, NY 10017-2398.

FIGURE 1: BASIC WIND SPEED (mph)

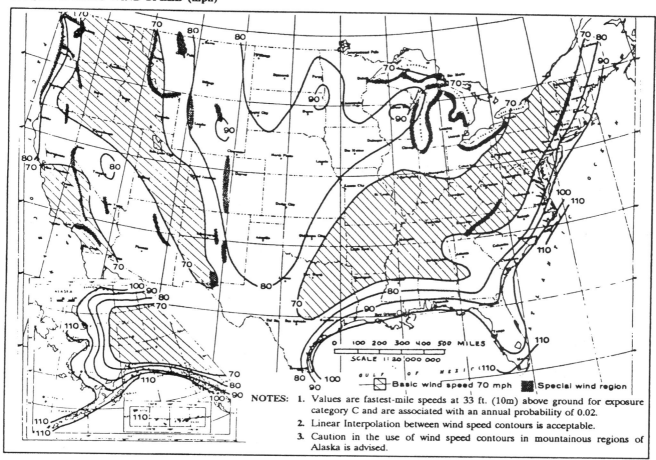

NOTES:
1. Values are fastest-mile speeds at 33 ft. (10m) above ground for exposure category C and are associated with an annual probability of 0.02.
2. Linear Interpolation between wind speed contours is acceptable.
3. Caution in the use of wind speed contours in mountainous regions of Alaska is advised.

TABLE 2: IMPORTANCE FACTORS

Nature of Occupancy	Category
All buildings and structures except those listed below.	I
Buildings and structures where the primary occupancy is one in which more than 300 people congregate in one area.	II
Buildings and structures designed as essential facilities including, but not limited to: Hospital and other medical facilities having surgery or emergency treatment areas Fire or rescue and police stations Structures and equipment in government Communication centers and other facilities required for emergency response Power stations and other utilities required in an emergency Structures having critical national defense capabilities Designated shelters for hurricanes	III
Buildings and structures that represent a low hazard to human life in the event of failure, such as agriculture buildings, certain temporary facilities, and minor storage facilities.	IV

FIGURE 2

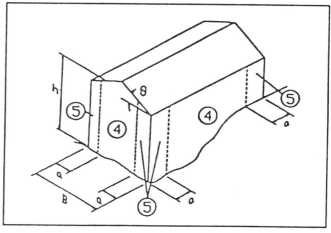

TABLE 3: DESIGN FACTORS

Category	Greater Than 100 Miles from Hurricane Oceanline	Less Than 100 Miles From Hurricane Oceanline
I	1.00	1.10
II	1.14	1.23
III	1.14	1.23
IV	0.90	1.00

EXAMPLE 1:

A 200 foot by 300 foot by 2 story (22 foot mean roof height) hospital is located in Kansas City, Kansas. What are the appropriate design wind load pressures for this building?

1A. Using this document:

Figure 1 shows that Kansas City lies between Basic Wind Speed isotachs of 70 and 80 mph, V = 80 mph. For this example, the higher of the two has been chosen. Enter Table 1, "Design Wind Load Tables," for a Basic Wind Speed of 80 mph at a mean roof height of 25 feet (the mean roof height has been rounded up from 22 feet to the next higher table increment). The positive pressure in all areas is +25.1 psf and the negative pressure is -34.3 psf in area 5 (building corners) and -26.7 psf in area 4 (remainder of the building).

The notation in Figure 2 defines the dimension "a". Ten percent of the minimum building width is 0.10 x 200 feet or 20 feet; forty percent of the mean roof height is 0.40 x 22 feet or 8.8 feet; four percent of the minimum building width is 0.04 x 200 feet or 8 feet. The width of area 5 (corners) is the smaller of 20 feet or 8.8 feet but not less than 8 feet or 3 feet, whichever is greater (in this case 8 feet).

Therefore, in this example, "a" is 8.8 feet. Since this building is a hospital, it falls under Category III from Table 2 (importance factor). The values from the Wind Load Tables are therefore multiplied by the Design Factor of 1.14 from Table 3.

All glass and glazing systems within 8.8 feet of the corners of the building (area 5) must withstand design wind loads of -39.1 psf outward and +28.6 psf inward. All other areas of the building (area 4) must meet design wind loads of +28.6 psf inward and -30.4 psf outward.

1B. Using the Local Code:

The local applicable code is the Uniform Building Code™. The Basic Wind Speed indicated in this code is between 70 and 80 mph.

For this example, the higher of the two has been chose, V = 80 mph. Using Exposure "C" and the 1991 edition of the Code, C_e = 1.19. C_q = 1.2 inward and outward for wall elements except at the corners where C_q = 1.5 outward and 1.2 inward.

The Wind Stagnation Pressure q_s = 16.4 psf. Hospitals require an Importance Factor, I = 1.15.

Therefore, all glass and glazing systems within 10 feet of the corners must withstand design wind loads of -33.7 psf outward and +26.9 psf inward. Remaining areas of the glass and glazing must withstand design wind loads of ±26.9 psf inward and outward.

Since the design wind loads from the local code are less severe, the designer might be well served to determine the design values required by the local code.

EXAMPLE 2:

The same 200 foot by 300 foot by 2 story (22 foot mean roof height) hospital is located in Philadelphia, Pennsylvania. What are the appropriate design wind load pressures for this building?

2A. Using this document:

Figure 1 shows that Philadelphia lies less than 100 miles from a hurricane coastline and between Basic Wind Speed isotachs of 70 and 80 mph. For this example, the higher of the two has been chosen, V = 80 mph. Enter Table 1, "Design Wind Load Table" for a Basic Wind Speed of 80 mph at a mean roof height of 25 feet (the mean roof height has been rounded up from 22 feet to the next highest table increment). The positive pressure in all areas is +25.1 psf and the negative pressure is -34.3 psf in area 5 (building corners) and -26.7 psf in area 4 (remainder of the building).

The notation in Figure 2 defines the dimension "a." Ten percent of the minimum building width is 0.10 x 200 feet or 20 feet; forty percent of the mean roof height is 0.40 x 22 feet or 8.8 feet; four percent of the minimum building width is 0.04 x 200 feet or 8 feet. The width of area 5 (corners) is the smaller of 20 feet or 8.8 feet but not less than 8 feet or 3 feet, whichever is greater (in this case 8 feet).

Therefore, in this example, "a" is 8.8 feet. Since this building is a hospital, it falls into Category III from Table 2 (importance factor). The values from the Wind Load Tables are therefore multiplied by the Design Factor of 1.23 (at hurricane oceanline) from Table 3.

All glass and glazing systems within 8.8 feet of the corners of the building (area 5) must withstand design wind loads of -42.2 psf outward and +30.9 psf inward. All other areas of the building (area 4) must meet design wind loads of +30.9 psf inward and -32.8 psf outward.

2B. Using the Local Code:

The local applicable code is the BOCA National Building Code. The Basic Wind Speed indicated in the code is between 70 and 80 mph.

For this example, the higher of the two was chosen. According to the 1990 edition of this Code, if the tributary area of the building element is less than 700 square feet (the AAMA document is based upon 10 square feet), the glass and glazing members must be designed using ASCE 7-88. This would result in the same design wind loads as calculated in part A above.

EXAMPLE 3:

The same 200 foot by 300 foot by 2 story (22 foot mean roof height) hospital is located in Corolla City, Currituck County, North Carolina. What are the appropriate design wind load pressures for this building?

3A. Using this document:

Figure 1 shows that Corolla City lies less than 100 miles from a hurricane coastline and between Basic Wind Speed isotachs of 90 and 100 mph. For this example, the higher of the two has been chosen, V = 100 mph. Enter Table 1, "Design Wind Load Tables" for a Basic Wind Speed of 100 mph at a roof height of 25 feet (the mean roof height has been rounded up from 22 feet to the next highest table increment). The positive pressure in all areas is +39.3 psf and the negative pressure is -53.6 psf in area 5 (building corners) and -41.7 psf in area 4 (remainder of the building).

The notation in Figure 2 defines the dimension "a." Ten percent of the minimum building width is 0.10 x 200 feet or 20 feet; forty percent of the mean roof height is 0.40 x 22 feet or 8.8 feet; four percent of the minimum building width is 0.04 x 200 feet or 8 feet. The width of area 5 (corners) is the smaller of 20 feet or 8.8 feet but not less than 8 feet or 3 feet, whichever is greater (in this case 8 feet).

Therefore, in this example, "a" is 8.8 feet. Since this building is a hospital, it falls into Category III from Table 2 (importance factor). The values from the Wind Load Tables are therefore multiplied by the Design Factor of 1.23 (at hurricane oceanline) from Table 3.

All glass and glazing systems within 8.8 feet of the corners of the building (area 5) must withstand design wind loads of -65.9 psf outward and +48.3 psf inward. All other areas of the building (area 4) must meet design wind loads of +48.3 psf inward and -51.3 psf outward.

3B. Using the Local Code:

From the 1991 North Carolina State Building Code, Table 1205.2A and Figure 1205.3, the Basic Design Wind Velocity for Corolla City is 120 mph. Then, from Table 1205.2B, velocity pressure can found as 29 psf for 120 mph basic design wind velocity. From statement 1205.3.3, for tributary areas of 200 ft^2 and less, the velocity pressure should be increased by 15% and becomes 29 x 1.15 = 33.35 psf. The shape factor can be obtained from Table 1205.5 as ±1.1. Therefore, the positive pressure in all areas shall be 33.35 x 1.1 = +36.7 psf and the negative pressure in all areas shall be 33.35 x (-1.1) = -36.7 psf.

The local building code is again less severe in this example.

GLASS TABLE

Required Nominal Thickness of Regular Plate, Float & Sheet Glass
Based on Minimum Thickness Allowed in ASTM C 1036-91
DESIGN FACTOR 2.5
MAXIMUM GLASS AREA IN SQUARE FEET (SQUARE METERS)

NOMINAL GLASS THICKNESS													
Design Pressure		SS (2.5mm)		DS (3mm)		5/32" (4mm)		3/16" (5mm)		7/32" (5.5mm)		1/4" (6mm)	
psf	(Pa)	ft²	m²	ft²	m²	ft²	m²	ft²	m²	ft²	m²	ft²	m²
10	478	26.8	(2.49)	38.2	(3.55)	60.3	(5.60)	73.0	(6.78)	91.8	(8.53)	107.0	(9.94)
15	718	17.8	(1.65)	25.4	(2.36)	39.8	(3.70)	48.8	(4.53)	58.5	(5.43)	71.0	(6.60)
20	958	13.4	(1.24)	19.1	(1.77)	30.2	(2.81)	36.5	(3.39)	45.9	(4.26)	54.5	(5.06)
25	1197	10.6	(.98)	15.0	(1.39)	24.0	(2.23)	29.1	(2.70)	36.6	(3.40)	43.3	(4.02)
30	1436	8.9	(.83)	12.7	(1.18)	20.0	(1.86)	24.4	(2.27)	30.6	(2.84)	36.2	(3.36)
35	1676	7.6	(.71)	10.9	(1.01)	17.4	(1.62)	20.8	(1.93)	26.3	(2.44)	30.9	(2.87)
40	1915	6.7	(.62)	9.5	(.88)	15.1	(1.40)	19.3	(1.79)	22.9	(2.13)	27.0	(2.51)
45	2155	5.9	(.55)	8.4	(.78)	13.5	(1.25)	16.2	(1.51)	20.3	(1.89)	23.9	(2.22)
50	2394	5.3	(.49)	7.6	(.71)	12.0	(1.11)	14.5	(1.35)	18.2	(1.69)	21.6	(2.01)
60	2873	4.4	(.41)	6.3	(.59)	10.0	(.93)	12.0	(1.11)	15.3	(1.42)	17.9	(1.66)
70	3352	3.8	(.35)	5.4	(.50)	8.5	(.79)	10.4	(.97)	13.0	(1.21)	15.4	(1.43)

NOMINAL GLASS THICKNESS											
Design Pressure		5/16" (8mm)		3/8" (10mm)		1/2" (12mm)		5/8" (15mm)		3/4" (19mm)	
psf	(Pa)	ft²	m²	ft²	m²	ft²	m²	ft²	m²	ft²	m²
10	478	154.0	(14.31)	–	–	–	–	–	–	–	–
15	718	102.8	(9.55)	148.8	(13.80)	–	–	–	–	–	–
20	958	77.0	(7.15)	111.6	(10.41)	165.8	(15.40)	–	–	–	–
25	1197	61.7	(5.73)	89.2	(8.29)	132.2	(12.30)	177.0	(16.40)	198.8	(18.50)
30	1436	51.4	(4.78)	74.3	(6.90)	110.3	(10.20)	148.4	(13.80)	198.8	(18.50)
35	1676	44.2	(4.11)	63.9	(5.94)	94.4	(8.77)	126.8	(11.80)	171.6	(15.90)
40	1915	38.5	(3.58)	55.8	(5.18)	82.9	(7.70)	110.5	(10.30)	149.0	(13.80)
45	2155	34.2	(3.18)	49.7	(4.62)	72.9	(6.77)	98.0	(9.10)	132.6	(12.30)
50	2394	30.8	(2.86)	44.6	(4.14)	65.6	(6.09)	88.2	(8.19)	119.2	(11.10)
60	2873	25.4	(2.36)	37.2	(3.46)	54.4	(5.05)	73.3	(6.81)	98.4	(9.14)
70	3352	22.0	(2.04)	31.8	(2.95)	46.5	(4.32)	63.0	(5.85)	85.0	(7.90)

A. *Allowable* Maximum Area Factors:
1. Tempered Glass   x 4.00
2. Heat Strengthened Glass   x 2.00
3. Sealed Insulating Glass
   Two Panes   x 1.70
   Three Panes   x 2.50

B. *Required* Maximum Area Factors:
1. Sand Blasted Annealed Glass   x 0.40
2. Wire Glass   x 0.50
3. Laminated Glass   x 0.75*

C. Areas shown are for width to height ratios between 1:5 and 1:1.

*Both plates must be identical in thickness and type: Use total glass thickness, not thickness of one ply.

References

1. Precast/Prestressed Concrete Institute, *Architectural Precast Concrete,* 2d ed., Chicago, 1989, p. 241.

2. E. B. J. Roos, *Building Construction Handbook,* Frederick S. Merritt (ed.), McGraw-Hill, Inc., New York, 1965, p. 18–8.

3. R. L. Quirouette, *The Difference Between a Vapour Barrier and an Air Barrier,* Building Practice Note #54, National Research Council Canada, Ottawa, 1985, p. 4.

4. Charles G. Ramsey and Harold R. Sleeper, *Architectural Graphic Standards,* 9th ed., John Wiley & Sons, Inc., New York, 1994.

5. S. V. Szokolay, *Handbook of Architectural Technology,* Henry J. Cowan (ed.), Van Nostrand Reinhold, New York, 1991, pp. 339–344.

6. Paul Weidlinger, "Visualizing the Effect of Earthquakes on the Behavior of Building Structures," *Architectural Record,* May 1977, pp. 139–142.

7. Christopher Arnold, AIA, and Henry Lagorio, AIA, "Chinese City Starts Over After Earthquake," *Architecture,* July 1987, p. 83.

8. *AIA Journal,* p. 35, June 1980.

9. Richard Saltus, "In a Quake, This Place Will Roll, Not Rock," *The Boston Globe,* April 18, 1994, p. 23.

10. Richard Rush, "Building in the Path of Nature's Wrath," *Progressive Architecture,* Penton Publishing, February 1980, p. 113.

11. Specialty Steel Industry of the United States, *Design Guidelines for the Selection and Use of Stainless Steel,* Washington, DC, 1993, p. 5.

12. Construction Publishers & Consultants, *R. L. Means Cost Guides,* published yearly.

13. Sweet's Group, The McGraw-Hill Companies, *General Building Renovation,* published yearly.

14. Sheet Metal and Air Conditioning Contractors National Association, Inc. (SMACNA), *Architectural Sheet Metal Manual,* 4th ed., Chantilly, VA, 1987, pp. 7 and 66.

15. J. K. Latta, *Walls, Windows and Roofs for the Canadian Climate,* National Research Council Canada, Ottawa, 1979, p. 74.

16. A. Dalgliesh and Garden, "Influence of Wind Pressures on Joint Performance," Technical Paper 264, National Research Council Canada. Ottawa, 1968.

17. Alan Dalgliesh, "Is Pressure Equalization a Worthwhile Goal?" A paper presented at Build Boston 1993, National Research Council Canada, Ottawa.

18. Brick Institute of America, *Technical Notes,* Tech. Note No. 28B, Revision II, 1987.

19. Building Officials and Code Administrators, International, Inc., *The BOCA National Codes,* 1993, p. 235.

20. Marble Institute of America, *Dimension Stone Design Manual IV,* "Installation—General Information," Marble Institute of America, 33505 State Street, Farmington, MI 48335, 810-476-5558, FAX 810-476-1630, 1991, p. 1.

21. M. S. Harriman, "Set in Stone," *Architecture,* February 1991, p. 79.

22. Michael Crosbie, "Finishing Touches," *Architecture,* December 1991, p. 100 and 101. (Paraphrasing approved by Ian Chin, vice-president Wiss Janney Elstner Associates, Chicago.)

23. Indiana Limestone Institute of America, Inc., *Indiana Limestone Handbook,* 19th ed., Bedford, IN, 1992, p. 28.

24. Forrest Wilson, "The Perils of Using Thin Stone," *Architecture,* February 1989, p. 96.

25. Based on Theodore Prudon, "Confronting Concrete Realities," *Progressive Architecture,* Penton Publishing, November 1981.

26. American Concrete Institute (Committee 303), *Guide to Cast-in-Place Architectural Concrete Practice* (ACI 303R-74), 1947, revised 1982, p. 10.

27. Sidney Freedman, "Curtain Call for Curtain Walls," *Architectural Technology,* October 1986, pp. 116–118.

28. Precast/Prestressed Concrete Institute, *Recommended Practice for Fiber Reinforced Concrete Panels,* 3d ed., 1993, p. 42.

29. Precast/Prestressed Concrete Institute, *Architectural Precast Concrete,* 2d ed., Chicago, 1989, p. 83.

30. Precast/Prestressed Concrete Institute, *Architectural Precast Concrete,* 2d ed., Chicago, 1989, Sec. 3.6.

31. Architectural Aluminum Manufacturers Association (currently the American Architectural Manufacturers Association), *Aluminum Curtain Wall Design Guide Manual,* 1979, p. 136.

32. Onkal K. (Duke) Guzey, "The Ongoing Revolution in Contract Documents," *Architectural Technology,* fall 1985.

Bibliography

GENERAL

Allen, Edward, *Fundamentals of Building Construction,* 2d ed., John Wiley & Sons, Inc., New York, 1990.

American Society of Heating, Refrigerating and Air Conditioning Engineers, *ASHRAE Handbook of Fundamentals,* Atlanta, GA, 1989.

Ballast, David Kent, *Architect's Handbook of Construction Detailing,* Prentice-Hall, Inc., Englewood Cliffs, NJ, 1990.

Ballast, David Kent, *Architect's Handbook of Formulas, Tables and Mathematical Calculations,* Prentice-Hall, Inc., Englewood Cliffs, NJ, 1988.

Bassler, Bruce (ed.), *Cladding,* Council on Tall Buildings and Urban Habitat, McGraw-Hill, Inc., New York, 1992.

Callendar, John, *Time Saver Standards for Architectural Design Data,* McGraw-Hill, Inc., New York, 1982.

Cowan, Henry J. (ed.), *Handbook of Architectural Technology,* Van Nostrand Reinhold, New York, 1991.

Kaminetsky, D., and F. Kaminetsky, et al., *Design and Construction Failures: Lessons from Forensic Investigations,* McGraw-Hill, Inc., New York, 1991.

Nashed, Fred, *Time-Saving Techniques for Architectural Construction Drawings,* Van Nostrand Reinhold, New York, 1993.

National Research Council Canada, "Cracks, Movements and Joints in Buildings," NRCC #15477, Ottawa, 1976.

Olin, Harold B., J. L. Schmidt, and W. H. Lewis, *Construction Principles, Materials and Methods,* 5th ed., Van Nostrand Reinhold, New York, 1990.

Ramsey, Charles G., and Harold R. Sleeper, *Architectural Graphic Standards,* 9th ed., John Wiley & Sons, Inc., New York, 1994.

Sands, Herman, *Wall Systems, Analysis by Detail,* McGraw-Hill, Inc., New York, 1986.

CHAPTER 1

Alexander, A., et al., *Road Traffic Noise,* John Wiley & Sons, Inc., New York, 1975.

Ambrose, James, and Dimitry Vergun, *Simplified Building Design for Wind and Earthquake Forces,* 2d ed., John Wiley & Sons, Inc., New York, 1990.

Architectural Record, "Engineering for Architects," mid-August 1976.

Arnold, Christopher, and Donald Geis, "Mexico City as Seismic Laboratory," *Architecture,* July 1987, p. 75 (revised 1982).

Arnold, Christopher, and Henry Lagorio, "Chinese City Starts Over After Earthquake," *Architecture,* July 1987, p. 83.

California Seismic Safety Commission, *Architectural Safety and Earthquake Hazards,* Sacramento, 1992.

Givoni, B., *Man, Climate and Architecture,* 2d ed., Van Nostrand Reinhold, New York, 1981.

Harris, C. W. (ed.), *Handbook of Noise Control,* McGraw-Hill, Inc., New York, 1957.

Jones, Robert St. Clair, *Noise and Vibration Control in Buildings,* McGraw-Hill, Inc., New York, 1984.

Kelly, James M., *Earthquake-Resistant Design with Rubber,* Springer-Verlag, New York, 1993.

Krinitzsky, Ellis L., *Fundamentals of Earthquake Resistant Construction*, John Wiley & Sons, Inc., New York, 1993.

Kubal, Michael T., *Waterproofing the Building Envelope*, McGraw-Hill, Inc., New York, 1993.

Maslow, P., *Chemical Materials for Construction*, McGraw-Hill, Inc., New York, 1982.

McQuiston, Faye C., and Jerald D. Parker, *Heating, Ventilating and Air Conditioning Analysis and Design*, 3d ed., John Wiley & Sons, Inc., New York, 1988.

Panek, Julian R., and J. P. Cook, *Construction Sealants and Adhesives*, John Wiley & Sons, Inc., New York, 1984.

Quirouette, R. L., *The Difference Between a Vapour Barrier and an Air Barrier*, Building Practice Note #54, National Research Council Canada, Ottawa, 1985.

Roos, E. B. J., *Building Construction Handbook*, Frederick S. Merritt (ed.), McGraw-Hill, Inc., New York, 1965.

Rush, Richard, "Building in the Path of Nature's Wrath," *Progressive Architecture*, Penton Publishing, February 1980, p. 106.

Saltus, Richard, "In a Quake, This Place Will Roll, Not Rock," *The Boston Globe*, April 18, 1994.

The Sealant and Waterproofers Institute, *Sealants: The Professional's Guide*, Chicago, 1987.

Szokolay, S. V., *Handbook of Architectural Technology*, Henry J. Cowan (ed.), Van Nostrand Reinhold, New York, 1991.

Weidlinger, Paul, "Visualizing the Effect of Earthquakes on the Behavior of Building Structures," *Architectural Record*, May 1977, p. 139.

CHAPTER 2

Coleman, R., *Structural Systems Design*, Prentice-Hall, Inc., Englewood Cliffs, N.J., 1983.

Feldman, Edwin B., *Building Design for Maintainability*, McGraw-Hill, Inc., New York, 1975.

Lin, T. Y., and S. D. Stotesley, *Structural Concepts and Systems for Architects and Engineers*, 2d ed., Van Nostrand Reinhold, New York, 1988.

Mann, Thornbjoern, *Building Economics for Architects*, Van Nostrand Reinhold, New York, 1992.

Salvadori, M., and M. Levy, *Structural Design in Architecture*, 2d ed., Prentice-Hall, Inc., Englewood Cliffs, N.J., 1981.

Stewart, Rodney D., *Cost Estimating*, John Wiley & Sons, Inc., New York, 1991.

Swineburne, Henry, *Design Cost Analysis for Architects and Engineers*, McGraw-Hill, Inc., New York, 1980.

Thornton, Charles H., *Exposed Structures in Building Design*, McGraw-Hill, Inc., New York, 1993.

Zimmerman, Larry W., and Glen D. Hart, *Value Engineering, A Practical Approach for Owner, Designers and Contractors*, Van Nostrand Reinhold, New York, 1982.

CHAPTER 3

American Architectural Manufacturers Association, *Aluminum Curtain Wall Design Guide Manual*, Chicago, 1979.

American Architectural Manufacturers Association, *Aluminum Storefront and Entrance Manual*, Chicago, 1987.

American Architectural Manufacturers Association, *Window Selection Guide*, Chicago, 1988.

Anderson, J. M., and J. R. Gill (eds.), *Rainscreen Cladding: A Guide to Design Principles and Practices*, Butterworth, London, 1988.

Brand, R., *Architectural Details for Insulated Buildings*, Van Nostrand Reinhold, New York, 1990.

Dalgliesh, Alan, "Is Pressure Equalization a Worthwhile Goal?" A paper presented at Build Boston 1993, National Research Council Canada, Ottawa.

Ganguli, U., and W. A. Dalgliesh, "Wind Pressures on Open Rain Screen Walls: Place Air Canada," *Journal of Structural Engineering*, vol. 114, no. 3, March 1988, National Research Council Canada 28859, Ottawa.

Johnson, Timothy E., *Low-E Glazing Design Guide*, Butterworth Architecture, Stoneham, MA, 1991.

Latta, J. K., *Walls, Windows and Roofs for the Canadian Climate*, National Research Council Canada, Ottawa, 1979.

National Research Council Canada, "Influence of Wind Pressures on Joint Performance," Technical Paper 264, Ottawa, 1968.

Olgyay, V., and A. Olgyay, *Solar Control and Shading Devices*, Princeton University Press, Princeton, N.J., 1975.

Pilkington Glass, *Glass in Buildings: A Guide to Modern Architectural Glass Performance*, Butterworth Architecture, Stoneham, MA, 1993.

CHAPTER 4
Masonry

Ambrose, James, *Simplified Design of Masonry Structures*, John Wiley & Sons, Inc., New York, 1991.

Beall, C., *Masonry Design and Detailing for Architects, Engineers and Builders*, 2d ed., McGraw-Hill, Inc., New York, 1987.

Brick Institute of America, Technical Notes, Reston, VA (updated periodically).

Elmiger, A., *Architectural and Engineering Concrete Masonry Details for Building Construction,* National Concrete Masonry Association, Herndon, VA, 1976.

National Concrete Masonry Association, *A Manual of Facts on Concrete Masonry,* Herndon, VA (updated periodically).

Panarese, W.C., S. H. Kosmatka, and F. A. Randall, Jr., *Concrete Masonry Handbook for Architects, Engineers and Builders,* 5th ed., Portland Cement Association, Skokie, IL, 1991.

Stone

Bordenaro, Michael, "Weighing Options for Stone Cladding Systems," *Building Design and Construction,* July 1992, p. 82.

Chin, Ian, "Finishing Touches," *Architecture,* December 1991, p. 99.

Corbella, Enrico, and Lucio Calenzani, *The Architect's Handbook of Marble, Granite and Stone,* Van Nostrand Reinhold, New York, 1990.

Crosbie, Michael, "Finishing Touches," *Architecture,* December 1991, pp. 100–101.

Donaldson, B. (ed.), *New Stone Technology, Design and Construction for Exterior Wall Systems,* American Society for Testing and Materials (ASTM), Philadelphia, PA, 1988.

Freeman, Allen, "Suddenly Building Stone is Everywhere," *Architecture,* March 1987, p. 72.

Harriman, M. S., "Set in Stone," *Architecture,* February 1991, p. 79.

Hook, Gail, "Look Out Below, The Amoco Building Cladding Failure," *Progressive Architecture,* Penton Publishing, February 1994, p. 58.

Indiana Limestone Institute of America, Inc., *Indiana Limestone Handbook,* 19th ed., Bedford, IN, 1992.

Lewis, Michael (ed.), *Standard Guide for the Design, Selection and Installation of Exterior Dimension Stone Anchors and Anchoring Systems,* American Society for Testing and Materials (ASTM), Philadelphia, PA, not dated.

Marble Institute of America, *Dimension Stone Design Manual IV,* "Installation—General Information," Farmington, MI, 1991.

Marble Institute of America, *Marble Design Manual,* Farmington, MI (updated periodically).

Rosan, Shira, "Sandstone," *Architecture,* November 1986, p. 111.

Wilson, Forrest, "The Perils of Using Thin Stone and the Safeguards Against Them," *Architecture,* February 1989, p. 96.

Yee, Roger, "Stonewalling It," *Progressive Architecture,* Penton Publishing, March 1976, p. 80.

Concrete

American Concrete Institute, *ACI Manual of Concrete Practice,* Detroit, 1993.

American Concrete Institute, *Building Code Requirements for Concrete Masonry Structures,* ACI 531, Detroit, 1983.

American Concrete Institute (Committee 303), *Guide to Cast-in Place Architectural Concrete Practice* (ACI 303R-74), Detroit, 1947, revised 1982.

The Concrete Society (UK), *Concrete Detail Design,* Butterworth Architecture, Stoneham, MA, 1986.

Freedman, Sidney, "Curtain Call for Curtain Walls," *Architectural Technology,* October 1986.

Hurd, M. K., *Formwork for Concrete,* 4th ed., American Concrete Institute, Detroit, 1979.

Precast/Prestressed Concrete Institute, *Architectural Precast Concrete,* 2d ed., Chicago, 1989.

Precast/Prestressed Concrete Institute, *GFRC Recommended Practice for Fiber Reinforced Concrete Panels,* 3d ed., Chicago, 1993.

Shaeffer, R. E., *Reinforced Concrete Design for Architects,* McGraw-Hill, Inc., New York, 1992.

Metal

Brookes, A. J., *Cladding of Buildings,* Construction Press, Longman, Inc., New York, 1983.

Copper Development Association, Inc., *Copper, Brass, Bronze Design Handbook,* Greenwich, CT (updated periodically).

Sheet Metal and Air Conditioning Contractors National Association, Inc. (SMACNA), *Architectural Sheet Metal Manual,* 4th ed., Chantilly, VA, 1987.

Specialty Steel Industry of the United States, *Design Guidelines for the Selection and Use of Stainless Steel,* Washington, DC, 1993.

Studs

Gorman, J. R., and S. Jaffe, et al., *Plaster and Drywall Systems Manual,* 3d ed., McGraw-Hill, Inc., New York, 1988.

Thomas, Robert G., *Exterior Insulation and Finish System Design Handbook,* CMD Associates, Inc., Vashon Island, WA, 1992.

Index

Index

Acoustics:
   and quality of life, 36
   See also Sound
Add alternates, 62
   defining, 69
Adhered waterproofing membranes, 14
Admixtures, concrete, table of, 167
Air:
   forces that move, 3–5
   upward migration of, 5
Air barriers, 5–6, 17, 223
   durability of, 5–6
   and vapor retarders, 16–17
Airborne sound, 48
Air currents, *see* Wind
Allowance, brick, 113
Aloha Stadium (Hawaii), 35–36
Aluminum storefronts, 87
Ames Building (Boston), 151
Amoco Building (Chicago), 161
Anchorage, stone walls, 161
Anchoring hardware, 151
Architectural Graphic Standards, 22
Architectural Manufacturers Association (AAMA), 90
Architectural orders, 146–147
Assemblies:
   brick, 136–137
   cement-based wall systems, 180
   CMU (concrete block), 137, 143
   EIFS systems, 23, 211–214
   glass block, 137, 142–145
   metal cladding, 198–199
   sandwich panels, 199
   sheet-metal and composite panels, 199
   siding panels, 198
   stone walls, 157–160
   stud-backed walls, 217–218
   unit masonry walls, 136–137
Asymmetrical buildings, and earthquakes, 28–29, 31
Attached columns:
   exterior, 51–53
   interior, 53–54

Back parging, 136
Bait, 99
Balloon frame, 206
Barrier-wall approach, 81
Barrier walls, 82
Base isolation, 32–34
Batt insulation, 23
Bedding plane, 161
Bee hives, 42
Bentonite, 15
Besser, Herman, 111
Bird nests, 41–42
Bowing, precast concrete panels, 183
Bracing, 49, 209
Brick:
   allowance, 113
   assemblies, 136–137
   bond patterns, 134, 136
   glass, 117
   grades, 113
   historical background, 109–110
   ingredients of, 111
   manufacturing methods, 113
   as ornamentation, 133–134
   sizes/shapes of, 111–113
   thin brick, 114
Bridging, 209
Brittle materials, cracking in, 7–8
Brittle veneers, 30
Budget:
   staying within, 69–70
   and wall system selection, 73
   See also Costs
Bug holes, 168
Building elements, thermal properties of, 26–27
Building type, and wall system selection, 73

Capacity insulation, 24–25
Capillary action, and water, 7–9
Cement-based systems, 165–188

Cement-based wall systems, 162–185
  assemblies, 180
  components, 164–179
  concrete, 166
  forms, 164–166
  GFRC panels, 69, 164, 172–174, 184–185
  historical background, 162–164
  insulation, 176–179
  ornamentation, 179–180
    color and texture of aggregates, 179–180
    veneers, 180
  panel supports, 174–176
  precast concrete panels, 163–164, 169–171, 182–184
  reinforcement, 166
  site-cast concrete, 163, 166–168, 180–182
  what can go wrong, 180–185
Cementitious fireproofing, 37
Cement waterproofing formulations, 15
Centered columns, 53
Ceramic tile, 217
  what can go wrong, 219
Chin, Ian, 161, 162
Citicorp Bank Tower (New York), 33, 35
Cladding, effects of deflection on, 48
Cladding support, 54–56
  masonry veneer support, 54–56
  panel support, 56
Clearances, 58–60
CMU (concrete block):
  assemblies, 137, 143
  and fire, 115–116
  historical background, 110–111
  ingredients of, 114
  as ornamentation, 134
  thermal expansion, 116–117
Coarse grout, 145
Column cover and spandrel system, 89
Columns:
  attached:
    exterior, 51–53
    interior, 53–54
  centered, 53
  expansion joints at, 63
  free-standing:
    exterior, 51
    interior, 54
  locations, 50–54
Concrete, 166
Concrete admixtures, table of, 167
Concrete block, *see* CMU (concrete block)
Condensation, 15
Con-Doc system, 70
Conduction, 21
Contingencies, and costs, 69–70
Control joints, 120–122, 169
Controlling costs, 62–64
Convection, 21
Coordination, and coss, 70
Copings, 133
Corbels, 134, 135
Cor-Ten Steel, 197
Cost evaluation methods, 64–68
  intuitive approach, 67–68
  life-cycle costs, 64
  value engineering, 66–67
  value of money, 64–66

Costs, 62–71
  controlling, 62–64
  cost evaluation methods, 64–68
  and design decisions, 68–69
    custom design, 69
    detailing, 68
    imported materials, 69
    weight factor, 69
  and discontinued products, 70
  labor and materials, 63–64
  and market conditions, 63
  shop drawings, checking, 71
  staying within budget, 69–70
    contingencies, 69–70
    coordination, 70
    defining add alternates, 69
Cracking, 146
  in brittle materials, 7–9
  causes of, 139–142
  GFRC (glass fiber reinforced concrete) panels, 185
  parapet, 140–142, 145
Creep, 13, 166
Cripples, 208
Crystal Palace (London), 185
Curtain walls, 81, 87–90
Custom design, cost of, 69

Dampproofing, 12, 222
  what can go wrong with, 19–20
Deflection, 46–50, 74
  in cantilevers, 47
  effects of, 48
  horizontal, 47–50
  precast concrete panels, 182–183
  vertical, 46–47
Design:
  custom, 69
  detailing, 68
  durability, 71
  imported materials, use of, 69
  maintenance, 71–73
  system selection, 73–74
  weight factor, 69
Destructive finishes, stone walls, 162
Detailing, 68
Details, 58–61
  clearances, 58–60
  horizontal joints, 60–61
  slab edge, 61–62
  vertical joints, 60
Dew point, 9, 15
Dimensions, hierarchy of, 227–229
Discoloration, GFRC (glass fiber reinforced concrete) panels, 184–185
Discontinued products, 70
Double glazing, 101
Drainage boards, 13–14
  types of, 14
Drawing the wall section:
  and CADD (computer-aided design and drafting), 232–233
  column centerline location, 229–230
  critical dimensions, 229–230
  drafting guidelines, 223–229
  drawing hierarchies, 223–229
  floor-to-floor height, 230
  information sources, 222

Drawing the wall section (*Cont.*):
  points to consider, 221–223
  procedure, 231–232
  sheet organization, 230–231
  wall defenses, 222–223
Dulles International Airport, 65
Durability, 46, 71
  of air barriers, 5–6
Dust-pressing process, 215
Dwight David Eisenhower Army Medical Center (Port Gordon, Ga.), 165

Earthquakes, 27–36
  epicenter, 27
  and irregular structures, 28–90
  mitigation measures, 30–35
    base isolation, 32–33
    future possibilities, 35
    protecting the cladding, 33–35
    stiff structures, 30–32
    tuned mass dampers, 33
  seismic movement, 27–28
  tectonic plates, 27
  what can go wrong, 35–36
Efflorescence, 72–73, 137–139, 146
Electrolysis, 3, 36, 38–39, 43
Epicenter, earthquakes, 27–28
Exfoliation, and stone walls, 161–162
Exposure, 90
Exterior attached columns, 51–53
Exterior free-standing columns, 51
Exterior insulation and finish system (EIFS) assemblies, 23, 211–214
  EIMA categories of, 212–213
  what can go wrong, 218–219
Exterior shading, windows, 106–107

Face panels, 187
Fast-track projects, 69
Federal Reserve Bank of Pittsburgh, 185–186
Fenestration, 84–107
  framing systems, 90–98
  glass treatments, 103–106
  glazing, 98–103
  window treatments, 106–107
  window types, 84–90
Field molded sealants, comparative characteristics/properties of, 13
Filed sub-bids, 199
Fine grout, 145
Finishes:
  metal, 194–198
    oxidation, 195–198
    paints, 195
    stainless steel, 198
  stud-backed walls, 209–217
    exterior insulation and finish system (EIFS) assemblies, 211–214
    stucco, 210–211, 216–217, 218
    wood siding, 209–210
Fire, 37–38
Fireproofing, 223
  cementitious, 37
  sprayed-on fiber, 37–38
Firestop, 206

Flashing, 7, 80, 128–129
  end dam, 129, 131
  materials, 130
Flex anchor, 178
Float glass, 99
Fluid-applied waterproofing membranes, 14
Foil-faced wallboard, as vapor retarder, 16
Forces of nature:
  earthquakes, 27–36
  electrolysis, 38–39
  fire, 37–38
  heat and cold, 20–27
  infestation, 41–42
  sound, 39–41
  and wall design, 3–43
  water, 6–20
  wind, 3–6
Forms, 164–166
Frames:
  balloon, 206
  metal, 93–95
  structural frame drift, 33–35, 49
  vinyl, 90–93
  wood, 90–93
Framing systems, 90–98
  metal frames, 93–95
  rubber gaskets, 98
  structural glazing, 95–98
  wood and vinyl frames, 90–93
Free-standing columns:
  exterior, 51
  interior, 54

Galvanic corrosion, *see* Electrolysis
GFRC (glass fiber reinforced concrete) panels, 69, 164, 172–174, 184–185
  and earthquakes, 35
  tolerances for, 177
  what can go wrong, 184–185
    cracking, 185
    discoloration, 184–185
Girt, 190
Glass:
  float, 99
  heat-absorbing, 104–106
  heat-strengthened, 99–100
  insulating, 101–102
  laminated, 100–101
  phase-changing, 106
  reflective, 106
  sheet, 99
  spandrel, 38, 105
  tempered, 100
  tinted, 104–106
Glass block:
  assemblies, 137, 142–145
  and fire, 117
  historical background, 111
  ingredients of, 117
  as ornamentation, 134–136
Glass brick, 117
Glass treatments, 103–106
  heat-absorbing and tinted glass, 104–106
  low-*e* (low-emissivity) glazing, 106

Glass treatments (*Cont.*):
  phase-change glass, 106
  reflective glass, 106
  windows, 103–106
Glazing, 98–103
  float glass, 99
  heat-strengthened glass, 99–100
  insulating glass, 101–102
  laminated glass, 100–101
  plastic glazing, 103
  sheet glass, 99
  tempered glass, 100
Goff, Bruce, 188
Government agencies, 254
Grades, brick, 113
Granite, 158–160
Gravity, and water, 7
Grout, 119–120, 145
Gypsum wallboard, as air barrier, 5

Hand-set stone walls, 155, 162
  common patterns for, 153
Hard low-*e* coat, 106
Headers, 58, 209
Heat-absorbing glass, 104–106
Heat and cold, 20–27
  heat transfer, 21–22
  methods of protection, 22–25
    capacity insulation, 24–25
    reflective insulation, 24
    resistive insulation, 22–23
  what can go wrong, 25–27
    foil-faced materials, 35
    overdesign, 25–27
    thermal bridging, 25
Heat-strengthened glass, 99–100
Heat transfer, 21–22
  conduction, 21
  convection, 21
  radiation, 21–22
Hierarchy of dimensions, 227–229
Hierarchy of notations, 224–227
Hierarchy of scales, 224
High-rise buildings:
  and stack effect, 4–5
  and wind pressure, 4
Honeycomb core panels, 188, 203
Horizontal deflection, 47–50
Horizontal joints, 60–61
House wrap, 12
Humidity, 9
Hurricanes, 3–4
Hydrostatic pressure, 9, 12
Hysteresis, and stone walls, 160–161

Impact damage, metal cladding, 203
Imported materials, cost of, 69
Infestation, 41–42
Insulated sandwich panels, 188
Insulating glass, 101–102
Insulation, 22, 101–102, 191
  batt, 23
  capacity, 24–25, 43

Insulation (*Cont.*):
  cement-based wall systems, 176–179
  exterior insulation and finish system (EIFS) assemblies, 23, 211–214, 218–219
  loose fit, 24
  reflective, 24, 43
  resistive, 22–24
  rigid, 23–24
  semirigid, 23
Interior attached columns, 53–54
Interior free-standing columns, 54
Interior shading, windows, 107
Ironite, 15

John Hancock Tower (Chicago), 52
Joints, 190–193
  control, 120–122, 169
  horizontal, 60–61
  sealants, 9–11
  seismic, 30
  vertical, 60
  width of, 10–11

Kinetic energy, and water, 7
Knights of Columbus Office Tower (New Haven, Conn.), 65
Kynar 500, 196

Labor and materials, cost of, 63–64
Laminated glass, 100–101
Lateral restraint supports, 56
Latta, J. K., 82
Leakage:
  metal cladding, 199–203
  stone walls, 161
LeCorbusier, 147
Lehr, 99
Lexan, 103
Life-cycle costs, 64
Life expectancy, and durability, 71
Light, 36–37
Liner panels, 187
Lintels:
  commonly used, 59
  loose, 56–58, 127–128
  sizes, 57
Liquidated damages, 63
Load-bearing supports, 56
Load-bearing walls, 79–81
Lo-boy truck, 170
Loose fit insulation, 24
Loose lintels, 56–58, 127–128
  alternate spanning methods, 57–58
  lintel sizes, 57
Louvre plaza pyramid (France), 73
Low-*e* (low-emissivity) glazing, 106

Maintenance, 71–73
  and durability, 71
  periodic, 72
  periodic inspection, 72–73
  preventive, 71–72

Marble, 149, 164
    anchoring hardware, 151
Market conditions, and costs, 63
Masonry anchors and reinforcement, 122–124
Masonry cavity walls, 83–84
Masonry veneer support, 54–56
Means Cost Guide, 64
Mechanical, electrical, plumbing (MEP) consultants, 64
Mechanical play, 123
Mechanical pressurization, wind, 5
Metal cladding, 185–205
    assemblies, 198–199
        sandwich panel systems, 188, 199
        sheet-metal and composite systems, 199
        siding panels, 198
    components, 186–193
    historical background, 185–186
    joints, 190–193
    ornamentation, 193–198
        articulation, 193
        finishes, 194–198
    panels, 188–193
    supporting structure, 190
    what can go wrong, 199–203
        impact damage, 203
        leakage, 199–203
        oil canning, 203, 205
Metal finishes, 194–198
    oxidation, 195–198
    paints, 195
    stainless steel, 198
Metal frames, 93–95
Metal panels, and joints, 11
Mile High Stadium (Denver), 35–36
Mitigation measures, earthquakes, 30–35
Moat, 33
Mockups, precast concrete panels, 169–170
Moisture migration, 9
Monadnock Building (Chicago), 110
Money, value of, 64–66
Monier, Joseph, 163, 166
Mortar, 117–119
Mortar parging, 12

Nervi, Pier Luigi, 163–164
Notations, hierarchy of, 227
Notre Dame Du Haut Cathedral, 163

Oil canning, metal cladding, 203, 205
Oolitic limestone, 149
Overdesign, 25–27
Oxidization, metal finishes, 195–198

Paint finishes, metal, 196–197
Palazzetto Dello Sport, 164, 165
Panels, 188–193
    honeycomb core panels, 188, 203
    insulated sandwich panels, 188
    sheet-metal and composite panels, 188–190
    siding panels, 186, 187–188
    stone, 155–160

Panel supports, 56
    concrete, 174–176
Panel system, 89
Panning, 85
Parapet cracking, 140–142, 145
Parging:
    back, 136
    mortar, 12
Periodic inspection, 72–73
Periodic maintenance, 72
Perlite, 24
Perret, Auguste, 163
Phase-change glass, 106
Pilkington Brothers Glass Company, 164
Pittsburgh Corning, 111, 117
Plastic glazing, 103
Platform framing system, 206
Plexiglas, 103
Polyethylene vapor retarder, as air barrier, 5
Pompidou Cultural Center (France), 73
Pozzolana, 163
Precast concrete panels, 163–164, 169–171, 182–184
    and earthquakes, 35
    mockups, 169–170
    what can go wrong, 182–184
        bowing, 183
        deflection, 182–183
        staining/streaking, 184
        structural frame shortening, 183–184
Prefabricated panels, stud-backed walls, 217–218
Pressure-equalized approach, 81
Pressure-equalized rain screen (PER), 84
Preventive maintenance, 71–72
Product evaluation matrix, 75
Punched windows, 85–86
P-wave, 27

Radiation, 21–22
Rain screen, defined, 82, 192
Rain screen joints, 10
Rain screen walls, 82–84
Redundancy, and durability, 71
Reflective glass, 106
Reflective insulation, 24
Reinforcement, 166
Relieving angles, *see* Shelf angles
Resistive insulation, 22–24, 43
    batt insulation, 23
    loose fit, 24
    rigid insulation, 23–24
    semirigid insulation, 23
Ribbon windows, 86
Rigid insulation, 23–24
River flood, defense against, 6
Rodents, 41–42
Ronchamp, chapel at, 147, 148
Rubber gaskets, 98
Rudolph, Paul, 111
Rustications, 46–47
R-value, 22–25

Saarinen, Eero, 196
Sandstone, 149

Sandwich panels, 188, 199
  assemblies, 199
  joints, 192
  supporting structure, 190
Scales, hierarchy of, 224
Sealants, 9–11
  improper application of, 19
  polyurethane, 213
  what can go wrong with, 19
Sealers, 11–12
  what can go wrong with, 19
Sears Tower (Chicago), 49, 52
Seismic movement, 27–28, 32
  and vertical joints, 60
Semirigid insulation, 23
Shear walls, 30, 74
  locations, 49
Sheathing, 209–211
Sheet glass, 99
Sheet-metal and composite panels, 188–190
  assemblies, 199
  joints, 192–193
  supporting structure, 190
Sheet waterproofing membranes, 14–15
Shelf angles, 54–56, 74, 124–127
Shop drawings, checking, 71
Shop-site assembly method, stud-backed walls, 217
Siding panels, 188–191
  assemblies, 198
  joints, 190–192
  supporting structure, 190
Sills, 133
Single sourcing, 199
Single-stage joints, 10
Site-case concrete, 163, 166–168, 180–182
  what can go wrong, 180–182
Slab edge, 61–62
Soffits:
  design, 4
  and vapor retarders, 17–18
  and wind pressure, 4
Soft low-*e* coat, 106
Soil conditions, and wall system selection, 73
Soleri, Paolo, 69
Sound, 39–41, 43
  airborne, 40
  sound-absorbing blocks, 116, 118
  STC rating, raising, 40–41
  structure-bound, 40
Sound-absorbing blocks, 116, 118
Span, 114
Spandrel beams, and deflection, 46–47
Spandrel glass, 38, 105
Sprayed-on fiber fireproofing, 37–38
Stack effect, 4–5
Staining, precast concrete panels, 184
Stainless steel finishes, metal, 198
Steel studs, 206
Stick built method, stud-back walls, 217
Stick system, 88
Stiff structures, and earthquakes, 30–32
Stone, 149–151
Stone, Edward Durell, 111
Stone ornamentation, 151–153
Stone walls, 146–165
  anchorage problems, 161
  anchoring hardware, 151

Stone walls (*Cont.*):
  assemblies, 153–160
    hand-set systems, 155
    panelized systems, 155–160
  components, 147–151
  destructive finishes, 162
  details, 153–160
  exfoliation, 161–162
  hand-set, patterns for, 153
  historical background, 146–147
  hysteresis, 160–161
  leakage, 161
  ornamentation, 151–153
  stone, 149–151
  thick, disadvantages of, 147
  what can go wrong, 160–162
Storefront systems, 87
Strip windows, 86
Structural frame drift, 33–35, 49
Structural frame shortening, precast concrete panels,
    183–184
Structural glazing, 95–98
Structural issues:
  cladding support, 54–56
  column locations, 50–54
  deflection, 46–50
  details, 58–61
  loose lintels, 56–58
  structure as an element of design, 61
Structure-bound sound, 48
Stucco, 210–211
  and EIFS, 218–219
  what can go wrong, 218
Stud-backed walls, 205–219
  assemblies, 217–218
  bracing/bridging, 208
  components, 206–215
  finishes, 209–215
    exterior insulation and finish system (EIFS) assemblies, 211–214
    stucco, 210–211, 216–217, 218
    wood siding, 209–210
  headers, 208
  historical background, 205–206
  ornamentation, 217
  sheathing, 209
  studs, 206–207, 218
  tracks, 207–208
  what can go wrong, 218–219
Studs, 206–207, 218
  steel, 206
Supporting structure, 190
Surface tension, and water, 7
S-wave, 27
Symmetrical buildings, and earthquakes, 28–29, 31
System selection, 73–74

Tectonic plates, 27, 30
  movements, types of, 31
Tempered glass, 100
Temple of Karnak (Egypt), Great Hall, 146
Thermal bridging, 21, 25
Thermal expansion, coefficients of, 12
Thermal properties of building elements, 26–27
Thick stone walls, disadvantages of, 147
Thin brick, 114
Tie spacing, 123, 125

Tile veneer, 215, 219
Tinted glass, 104–106
Tolerances, 60
Tornados, 3–4
Tracks, 208–209
Trade associations, 251–254
Trass, 166
Tsunami, 6
Tuned mass dampers, 33
Two-stage joints, 10
Tyvek, 5

Underwriters Laboratories (U.L.), 37
    Building Materials Directory, 117
    Fire-Resistance Directory, 90
Unit-and-mullion system, 88
Unit masonry, definition of, 109
Unit masonry walls, 109–146
    assemblies, 136–137
    brick, 109–114, 133–134, 136–137
    CMU (concrete block), 110–111, 115–117, 134, 137, 143
    components, 111–133
    glass block, 111, 117, 134–136, 144
    historical background, 109–111
    ornamentation, 133–136
    what can go wrong, 137–146
Unit system, 88
Unity Church and Parish House (Oak Park, Ill.), 164
Urban concept, and wall system selection, 73
U-value, 21

Value engineering, 66–67
Value of money, 64–66
Vapor retarders, 15–19, 223
    and air barriers, 16–17
    foil-faced wallboard as, 16
    and soffit areas, 17–18
    what can go wrong with, 20
Veneers:
    brittle, 30
    cement-based wall systems, 180
    masonry veneer support, 54–56
    stud-backed walls, 215, 218–219
    vertical expansion of, 55
Vermiculite, 24
Vertical deflection, 46–47
Vertical joints, 60
Vinyl frames, 90–93

Wall assemblies:
    cement-based systems, 165–188
    metal cladding, 185–205
    stone walls, 146–165
    stud-backed walls, 205–219
    unit masonry walls, 109–146
    what can go wrong:
        cracking, 139–142
        efflorescence, 137–139
Wall design:
    factors influencing, 1–76
    and forces of nature, 3–43
    philosophies, 81–84

Walls:
    barrier, 82
    cement-based wall systems, 162–185
    curtain, 81, 87–90
    hand-set stone, 155, 162
        common patterns for, 153
    load-bearing, 79–81
    masonry cavity, 83–84
    rain screen, 82–84
    shear, 30, 49, 74
    stone, 146–165
    stud-backed, 205–219
    unit masonry, 109–146
Wall system selection, 73–74
Wall types, 79–84
    curtain walls, 81
    load-bearing walls, 79–81
Wasp hives, 42
Water, 6–20
    and capillary action, 7–9
    forces that move, 6–9
    and gravity, 7
    and hydrostatic pressure, 9
    and kinetic energy, 7
    leakage, causes of, 81–82
    methods of protection from, 9–19
        dampproofing, 12
        sealants, 9–11
        sealers, 11–12
        waterproofing, 10–15
    moisture migration, 9
    and surface tension, 7
    vapor retarders, 15–19
    what can go wrong, 19–20
        with dampproofing, 19–20
        with sealants, 19
        with sealers, 19
        with vapor retarders, 20
        with waterproofing, 20
Waterproofing, 10–15
    drainage panels, 13
    membranes, types of, 14
    waterstop, 13
    what can go wrong with, 20
Water repellents, 11–12
    what can go wrong, 19
Waterstop, 13–14
Water table, 9
Weather conditions, and wall system selection, 73
Weathering steel, 195–196
Weepholes and vents, 129–133
Weight factor, and costs, 69
Wilkinson, William B., 163
Wilson, Forrest, 164
Wind, 3–6
    air barriers, 5–6
    effect on cavities, 81
    mechanical pressurization, 5
    speed, and terrain/altitude, 3–4
    stack effect, 4–5
    what can go wrong, 6
    wind pressure, 3–4
Window treatments, 106–107
    exterior shading, 106–107
    interior shading, 107
Window types, 84–90
    curtain walls, 87–90

Window types (*Cont.*):
    punched windows, 85–86
    storefronts, 87
    strip windows, 86
Wind pressure, 3–4
Wood, infestation of, 41
Wood frames, 90–93
Wood lintels, *see* Headers

Wood siding:
    stud-backed walls, 209–210
    what can go wrong, 218
Wright, Frank Lloyd, 32, 69, 111, 163

Zayas, Victor, 33
Zibell Anchoring System, 155–157

About the Author

Fred Nashed is the founder of Architectural Consulting Services (ACS), a firm located in Canton, Massachusetts specializing in helping major architectural offices to optimize the process of producing construction drawings. He is a member of the AIA and the Boston Society of Architects, is NCARB certified, and has a master's degree in architecture from the University of Texas at Austin where he worked part time as a teaching assistant. He has 40 years of experience in architectural offices in Texas, North Carolina, Massachusetts, and abroad. Prior to establishing his own firm, he was in charge of several multimillion dollar projects that included industrial, commercial, high-rise, and educational buildings. His design of the Houston Bus Maintenance Facility won a design award from the Texas Society of Architects and was published in *Progressive Architecture*, *Architectural Record*, and *Texas Architect*. Mr. Nashed is currently providing consulting services for Shepley Bulfinch Richardson and Abbott, a 185-person firm established in Boston in 1874.